D1381225

LEABHARLANNA CHONDAE LUGHAÍ
(Louth County Libraries)

Acc. No. _1064208._   Class No. _R 798.4_

2 ·

FOR
REFERENCE ONLY

Books are due for return on or before last date entered above.
Fines for overdue books:- 20p for each week or portion of a
week plus cost of postage incurred in recovery.

Travelling the Turf

Artist: **Terence Gilbert** **THE JOCKEY** Courtesy of: **The Artist**

KENSINGTON WEST PRODUCTIONS

HEXHAM ENGLAND

Kensington West Productions Ltd,
5 Cattle Market, Hexham,
Northumberland NE46 1NJ
Tel: (01434) 609933 Fax: (01434) 600066
e mail: kwp@kensingtonwest.co.uk
web site: www.kensingtonwest.co.uk
or visit: www.amazon.co.uk
www.racecourseguide.co.uk

Editor
Julian West

British Racecourse Editor
Nicola Clements

Travelling the Turf Around the World Editor
Barry Roxburgh

Research
Joanna Clements

Marketing & Advertising
Mark Scandle

Design & Production
Diane Ridley, Nick Ridley

Origination
Pre Press, Hong Kong

Printing
Estudios Gráficos Zure S.A., Spain

Front cover
Artist: Peter Smith, THUNDERING HOME
Courtesy of: Frost & Reed

Acknowledgements

The sixteenth edition of Travelling the Turf sees a new look for the new millennium with a significant change in design. As ever we are extremely grateful to many people: Racecourse managers who have supplied us with our information, Betty O'Connell, her team and the racecourses of Ireland, not to mention those who work to promote racing furlongs further away. Fine art has always played a key role in our publication and we have introduced a rare collection of old and new work this year. My thanks go to the numerous artists and galleries who have helped us collate this collection. In addition we are grateful to the hoteliers who have helped us with the local favourites section. Special thanks also to Tony McCoy and Ronnie Beggan for writing a foreword when so busy.

Finally, I would like to thank my friends and family who have supported Travelling the Turf over the years particularly Nicola Clements and Barry Roxburgh for working so hard to improve our copy.

For Mowel, Rory, Izzy, Millie and Honor.

All rights reserved. No part of this publication may be reproduced, stored in a retrieval system, or transmitted in any form or by any means, electronic, mechanical, photocopying, recording or otherwise, without the prior permission of Kensington West Productions Ltd. While every effort has been made to ensure the accuracy of the facts and data contained in this publication, no responsibility can be accepted by the editor, or Kensington West Productions Ltd, for errors or omissions or their consequences.

© Copyright 2000
Kensington West Productions Ltd

Artist: Peter Curling THE HEAD LAD
Courtesy of: Rosenstiel's

Foreword

The busy fixture list has again ensured a full year of competitive action for the year 2001 and with Travelling the Turf in its 16th year as the most invaluable racecourse guide, a day out at the races has never been more informative and pleasurable.

This excellent edition of Travelling the Turf is the best yet, packed with more information than ever including maps of the racecourses and the surrounding areas, giving the racegoer helpful hints for eating, drinking and resting up close by to your favourite tracks.

Whether you prefer the national hunt scene or the pomp and ceremony of the flat race meetings this guide is a celebration of both horse racing strands and will provide you with more information than any other. Whether you are cheering on your own colours or have simply come for a fun day out Travelling the Turf is packed with a mass of information for you.

I hope that you enjoy the 2001 racing season and that this fantastic guide makes your racing experiences even more enjoyable.

Good luck

Tony McCoy

Contents

Artist: **Katie O'Sullivan** **SADDLES** *Courtesy of:* **Osborne Studio Gallery**

Some racecourses have good years, some bad - some are well run, others are let down by the people who are fortunate enough to be charged with their prosperity. In the last 15 years since Travelling the Turf has been published some racecourses have gone from smug and snooty to welcoming and worldly wise. There are a few racecourses which, as hard as people may have tried, remain predictable and ordinary; and there are others who against the odds have developed themselves to near dizzy heights.

Of the major courses, Cheltenham, York and Haydock Park stand out. While others offer a decent if slightly inconsistent shout when seeking a vote of commendation. While assessing British Racecourses in the past we have tended to be drawn to the twin magnets of size and quality. Cheltenham remains as outstanding; Ascot, York and Newbury always knock on the door because their door is always open. Even Epsom, so troubled and dogged by criticism, has improved beyond belief and is showing signs of class to add to her fine heritage. Amidst this larger group of racecourses, however, there has been one country course that independently has always knocked on the door - not in the way of a Doncaster or Goodwood, but more humbly; this course is Uttoxeter. In our 15 years of publishing the bridesmaid has grown up, matured and remained consistently acceptable. She

has also remained attractive, reliable and consistent and through the years she has become one of the most dependable courses in Britain. As a result of this excellence we are delighted to award the first of Britain's smaller courses - The Travelling the Turf Racecourse of the Year.

Top 5 Racecourses

Uttoxeter • Cheltenham • Haydock Park • York • Aintree

Previous Winners

1990 - Cheltenham
1991 - Newmarket
1992 - Aintree
1993 - Goodwood
1994 - Chester
1995 - Newbury
1996 - Ascot
1997 - York
1998 - Haydock Park
1999 - Kempton Park
2000 - Haydock Park
15 Years of Excellence - Cheltenham

Artist: **Hubert De Watrigant** *JOCKEYS* *Courtesy of:* **Osborne Studio Gallery**

In essence Uttoxeter has over the years demonstrated what can be done with a smaller racecourse. This has admittedly been backed up with significant investment - some £6 million pounds - but the cash has been spent wisely and racegoers are extremely well looked after in all enclosures. Equally importantly, investment at the track has been matched by substantially increased prize money with 22 National Hunt meetings offering over £1 million; this is a tremendous achievement. This has ensured good support from numerous yards and also the attention of both the BBC and Channel 4. While this emphasises the progress made in covering racing, particularly by Channel 4, it is another demonstration of the strides that have been made at Uttoxeter.

While the racecourse has been improved across the board the atmosphere remains vibrant, and there is absolutely no doubt that the racing public whether they are owner, trainer or first time racegoer, are customers and that they all matter. It is no surprise that every racecourse of the year that Travelling the Turf has nominated has seen this element of racecourse management as crucial. Furthermore, the facilities offer something at every turn - there are no eyesores. Every aspect of the course gives something back to the racegoer. Sadly too many racecourses have these miserable spots which don't seem to matter. Ironically this lack of attention is completely misjudged. At Uttoxeter each building, whatever shape or size, offers a place to entertain, or a bar to have a quiet beverage before assessing the form.

There are boxes around the Paddock, the Hunters Room, The Paddock Pavilion and numerous other facilities, so you can bring a party of just about any size to the races. Marquees are available and in the Staffordshire Stand which lies at the heart of the course there are rooms for parties from 20 to 160 guests. I would not usually dwell on the potential for parties so much but the point that is so valid here is that the management and staff at Uttoxeter have worked incredibly hard to ensure that everything works, that packages are good value and not a hassle and that every aspect of racing has fizz from flowers on the table to the course enclosure, which can be visited for £5 per day.

Annual membership to the racecourse remains good value at £180 (£265 double badges - lady & gentleman) with discounts offered to senior citizens and juniors. In addition to the 22 meetings at Uttoxeter a staggering 100 reciprocal days have been arranged at other racecourses. Certainly if you have a little time on your hands this is a most excellent opportunity. It also further demonstrates the enthusiasm that Uttoxeter have to give the customer, in this case the annual member, real value for money.

The course is conveniently located off the A50 between Burton on Trent and Stoke on Trent with good facilities for parking. The success of the course can cause traffic problems, but even here the racecourse has, like Cheltenham, tried to establish a fast and direct route from all regions.

Uttoxeter has received numerous accolades for being the best regional racecourse from the Racegoers Club and rightly so. However, we feel that this sustained excellence merits our Travelling the Turf National Racecourse of the Year award because Uttoxeter shows clearly you don't have to be big to be beautiful. Their aspirations also reflect closely those of our own for racing excellence.

When I wrote to Uttoxeter and Northern Racing's supremo Stan Clarke to offer him our award I was delighted when he telephoned back. He is a very successful man but one could sense he was genuinely pleased to receive another accolade because he knows that this is one further demonstration that the team at Uttoxeter have done so much and are continuing to improve this outstanding racecourse. We wish them well in 2001 and beyond in their efforts to try to maintain the superb standards for yet another decade.

So the millennium came, strutted its stuff and has gone and now as we begin our odyssey into the next 1000 years where does British Racing find itself? Well in many ways the year 2000 was a particularly vibrant one with the scrapping of the historic Levy system. It has also seen vast growth in off track online betting, an agreement from Government to sell off the Tote to 'British Racing PLC' and an agreement which remains only in principle at the time of writing on the vexed issue of media rights.

On the negative side a Morrison Stoneham survey of trainers, racegoers, owners and jockeys found that confidence in racing's future had dipped from 87% in 1994 to 67% in 2000. Areas of major concern were staffing the industry and the failure to gain sufficient sponsorship for racing. Another problem to throw into the melting pot is the issue of the racing calendar with particular reference to weekend racing. In essence the high summer of racing doesn't stop for a day. However, while stables must continue to be run, I fail to see why trainers should feel pressured to race every day and jockeys, even if retainers are an issue, should have the sense to have the odd day off . . . it must make sense. This may sound a little simplistic and certainly at the foot of the jockeys' table where financial pressures are toughest this may sound naive but frankly it just seems logical that a topflight sportsman/woman particularly in a dangerous sport should not push themselves over the top.

It is clear that Sunday racing is a success with large crowds voting with their feet to attend meetings up and down the country. What foxes me though is the removal of some Saturday evening fixtures - this is barmy. Certainly the team that made that decision were failing to consider one of racing's other aspirations–namely to target a younger audience. This group certainly could have had no knowledge of the behaviour of your average adolescent - Saturday night = fun, Sunday = crashed out. What's more many other groups find Saturday night and Friday night as their key nights for going out . . . and if racing is going to drive itself from sport into the realms of entertainment then Friday and Saturday nights are key.

Over the year the issue that I have found most compelling is that of media rights. I recently spoke to one of the industry's more energetic and hard hitting men and he sounded positively drained by the whole process. However, and negotiations are still under way, it appears that most elements of the racing industry are now working together for the good of the sport. Christopher Spence, something of a good sort in the industry, expressed it particularly well in The Times "We remain totally behind the BHB position on pooling rights and I hope the courses come up with a proposal for the benefit of racing as a whole. We need to put aside all the egotism and adopt a united position". Certainly there is a massive opportunity for racing to get its financial house in order and also when the negotiations take place with the bookmakers over SIS (live pictures of racing into betting shops), then the future of racing should be strengthened considerably with the bookmaking industry finally submitting a reasonable contribution to racing's coffers.

Certainly live pictures demonstrate the value of the sport as a betting medium which sadly seems lost on the sports producers at the 'Beeb' who have been happy to show the minimum of racing, often you'll only see a recording which is simply not that attractive to most punters. Let's hope that racing is not given up by the Beeb because the sport needs good coverage and in Balding and Carson etc they have a good team. Mind you the BBC also needs to show sport and there are few more striking than well televised racing.

So we wait with bated breath to see if Arena Leisure's bid for interactive rights, worth a guaranteed £178 million over 10 years to racecourses (that's before terrestrial TV rights of some £150 million), comes off. If it brings about a unity of the sport well that will be a break through in itself. What I hope, though, is that as with the deal which was struck with the bookmakers many, many moons ago racing is not selling itself to a bookmaker of the future . . time will tell.

On a more positive note it is tremendous to hear of the opening of two new racecourses, one on the outskirts of London to keep the East London and Essex tribes happy, and one in South Wales. We wish the courses concerned good fortune. Finally, despite the sad injury to Dubai Millennium's leg I think we should be grateful to have seen in both this horse and Montjeu two exceptional colts. Indeed I suspect the year 2000 will be a good one for racing both on and off the track . . . I wonder where we shall journey next? And that, dear reader, is the pleasure of this book, where to next . . . happy Travelling the Turf in 2001.

Artist: **Graham Isom** **ISTABRAQ AT CHELTENHAM** *Courtesy of:* **Rosenstiel's**

Racing Calendar

Artist: **Henry Koehler** COLOURS Courtesy of: **Rosenstiel's**

JANUARY 2001

Date	Racecourse	Race Type	Race Name
1	*Cheltenham*	Chase	Unicoin Handicap Chase
1	*Cheltenham*	Hurdle	Tote Scoop6 Hurdle (Handicap)
6	*Sandown Park*	Chase	Coral Mildmay Cazalet Handicap Chase
6	*Sandown Park*	Hurdle	Sun 'King of the Punters' Tolworth Novice Hurdle
6	*Uttoxeter*	Chase	ukbetting.com Chase (Handicap)
13	*Ascot*	Chase	Victor Chandler Chase (Handicap)
13	*Lingfield Park*	AWT	Ladbroke All-Weather Trophy Final (Handicap)
13	*Newcastle*	Chase	Castle Eden Brewery Dipper Novice Chase
13	*Warwick*	Chase	Tote Scoop6 Warwick National Handicap Chase
13	*Ascot*	Chase	P.M.L. Lightning Novice Chase
14	*Leopardstown*	Hurdle	Leopardstown Handicap Hurdle
20	*Haydock Park*	Chase	Bet Direct Peter Marsh Chase (Limited Handicap)
20	*Haydock Park*	Hurdle	Red Square Energising Champion Hurdle Trial
20	*Haydock Park*	Hurdle	Tote Exacta Long Distance Hurdle
20	*Kempton Park*	Hurdle	Tote Scoop 6 Lanzarote Hurdle
21	*Leopardstown*	Hurdle	AIG Europe Champion Hurdle
25	*Gowran Park*	Chase	Thyestes Chase
27	*Cheltenham*	Hurdle	Marchpole Cleeve Hurdle
27	*Cheltenham*	Chase	Pillar Property Chase
27	*Cheltenham*	Chase	Ladbroke Trophy Chase (Handicap)
27	*Cheltenham*	Hurdle	Wragge & Co Finesse 4yo Novice Hurdle
27	*Doncaster*	Chase	Pertemps Great Yorkshire Handicap Chase
27	*Doncaster*	Hurdle	River Don Novice Hurdle

Artist: **Philip Toon** *CRISP EVENING* *Courtesy of:* **The Artist**

JANUARY 2001

		North	Midlands	South	
1	Monday (Bank Holiday)	Catterick Bridge	Cheltenham Leicester SOUTHWELL (AWT) WOLVERHAMPTON (AWT)	Exeter Plumpton	Monday (Bank Holiday)
2	Tuesday	Ayr		Folkestone	Tuesday
3	Wednesday	Musselburgh		LINGFIELD PARK (AWT)	Wednesday
4	Thursday	Sedgefield	WOLVERHAMPTON (AWT) Ludlow	Taunton	Thursday
5	Friday		SOUTHWELL (AWT) Towcester		Friday
6	Saturday	Haydock Park Uttoxeter	Huntingdon Sandown Park †WOLVERHAMPTON (AWT)	LINGFIELD PARK (AWT)	Saturday
8	Monday		Fakenham (R) SOUTHWELL (AWT)	Fontwell Park	Monday
9	Tuesday		Hereford (R) Leicester WOLVERHAMPTON (AWT)		Tuesday
10	Wednesday	Catterick Bridge	LINGFIELD PARK (AWT)	Kempton Park	Wednesday
11	Thursday	Wetherby	WOLVERHAMPTON (AWT)	Wincanton	Thursday
12	Friday	Musselburgh	SOUTHWELL (AWT)	Folkestone	Friday
13	Saturday	Newcastle	Warwick LINGFIELD PARK (AWT)	Ascot	Saturday
15	Monday	Doncaster (R)	SOUTHWELL (AWT)	Plumpton	Monday
16	Tuesday	Carlisle	WOLVERHAMPTON (AWT)		Tuesday
17	Wednesday	Newcastle	Huntingdon	LINGFIELD PARK (AWT)	Wednesday
18	Thursday	WOLVERHAMPTON (AWT)	Ludlow	Taunton	Thursday
19	Friday	Kelso Uttoxeter	SOUTHWELL (AWT)		Friday
20	Saturday	Catterick Bridge Haydock Park	†WOLVERHAMPTON (AWT)	Kempton Park LINGFIELD PARK (AWT)	Saturday
22	Monday	Wetherby (R)	SOUTHWELL (AWT)		Monday
23	Tuesday		Leicester WOLVERHAMPTON (AWT)	Fontwell Park (R)	Tuesday
24	Wednesday	Sedgefield	Southwell (R)	LINGFIELD PARK (AWT)	Wednesday
25	Thursday		Warwick WOLVERHAMPTON (AWT)	Wincanton	Thursday
26	Friday	Doncaster	SOUTHWELL (AWT)	Folkestone	Friday
27	Saturday	Ayr Doncaster	Cheltenham	LINGFIELD PARK (AWT)	Saturday
29	Monday		SOUTHWELL (AWT) Plumpton	Kempton Park (R)	Monday
30	Tuesday	Musselburgh	WOLVERHAMPTON (AWT)	Taunton (R)	Tuesday
31	Wednesday	Newcastle	Leicester	LINGFIELD PARK (AWT)	Wednesday

CAPITALS: Flat racing   Lower Case: National Hunt   AWT: (All weather track)   †: Evening Meeting

FEBRUARY 2001

Date	Racecourse	Race Type	Race Name
3	*Sandown Park*	Hurdle	Tote Scoop6 Sandown Hurdle (Handicap)
3	*Sandown Park*	Chase	Weatherbys Scilly Isles Novice Chase
3	*Sandown Park*	Chase	Agfa Diamond Chase (Handicap)
3	*Uttoxeter*	Chase	Singer & Friedlander National Trial Chase (Handicap)
3	*Uttoxeter*	Hurdle	Classic Novice Hurdle
3	*Wetherby*	Hurdle	Totty Construction Rossington Main Novice Hurdle
3	*Wetherby*	Chase	Towton Novice Chase
4	*Leopardstown*	Chase	Hennessy Cognac Gold Cup Chase
8	*Wincanton*	Hurdle	Dick Reynolds 'NH' Auction Novice Hurdle
10	*Newbury*	Hurdle	Tote Gold Trophy Hurdle (Handicap)
10	*Newbury*	Chase	Mitsubishi Shogun Game Spirit Chase
10	*Newbury*	Chase	AON Chase
17	*Ascot*	Chase	Mitsubishi Shogun Ascot Chase
17	*Ascot*	Chase	Gerrard Group Reynoldstown Novice Chase
17	*Ascot*	Hurdle	William Hill Internet - No Tax Handicap Hurdle
17	*Newcastle*	Chase	Tote Northern National Chase (Handicap)
17	*Warwick*	Chase	Michael Page International Kingmaker Novice Chase
22	*Wincanton*	Hurdle	Axminster 100 Kingwell Hurdle
22	*Wincanton*	Chase	Jim Ford Challenge Cup Chase
23	*Kempton Park*	Hurdle	Rendlesham Hurdle (Limited Handicap)
24	*Haydock Park*	Chase	De Vere Gold Cup Chase (Handicap)
24	*Kempton Park*	Chase	Racing Post Chase (Handicap)
24	*Kempton Park*	Chase	luvbet.com Pendil Novice Chase
24	*Kempton Park*	Hurdle	Voice Newspaper Adonis Juvenile Novice Hurdle
24	*Kempton Park*	Hurdle	thehorsesmouth.co.uk Dovecote Novice Hurdle
24	*Lingfield Park*	AWT	Bet Direct Winter Derby Trial
28	*Chepstow*	Hurdle	St David's Day Prestige Novice Hurdle

Artist: **Philip Toon** *TIME FOR A CHAT* *Courtesy of:* **The Artist**

FEBRUARY 2001

		North	Midlands	South	
1	Thursday	Kelso	Towcester		Thursday
			WOLVERHAMPTON (AWT)		
2	Friday	Catterick Bridge	SOUTHWELL (AWT)	Folkestone	Friday
3	Saturday	Wetherby	Uttoxeter	LINGFIELD PARK (AWT)	Saturday
			†WOLVERHAMPTON (AWT)	Sandown Park	
5	Monday	Musselburgh	SOUTHWELL (AWT)	Fontwell Park	Monday
6	Tuesday	Carlisle	Market Rasen		Tuesday
			WOLVERHAMPTON (AWT)		
7	Wednesday		Ludlow	Chepstow	Wednesday
				LINGFIELD PARK (AWT)	
8	Thursday		Huntingdon	Wincanton	Thursday
			WOLVERHAMPTON (AWT)		
9	Friday		Bangor-on-Dee	Newbury	Friday
			SOUTHWELL (AWT)		
10	Saturday	Ayr		LINGFIELD PARK (AWT)	Saturday
		Catterick Bridge		Newbury	
		Haydock Park			
12	Monday		Hereford	Plumpton	Monday
			SOUTHWELL (AWT)		
13	Tuesday	Sedgefield	WOLVERHAMPTON (AWT)	Folkestone	Tuesday
14	Wednesday	Musselburgh	Leicester	LINGFIELD PARK (AWT)	Wednesday
15	Thursday		WOLVERHAMPTON (AWT)	Sandown Park	Thursday
				Taunton	
16	Friday		Fakenham	Sandown Park	Friday
			SOUTHWELL (AWT)		
17	Saturday	Newcastle	Warwick	Ascot	Saturday
			†WOLVERHAMPTON (AWT)	LINGFIELD PARK (AWT)	
19	Monday	Carlisle (R)	SOUTHWELL (AWT)	Fontwell Park	Monday
20	Tuesday	Sedgefield	WOLVERHAMPTON (AWT)	Folkestone	Tuesday
21	Wednesday	Doncaster	Ludlow (R)	LINGFIELD PARK (AWT)	Wednesday
22	Thursday		Huntingdon	Wincanton	Thursday
			WOLVERHAMPTON (AWT)		
23	Friday		SOUTHWELL (AWT)	Kempton Park	Friday
			Warwick		
24	Saturday	Haydock Park		Kempton Park	Saturday
		Musselburgh		LINGFIELD PARK (AWT)	
26	Monday	Newcastle	SOUTHWELL (AWT)	Plumpton	Monday
27	Tuesday	Catterick Bridge	Leicester		Tuesday
			WOLVERHAMPTON (AWT)		
28	Wednesday	Wetherby		Chepstow	Wednesday
				LINGFIELD PARK (AWT)	

CAPITALS: Flat racing   Lower Case: National Hunt   AWT: (All weather track)   †: Evening Meeting

13

MARCH 2001

Date	Racecourse	Race Type	Race Name
3	**Doncaster**	Chase	Velka Pardubicka Grimthorpe Chase (Handicap)
10	**Sandown Park**	Hurdle	Sunderlands Imperial Cup Hurdle (Handicap)
10	**Sandown Park**	Hurdle	European Breeders Fund 'NH' Novice Final Hurdle (Handicap)
10	**Wolverhampton**	AWT	Ed Weetman Haulage Lincoln Trial (Handicap)
13	**Cheltenham**	Hurdle	Smurfit Champion Challenge Trophy Hurdle
13	**Cheltenham**	Chase	Irish Independent Arkle Challenge Trophy Novice Chase
13	**Cheltenham**	Hurdle	Capel Cure Sharp Supreme Novice Hurdle
13	**Cheltenham**	Chase	Fulke Walwyn Kim Muir Challenge Cup Chase (Handicap)
13	**Cheltenham**	Hurdle	Ladbroke Casinos Final Hurdle (Handicap)
13	**Cheltenham**	Chase	William Hill NH Chase (Handicap)
14	**Cheltenham**	Chase	Queen Mother Champion Chase
14	**Cheltenham**	Chase	Royal & SunAlliance Novice Chase
14	**Cheltenham**	Hurdle	Royal & SunAlliance Novice Hurdle
14	**Cheltenham**	Hurdle	Coral Cup Hurdle (Handicap)
14	**Cheltenham**	NHF	Weatherbys Champion Bumper
14	**Cheltenham**	Chase	NH Challenge Cup Chase
14	**Cheltenham**	Chase	Mildmay of Fleet Challenge Cup Chase (Handicap)
15	**Cheltenham**	Chase	Tote Cheltenham Gold Cup Chase
15	**Cheltenham**	Hurdle	Bonusprint Stayers' Hurdle
15	**Cheltenham**	Hurdle	Elite Racing Club Triumph Novice Hurdle
15	**Cheltenham**	Hurdle	Vincent O'Brien County Hurdle (Handicap)
15	**Cheltenham**	Chase	Cathcart Challenge Cup Chase
15	**Cheltenham**	Chase	Cheltenham Grand Annual Challenge Cup Chase (Handicap)
15	**Cheltenham**	Chase	Christie's Foxhunter Challenge Cup Chase
17	**Lingfield Park**	AWT	Bet Direct Winter Derby
17	**Uttoxeter**	Chase	Marstons Pedigree Midlands Grand National Chase (Handicap)
17	**Uttoxeter**	Chase	Tote Placepot Novice Handicap Chase
17	**Uttoxeter**	Chase	EBF Tattersalls (Ireland) Mares Novice Chase (Handicap)
22	**Doncaster**	Flat	Tote Exacta 1-2 Stakes (Handicap)
22	**Doncaster**	Flat	Doncaster Mile
23	**Doncaster**	Flat	Worthington Spring Mile (Handicap)
23	**Kelso**	Chase	Ashleybank Investments Scottish Border National (Handicap) Chase
24	**Doncaster**	Flat	Worthington Lincoln (Handicap)
24	**Doncaster**	Flat	Victor Chandler Cammidge Trophy
24	**Newbury**	Hurdle	EBF Crandon Park Stud Mares 'NH' Novice Final Hurdle (Handicap)
30	**Carlisle**	Chase	'Tote Bookmakers Fullstop' Novice Chase (Handicap)
31	**Ascot**	Hurdle	Grosvenor Casinos Long Distance Hurdle

Artist: **Peter Curling ISTABRAQ** *Courtesy of:* **Rosenstiel's**

MARCH 2001

		North	Midlands	South	
1	Thursday		Ludlow	Taunton	Thursday
2	Friday	Doncaster	WOLVERHAMPTON (AWT)	Newbury	Friday
		Kelso			
3	Saturday	Doncaster	Huntingdon	LINGFIELD PARK (AWT)	Saturday
			†WOLVERHAMPTON (AWT)	Newbury	
5	Monday		SOUTHWELL (AWT)	Fontwell Park	Monday
6	Tuesday	Sedgefield	Leicester	Exeter	Tuesday
7	Wednesday	Catterick Bridge	Bangor-on-Dee	LINGFIELD PARK (AWT)	Wednesday
8	Thursday	Carlisle	Towcester	Wincanton	Thursday
9	Friday	Ayr	Hereford	Sandown Park	Friday
10	Saturday	Ayr	Warwick	Chepstow	Saturday
			WOLVERHAMPTON (AWT)	Sandown Park	
12	Monday		Stratford-on-Avon	Plumpton	Monday
				Taunton	
13	Tuesday	Sedgefield	Cheltenham		Tuesday
			SOUTHWELL (AWT)		
14	Wednesday		Cheltenham	Newton Abbot	Wednesday
				Huntingdon	
15	Thursday	Hexham	Cheltenham		Thursday
			WOLVERHAMPTON (AWT)		
16	Friday		Fakenham		Friday
			SOUTHWELL (AWT)		
			Worcester		
17	Saturday	Newcastle	Market Rasen	Lingfield Park (Mixed AWT)	Saturday
			Uttoxeter		
19	Monday		SOUTHWELL (AWT)	Folkestone	Monday
20	Tuesday	Sedgefield		Exeter	Tuesday
				Fontwell Park	
21	Wednesday		Ludlow	Chepstow	Wednesday
			Towcester		
22	Thursday	DONCASTER	WOLVERHAMPTON (AWT)	Wincanton	Thursday
23	Friday	DONCASTER		Newbury	Friday
		Kelso			
24	Saturday	DONCASTER	Bangor-on-Dee	KEMPTON PARK	Saturday
			†WOLVERHAMPTON (AWT)	Newbury	
26	Monday		SOUTHWELL (AWT)	WINDSOR	Monday
27	Tuesday	NEWCASTLE	WOLVERHAMPTON (AWT)		Tuesday
28	Wednesday	CATTERICK BRIDGE	NOTTINGHAM	LINGFIELD PARK (AWT)	Wednesday
29	Thursday	MUSSELBURGH	LEICESTER	Exeter	Thursday
30	Friday	Carlisle	SOUTHWELL		Friday
					Uttoxeter
31	Saturday	HAYDOCK PARK(MXD)	Market Rasen	Ascot	Saturday
		Hexham			

CAPITALS: Flat racing   Lower Case: National Hunt   AWT: (All weather track)   †: Evening Meeting

15

APRIL 2001

Date	Racecourse	Race Type	Race Name
5	*Aintree*	Chase	Martell Cup Chase
5	*Aintree*	Chase	Sandeman Maghull Novice Chase
5	*Aintree*	Hurdle	Glenlivet Anniversary Novice Hurdle
5	*Aintree*	Hurdle	Barton & Guestier Top Novice Hurdle
6	*Aintree*	Chase	Mumm Melling Chase
6	*Aintree*	Chase	Mumm Mildmay Novice Chase
6	*Aintree*	Hurdle	Belle Epoque Sefton Novice Hurdle
6	*Aintree*	Chase	John Hughes Trophy Chase (Handicap)
6	*Aintree*	Hurdle	Martell Mersey Novice Hurdle
7	*Aintree*	Chase	Martell Grand National Chase (Handicap)
7	*Aintree*	Hurdle	Martell Aintree Hurdle
7	*Aintree*	Chase	Martell Red Rum Chase (Limited Handicap)
7	*Aintree*	Hurdle	Cordon Bleu Handicap Hurdle
7	*Aintree*	NHF	Martell Champion Standard Bumper
14	*Haydock Park*	Flat	Field Marshal Stakes
14	*Kempton Park*	Flat	Sovereign Bookmakers Easter Stakes (colts & geldings)
14	*Kempton Park*	Flat	Sovereign Bookmakers Masaka Stakes (fillies)
16	*Chepstow*	Hurdle	Welsh Champion Hurdle (Limited Handicap)
16	*Fairyhouse*	Chase	Powers Gold Label Irish Grand National Chase
16	*Kempton Park*	Flat	Coral Rosebery Handicap Stakes
16	*Kempton Park*	Flat	kickon.com Magnolia Stakes
17	*Fairyhouse*	Chase	Powers Gold Cup Chase
17	*Newmarket*	Flat	Shadwell Stud Nell Gwyn Stakes (fillies)
17	*Newmarket*	Flat	NGK Spark Plugs Abernant Stakes
18	*Cheltenham*	Hurdle	betinternet.com 'NH' Auction Novice Hurdle
18	*Cheltenham*	Chase	Faucets for Mira Rada Showers Silver Trophy Chase
18	*Newmarket*	Flat	Weatherbys Earl of Sefton Stakes
18	*Newmarket*	Flat	Victor Chandler European Free Handicap
19	*Cheltenham*	NHF	EBF/Doncaster Bloodstock Sales Mares Bumper Final
19	*Newmarket*	Flat	John Mowlem Feilden Stakes
19	*Newmarket*	Flat	thehorsesmouth.co.uk Craven Stakes (colts & geldings)
20	*Newbury*	Flat	Dubai Duty Free Stakes (fillies)
21	*Ayr*	Chase	Ladbroke Casinos Scottish Grand National Chase (Handicap)
21	*Ayr*	Chase	Ashleybank Investments Future Champion Novice Chase
21	*Ayr*	Chase	Doubleprint Novice Handicap chase
21	*Ayr*	Hurdle	Samsung Electronics Scottish Champion Hurdle (Limited Handicap)
21	*Newbury*	Flat	Watership Down Stud John Porter Stakes
21	*Newbury*	Flat	Lane's End Greenham Stakes (colts & geldings)
21	*Thirsk*	Flat	Stanley Racing Thirsk Classic Trial
24	*Punchestown*	Chase	BMW Chase
24	*Punchestown*	Hurdle	Evening Herald Champion Novice Hurdle
25	*Punchestown*	Chase	Heineken Gold Cup Chase
25	*Punchestown*	Hurdle	Stanley Cooker Champion Novice Hurdle
26	*Punchestown*	Hurdle	IAWS Champion 4-year old Hurdle
26	*Punchestown*	Hurdle	Ballymore Properties Champion Stayers Hurdle
26	*Punchestown*	Chase	Swordlestown Cup Novice Chase
27	*Punchestown*	Hurdle	Shell Champion Hurdle
27	*Punchestown*	Chase	David Austin Memorial Chase
28	*Sandown Park*	Flat	KLM UK Mile
28	*Leicester*	Flat	Leicestershire Stakes
28	*Sandown Park*	Chase	Whitbread Gold Cup Chase (Handicap)
28	*Sandown Park*	Chase	Pizza Hut Novice Chase
28	*Sandown Park*	Chase	Brewers Fayre Novice Handicap Chase
28	*Sandown Park*	Flat	Thresher Classic Trial
28	*Sandown Park*	Flat	Marriott Hotels Stakes
28	*Sedgefield*	Chase	Foster's Durham National Chase (Handicap)

APRIL 2001

		North	Midlands	South	
2	Monday	Kelso	WARWICK	LINGFIELD PARK (AWT)	Monday
3	Tuesday	Newcastle	NOTTINGHAM		Tuesday
4	Wednesday	RIPON	Ludlow	Ascot	Wednesday
5	Thursday	Aintree	LEICESTER	Taunton	Thursday
6	Friday	Aintree		LINGFIELD PARK	Friday
		Sedgefield			
7	Saturday	Aintree	Hereford		Saturday
		HAMILTON PARK			
9	Monday		SOUTHWELL	WINDSOR	Monday
10	Tuesday	PONTEFRACT	WOLVERHAMPTON (AWT)	Exeter	Tuesday
11	Wednesday		WARWICK	Chepstow	Wednesday
				LINGFIELD PARK (AWT)	
12	Thursday	MUSSELBURGH	Ludlow	BRIGHTON	Thursday
14	Saturday	Carlisle	Towcester	KEMPTON PARK	Saturday
		HAYDOCK PARK		Newton Abbot	
				Plumpton	
16	Monday	Carlisle	Fakenham	Chepstow	Monday
	(Bank Holiday)	NEWCASTLE	Hereford	KEMPTON PARK	(Bank Holiday)
		Wetherby	Huntingdon	Plumpton	
			Market Rasen	Wincanton	
			NOTTINGHAM		
			Towcester		
			Uttoxeter		
			WARWICK		
17	Tuesday		NEWMARKET		Tuesday
			SOUTHWELL (AWT)		
			Uttoxeter		
18	Wednesday	BEVERLEY	Cheltenham		Wednesday
			NEWMARKET		
19	Thursday	RIPON	Cheltenham		Thursday
			NEWMARKET		
20	Friday	Ayr		NEWBURY	Friday
		THIRSK			
21	Saturday	Ayr	Bangor-on-Dee	NEWBURY	Saturday
		THIRSK	Stratford-on-Avon		
			†WOLVERHAMPTON (AWT)		
23	Monday	Hexham		WINDSOR	Monday
		PONTEFRACT			
24	Tuesday			Exeter	Tuesday
				FOLKESTONE	
25	Wednesday	CATTERICK BRIDGE		EPSOM DOWNS	Wednesday
		Perth			
26	Thursday	BEVERLEY		Fontwell Park	Thursday
		Perth			
27	Friday	Perth	WOLVERHAMPTON (AWT)	SANDOWN PARK	Friday
28	Saturday	RIPON	LEICESTER	SANDOWN PARK (MIXED)	Saturday
		Sedgefield	Market Rasen		
30	Monday	†Newcastle	SOUTHWELL (AWT)	Plumpton	Monday
			Towcester	†WINDSOR	

CAPITALS: Flat racing   Lower Case: National Hunt   AWT: (All weather track)   †: Evening Meeting

MAY 2001

Date	Racecourse	Race Type	Race Name
1	*Bath*	Flat	European Breeders Fund Lansdown Stakes (fillies)
2	*Ascot*	Flat	Bovis Homes Sagaro Stakes
2	*Ascot*	Flat	Sodexho Victoria Cup (Handicap)
2	*Ascot*	Flat	Sodexho Pavillion Stakes
2	*Ascot*	Flat	Woodcote Stud Swinley Stakes (fillies)
4	*Newmarket*	Flat	Sagitta Jockey Club Stakes
4	*Newmarket*	Flat	Green Ridge Stables Newmarket Stakes (colts)
4	*Newmarket*	Flat	Charles Heidsieck Champagne Dahlia Stakes (fillies)
5	*Haydock Park*	Hurdle	Crowther Homes Swinton Hurdle (Handicap)
5	*Haydock Park*	Flat	Crowther Homes Spring Trophy (Rated)
5	*Newmarket*	Flat	Sagitta 2000 Guineas Stakes (colts & fillies)
5	*Newmarket*	Flat	Ladbrokes Handicap
5	*Newmarket*	Flat	Victor Chandler Palace House Stakes
6	*Newmarket*	Flat	Sagitta 1000 Guineas Stakes (fillies)
6	*Newmarket*	Flat	R.L. Davison Pretty Polly Stakes (fillies)
7	*Kempton Park*	Flat	Doubleprint Handicap
8	*Chester*	Flat	Victor Chandler Chester Vase
8	*Chester*	Flat	Stanley Leisure Handicap
9	*Chester*	Flat	Tote Chester Cup (Handicap)
9	*Chester*	Flat	Shadwell Stud Cheshire Oaks (fillies)
10	*Chester*	Flat	Ormonde Stakes
10	*Chester*	Flat	Smartestates 187th Year of the Dee Stakes
10	*Chester*	Flat	Huxley Stakes
12	*Lingfield Park*	Flat	Gartner Derby Trial Stakes (colts & geldings)
12	*Lingfield Park*	Flat	Tote Scoop6 Sprint Handicap Stakes
12	*Lingfield Park*	Flat	Victor Chandler Oaks Trial Stakes (fillies)
12	*Lingfield Park*	Flat	MER Car Polish Chartwell Stakes (fillies)
14	*Windsor*	Flat	Coral Eurobet Royal Windsor Stakes
15	*York*	Flat	Tattersalls Musidora Stakes (fillies)
15	*York*	Flat	Newton Investment Management Rated Stakes (Handicap)
15	*York*	Flat	williamhillcasino.com Handicap Stakes
16	*York*	Flat	JWE Telecom Dante Stakes
16	*York*	Flat	PricewaterhouseCoopers Hambleton Rated Stakes (Handicap)
16	*York*	Flat	Brewin Dolphin Securities Middleton Stakes (fillies)
16	*York*	Flat	Sony Telecom Service Handicap Stakes
17	*York*	Flat	Merewood Homes Yorkshire Cup
17	*York*	Flat	Duke of York Victor Chandler Stakes
17	*York*	Flat	Michael Seely Memorial Glasgow Stakes
17	*York*	Flat	Guilbert UK Rated Stakes (Handicap)
18	*Newbury*	Flat	Ashbury Fillies' Trial Stakes
19	*Newbury*	Flat	Juddmonte Lockinge Stakes
19	*Newbury*	Flat	Grundon Recycle Aston Park Stakes
19	*Nottingham*	Flat	Victor Chandler Kilvington Stakes (fillies)
22	*Goodwood*	Flat	Tote Trifecta Handicap Stakes
22	*Goodwood*	Flat	Compass UK Leisure Predominate Stakes (colts & geldings)
23	*Goodwood*	Flat	ABN Amro Handicap Stakes
23	*Goodwood*	Flat	Victor Chandler Lupe Stakes (fillies)
24	*Goodwood*	Flat	Badger Brewery Festival Stakes
24	*Goodwood*	Flat	European Breeders Fund Conqueror Stakes (fillies)
26	*Curragh*	Flat	Entenmann's 2000 Guineas Stakes
26	*Haydock Park*	Flat	Tote Credit Club Silver Bowl (Handicap)
26	*Haydock Park*	Flat	Sandy Lane Stakes (Rated)
26	*Kempton Park*	Flat	sportingodds.com Heron Stakes
26	*Kempton Park*	Flat	sportingindex.com Achilles Stakes
27	*Curragh*	Flat	Entenmann's 1000 Guineas Stakes
28	*Redcar*	Flat	Zetland Gold Cup (Handicap)
28	*Sandown Park*	Flat	Tripleprint Temple Stakes
28	*Sandown Park*	Flat	Doubleprint Rated Stakes (Handicap)
28	*Sandown Park*	Flat	Bonusprint Stakes
29	*Sandown Park*	Flat	Credit Suisse First Boston Brigadier Gerard Stakes
29	*Sandown Park*	Flat	Credit Suisse First Boston National Stakes

		North	Midlands	South	
1	Tuesday		NOTTINGHAM	BATH	Tuesday
2	Wednesday	†Kelso PONTEFRACT	†Cheltenham Exeter	ASCOT	Wednesday
3	Thursday	REDCAR	WOLVERHAMPTON (AWT)	BRIGHTON	Thursday
4	Friday	MUSSELBURGH †Sedgefield	†Bangor-on-Dee NEWMARKET	Folkestone	Friday
5	Saturday	HAYDOCK PARK (MXD) Hexham THIRSK	Hereford NEWMARKET Uttoxeter	Saturday	
6	Sunday	HAMILTON PARK	NEWMARKET	SALISBURY	Sunday
7	Monday (Bank Holiday)	DONCASTER NEWCASTLE	Ludlow Towcester WARWICK	Fontwell Park KEMPTON PARK	Monday (Bank Holiday)
8	Tuesday		CHESTER	BRIGHTON †Taunton †WINDSOR	Tuesday
9	Wednesday	Kelso †Wetherby	CHESTER †Fakenham	Chepstow	Wednesday
10	Thursday		CHESTER Southwell		Thursday
11	Friday	CARLISLE †HAMILTON PARK	NOTTINGHAM	LINGFIELD PARK †Wincanton	Friday
12	Saturday	BEVERLEY Hexham †THIRSK	†Huntingdon †Warwick Worcester	LINGFIELD PARK	Saturday
14	Monday	REDCAR	SOUTHWELL (AWT) †Towcester Hereford	†WINDSOR	Monday
15	Tuesday	YORK			Tuesday
16	Wednesday	†Perth YORK		BRIGHTON Exeter †Folkestone	Wednesday
17	Thursday	Perth YORK		SALISBURY	Thursday
18	Friday	†Aintree †HAMILTON PARK	NOTTINGHAM	NEWBURY	Friday
19	Saturday	THIRSK	†Stratford-on-Avon Bangor-on-Dee NOTTINGHAM †Warwick †WOLVERHAMPTON (AWT)	†Lingfield Park NEWBURY	Saturday
21	Monday	†MUSSELBURGH	SOUTHWELL (AWT)	BATH †WINDSOR	Monday
22	Tuesday	BEVERLEY		GOODWOOD	Tuesday
23	Wednesday	Kelso	†Uttoxeter Worcester	†BRIGHTON GOODWOOD	Wednesday
24	Thursday	NEWCASTLE Wetherby		GOODWOOD	Thursday
25	Friday	HAYDOCK PARK †PONTEFRACT	SOUTHWELL (AWT) †Towcester	BRIGHTON	Friday
26	Saturday	Cartmel DONCASTER HAYDOCK PARK Hexham	†Market Rasen †WARWICK	KEMPTON PARK †LINGFIELD PARK (AWT)	Saturday
28	Monday (Bank Holiday)	Cartmel REDCAR	Hereford Huntingdon LEICESTER Uttoxeter	CHEPSTOW Fontwell Park SANDOWN PARK	Monday (Bank Holiday)
29	Tuesday	†Hexham REDCAR	LEICESTER	†SANDOWN PARK	Tuesday
30	Wednesday †RIPON	Cartmel YARMOUTH	SOUTHWELL	†NEWBURY	Wednesday
31	Thursday	AYR †Wetherby	†Huntingdon Newton Abbot	GOODWOOD	Thursday

CAPITALS: Flat racing   Lower Case: National Hunt   AWT: (All weather track)   †: Evening Meeting

JUNE 2001

Date	Racecourse	Race Type	Race Name
2	*Windsor*	Flat	Bet Direct from Littlewoods Leisure Stakes
2	*Newmarket*	Flat	Coral Europrint Sprint Stakes (Handicap)
2	*Newmarket*	Flat	Milcars King Charles II Stakes
2	*Stratford-on-Avon*	Chase	Intrum Justitia (Horse and Hound) Cup Champion Chase (Hunters)
8	*Epsom Downs*	Flat	Vodafone Oaks (fillies)
8	*Epsom Downs*	Flat	Vodafone Coronation Cup
8	*Epsom Downs*	Flat	Vodafone Victress Stakes (fillies)
8	*Epsom Downs*	Flat	Vodafone Surrey Stakes
8	*Epsom Downs*	Flat	Vodafone Network Handicap Stakes
8	*Epsom Downs*	Flat	Vodafone Distribution Handicap Stakes
8	*Epsom Downs*	Flat	Vodafone Paging Handicap Stakes
9	*Epsom Downs*	Flat	Vodafone Derby (colts & fillies)
9	*Epsom Downs*	Flat	Vodafone International Stakes (Rated)
9	*Epsom Downs*	Flat	Vodafone Data Network Handicap Stakes
9	*Epsom Downs*	Flat	Vodafone Diomed Stakes
9	*Epsom Downs*	Flat	Vodafone 'Dash' Stakes (Rated)
9	*Epsom Downs*	Flat	Vodafone Woodcote Stakes
9	*Epsom Downs*	Flat	EDS Handicap Stakes
9	*Haydock Park*	Flat	Halliwell Landau John of Gaunt Stakes
9	*Haydock Park*	Flat	Cecil Frail Stakes(fillies)
10	*Worcester*	Hurdle	Tote Credit Club Handicap Hurdle
10	*Newmarket*	Flat	Charles Heidsieck Champagne Fairway Stakes
14	*Newbury*	Flat	Ballymacoll Stud Stakes
16	*York*	Flat	William Hill Trophy
17	*Leicester*	Flat	Mercury Leicester Stakes
19	*Royal Ascot*	Flat	St James's Palace Stakes (colts)
19	*Royal Ascot*	Flat	King's Stand Stakes
19	*Royal Ascot*	Flat	Queen Anne Stakes
19	*Royal Ascot*	Flat	Coventry Stakes
19	*Royal Ascot*	Flat	Queen's Vase Stakes
19	*Royal Ascot*	Flat	Duke of Edinburgh Stakes (Handicap)
20	*Royal Ascot*	Flat	Ascot Stakes (Handicap)
20	*Royal Ascot*	Flat	Prince of Wales's Stakes
20	*Royal Ascot*	Flat	Royal Hunt Cup (Handicap)
20	*Royal Ascot*	Flat	Jersey Stakes
20	*Royal Ascot*	Flat	Chesham Stakes
20	*Royal Ascot*	Flat	Queen Mary Stakes (fillies)
21	*Royal Ascot*	Flat	Gold Cup
21	*Royal Ascot*	Flat	Ribblesdale Stakes (fillies)
21	*Royal Ascot*	Flat	Cork and Orrery Stakes
21	*Royal Ascot*	Flat	King George V Stakes (Handicap)
21	*Royal Ascot*	Flat	Norfolk Stakes
21	*Royal Ascot*	Flat	Britannia Stakes (Handicap) (colts & geldings)
22	*Royal Ascot*	Flat	Coronation Stakes (fillies)
22	*Royal Ascot*	Flat	Hardwicke Stakes
22	*Royal Ascot*	Flat	King Edward VII Stakes (colts & geldings)
22	*Royal Ascot*	Flat	Wokingham Stakes (Handicap)
22	*Royal Ascot*	Flat	Queen Alexandra Stakes
22	*Royal Ascot*	Flat	Windsor Castle Stakes
23	*Ascot*	Flat	Ladbrokes Handicap
23	*Ascot*	Flat	Palan Stakes (Handicap)
23	*Ascot*	Flat	Milcars New Stakes
23	*Ascot*	Flat	London Clubs Fern Hill Stakes (Rated)
24	*Perth*	Chase	City of Perth Gold Cup Chase
27	*Carlisle*	Flat	Crowther Homes Carlisle Bell Stakes (Handicap)
27	*Kempton Park*	Flat	Mowlem Gala Stakes
28	*Carlisle*	Flat	UCB Films Cumberland Plate (Handicap)
29	*Newcastle*	Flat	Northern Rock Gosforth Park Cup (Handicap)
29	*Newcastle*	Flat	European Breeders Fund Stakes
30	*Newcastle*	Flat	Foster's Lager Northumberland Plate (Handicap)
30	*Newcastle*	Flat	EBF/UK Land Estates Hoppings Stakes (fillies)
30	*Newcastle*	Flat	John Smith's Extra Smooth Chipchase Stakes
30	*Newcastle*	Flat	Tote Exacta Northern Sprint Stakes (Handicap)
30	*Newmarket*	Flat	Van Geest Criterion Stakes
30	*Newmarket*	Flat	Hole In The Wall Fred Archer Stakes
30	*Newmarket*	Flat	High Havens Empress Stakes (fillies)

JUNE 2001

		North	Midlands	South	
1	Friday	AYR	NOTTINGHAM	†BATH	Friday
2	Saturday	CATTERICK BRIDGE	†Stratford-on-Avon	†BRIGHTON	
		CATTERICK BRIDGE	NEWMARKET	WINDSOR	Saturday
		MUSSELBURGH	Stratford-on-Avon		
3	Sunday	PONTEFRACT	Fakenham	WINDSOR	Sunday
4	Monday	CARLISLE	LEICESTER	†WINDSOR	Monday
		†THIRSK			
5	Tuesday			LINGFIELD PARK	Tuesday
				Newton Abbot	
6	Wednesday	†BEVERLEY	†CHESTER	†KEMPTON PARK	Wednesday
		NEWCASTLE	Market Rasen		
7	Thursday	HAYDOCK PARK	†Uttoxeter	CHEPSTOW	Thursday
		Perth		†NEWBURY	
8	Friday	CATTERICK BRIDGE	SOUTHWELL (AWT)	EPSOM DOWNS	Friday
		†HAYDOCK PARK		†GOODWOOD	
		†Perth			
9	Saturday	DONCASTER	Worcester	EPSOM DOWNS	Saturday
		HAYDOCK PARK			
10	Sunday	RIPON	NEWMARKET		Sunday
			Worcester		
11	Monday	†PONTEFRACT	NOTTINGHAM	Newton Abbot	Monday
				†WINDSOR	
12	Tuesday	REDCAR		SALISBURY	Tuesday
13	Wednesday	BEVERLEY	Hereford	†KEMPTON PARK	Wednesday
		†HAMILTON PARK		LINGFIELD PARK	
14	Thursday	HAMILTON PARK	†Uttoxeter	†BRIGHTON	Thursday
			YARMOUTH	NEWBURY	
15	Friday	YORK	SOUTHWELL (AWT)	†CHEPSTOW	Friday
				†GOODWOOD	
				†Newton Abbot	
				SANDOWN PARK	
16	Saturday	Hexham	NOTTINGHAM	BATH	Saturday
		YORK		SANDOWN PARK	
17	Sunday	CARLISLE	LEICESTER	SALISBURY	Sunday
18	Monday	MUSSELBURGH	†WARWICK	BRIGHTON	Monday
				†WINDSOR	
19	Tuesday	THIRSK		ASCOT	Tuesday
20	Wednesday	HAMILTON PARK	WOLVERHAMPTON (AWT)	ASCOT	Wednesday
		†RIPON	†Worcester		
21	Thursday	RIPON	SOUTHWELL (AWT)	ASCOT	Thursday
22	Friday	AYR	†NEWMARKET	ASCOT	Friday
		†Hexham		†GOODWOOD	
		REDCAR			
23	Saturday	AYR	Market Rasen	ASCOT	Saturday
		REDCAR		Newton Abbot	
24	Sunday	Perth		LINGFIELD PARK	Sunday
				PONTEFRACT	
25	Monday	MUSSELBURGH	NOTTINGHAM	†WINDSOR	Monday
			†YARMOUTH		
26	Tuesday	BEVERLEY		LINGFIELD PARK	Tuesday
27	Wednesday	CARLISLE	WARWICK	†BATH	Wednesday
		†HAMILTON PARK		†KEMPTON PARK	
				SALISBURY	
28	Thursday	CARLISLE		SALISBURY	Thursday
29	Friday	†NEWCASTLE	NEWMARKET	FOLKESTONE	Friday
			SOUTHWELL (AWT)	†GOODWOOD	
			†Stratford-on-Avon		
30	Saturday	†DONCASTER	CHESTER	†LINGFIELD PARK	Saturday
		NEWCASTLE	NEWMARKET	†Newton Abbot	
			Worcester		

CAPITALS: Flat racing   Lower Case: National Hunt   AWT: (All weather track)   †: Evening Meeting

JULY 2001

Date	Racecourse	Race Type	Race Name
1	*Curragh*	Flat	Budweiser Irish Derby
1	*Goodwood*	Flat	'On The House' Stakes
1	*Uttoxeter*	Chase	Britannia Building Society English Summer National Chase(Hcap)
6	*Sandown Park*	Flat	Tote Exacta Stakes (Handicap)
7	*Haydock Park*	Flat	Letheby & Christopher Old Newton Cup (Handicap)
7	*Haydock Park*	Flat	Unigate Foodservice Lancashire Oaks (fillies)
7	*Haydock Park*	Flat	Charlton Group July Trophy (colts & geldings)
7	*Sandown Park*	Flat	Coral-Eclipse Stakes
7	*Sandown Park*	Flat	Rio De Janeiro Handicap Stakes
7	*Sandown Park*	Flat	Porcelanosa Sprint Stakes
8	*Sandown Park*	Flat	Dragon Stakes
8	*Sandown Park*	Flat	Victor Chandler 'Raceday' Stakes (Handicap)
10	*Newmarket*	Flat	Princess of Wales's Stakes
10	*Newmarket*	Flat	thehorsesmouth.co.uk Cherry Hinton Stakes (fillies)
11	*Newmarket*	Flat	sportingodds.com Falmouth Stakes (fillies)
11	*Newmarket*	Flat	TNT July Stakes (colts & geldings)
11	*Newmarket*	Flat	Bonusprint Stakes (Handicap)
11	*Newmarket*	Flat	Bahrain Trophy
12	*Newmarket*	Flat	Darley July Cup
12	*Newmarket*	Flat	Ladbroke Bunbury Cup (Handicap)
12	*Newmarket*	Flat	Weatherbys Superlative Stakes
13	*York*	Flat	Stanley Racing Summer Stakes (fillies)
14	*Ascot*	Flat	Michael Page International Silver Trophy
14	*Ascot*	Flat	Maxims Casino Club Handicap Stakes
14	*Chester*	Flat	Jani City Wall Stakes
14	*York*	Flat	John Smith's Cup (Handicap)
14	*York*	Flat	Foster's Silver Cup Rated Stakes(Handicap)
15	*Curragh*	Flat	Kildangan Stud Irish Oaks
16	*Ayr*	Flat	Sodexho Prestige Scottish Classic
21	*Newbury*	Flat	Weatherbys Super Sprint Stakes
21	*Newbury*	Flat	Steventon Stakes
21	*Newbury*	Flat	Ruinart Champagne Hackwood Stakes
21	*Newbury*	Flat	Rose Bowl Stakes
21	*Newmarket*	Flat	Foodbrokers Animal Health Trust Trophy (Rated)
21	*Newmarket*	Flat	Foodbrokers Aphrodite Stakes (fillies)
21	*Market Rasen*	Chase	Tote Summer Special Handicap chase
21	*Market Rasen*	Hurdle	Summer Special Handicap Hurdle
26	*Sandown Park*	Flat	Milcars Star Stakes (fillies)
27	*Chepstow*	Flat	Fawley Stud Golden Daffodil Stakes (fillies)
28	*Ascot*	Flat	King George VI and Queen Elizabeth Diamond Stakes
28	*Ascot*	Flat	Tote International Stakes (Handicap)
28	*Ascot*	Flat	Princess Margaret Stakes (fillies)
28	*Ascot*	Flat	Millennium Star Diamond Rated Stakes (Handicap)
29	*Ascot*	Flat	Hong Kong Jockey Club Sprint Stakes (Handicap)
29	*Newmarket*	Flat	Tote Bookmakers NSPCC Handicap Stakes
31	*Goodwood*	Flat	Money Guru Stakes (Handicap)
31	*Goodwood*	Flat	Peugeot Gordon Stakes
31	*Goodwood*	Flat	King George Stakes

Artist: **John King** *THE WORK RIDERS* *Courtesy of:* **Osborne Studio Gallery**

JULY 2001

		North	Midlands	South	
1	Sunday	DONCASTER	Uttoxeter	GOODWOOD	Sunday
2	Monday	†MUSSELBURGH	SOUTHWELL (AWT)	†WINDSOR	Monday
		PONTEFRACT			
3	Tuesday	HAMILTON PARK	YARMOUTH		Tuesday
4	Wednesday	CATTERICK BRIDGE	†YARMOUTH	BRIGHTON	Wednesday
				†KEMPTON PARK	
5	Thursday	CATTERICK BRIDGE		CHEPSTOW	Thursday
		HAYDOCK PARK		† EPSOM DOWNS	
				†NEWBURY	
6	Friday	†BEVERLEY	WARWICK	†SALISBURY	Friday
		†HAYDOCK PARK	Wolverhampton	SANDOWN PARK	
7	Saturday	BEVERLEY	LEICESTER	CHEPSTOW	Saturday
		HAYDOCK PARK		SANDOWN PARK	
8	Sunday	NEWCASTLE	Market Rasen	SANDOWN PARK	Sunday
9	Monday	MUSSELBURGH		BATH	Monday
		†RIPON		†WINDSOR	
10	Tuesday	PONTEFRACT	NEWMARKET		Tuesday
11	Wednesday	DONCASTER	NEWMARKET	†KEMPTON PARK	Wednesday
			†Worcester	LINGFIELD PARK	
12	Thursday	†DONCASTER	NEWMARKET	†EPSOM DOWNS	Thursday
			WOLVERHAMPTON (AWT)	FOLKESTONE	
13	Friday	†HAMILTON PARK	†CHESTER	†CHEPSTOW	Friday
		YORK	SOUTHWELL (AWT)	LINGFIELD PARK	
14	Saturday	YORK	CHESTER	ASCOT	Saturday
			NOTTINGHAM	SALISBURY	
15	Sunday	HAYDOCK PARK	Stratford-on-Avon	BATH	Sunday
16	Monday	AYR	†Wolverhampton	Newton Abbot	Monday
				†WINDSOR	
17	Tuesday	BEVERLEY		BRIGHTON	Tuesday
18	Wednesday	CATTERICK BRIDGE	†Worcester	†KEMPTON PARK	Wednesday
		†DONCASTER	YARMOUTH	LINGFIELD PARK	
19	Thursday	HAMILTON PARK	LEICESTER	†EPSOM DOWNS	Thursday
		†Sedgefield			
20	Friday	CARLISLE	†NEWMARKET	NEWBURY	Friday
		†HAMILTON PARK	SOUTHWELL (AWT)		
		†PONTEFRACT			
21	Saturday	RIPON	Market Rasen	NEWBURY	Saturday
			NEWMARKET		
			WARWICK		
22	Sunday	REDCAR	Southwell	KEMPTON PARK	Sunday
23	Monday	AYR		BRIGHTON	Monday
		†BEVERLEY		†WINDSOR	
24	Tuesday	AYR	YARMOUTH		Tuesday
25	Wednesday	CATTERICK BRIDGE	†LEICESTER	LINGFIELD PARK	Wednesday
			Worcester	†SANDOWN PARK	
26	Thursday	Sedgefield		BATH	Thursday
				SANDOWN PARK	
27	Friday	THIRSK	†NEWMARKET	ASCOT	Friday
			SOUTHWELL (AWT)	†CHEPSTOW	
				†SALISBURY	
28	Saturday	NEWCASTLE	NOTTINGHAM	ASCOT	Saturday
		REDCAR	Stratford-on-Avon		
29	Sunday		NEWMARKET	ASCOT	Sunday
				Newton Abbot	
30	Monday	NEWCASTLE	†YARMOUTH	FOLKESTONE	Monday
				†WINDSOR	
31	Tuesday	BEVERLEY		GOODWOOD	Tuesday

CAPITALS: Flat racing   Lower Case: National Hunt   AWT: (All weather track)   †: Evening Meeting

AUGUST 2001

Date	Racecourse	Race Type	Race Name
1	*Galway*	Chase	Compaq Galway Plate Handicap Chase
1	*Goodwood*	Flat	Champagne Lanson Sussex Stakes
1	*Goodwood*	Flat	Tote Gold Trophy (Handicap)
1	*Goodwood*	Flat	Champagne Lanson Vintage Stakes
1	*Goodwood*	Flat	Marriott Hotels Goodwood Stakes (Handicap)
2	*Galway*	Hurdle	Guinness Galway Handicap Hurdle
2	*Goodwood*	Flat	William Hill Mile (Handicap)
2	*Goodwood*	Flat	J.P. Morgan Goodwood Cup
2	*Goodwood*	Flat	Richmond Stakes (colts & geldings)
2	*Goodwood*	Flat	Oak Tree Stakes (fillies)
3	*Goodwood*	Flat	Volvo Truck Globetrotter Stakes (Handicap)
3	*Goodwood*	Flat	Tioman Island Glorious Stakes (Rated)
3	*Goodwood*	Flat	Queen Elizabeth Molecomb Stakes
3	*Goodwood*	Flat	Stewards' Sprint Stakes (Handicap)
3	*Goodwood*	Flat	Bonusprint Stakes (Handicap)
3	*Goodwood*	Flat	Theo Fennell Lennox Stakes
4	*Goodwood*	Flat	Vodafone Stewards' Cup (Handicap)
4	*Goodwood*	Flat	Vodafone Nassau Stakes (fillies)
4	*Goodwood*	Flat	Vodafone Thoroughbred Stakes
4	*Newmarket*	Flat	Sporting Index Nursery Handicap Stakes
5	*Chester*	Flat	Family Funday Queensferry Stakes
5	*Chester*	Flat	Curzon Park Rated Stakes (Handicap)
5	*Newbury*	Flat	Chalice Stakes (fillies)
11	*Ascot*	Flat	Shergar Cup Day
11	*Haydock Park*	Flat	Petros Rose of Lancaster Stakes
11	*Newmarket*	Flat	Joe Jennings Bookmakers Stakes (Handicap)
11	*Newmarket*	Flat	Milcars Sweet Solera Stakes (fillies)
12	*Ascot*	Flat	betinternet.com E.B.F. Valiant Stakes (fillies)
12	*Leopardstown*	Flat	Independent Heinz 57 Phoenix Stakes
15	*Salisbury*	Flat	European Breeders Fund Upavon Stakes (fillies)
16	*Salisbury*	Flat	Sovereign Stakes (colts & geldings)
17	*Newbury*	Flat	thehorsesmouth.co.uk Hungerford Stakes
17	*Newbury*	Flat	Doncaster Bloodstock Sales Washington Singer Stakes
18	*Newbury*	Flat	thehorsesmouth.co.uk Geoffrey Freer Stakes
18	*Newbury*	Flat	St Hugh's Stakes (fillies)
18	*Ripon*	Flat	William Hill Great St Wilfred Stakes (Handicap)
18	*Wolverhampton*	Flat	Weatherbys Dash
19	*Pontefract*	Flat	Slatch Farm Stud Flying Fillies' Stakes
21	*York*	Flat	Juddmonte International Stakes
21	*York*	Flat	Great Voltigeur Stakes (colts & geldings)
21	*York*	Flat	Weatherbys Insurance Lonsdale Stakes
21	*York*	Flat	Breckenbrough Racing Acomb Stakes
21	*York*	Flat	Ladbroke Knavesmire Stakes (Handicap)
22	*York*	Flat	Aston Upthorpe Yorkshire Oaks (fillies)
22	*York*	Flat	Scottish Equitable Gimcrack Stakes (colts & geldings)
22	*York*	Flat	Tote Ebor (Handicap)
22	*York*	Flat	Costcutter Roses Stakes (colts & geldings)
22	*York*	Flat	Motability Rated Stakes (Handicap)
23	*York*	Flat	Peugeot Lowther Stakes (fillies)
23	*York*	Flat	Nunthorpe Stakes
23	*York*	Flat	Bradford & Bingley Rated Stakes (Handicap)
23	*York*	Flat	Charles Heidsieck Champagne Melrose Rated Stakes (Handicap)
23	*York*	Flat	European Breeders Fund Galtres Stakes (fillies)
23	*York*	Flat	McArthurglen Designer Outlet City of York stakes
24	*Newmarket*	Flat	Charles Heidsieck Champagne Hopeful Stakes
25	*Goodwood*	Flat	Celebration Mile
25	*Goodwood*	Flat	Ladbroke Racing Sprint (Handicap)
25	*Goodwood*	Flat	Sport On 5 March Stakes
25	*Newmarket*	Flat	Tote Nursery Handicap Stakes
25	*Windsor*	Flat	Winter Hill Stakes
26	*Goodwood*	Flat	Link Mobile Phone Prestige Stakes (fillies)
27	*Epsom Downs*	Flat	Tote Bookmakers Sprint (Handicap)
27	*Newcastle*	Flat	Blaydon Stakes (Nursery Handicap)
27	*Newcastle*	Flat	Chisholm Bookmakers Virginia Stakes (Rated)
27	*Ripon*	Flat	Ripon Champion Two Yrs Old Trophy
31	*Epsom Downs*	Flat	Michael J Lonsdale Fortune Stakes

AUGUST 2001

		North	Midlands	South	
1	Wednesday	CARLISLE †MUSSELBURGH	†LEICESTER	GOODWOOD †KEMPTON PARK Newton Abbot	Wednesday
2	Thursday	Sedgefield	Stratford-on-Avon	GOODWOOD	Thursday
3	Friday	†AYR THIRSK	Bangor-on-Dee †NEWMARKET †NOTTINGHAM	GOODWOOD	Friday
4	Saturday	DONCASTER THIRSK	NEWMARKET Worcester	GOODWOOD	Saturday
5	Sunday		CHESTER	NEWBURY Market Rasen	Sunday
6	Monday	†CARLISLE RIPON		Newton Abbot †WINDSOR	Monday
7	Tuesday	CATTERICK BRIDGE		BATH	Tuesday
8	Wednesday	NEWCASTLE PONTEFRACT	†LEICESTER †YARMOUTH	BRIGHTON †SANDOWN PARK	Wednesday
9	Thursday	HAYDOCK PARK		BRIGHTON CHEPSTOW	Thursday
10	Friday	†HAYDOCK PARK	†NEWMARKET WOLVERHAMPTON (AWT) †Worcester	LINGFIELD PARK	Friday
11	Saturday	HAYDOCK PARK REDCAR	NEWMARKET Stratford-on-Avon	ASCOT	Saturday
12	Sunday	REDCAR	LEICESTER	ASCOT	Sunday
13	Monday	†THIRSK	Southwell	FOLKESTONE †WINDSOR	Monday
14	Tuesday			BRIGHTON Newton Abbot	Tuesday
15	Wednesday	BEVERLEY †HAMILTON PARK	YARMOUTH	†EPSOM DOWNS SALISBURY	Wednesday
16	Thursday	BEVERLEY		EPSOM DOWNS SALISBURY	Thursday
17	Friday	†CATTERICK BRIDGE NEWCASTLE	†NEWMARKET	FOLKESTONE NEWBURY	Friday
18	Saturday	†HAYDOCK PARK Perth RIPON	Bangor-on-Dee †WOLVERHAMPTON (AWT)	†LINGFIELD PARK NEWBURY	Saturday
19	Sunday	PONTEFRACT		BATH SANDOWN PARK	Sunday
20	Monday		NOTTINGHAM	BRIGHTON	Monday
21	Tuesday	HAMILTON PARK YORK			Tuesday
22	Wednesday	CARLISLE YORK		LINGFIELD PARK	Wednesday
23	Thursday	MUSSELBURGH		FOLKESTONE YORK	Thursday
24	Friday	†NEWCASTLE THIRSK	NEWMARKET †Uttoxeter	†BATH Fontwell Park	Friday
25	Saturday	BEVERLEY Cartmel †REDCAR	NEWMARKET †Worcester	GOODWOOD †WINDSOR	Saturday
26	Sunday	BEVERLEY	YARMOUTH	GOODWOOD	Sunday
27	Monday (Bank Holiday)	Cartmel NEWCASTLE RIPON	Huntingdon Southwell WARWICK	CHEPSTOW EPSOM DOWNS FOLKESTONE Fontwell Park Newton Abbot	Monday
28	Tuesday	RIPON	Uttoxeter		Tuesday
29	Wednesday	CATTERICK BRIDGE		BRIGHTON	Wednesday
30	Thursday			LINGFIELD PARK SALISBURY	Thursday
31	Friday	AYR	CHESTER	EPSOM DOWNS	Friday

CAPITALS: Flat racing   Lower Case: National Hunt   AWT: (All weather track)   †: Evening Meeting

SEPTEMBER 2001

Date	Racecourse	Race Type	Race Name
1	Chester	Flat	Chester Stakes (Rated)
1	Sandown Park	Flat	Ford Solario Stakes
1	Sandown Park	Flat	Philishave Atalanta Stakes (fillies)
2	Curragh	Flat	Moyglare Stud Stakes
2	York	Flat	Sunday Stakes (Handicap)
5	York	Flat	Travel Trade Gazette Strensall Stakes
5	York	Flat	Lawrence Batley Rated Stakes (Handicap)
7	Kempton Park	Flat	Sirenia Stakes
8	Haydock Park	Flat	Stanley Leisure Sprint Cup
8	Haydock Park	Flat	Newtonborough Handicap Stakes
8	Kempton Park	Flat	Milcars September Stakes
8	Leopardstown	Flat	Esat Digifone Irish Champion Stakes (part of the Emirates World Series Racing Championship)
12	Doncaster	Flat	£200,000 St Leger Yearling
12	Doncaster	Flat	Rothmans Royals Park Hill Stakes (fillies)
12	Doncaster	Flat	Tote Trifecta Portland Stakes (Handicap)
12	Doncaster	Flat	E.B.F. Carrie Red Stakes (fillies) (Nursery Handicap)
13	Doncaster	Flat	Great North Eastern Railway Doncaster Cup
13	Doncaster	Flat	G.N.E.R. Park Stakes
13	Doncaster	Flat	Rothmans Royals May Hill Stakes (fillies)
13	Doncaster	Flat	Kyoto Sceptre Stakes (fillies)
13	Doncaster	Flat	Scarbrough Stakes
14	Doncaster	Flat	thehorsesmouth.co.uk Champagne Stakes (colts & geldings)
14	Doncaster	Flat	DBS St Leger Yearling Stakes
14	Doncaster	Flat	Rothmans Royals Mallard Stakes (Handicap)
14	Doncaster	Flat	Terex Troy Stakes
14	Goodwood	Flat	Bellway Homes Stardom Stakes
15	Curragh	Flat	Jefferson Smurfit Memorial Irish St. Leger Stakes
15	Doncaster	Flat	Rothmans Royals St Leger Stakes (colts & fillies)
15	Doncaster	Flat	Polypipe Plc Flying Childers Stakes
15	Doncaster	Flat	Constant Security Handicap Stakes
15	Goodwood	Flat	Select Stakes
16	Curragh	Flat	Aga Khan Studs National Stakes
18	Yarmouth	Flat	John Musker Stakes (fillies)
20	Ayr	Flat	Sun Life of Canada Harry Rosebery Stakes
21	Newbury	Flat	Dubai Arc Trial
21	Newbury	Flat	Dubai Airport World Trophy
22	Ayr	Flat	Ladbroke (Ayr) Gold Cup Stakes (Handicap)
22	Ayr	Flat	Ladbrokes Ayrshire Handicap Stakes
22	Ayr	Flat	Doonside Cup Stakes
22	Ayr	Flat	Faucets First for Faucets Firth of Clyde Stakes (fillies)
22	Newbury	Flat	Courage Best Handicap Stakes
22	Newbury	Flat	Dubai Duty Free Mill Reef Stakes
22	Newbury	Flat	Tote Sporting Index Autumn Cup (Handicap)
22	Newbury	Flat	Dubai Duty Free Cup
22	Newmarket	Flat	Abu Dhabi Rated Stakes (Handicap)
24	Hamilton Park	Flat	Tote Hamilton Park Buttonhook Handicap Stakes
26	Goodwood	Flat	Caffrey's Premium Ale Foundation Stakes
26	Listowel	Chase	Guinness Kerry National Handicap Chase
27	Goodwood	Flat	Charlton Hunt Supreme Stakes
29	Ascot	Flat	Queen Elizabeth II Stakes
29	Ascot	Flat	Meon Valley Stud Fillies' Mile
29	Ascot	Flat	Tote Trifecta Handicap Stakes
29	Ascot	Flat	John Hopkins Cumberland Lodge Stakes
29	Ascot	Flat	Sodexho Rosemary Stakes (Rated)(fillies)
30	Ascot	Flat	Serpentine Gallery Royal Lodge Stakes
30	Ascot	Flat	Sodexho Diadem Stakes
30	Ascot	Flat	Ritz Club Handicap Stakes
30	Ascot	Flat	Mail On Sunday Mile Final (Handicap)
30	Ascot	Flat	Riggs Bank Harvest Stakes (fillies)
30	Ascot	Flat	Singapore Turf Club Rated Stakes (Handicap)

SEPTEMBER 2001

		North	Midlands	South	
1	Saturday	RIPON	CHESTER Market Rasen	SANDOWN PARK	Saturday
2	Sunday	HAMILTON PARK YORK		SANDOWN PARK	Sunday
3	Monday	HAMILTON PARK		FOLKESTONE	Monday
4	Tuesday	MUSSELBURGH	YARMOUTH	BRIGHTON	Tuesday
5	Wednesday	YORK		LINGFIELD PARK Newton Abbot	Wednesday
6	Thursday	REDCAR	WOLVERHAMPTON (AWT)	SALISBURY	Thursday
7	Friday	HAYDOCK PARK Sedgefield		KEMPTON PARK	Friday
8	Saturday	HAYDOCK PARK THIRSK	Stratford-on-Avon †WOLVERHAMPTON (AWT)	KEMPTON PARK	Saturday
10	Monday	NEWCASTLE	NOTTINGHAM	BATH	Monday
11	Tuesday		LEICESTER	LINGFIELD PARK	Tuesday
12	Wednesday	DONCASTER	Hereford	EPSOM DOWNS	Wednesday
13	Thursday	DONCASTER	Uttoxeter	CHEPSTOW	Thursday
14	Friday	DONCASTER	Worcester	GOODWOOD	Friday
15	Saturday	DONCASTER	Bangor-on-Dee Worcester	GOODWOOD	Saturday
17	Monday		WARWICK	Plumpton	Monday
18	Tuesday	Sedgefield	YARMOUTH	CHEPSTOW	Tuesday
19	Wednesday	BEVERLEY	YARMOUTH	SANDOWN PARK	Wednesday
20	Thursday	AYR	YARMOUTH	PONTEFRACT	Thursday
21	Friday	AYR	NOTTINGHAM	NEWBURY	Friday
22	Saturday	AYR CATTERICK BRIDGE	NEWMARKET †WOLVERHAMPTON (AWT)	NEWBURY	Saturday
24	Monday	HAMILTON PARK	LEICESTER	KEMPTON PARK	Monday
25	Tuesday	BEVERLEY		Fontwell Park	Tuesday
26	Wednesday	Perth	CHESTER	GOODWOOD	Wednesday
27	Thursday	Perth PONTEFRACT		GOODWOOD	Thursday
28	Friday	HAYDOCK PARK REDCAR		ASCOT	Friday
29	Saturday	HAYDOCK PARK	Market Rasen	ASCOT Plumpton	Saturday
30	Sunday	MUSSELBURGH	Huntingdon	ASCOT BRIGHTON	Sunday

CAPITALS: Flat racing   Lower Case: National Hunt   AWT: (All weather track)   †: Evening Meeting

OCTOBER 2001

Date	Racecourse	Race Type	Race Name
2	Newmarket	Flat	£400,000 Tattersalls Houghton Sales
2	Newmarket	Flat	Shadwell Stud Cheveley Park Stakes (fillies)
2	Newmarket	Flat	E.B.F. Jersey Lily Nursery Handicap Stakes (fillies)
4	Newmarket	Flat	Middle Park Stakes (colts)
4	Newmarket	Flat	Joel Stakes
4	Newmarket	Flat	JRA Nakayama Rous Stakes
5	Newmarket	Flat	Somerville Tattersall Stakes (colts & geldings)
5	Newmarket	Flat	Fishpools Furnishings Godolphin Stakes
6	Newmarket	Flat	Tote Cambridgeshire Stakes (Handicap)
6	Newmarket	Flat	Peugeot Sun Chariot Stakes (fillies)
6	Newmarket	Flat	Oh So Sharp Stakes (fillies)
6	Redcar	Flat	Redcar Two-Year-Old Trophy Stakes
13	Ascot	Flat	Princess Royal Willmott Dixon Stakes (fillies)
13	Ascot	Flat	Willmott Dixon Cornwallis Stakes
13	Ascot	Flat	Financial Dynamics October Stakes (fillies)
13	Ascot	Flat	Kleenex Stakes (Handicap)
13	Ascot	Flat	Tom McGee Autumn Stakes
13	York	Flat	Coral Sprint Trophy Stakes (Handicap)
13	York	Flat	Coldstream Guards Rockingham Stakes
18	Newmarket	Flat	Grangewood Severals Stakes (fillies)
19	Newmarket	Flat	£100,000 Tattersalls Autumn Auction Stakes
19	Newmarket	Flat	Egerton Stud Darley Stakes
19	Newmarket	Flat	Bentinck Stakes
20	Newmarket	Flat	Dubai Champion Stakes
20	Newmarket	Flat	Darley Dewhurst Stakes (colts & fillies)
20	Newmarket	Flat	Tote Cesarewitch Stakes (Handicap)
20	Newmarket	Flat	Victor Chandler Challenge Stakes
20	Newmarket	Flat	Owen Brown Rockfel Stakes (fillies)
20	Newmarket	Flat	Jockey Club Cup
20	Newmarket	Flat	Melbourn Handicap Stakes
22	Pontefract	Flat	Tote Silver Tankard Stakes
26	Doncaster	Flat	DBS October Yearling Stakes
26	Newbury	Flat	Vodafone Horris Hill Stakes (colts & geldings)
27	Doncaster	Flat	Racing Post Trophy Stakes (colts & fillies)
27	Doncaster	Flat	Doncaster Stakes
27	Kempton Park	Chase	Charisma Gold Cup Chase (Handicap)
27	Newbury	Flat	Perpetual St Simon Stakes
27	Newbury	Flat	Swettenham Stud Radley Stakes (fillies)
28	Wincanton	Chase	Axminster 100 Desert Orchid SW Pattern Chase (Limited Handicap)

Artist: **Peter Smith** *HEAVY GOING, AYR* *Courtesy of:* **Frost & Reed**

OCTOBER 2001

Date	Day	North	Midlands	South	Day
1	Monday		SOUTHWELL (AWT)	BATH	Monday
2	Tuesday	Sedgefield	NEWMARKET	Exeter	Tuesday
3	Wednesday	NEWCASTLE		BRIGHTON SALISBURY	Wednesday
4	Thursday		Hereford NEWMARKET NOTTINGHAM		Thursday
5	Friday	Hexham	NEWMARKET	LINGFIELD PARK	Friday
6	Saturday	REDCAR	NEWMARKET Uttoxeter †WOLVERHAMPTON (AWT)	Chepstow SANDOWN PARK	Saturday
7	Sunday	Kelso	Market Rasen	Fontwell Park	Sunday
8	Monday	PONTEFRACT		WINDSOR	Monday
9	Tuesday	CATTERICK BRIDGE	Southwell WOLVERHAMPTON (AWT)		Tuesday
10	Wednesday		Towcester	Exeter LINGFIELD PARK	Wednesday
11	Thursday	YORK	Ludlow	Wincanton	Thursday
12	Friday	Carlisle YORK	Huntingdon		Friday
13	Saturday	Hexham YORK	Bangor-on-Dee Southwell	ASCOT	Saturday
15	Monday	AYR	LEICESTER	Folkestone	Monday
16	Tuesday	AYR Sedgefield	LEICESTER		Tuesday
17	Wednesday	HAYDOCK PARK Wetherby		LINGFIELD PARK	Wednesday
18	Thursday		NEWMARKET SOUTHWELL (AWT)	Taunton	Thursday
19	Friday	REDCAR	Hereford NEWMARKET		Friday
20	Saturday	CATTERICK BRIDGE Kelso	Market Rasen NEWMARKET Stratford-on-Avon †WOLVERHAMPTON (AWT)		Saturday
22	Monday	PONTEFRACT	SOUTHWELL (AWT)	Plumpton	Monday
23	Tuesday		WOLVERHAMPTON (AWT) YARMOUTH	Exeter	Tuesday
24	Wednesday	NEWCASTLE	NOTTINGHAM	Chepstow	Wednesday
25	Thursday		Ludlow	BATH BRIGHTON	Thursday
26	Friday	DONCASTER	Fakenham	NEWBURY	Friday
27	Saturday	Carlisle DONCASTER	Southwell	Kempton Park NEWBURY	Saturday
28	Sunday	Aintree	Towcester	Wincanton	Sunday
29	Monday		Bangor-on-Dee LEICESTER	WINDSOR	Monday
30	Tuesday	REDCAR	Cheltenham NOTTINGHAM		Tuesday
31	Wednesday		Cheltenham YARMOUTH	Fontwell Park	Wednesday

CAPITALS: Flat racing   Lower Case: National Hunt   AWT: (All weather track)   †: Evening Meeting

NOVEMBER 2001

Date	Racecourse	Race Type	Race Name
2	Newmarket	Flat	NGK Spark Plugs Stubbs Stakes (Rated)
2	Newmarket	Flat	James Seymour Stakes
3	Ascot	Chase	United House Construction Handicap Chase
3	Newmarket	Flat	Ladbroke Autumn Handicap Stakes
3	Newmarket	Flat	Ben Marshall Stakes
3	Newmarket	Flat	Zetland Stakes
3	Newmarket	Flat	European Breeders Fund Montrose Stakes (fillies)
3	Wetherby	Chase	Peterhouse Group Charlie Hall Chase
3	Wetherby	Hurdle	John Smith's West Yorkshire Hurdle
3	Wetherby	Hurdle	Stanley Racing Wensleydale Juvenile Novice Hurdle
6	Exeter	Chase	William Hill Haldon Gold Cup Chase (Limited Handicap)
10	Chepstow	Hurdle	Tote Silver Trophy Hurdle (Handicap)
10	Chepstow	Chase	Courage Best Bitter Rising Stars Novice Chase
10	Chepstow	Hurdle	Persian War Novice Hurdle
10	Doncaster	Flat	Tote Scoop6 November Stakes (Handicap)
10	Doncaster	Flat	CIU Serlby Stakes
10	Doncaster	Flat	Charles Sidney Mercedes Benz Wentworth Stakes
10	Down Royal	Chase	John Nicholson Steeplechase
10	Wincanton	Chase	Badger Beer Handicap Chase
10	Wincanton	Hurdle	Tanglefoot Elite Hurdle (Limited Handicap)
16	Cheltenham	Chase	Sporting Index Chase (Cross Country)
16	Cheltenham	Hurdle	Capel Cure Sharp Novice Hurdle
17	Cheltenham	Chase	Thomas Pink Gold Cup Chase (Handicap)
18	Haydock Park	Chase	Edward Hanmer Memorial Chase (Limited Handicap)
18	Cheltenham	Hurdle	Eastleach Hurdle (Handicap)
18	Cheltenham	Hurdle	Ladbroke Casinos Hurdle (Intermediate Race)
18	Cheltenham	Chase	Greyhounds as Pets November Novice Chase
23	Ascot	Hurdle	PricewaterhouseCoopers Ascot Hurdle
24	Ascot	Chase	First National Gold Cup Chase (Limited Intermediate Handicap)
24	Huntingdon	Chase	Victor Chandler Peterborough Chase
24	Lingfield Park	AWT	Churchill Stakes
25	Aintree	Chase	Tote Becher Chase (Handicap)
30	Newbury	Chase	Elizabeth Hitchins Worcester Chase

Artist: **Heather St Clair Davis** **WINNERS ENCLOSURE** *Courtesy of:* **Frost & Reed**

NOVEMBER 2001

		North	Midlands	South	
1	Thursday	Sedgefield	Stratford-on-Avon	LINGFIELD PARK	Thursday
2	Friday	Wetherby	NEWMARKET	BRIGHTON	Friday
3	Saturday	Kelso	NEWMARKET	Ascot	Saturday
		Wetherby	†WOLVERHAMPTON (AWT)		
5	Monday	REDCAR	NOTTINGHAM	Plumpton	Monday
6	Tuesday	CATTERICK BRIDGE	Warwick	Exeter	Tuesday
7	Wednesday	MUSSELBURGH		Kempton Park	Wednesday
				Newton Abbot	
8	Thursday	Haydock Park	Towcester	WINDSOR	Thursday
9	Friday	DONCASTER	Uttoxeter		Friday
		Hexham			
10	Saturday	DONCASTER		Chepstow	Saturday
				Sandown Park	
				Wincanton	
12	Monday	Carlisle	SOUTHWELL (AWT)	Fontwell Park	Monday
13	Tuesday	Sedgefield	Huntingdon	LINGFIELD PARK (AWT)	Tuesday
14	Wednesday	Kelso		Folkestone	Wednesday
				Newbury	
15	Thursday		Ludlow	LINGFIELD PARK (AWT)	Thursday
				Taunton	
16	Friday	Newcastle	Cheltenham		Friday
			SOUTHWELL (AWT)		
17	Saturday	Ayr	Cheltenham		Saturday
		Wetherby	Uttoxeter		
			†WOLVERHAMPTON (AWT)		
18	Sunday	Ayr	Cheltenham		Sunday
		Haydock Park			
19	Monday		Leicester		Monday
			SOUTHWELL (AWT)		
20	Tuesday		Hereford	LINGFIELD PARK (AWT)	Tuesday
				Newton Abbot	
21	Wednesday	Hexham	WOLVERHAMPTON (AWT)	Kempton Park	Wednesday
22	Thursday	Sedgefield	Warwick	Wincanton	Thursday
23	Friday		SOUTHWELL (AWT)	Ascot	Friday
				Exeter	
24	Saturday	Catterick Bridge	Huntingdon	Ascot	Saturday
				LINGFIELD PARK (AWT)	
25	Sunday	Aintree	Fakenham	Plumpton	Sunday
26	Monday	Newcastle	Ludlow		Monday
			SOUTHWELL (AWT)		
27	Tuesday		Market Rasen		Tuesday
			Towcester		
			WOLVERHAMPTON (AWT)		
28	Wednesday	Wetherby		Chepstow	Wednesday
				LINGFIELD PARK (AWT)	
29	Thursday	Carlisle	Uttoxeter	Taunton	Thursday
30	Friday		Bangor-on-Dee	Newbury	Friday
			SOUTHWELL (AWT)		

CAPITALS: Flat racing   Lower Case: National Hunt   AWT: (All weather track)   †: Evening Meeting

31

DECEMBER 2001

Date	Racecourse	Race Type	Race Name
1	*Newbury*	Chase	Hennessy Cognac Gold Cup Chase (Handicap)
1	*Newbury*	Chase	Ladbroke Handicap Chase
1	*Newbury*	Hurdle	RBI Promotions Gerry Feilden Hurdle (Limited Handicap)
1	*Newbury*	Hurdle	EDS Long Distance Hurdle
1	*Newcastle*	Hurdle	Pertemps 'Fighting Fifth' Hurdle
2	*Fairyhouse*	Hurdle	Hatton's Grace Hurdle
2	*Fairyhouse*	Chase	Drinmore Novice Chase
2	*Fairyhouse*	Chase	Royal Bond Novice Chase
7	*Sandown Park*	Hurdle	Bovis Europe Winter Novice Hurdle
8	*Chepstow*	Chase	Coral Rehearsal Chase (Limited Handicap)
8	*Sandown Park*	Chase	Mitsubishi Shogun Tingle Creek Trophy Chase
8	*Sandown Park*	Hurdle	William Hill Hurdle (Handicap)
8	*Sandown Park*	Chase	Extraman Trophy Novice Chase
9	*Punchestown*	Chase	John Durkan Memorial Chase
15	*Cheltenham*	Chase	Tripleprint Gold Cup Chase (Handicap)
15	*Cheltenham*	Hurdle	Bonusprint Bula Hurdle
15	*Cheltenham*	Hurdle	Chubb Bristol Hurdle
15	*Haydock Park*	Chase	Tommy Whittle Chase
15	*Lingfield Park*	Chase	Arena Leisure December Novice Chase
15	*Lingfield Park*	Hurdle	Summit Junior Hurdle
22	*Ascot*	Hurdle	Cantor Fitzgerald Long Walk Hurdle
22	*Ascot*	Chase	Tote Silver Cup Chase (Handicap)
22	*Ascot*	Chase	Mitie Group Noel Novice Chase
22	*Ascot*	Hurdle	Capel Cure Sharp Kennel Gate Novice Chase
26	*Kempton Park*	Chase	Pertemps King George VI Chase
26	*Kempton Park*	Chase	Pertemps Partnership Feltham Novice Chase
26	*Leopardstown*	Chase	Denny Gold Medal Chase
26	*Wetherby*	Chase	Castleford Chase (Limited Handicap)
27	*Chepstow*	Chase	Coral Welsh National Chase (Handicap)
27	*Chepstow*	Hurdle	Finale Junior Hurdle
27	*Chepstow*	NHF	Chepstow Championship Bumper
27	*Kempton Park*	Hurdle	Pertemps Christmas Hurdle
27	*Leopardstown*	Chase	Paddy Power Handicap Chase
27	*Wetherby*	Chase	Rowland Meyrick Chase (Handicap)
28	*Leopardstown*	Chase	Ericsson Chase
29	*Newbury*	Hurdle	Challow Hurdle
31	*Cheltenham*	Chase	Windrush Chase (Handicap)
31	*Fontwell Park*	Chase	Victor Chandler Sussex National Chase (Handicap)

Artist: **Philip Toon** *LAST SNOW* *Courtesy of:* **The Artist**

DECEMBER 2001

		North	Midlands	South	
1	Saturday	Haydock Park Newcastle	Warwick †WOLVERHAMPTON (AWT)	Newbury	Saturday
3	Monday	Kelso	SOUTHWELL (AWT)	Folkestone	Monday
4	Tuesday		Hereford	LINGFIELD PARK (AWT) Newton Abbot	Tuesday
5	Wednesday	Catterick Bridge	WOLVERHAMPTON (AWT)	Plumpton	Wednesday
6	Thursday		Leicester Market Rasen	Wincanton	Thursday
7	Friday		Southwell	Exeter Sandown Park	Friday
8	Saturday	Wetherby	Towcester †WOLVERHAMPTON (AWT)	Chepstow Sandown Park	Saturday
10	Monday	Ayr	SOUTHWELL (AWT)	Folkestone	Monday
11	Tuesday	Sedgefield	WOLVERHAMPTON (AWT)	Fontwell Park	Tuesday
12	Wednesday	Hexham	Leicester	LINGFIELD PARK (AWT)	Wednesday
13	Thursday		Huntingdon Ludlow	Taunton	Thursday
14	Friday	Doncaster	Cheltenham SOUTHWELL (AWT)		Friday
15	Saturday	Doncaster Haydock Park	Cheltenham SOUTHWELL (AWT) †WOLVERHAMPTON (AWT)	Lingfield Park	Saturday
17	Monday		SOUTHWELL (AWT) Towcester	Plumpton	Monday
18	Tuesday	Musselburgh	Hereford WOLVERHAMPTON (AWT)		Tuesday
19	Wednesday		Bangor-on-Dee	LINGFIELD PARK (AWT) Newbury	Wednesday
20	Thursday	Catterick Bridge	Ludlow	Exeter	Thursday
21	Friday		SOUTHWELL (AWT) Uttoxeter	Ascot	Friday
22	Saturday	Newcastle	Uttoxeter Warwick	Ascot LINGFIELD PARK (AWT)	Saturday
26	Wednesday (Bank Holiday)	Ayr Sedgefield Wetherby	Hereford Huntingdon Market Rasen Towcester WOLVERHAMPTON (AWT)	Kempton Park Wincanton	Wednesday (Bank Holiday)
27	Thursday	Wetherby	Leicester	Chepstow Kempton Park	Thursday
28	Friday	Haydock Park Musselburgh		Taunton	Friday
29	Saturday	Carlisle	Southwell Stratford-on-Avon	Newbury	Saturday
31	Monday	Catterick Bridge	Cheltenham Warwick	Fontwell Park	Monday

CAPITALS: Flat racing   Lower Case: National Hunt   AWT: (All weather track)   †: Evening Meeting

33

Scotland

The North

© *MAP IN MINUTES™ (2000)*

Yorkshire

The North West

© *MAP IN MINUTES™(2000)*

_East
Midlands &
East Anglia_

The Midlands & South Wales

© _MAP IN MINUTES™ (2000)_

London & The South

The South West

© *MAP IN MINUTES™ (2000)*

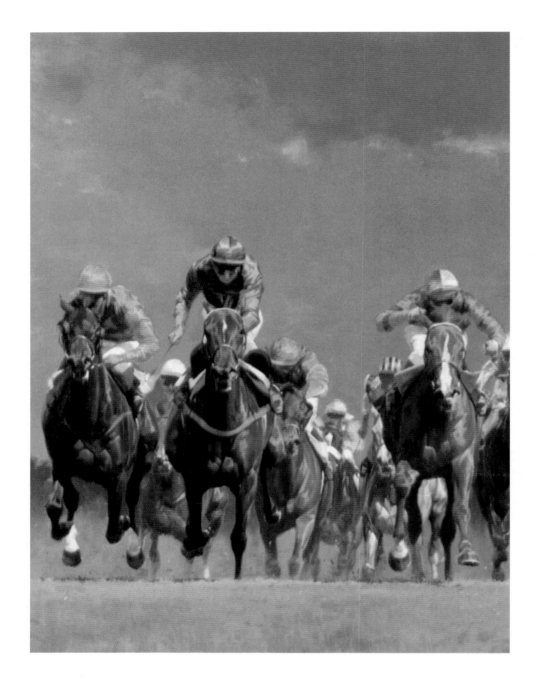

racecourseguide.com

Travelling the Turf goes online from December 2000

* Racing in Britain • Racing in Ireland
* Racing around the world • Racing Calendar
* Point-to-Pointing • A day at the races
* Special offers at racecourses and hotels
* Competitions

British Racecourses

Artist: **D M Dent** **THE 1999 DERBY** Courtesy of: **The Artist**

Aintree is in the capable and safe hands of **Charles Barnett**, who acts as the **Managing Director. Ian Renton** is the **Clerk of the Course** and the **Operations Manager** is **Alastair Warwick** with **Dickon White** as **Marketing Manager**. If you wish to make enquiries with reference to the Grand National Festival, please write to **Aintree Racecourse Co Ltd, Aintree, Liverpool L9 5AS. Tel 0151 523 2600 Fax 0151 522 2920. web site: www.aintree.co.uk**

The racecourse itself lies seven miles from the centre of Liverpool in the suburb of Aintree and approximately one mile from the end of the M58 and M57. Travellers coming up from London should expect a journey of some 213 miles. The M1/M6 double is the answer for these southerners, while visitors from north of Merseyside might care to use another motorway double—the M6 followed by the M58. Northbound travellers from Birmingham should use the M5 before joining the M6/M57. If you are a train traveller then the Euston line is the one to be on. From Liverpool Central take the Merseyrail to Aintree. The station is opposite the course entrance. The No 5 bus from Lime Street also stops next to the track. Car drivers should note that there are over 230 acres in which to park your car or coach—follow the signs for your chosen enclosure and arrive early to see the non-race entertainment and avoid the queues! Perhaps a better idea is to use the free 'park and ride' system which was successfully launched in 1998. Coach parking is no longer allowed in the central enclosure, giving much improved viewing on the Mildmay course. The Steeplechase enclosure has seated viewing for 600 and a total capacity of 25,000. The cost of parking varies from £5 to £25 on the Saturday. If you prefer to fly, (helicopters only please), do contact the course in advance. You will need written permission from Philip Pickford. Contact him on 0161 799 6967.

The Aintree Festival lasts three days, during which racing of the highest quality is guaranteed. Each day features pattern races, and champions and old favourites reappear every year, particularly in the National with many horses seeming to love the big day and being kept in reserve just for the occasion. Some come straight from the Cheltenham Festival, attempting to enhance or redeem reputations. As the shrewd punter knows, Cheltenham form can be well and truly reversed at Aintree. During the meeting, racing takes place over three different courses—the Grand National course, the Mildmay course and the Hurdle course. Friday features the John Hughes Memorial Race over the National fences, whetting the appetite for the big day. You also have a sight of the Grand National fences on the Thursday, during the Martell Foxhunters Chase, and prospective star hurdlers appear in the Glenlivet Hurdle.

Aintree has a members' scheme, the Grand National Club which offers a private room, choice of badge, four course lunch, champagne reception, and private parking. Costs are £275 single, £495 joint. At time of going to press, admission charges were not confirmed for the 2001 Grand National meeting but in 2000 they varied from £20-25 for the County enclosure on Thursday, rising to £65 for a place in the Princess Royal, Queen Mother or County stands on Grand National Day. Three day badges were also available and if you bought them before January 1st the price dropped from £105 to £95 for the Princess Royal and Queen Mother stands with similar discounts for the County, Glenlivet stands and Tattersalls. But you don't have to spend this much to enjoy the wonders of Aintree on National Day as a mere £7 will get you into the Steeplechase enclosure and you can bring the kids for a modest £2 a head; excellent value considering you will be closer to

Artist: **Peter Smith HE'S DONE IT AGAIN!** _Courtesy of:_ **Frost & Reed**

the action than many others attending. The Steeplechase and Tattersalls Enclosures have bookmaking and Tote facilities, and an arcade of shops. Entry to these enclosures costs between £5 and £16, depending on the day. Transfer badges may be purchased daily subject to availability. Various discounts are available for parties of 25 or more if you contact the course well in advance. For all other meetings a one admission price policy of £12 has been introduced, allowing access to all public areas, with accompanied children aged 16 and under admitted free.

One sensible addition to Aintree's facilities is the starvision screens, of which there are six on National Day, giving you a life size view of the action—essential for some if they are to see the racing, given the large crowds that attend. The November Becher's meeting is also a first class event, and the May evening meeting has also become a regular fixture, which is a pleasure to report. A new visitor attraction, The Grand National Experience, opened in July 1999, which gives people the chance to ride out their own winner in the Grand National virtual reality ride!

Aintree is continually improving itself and the latest addition to the facilities is the new Princess Royal Stand which was opened on Martell Grand National Day in 1998. It includes a large ground floor Irish Bar, incorporating a betting shop and food and drink outlets for Tattersalls racegoers. There is seating for 1,000 people, plus standing room for a further 2,000, with access to the Mumm Champagne Bar. There are also 16 private rooms in the new stand, 10 of which overlook the racecourse. On the top floor is the magnificent Martell Suite which is a restaurant seating 350 with its own private viewing balcony for patrons and unrivalled views of the course. Other new facilities in Tattersalls include the Chair Pavilion which overlooks the Chair fence, bringing extra coffee shop facilities to Tatts patrons.

Other restaurants at Aintree are the County Reserved Dining Room (advance bookings only) and the Rendezvous (with wheelchair access) where you can expect to pay between £17 and £20 per head. Catering at all on-course eateries is by racecourse specialists Letheby & Christopher.

There is little doubt that the connection between racing, both flat and over the jumps, on both sides of the Irish Sea has grown stronger in recent years and nowhere has this been better highlighted than the emotional victory of the Irish trained Papillon in the 2000 Grand National. The lightly raced Mely Moss was the only real danger as the winning post loomed, but Ruby Walsh kept it in the family as he rode Papillon, trained by his prolific father Ted, to a popular and exhilarating win. As dedicated National Hunt followers well know, the thrill of victory is never far away from the agony of witnessing a favourite horse make the ultimate sacrifice to the sport. Aintree has done just about everything conceivable to ensure the welfare of horses and riders taking on its still formidable obstacles and yet an unprecedented string of fatalities at the Grand National meeting prompted renewed calls for action, or, heaven forbid, a ban on National Hunt racing. We hope that wise counsel will prevail in the future, and that those who make their profits out of racing, including the bookmaking fraternity, will rally round the BHBs initiative on racehorse welfare.

*Artist: **David Dent** **GRAND NATIONAL 2000 PAPILLON** Courtesy of: **Arlington Gallery***

In Liverpool, the more luxurious hotels include the **Thistle Atlantic Tower** 0151 227 4444, which boasts two especially remarkable sights: the docklands of the river Mersey and a giant statue of one of Liverpool's best known sons, John Lennon. Other good smaller hotels include The **Park** 0151 525 7555 and **Devonshire House** 0151 280 3903. A good place for a pre-race celebration can be found at the **Trials Hotel** 0151 227 1021—an excellent atmosphere to savour here. **The Crowne Plaza** 0151 243 8000 and **The Swallow Hotel** 0151 476 8000 are also two good bets. The **Liverpool Moat House** 0151 471 9988 is also a good runner in this national field. A perfect restaurant for visiting racegoers is the well thought of **Becher's Brook** 0151 707 0005.

From a mind-boggling selection of establishments one prominent example is the **Aachen House** 0151 709 3477. In Liverpool there are a number of restaurants to sample and an extremely popular bistro for lunch or dinner is **Baritalia** 0151 236 3375. Finally, a marvellous pub to visit is the celebrated **Philharmonic** 0151 709 1163—a great place to assess the form on Grand National Eve.

The Lancashire coast yields some excellent golf courses: Royal Liverpool, Royal Birkdale and Royal Lytham St Annes. In Lytham, the **Clifton Arms** (01253) 739898 is a thoughtfully modernised Edwardian hotel. In Lytham St Anne's, the **Dalmeny Hotel** (01253) 712236 is well turned out and the restaurant is well thought of. The **Grand** (01253) 721288, the **Bedford** (01253) 724636 and the **Glendower** (01253) 723241 are also worthy candidates. Further south, in Southport with its gorgeous sands where Red Rum used to gallop, there are a number of good pubs and a hotel of note is the **Scarisbrick** (01704) 543000. The **Prince of Wales** Hotel (01704) 536688 also merits a pre-race inspection and for a budget break, the **Ambassador** (01704) 543998 will almost certainly lead to a return visit. A restaurant to consider is **Ho'Lee**

Chow's (01704) 551167. Those coming from the south, wishing to break their journey prior to Aintree might consider either the **Jolly Thresher** (01925) 752265, Broomedge or the **Spinner and Bergamot** (01606) 891307, Comberbach or the **George and Dragon** (01606) 891317, Great Budworth.

It may well be that our golfing supremo might have wished to visit Hoylake. If this was the case, then he might have been tempted to stay at the **Bowler Hat Hotel**, Birkenhead 0151 652 4931. The **Lord Daresbury Hotel** (01925) 267331, handily situated near to Warrington is also one to consider. Also near Warrington the **Park Royal International Hotel** (01925) 730706 does special racing breaks including racing papers and transport to and from the racecourse. If you are envisaging a particularly good day and don't mind a trip, **Paul Heathcote's Restaurant** (01772) 784969 is outstanding and can be found in Longridge near Preston.

For those who want to make a weekend of it, there are many places to visit slightly further afield. The **Inn at Whitewell**, (01200) 448222 in Whitewell to the north of Aintree is a splendid ancient inn, whilst at Knutsford the **Cottons Hotel**, (01565) 650333 is well worth a look. In Cheshire, the **Hartford Hall Hotel**, (01606) 75711 at Northwich offers 16th century charm along with 20th century comfort. **Nunsmere Hall** (01606) 889100 is an excellent stayer where the Garden Room Restaurant is first class. What's more, the hotel is almost entirely surrounded by a lake—ideal for throwing oneself in if the big ante-post bet on the National falls at the first and brings down the wife's selection! At Woolton, The **Woolton Redbourne** 0151 421 1500 is a top notch hotel to start and end a great sporting weekend. Finally, if any more suggestions are needed, then turn to the Haydock Park section for inspiration.

Artist: **Hubert de Watrigant** **THE WEIGHING ROOM, AINTREE 98** _Courtesy of:_ **Osborne Studio Gallery**

Sporting Fine Art

Istabraq

Image size 18" x 21", edition size 650
Each print is individually signed
by the jockey Charlie Swan and the trainer Aidan O'Brien
and signed and numbered by the artist, Stephen Smith

Sporting Fine Art
88 Gloucester Crescent, Rushden, Northamptonshire NN10 0BN
Tel: (01933) 355248
Fax: (01933) 357187

Ascot is a really outstanding sporting venue. It used to suffer from a terribly stuffy image, but all that has gone now. Today, Ascot provides style and class but is most certainly not aloof. It is also interesting to note that the racecorse is endeavouring to use its brand logo - a relatively recent mark when compared with others - to enhance star products; an interesting concept amongst a plethora of new ideas from a thoroughly progressive team whom we wish well.

The management team includes **Douglas Erskine Crum,** the **Chief Executive; Nicholas Cheyne**, the **Clerk of the Course; Jane Macdonald,** as **Operations Director** and **David Demolder** who is the **Events Director. Her Majesty's Representative** is **Lord Hartington**. The authorities can be contacted at **Ascot Racecourse, Ascot, Berkshire. Tel (01344) 622211. Fax (01344) 628299**. There is a credit card hotline for all bookings on **(01344) 876876** and car park details are dealt with on **(01344) 20768. Website: www.ascot.co.uk E mail: enquiries@ascot.co.uk.**

The racecourse lies approximately midway between the M3 and the M4. Travellers from the west should use the M4, exiting at junction 10 taking the A329 signed to Bracknell, following the signs to the course. From the south and east, the M3 is recommended, leaving at junction 3 onto the A332 to Bracknell and following the signs to Ascot. From London and the north, exit at junction 6 of the M4 and turn onto the A332 Windsor by-pass. The traffic for the big meetings is usually heavy so an early start is recommended. Indeed, so much so, that the train is often a sensible alternative. Although the station is a fairly stiff three furlongs uphill to the grandstand, one is generally rewarded by a smooth trip from both Waterloo and Reading giving you plenty of time to peruse the form before the

racing. Helicopters are permitted to land during major meetings through Helicopter Aviation Services: (01279) 850 750

The course hosts some 24 racedays and these range from high quality midweek jump meetings in winter to the summer heat of the King George VI and Queen Elizabeth Diamond Stakes, the Festival and Royal Ascot. The Royal Meeting is one of the social occasions of the year with the Royal Family parading down the centre of the course before the racing on all four days. The popularity of the event is staggering: picnics in the car park are always a feast and there is a constant popping of champagne corks before, and after, the racing. As in 2000, the 2001 Festival of British Racing will be run over two days.

It should be emphasised that people who attend the royal event merely for the binge are really missing out. The four days of equine excellence are purely and simply the best in the racing year. Tickets to the Royal Enclosure are available provided you follow the proper formalities. All enquiries should be made in writing to Her Majesty's Representative, Ascot Office, St James's Palace, London SW1A 1BP. Visitors from abroad should apply to their embassies. Admission to other enclosures is less demanding and less formal, and racegoers can still enjoy the pomp of the occasion. As a spectacle of elegance, the meeting really takes some beating, and as a race meeting there is no match!

Apart from the Royal Meeting which is at its busiest on Thursday, Gold Cup Day, the Queen Elizabeth II Stakes at the Festival, and Diamond Day in July, there are some excellent jump meetings. These include the Victor Chandler Steeplechase

Artist: ***Klaus Philipp*** ***STEEPLECHASE FINISH*** *Courtesy of:* ***The Artist***

in January, the First National Day in November and the Cantor Fitzgerald Day in December.

Whichever day you decide to go, there are definite advantages in becoming an Annual Member—special rooms and viewing areas are reserved for convenience; the Club dining room and Garden room are two examples. The Annual Membership in 2000 was £150 although it does not admit you to the Royal Meeting. Members may also purchase a guest's transferable badge which is priced at £118. Younger racing enthusiasts (17-25 year olds) should not mind the first rate junior membership price of £50. Everyone is welcome at Ascot and you can book in advance for the Royal Meeting for the Grandstand and Paddock from January 2nd 2001. In 2000 prices for the Members for Royal Ascot were £37.50 for Tuesday and Wednesday while Thursday and Friday were £45. Be sure to book well in advance. For the Festival meeting and Diamond Day, a charge of £27 was asked for the Members, while £16 allowed you into the Grandstand and £6 the Silver Ring, which is good value. On all other days throughout the year, the Silver Ring was £6, the Grandstand and Paddock £11 and the Members £16. Prices have yet to be confirmed for 2001.

All of Ascot's enclosures have good facilities and good viewing. The course has made some improvements during the past year and the first floor of the Grandstand has been fully refurbished, as have a number of public bars. The course offers reductions of up to 25 per cent on admission charges on certain days and there are a huge number of boxes at the course but—and here's the catch—there is between a 3 and 17 year waiting list! However, they are often leased on a daily basis. Ascot have recently built two new boxes, the Cumberland Box and the Millennium Box, both of which command great views of the racecourse. Contact the racecourse to make general enquiries with regard to dates, availability, size etc (01344) 622211. There are numerous rooms, bars and snack outlets in which to indulge—most named after champions that have graced Ascot's turf. There is now a large area set aside for owners and trainers. The food ranges from four course, waitress served, luncheons to hot snacks and sandwiches. Facilities for the disabled are very good and there is a playground for under 11s and a free crèche for under 8s. A Barclays Bank is also open in the Grandstand, together with several shops.

It is great to hear of plans to redevelop the vast stands of Ascot. Let's hope the success of these developments is as profound as the atmosphere at the racecourse itself. The racecourse, owned by the Crown, should also consider as well as nurturing its own young brand, an association similar to that found at Wimbledon with truly excellent trademarks. The Royal Family is being encouraged to fund itself more progressively and if done sensitively this will be a wonderful way of incorporating revenue without detracting from the style of this outstanding racecourse.

The consistently high calibre of racing presented at the Royal meeeting apart, once again the highlight of the year was the devastating victory of Montjeu in the King George VI and Queen Elizabeth Diamond Stakes in July. With all other competition now firmly beaten, the winner was now surely poised to take on a fellow superstar in Dubai Millennium. Unfortunaely we will never know the outcome of this tantalising prospect as the Godolphin flag-bearer saw his racing days ended with injury on the gallops. A few weeks later though, Ascot successfully staged the second Shergar Cup meeting, a challenge match between jockeys from Europe versus the rest of the world. Everyone seems to agree that the concept needs some fine tuning to become a truly competitive event, but as an entertainment spectacle it surely sent the pulses racing of the nearly 20,000 who sweltered under the summer sun, many of them first time racegoers.

*Artist: **David Trundley** ROYAL ASCOT Courtesy of: **The Artist***

There are numerous excellent hostelries in Berkshire's leafy countryside making ideal ports of call for a pre or post-race chat. We start our Ascot recommendations with a pub and restaurant double, the **Winkfield** (01344) 883498 in Winkfield Row—there is fine bar food here and a cosy restaurant. Another good eating establishment located in Ascot is the **Thatched Tavern** (01344) 620874—a great atmosphere here as well with first rate beer. The **Rose and Crown** (01344) 882051 has some rooms and good food, it's very handy for the racecourse.

Back in Winkfield, one finds the **Olde Hatchet** (01344) 899910 which is both handy and friendly and the small restaurant is well worth considering. Another pub with a restaurant is the **White Hart** (01344) 882415—the bar snacks here are good. Further west, and in Waltham St Lawrence, the **Bell** (0118) 9341788 is a pub restaurant with a beautifully relaxed atmosphere, ideal for explaining the disastrous losses of the afternoons racing to one's better half! (but don't take the children).

Binfield has more than its fair share of good boozers—the **Stag and Hounds** (01344) 483553 and the **Victoria Arms** (01344) 483856 are two of several that should be sampled.

At Bray, the **Monkey Island Hotel** (01628) 623400, securely anchored on its own private island, is an idyllic retreat from the bustle of Ascot. The **Fat Duck** restaurant (01628) 580333 is also one that comes highly recommended. The **Hinds Head** here is a popular pub to shortlist. Another jewel is the **Brickmakers Arms** (01276) 472267 - very good fayre here as is **The Fish** (01628) 781111 which serves sumptuous seafood meals.

There are many people who will dash straight home after racing but for people wishing to stay locally there are a number of possibilities; the **Berystede Hotel** (01344) 623311 on the Bagshot Road in Ascot, or in Bagshot itself, the **Pennyhill Park Hotel** (01276) 471774 a grand country mansion which also has a commendable restaurant. An alternative which is less pricey is the **Cricketers**, also in Bagshot (01276) 473196. A little further

Artist: **Terence Gilbert** *JOCKEY SILKS* *Courtesy of:* **The Artist**

south one arrives in Camberley. Here, the **Frimley Hall Hotel** (01276) 28321 is not cheap but most comfortable. Other places that are well worth considering include a brace of hotels in Egham, in neighbouring Surrey. Neither is particularly cheap, but both are extremely comfortable. They are **Great Fosters** (01784) 433822, an outstandingly elegant former hunting lodge with good facilities, and the **Runnymede** (01784) 436171 where a Thames-side setting adds scenic splendour—a warm favourite for racegoers. A jolly restaurant in Egham should also be noted when visiting the races or bloodstock sales—The **Olive Grove** (01784) 439494, where Mediterranean cuisine is the order of the day. Maidenhead is also handy for the course and **Fredrick's Hotel** (01628) 581000 is well worth a visit (a superb restaurant here as well). The **Holiday Inn Maidenhead** (01628) 506000 is another worthy option. In Sonning, **The Great House** (01734) 692277 comes particularly well recommended for both service and value as does **French Horn** (01189) 692204 which commands a great view over the Thames. While in Hurley, **Ye Olde Bell** (01628) 825881 boasts a wealth of charming features and extremely comfortable bedrooms. Further out in Pingewood, the **Hannover International Hotel** (0118) 9500885, offers a spectacular lakeside situation, but is modern by comparison. Another modern and excellently equipped hotel is the Swiss

styled **Coppid Beech** (01344) 303333—a good restaurant here as well.

In Ascot itself, the **Royal Berkshire Hotel** (01344) 623322, is a superb Queen Anne mansion with excellent restaurants and is worth noting when visiting this esteemed course. Ascot is synonymous with style and if one wishes to experience the real glamour of days gone by, then a visit to the singularly magnificent **Cliveden** (01628) 668561 is in order. Former home of the Astor family, the house is now an hotel of unrivalled elegance. Another handy local favourite is the **Stirrups Hotel** (01344) 882284 at Maidens Green near Bracknell, a hotel and restaurant combination with prominent racing themes. A night spent in Ascot does not have to be extravagantly expensive. For affordable comfort try the **Highclere Hotel** (01344) 625220 at Sunninghill. The **Jade Fountain** (01344) 627070, in the High Street is also a good choice for those who enjoy Chinese cooking. Other ideas for the Ascot racegoer can be found in the Windsor, Sandown and Kempton sections of this book. Whatever happens at the racetrack there are numerous fine hostelries at which to celebrate or commiserate in and around Ascot—a thoroughbred racecourse.

*Artist: **Terence Gilbert** LADIES DAY, ROYAL ASCOT Courtesy of: **The Artist***

The **Clerk of the Course** and **General Manager** at Ayr can be contacted at **2 Whitletts Road, Ayr, KA8 0JE. Tel (01292) 264179. Fax (01292) 610140. E mail: info@ayr-racecourse.co.uk web site: www.ayr-racecourse.co.uk** On racedays there is an on-course office at the main Eglinton Stand entrance.

The track is situated just outside Ayr and is easily accessible via the dual carriageway which bypasses the town centre. The course is about 400 miles from London but the motorway network should see you through smoothly and the A713, the A70 and the A77 will carry you to Ayr from Glasgow on the latter stages of your journey to the large, free car parks. If the car journey sounds too much like hard work, then Prestwick Airport is located only 15 minutes away from the racecourse while Glasgow International Airport is only 45 minutes from Ayr. The airstrip in the centre of the course is suitable only for helicopters but please notify the racecourse of your intended arrival. Trains depart from London Euston and the station at Ayr is a mile from the course where a bus trip will complete your journey.

The management have been very successful in attracting sponsorship at Scotland's premier racecourse. There are several races to look out for, including the Stakis Casinos Scottish National in April, the Tennant Caledonian Brewery Scottish Classic in July and the popular Western Meeting in September which features the Ladbroke Ayr Gold Cup. This three day meeting provides excellent racing and the ideal excuse for a jaunt to the superb Ayrshire coast.

The daily admission rates vary from meeting to meeting. Daily entrance in 2001 to the Club Enclosure is priced from £14 - £25, while entrance to the Grandstand and Paddock costs between £7 and £10. OAPs and students with the appropriate identification are welcomed to the racecourse at £4 for most meetings with children under 16 of course admitted free. Ayr

have introduced some innovative ways to get people to "Come Racing!" including Family Newcomers Days when £7 admits you to all enclosures and a Ladies Evening in August where the same price admits the fairer sex to the Members. Two day badges cost £35 for the Members and £15 for the Grandstand for the Scottish National Meeting and £48 and £20 respectively for the Gold Cup meeting in September. For parties of ten or more there is a special offer of £13 to include admission to the Grandstand and lunch in the Eglinton Suite. If you wish to become an Annual Member, a double badge together with a complimentary parking pass in the Western House Car Park will cost around £200. A joining fee of £100 is also required. This will allow you to attend Ayr's annual fixtures as well as reciprocal meetings at other racecourses.

The on-course catering facilities, managed by Sodexho Prestige, are comprehensive, ranging from a full tented village to the Western House which caters for parties of 60 to 200, and the Eglinton Rooms which can hold up to 400 guests. The Princess Royal Stand offers twelve private boxes for groups of up to 20 close to the winning post and two large sponsors' rooms which can hold up to 90 guests. Private rooms and private boxes are also available for daily hire in the recently refurbished Craigie Stand accomodating from 14 to 90 guests. There are various restaurants and snack bars at Ayr including the club restaurant in the Western House, a champagne bar in the Princess Royal Stand with spectacular views of the track, the Eglinton Restaurant in the Grandstand and the totally redecorated Chancellor Bar.

Facilities for the disabled include viewing ramps and lavatories in all enclosures and ground floor bars. There is a Ladbrokes betting shop in the Grandstand. Ayr is a fine racecourse boasting competitive racing and some spectacular betting events. All in all, this is an excellent racecourse.

*Artist: **Peter Smith** EARLY MORNING, CREE LODGE Courtesy of: **Frost & Reed***

There are all manner of guesthouses in and around Ayr and the local tourist board will help with any enquiries. People wishing for hotel accommodation also have a good choice when visiting West Scotland and Ayr racecourse.

The **Turnberry Hotel** (01655) 331000 is an extremely stylish place to stay with an array of leisure facilities, including two world-famous golf courses, the Ailsa and the Arran. The **Blairquhan Castle** (01655) 770239 is also worth a visit and is especially good for group bookings. Ayr itself is a busy market town which overlooks the Firth of Clyde. The coastline reveals some charming sandy beaches and attractive fishing villages. The town has many restaurants, bars and hotels but two hotels which stand out particularly are **Fairfield House** (01292) 267461 and **Manor Park Hotel** (01292) 479365, recently refurbished and offering excellent cuisine. At Alloway, the **The Ivy House** (01292) 442336 and the **Brig O'Doon House** (01292) 442466 merit consideration. **Ladyburn** (01655) 740585 at Maybole lies within easy reach of Ayr and also many of the renowned local golf courses and is family run, welcoming and offers excellent food. Good fare can also be found in Ayr at **Fouters Bistro** (01292) 261391 and **The Stables** (01292) 283704—good Scottish cooking. **Highgrove House** (01292) 312511 is a good restaurant with rooms to note in Troon.

More golf is available in Prestwick and, as you might imagine, the town is also well placed for the nearby airport of the same name. **Fairways Hotel** (01292) 470396 is a convenient guesthouse. But if it's racing you are after, an ideal place to stay near the racecourse is the **Carlton Toby** (01292) 476811 on the Ayr road. The bedrooms are comfortable and the bars and restaurant should also be visited. Further north still, one arrives at yet another golfing delight, Troon. Three more hotels to note are the **Marine** Hotel (01292) 314444 which overlooks the golf course and the Isle of Arran. This is a well equipped and comfortable hotel with a superb bistro. Secondly, visit **Piersland House** (01292) 314747 and **Lochgreen House** (01292) 313343 is also first-class. A short way from Irvine in the Montgreenan Estate, near Kilwinning, lies the **Montgreenan Mansion House** (01294) 557733, former home of Lord Glasgow. Two miles from the village of Stewarton, amid the valleys and countryside, is the splendid **Chapeltoun House Hotel** (01560) 482696—quite tremendous. Our final thoughts are situated someway south of Ayr. **Knockinaam Lodge** (01776) 810471, Portpatrick, is an outstanding hotel with a first-class restaurant—a real favourite. Alternatively for those on their way south **Farlam Hall** (016977) 46234, near Brampton is another good tip. A very warm welcome, outstanding food and comfortable bedrooms—a winning treble.

Artist: **Barry Linklater** _JOCKEYS UP_ _Courtesy of:_ **W H Patterson Gallery**

The **Secretary** and **Clerk of the Course** is **Major Michael Webster**, who can be contacted by writing to **The Racecourse Office, Overton Road, Bangor-on-Dee, Wrexham LL13 0DA. Tel (01978) 780323 Fax (01978) 780985. Sponsorship** and **corporate hospitality Manager** is **Jeannie Chantler Tel (01978) 780323. E mail: racing@bangordee.sagehost.co.uk web site: www.bangor dee.co.uk**

The course is located in the Bryn y Pys estate near Bangor-on-Dee on the Welsh border. Chester is some 15 miles to the north and Shrewsbury some 25 miles south. London is a full 180 miles away. The major routes to the course are the A525 from Stoke and the M6. The A41 to Wolverhampton, and the M54 and A41 north towards Chester, can be used to link with the M56 network of the north west. The course itself lies on the A525, but to reach the course it is necessary to turn off the bypass, drive through the village, and onto the B5069 for Overton-on-Dee. There are also a number of minor routes, the B5130 for instance, which can be taken in preference to the A roads to enjoy the border countryside. There is plenty of free parking at the course. The A5 from Llangollen will assist people travelling from inland Wales. Wrexham and its rail network is four miles away and is part of the Euston line, as are nearby Chester and Shrewsbury. A free bus service is provided by the racecourse, leaving Wrexham Station one and a half hours before the first race and returning after racing. If you wish to make a speedy entry/departure then your helicopter is welcomed, though please contact the Clerk of the Course.

Among the major racing highlights are the Wynnstay Hunt evening, the North Western Area point-to-point championship final in May, and the Countryside Charity Day in October. If you do make the excellent decision to embark on a day at Bangor-on-Dee, then you will not be too shocked by the entrance prices that await you: £10 for the Paddock and £6 for the Course Enclosure. If you are intent on making regular visits to the track then you ought to consider an Annual Members badge: £100 is the asking price and it is worth noting that the members' car park has one of the best vantage points from which to view the racing. In addition to the days at Bangor, there are 14 reciprocal meetings at some exceptional racecourses. If you are planning to take a party racing at Bangor, discounts of 25 per cent are available for groups of 12 or more and a free racecard and betting vouchers come with all advance bookings.

A new building houses the impressive Owners, Trainers and Bangor Annual Members bar, and the Sponsors' suite. A new seafood and wine bar (Bookings 01676 535237) is also popular with Owners and Trainers while an enlarged restaurant offers a wide range of meals, including tables for owners and trainers. Larger parties should note that marquees are available. The course authorities have pointed out that they will accept race sponsorship for as little as £500 for personal, family etc occasions but, naturally, would expect more from commercial enterprises looking to sponsor a race. The sponsor's package includes a return of ten per cent of the sponsorship contribution in free badges and additional badges can be purchased at a reduced rate. There is a restaurant in the Paddock enclosure and the caterers are Hughes of Welshpool (01938) 553366 if you wish to make bookings. There are also snacks available at the bars, where you can munch roast beef sandwiches whilst watching the closed circuit television.

Artist: **Malcolm Coward** **GOING WELL** *Courtesy of:* **Sally Mitchell Fine Arts**

Children and wheelchair-bound racegoers are admitted free and the latter have the benefit of a wheelchair viewing stand. There is ample car parking overlooking the course where a reserved space may be booked by phoning the racecourse. There are public telephones and betting shops in the Paddock enclosure and a 'walk in' Tote betting office. The whole course delights with its country setting and splendid atmosphere. If you are seeking a fun day out in 2001 at one of Britain's idyllic national hunt courses, make sure that Bangor is on the shortlist.

Local Favourites

This is an area rife with hotels and hostelries. A favourite establishment with the racing fraternity is the **Cross Foxes Inn** (01978) 780380. The **Carden Park Hotel** (01829) 731000 also comes highly recommended and is ideal for combining a day at the races with a spot of golf. A favourite local pub is the **Royal Oak** (01978) 780289 in Bangor.

Some of the best places to stay are in Llangollen, home of the Eisteddfod festival of song and dance for those who appreciate a fiesta as well as a flutter. The **Hand Hotel** (01978) 860303 affords an extremely comfortable stay, while in Bridge Street, the **Royal Hotel** (01978) 860202 enjoys a fine setting over the River Dee. The restaurant here is good and the bar's ideal for a leisurely chat before racing. **Rhydonnen Ucha Rhewl** (01978) 860153 is modestly priced and can also offer shooting and trout fishing. Three miles east, the **Bryn Howel Hotel** (01978) 860331 is another cosy place. One of the most strikingly pretty spots is the Horseshoe Pass where the **Britannia Inn** (01978) 860144 is a pleasant place to relax. If you are merely looking for a restaurant with views over the waters of the Dee, then **Caesars** (01978) 860133, where an imaginative menu makes good use of fresh local produce, is an excellent idea. If you prefer a wine bar, **Gales** (01978) 860089 is well thought of and ideal for an early lunch, though it has a few bedrooms too Another good performer is the **Cross Lanes** (01978) 780555—extremely convenient and increasingly popular with the racing fraternity, it offers special racing breaks.

In Llanarmon Dyffryn Ceiriog, the **West Arms** (01691) 600665 is over 400 years old and remains a charming place to stay. The **Hand** (01691) 600264 is also most welcoming. In Llanyblodwell, the **Horseshoe** is particularly recommended for people who might wish to take in some fishing, good bar food and good value accommodation. Closer to hand and quite appropriately titled, the **Stableyard Country Restaurant** (01978) 780642 is another fine local performer. Also close at hand is the **Buck House Hotel** (01978) 780336, extremely handy for the racecourse for those of you who prefer not to travel too far to the races.

Further south in the quiet town of Oswestry, the **Wynnstay** (01691) 655261 is an appealing Georgian inn. And in Morda, a little south of Oswestry, the **Sweeney Hall Hotel** (01691) 652450 has a beautiful parkland setting and a good restaurant. Finally, **Dearnford Hall** (01948) 662319 is a first rate classy performer.

Artist: **Katy Sodeau** **THE LAST RACE** *Courtesy of:* **The Artist**

Bath

The **Secretary** of this beautiful track outside Bath is **Sylvia Wilcox**, who can be contacted at **The Bath Racecourse Co Ltd**, Lansdown, Bath BA1 9BU Tel (01225) 424609/(01295) 688030 Fax (01225) 444415/(01295) 688211 **Rodger Farrant** is **Clerk of the Course** and can be contacted on (01398) 332410.

In order to reach Bath racecourse several points should be noted: London is approximately 100 miles away, Bath three miles away and Bristol ten miles yonder. The M4 route is quick but rather boring while the A4 is more interesting but can be fairly congested. Junction 18 off the M4 is the appropriate exit point. The course is well signposted from here, nestling amidst the villages of Kelston, Charlcombe, Swainswick and North Stoke. For travellers from the north and west the M5/M4 is the better route while the A46 is an alternative if time is not so pressing. If, however, time is of the essence and you decide to take a helicopter, then please land at the north end of the coach park. Car parking areas abound and are free although if you wish to park in the centre of the course, a charge of £5 is levied—which admits the driver only. All additional occupants will also be charged. Members are entitled to reserved parking. The railway station in Bath is on the main Paddington-South Wales line and buses from the station go to the racecourse.

The 2001 fixture list is expected to follow a similar pattern to last year with 14 flat race meetings. The course's feature race remains the Somerset Stakes. Although crowds are always fairly good at Bath, the course is, not surprisingly, at its busiest during its weekend fixtures. The charge for a day's racing at Bath is £14 for a Daily Members badge, £10 if you prefer the Tattersalls and £5 or £2 if you have a hankering for the Silver Ring or the Course Enclosures. The Annual Members badge is priced at £99 whilst a double badge can be ordered for £198. Junior Members (21 and under) are asked to part with £25 which is good value. Annual Members also enjoy thirteen reciprocal race meetings. One final point worth noting is that if you want to organise a larger gathering a 20 per cent saving can be made on parties of 20 or more, but this applies only to the Tattersalls and Silver Ring enclosures.

There are nine private boxes available for hire and betting vouchers in units of two or five can be pre-arranged in advance for guests. Should you wish to take a larger party, there are two rooms available for entertaining. Catering is organised by Letheby & Christopher (01242) 523203. These facilities are well used so you are advised to book well in advance. If you would prefer a marquee then these can be erected—please contact the racecourse office for further details. You can also make bookings for lunch in the Members Restaurant—indeed, this is sometimes advisable. One final point that should be noted is that there is access to the stand roof which makes for an interesting vantage point.

If you are disabled or taking a disabled friend racing, then do contact the course and they will make life as easy as possible for you. Telephones can be found at various points on the course and there is a betting shop serving Tatts and the Silver Ring.

Artist: **Peter Smith THE LAST FURLONG** *Courtesy of:* **Frost & Reed**

Local Favourites

Bath is a beautiful city with many good hotels and restaurants among its attractions. An excellent hotel is the **Priory** (01225) 331922, where the French cuisine is superb and the Georgian mansion exudes luxury. The **Lansdown Grove** (01225) 483888 is also charming and slightly less expensive!

Bargain seekers will also find solace at the **Laura Place Hotel** (01225) 463815, **Orchard Lodge Hotel** (01225) 466115 and **Paradise House Hotel** (01225) 317723. If money is no object, two for the shortlist are the **Bath Spa** (01225) 444424 and the majestic **Royal Crescent** (01225) 823333. Heading south out of town quickly brings you to the excellent **Combe Grove Manor** (01225) 834644 at Monkton Combe. There are some excellent leisure facilities here as well.

The hotel and fine restaurant of **Ston Easton Park** (01761) 241631 is one for the notebook—an outstanding pedigree well worth a detour if your funds are in plentiful supply. In Hinton Charterhouse, **Homewood Park** (01225) 723731 and **Green Lane House** (01225) 723631 are both good. The former is extremely grand, the latter far less so but most pleasant. In Hunstrete, the **Hunstrete House Hotel** (01761) 490490 boasts an outstanding restaurant in a distinguished Georgian manor house set in rolling parkland. Nearby Chelwood houses the first class **Chelwood House** (01761) 490730. **Lucknam Park** (01225) 742777 at Colerne near Bath is another Georgian manor house, quite unsurpassed in luxury and cuisine. There are all manner of restaurants to sample in Bath among the best are **Lettonie** (01225) 446676, the **Hole in the Wall** (01225) 425242 and **Clos du Roy** (01225) 444450.

Less pricey, but extremely comfortable accommodation can be discovered in Limpley Stoke, at the **Cliffe** (01225) 723226 which has a tremendous restaurant. In Beanacre, **Beechfield House** (01225) 703700 is outstanding. A similar summary could be applied to the **Old Bell** (01666) 822344 in Malmesbury

which is a rapidly improving type and well worth considering. In Winterbourne, the **Jarvis Grange Hotel** at Northwoods (01454) 777333 is an elegant place to stay with good leisure facilities and in Dunkirk, the **Petty France** (01454) 238361 is also good. But people who are content with a bar snack or just a post-race pint may care to try any of the following gems. Stanton Wick offers the **Carpenter's Arms** (01761) 490202 a tremendous all rounder, good ales, excellent food, bar meals and restaurant, even some cosy bedrooms if required. The **George** (01373) 834224 at Norton St Philip is charming. **The Plaine** (01373) 834723 is a delightful place to stay near here. **The Inn** (01225) 722250 at Freshford is appealing, and returning to Hinton Charterhouse, the **Stag** has style. The **Royal Oak**, Winsford, has a delightful country setting, and nearby in Ford, the **White Hart** (01249) 782213 is a welcoming pub with a pleasant restaurant and some bedrooms. Another splendid **White Hart** lies in the charming village of Castle Combe. Our final selection is the **Manor House** (01249) 782206 also at Castle Combe. Romance is in the air here and racegoers with a conscience should consider it a firm favourite for their less enthusiastic partners, particularly if they also enjoy golf!

Artist: **Peter Smith** **THEY'RE ALL IN WITH A CHANCE** *Courtesy of:* **Frost & Reed**

The people to contact at this excellent track are headed by **Miss Sally Igguiden**, who acts as **Manager. Mrs J Parry** is the **Secretary**, and **Mrs Jane Johnson** is in charge of sponsorship, marketing and other bookings. Contact them at: **The Racecourse, York Road, Beverley, HU17 8QZ. Tel (01482) 867488/882645. Fax (01482) 863892. Website: www.beverley-racecourse.co.uk.**

Beverley itself is situated to the south east of York and north west of the Humber estuary. The southbound traveller should make best use of the A1, the A19 and the A1079. If one is travelling from the south or east make your way via the A1(M) to the M62, exit left through North Cave (junction 38) and from there pursue the B1230. From Lincolnshire, the A15 Humber Bridge followed by the A164 is probably a good each-way bet. There are a number of routes east of Beverley. Should one be venturing from that part of the country, the A1035 looks to be the obvious choice. When it comes to a train journey the best idea is to go to Beverley itself, although it may be prudent to journey via York or Doncaster and thus catch a faster train. An intermittent bus service runs from Beverley station when you reach that destination. For more speedy journeys, helicopters will come in handy. If you happen to have one available you are welcome to land it in the centre of the course. Parking for your helicopter is free, as it is for your car. There is a separate car park for Members at the course.

The 2001 fixture list will probably contain about the same number of fixtures as 2000. The first July meeting is a popular occasion—well worth attending. The feature races are now worth approximately £15,000 each and they are two of the well established ones: the Brian Yeardley Continental Two Year Old Trophy and the Hilary Needler Trophy.

For 2001, the daily fee will be £14 for admission to the Members Enclosure (£9 for 16-21 year olds), £9 for Tattersalls, £3 for the Silver Ring and £2 for the Course. Party rates are offered for all enclosures with groups of 20 or more being charged £12 to the Club Enclosure, groups of between 10 and 30 being offered admission to Tatts for £8 and groups of more than 30 for £7. Annual Members at Beverley pay £100 for a single badge. An Associate Membership (two people) is £170 and Junior Members can purchase discounted subscriptions of £60 per annum. Under 16s are admitted free of charge provided they are accompanied.

Artist: **Philip Toon SLIGHT DELAY** _Courtesy of:_ **The Artist**

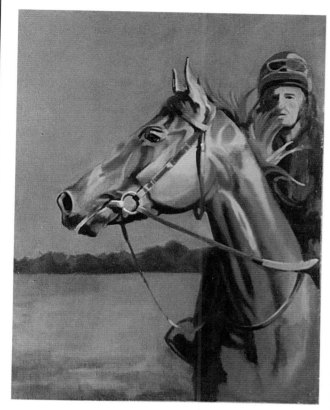

*Artist: **Alison Ruth Wilson** HEAD OF A CHESTNUT*
*Courtesy of: **The Artist***

The main grandstand has been extended to include a larger club dining room with a suite of three entertaining boxes which may be taken as one to accommodate a large party. On the second floor there is a box suitable for parties of up to 50 in addition to the four original boxes. Prices are available on application to Mrs Johnson at the racecourse office. A recent addition to the facilities is a new weighing room with a Paddock Bar perched above it which offers wonderful views of the racecourse and the surrounding countryside. Bookings can be made for the restaurants and should you need to make any catering enquiries then Craven Gilpin, the racecourse caterers, 0113 287 6387, are the chaps to contact. If you really want to push the boat out, the racecourse staff will be happy to organise the erection of a marquee.

There are three telephones at the course—vital for placing those bets should you be out of cash as there is no bank here. There are however two betting shops, in Tattersalls and the Silver Ring, should you wish to lighten your purse, or hopefully add to it.

Local Favourites

Beverley is a flourishing market town surrounded by outstanding countryside. To the north, the Wolds and the Yorkshire Moors. To the west, the Pennines and to the east, ragged coastline. The 17th century **Beverley Arms Hotel** (01482) 869241 is an extremely comfortable inn in which to stay and a good place from which to explore.

Aside from the Beverley Arms, the **White Horse** (01482) 868103, better known as Nellies, has a superbly traditional pub atmosphere. The **Kings Head** (01482) 868103 is also a good pub

to put the racegoer in the right spirit before racing—or equally after the racing is over as it has some satisfactory bedrooms. **Lairgate** (01482) 882141 is also a worthy contender. **Cerutti 2** (01482) 866700 is a restaurant with good form. Nearby, a number of welcoming hotels include the **Tickton Grange Hotel** (01964) 543666 a superb Georgian country house two miles from Beverley. Slightly further afield in Driffield one finds the **Bell Hotel** (01377) 256661, a pleasant inn in the market place—ideal for a post-race bar snack or dinner in the restaurant.

Alternatives to the south of Beverley include **Rowley Manor** (01482) 848248 at Little Weighton—a splendid parkland setting with a particularly relaxing bar, ideal for studying overnight declarations in style. There is further comfort to be found with another manor, this time in Willerby, the **Willerby Manor** (01482) 652616; a mention here also for the **Grange Park Hotel** (01482) 656488, just to the south of Beverley—well-equipped and comfortable. If you are lured into Hull then an excellent restaurant in which to have a bite is **Ceruttis** (01482) 328501, a harbourside spot with first rate seafood.

In Brandesburton, the **Dacre Arms** (01964) 542392 appeals—note the Wensleydale Ploughmans, and Burton Lodge (01964) 542847 is worth a visit, while in Bishop Burton, the **Altisidora** is a friendly pub with a delightful setting. The pub takes its name from the 1813 St Leger winner. In South Dalton, the **Pipe and Glass** (01430) 810246 has great character and serves good food while in Market Weighton, the **Londesborough Arms** (01430) 872214 also has bedrooms and is a very friendly place to stay. The **Triton** in Sledmere (01377) 236644 is very popular and ideally situated for **Sledmere House**—well worth a post-race inspection. Yorkshire Pudding lovers should note the **Half Moon** (01482) 843403 at Skidby. The **Manor House** (01482) 881645 at Walkington is very relaxing and the restaurant is first class. Our final recommendation for all 'foodies' is the **Winteringham Fields** (01724) 733096. Here the food is fantastic and there are some delightful bedrooms as well—one for the notebook for those of you considering a trip to Beverley races in 2001.

*Artist: **Alison Ruth Wilson** READY FOR OFF*
*Courtesy of: **The Artist***

A new team has taken over at Brighton recently, reflecting the partnership that now runs the course between Northern Racing Limited and Brighton and Hove Council. **Jeremy Martin** is **Clerk of the Course**, **Phil Bell** is **General Manager**, **Judy Welsh** is **Customer Services** and **Marie Norman** is **Senior Commercial Executive**. They can be contacted on **(01273) 603580** by **Fax (01273) 673267**. Should you wish to write, the address is **Brighton Racecourse Company Limited, Brighton Racecourse, Freshfield Road, Brighton, East Sussex, BN2 2XZ. Email: info@brighton-racecourse.co.uk. Website: www.brighton-racecourse.co.uk.**

The course is situated in one of Brighton's eastern suburbs, high up on White Hawk Hill and about a 60 mile journey from the capital. If you are coming from outside Brighton, head towards Sussex University on the A27 and take the exit for Woodingdean. In the centre of Woodingdean, turn right at the traffic lights and a mile down the road lies the racecourse. Alternatively, however, you can take the A23 and follow the signs to the racecourse through the town centre, which may take a little longer. The London-Brighton Victoria rail line is most efficient and there is a courtesy bus service from the station to the racecourse on racedays with two trips back after the last. The Brighton/Hove buses all stop near the course too. There is plenty of space for car parking which is provided free.

Under the leadership of Chairman Stan Clarke, £3 million has been spent on improving facilities at the course in the last two years. A £1.5 million Grandstand redevelopment scheme was completed in April 2000 as well as renovations to Tattersalls and Members with new bars, food outlets, toilets, Tote and ladbrokes betting facilities. Considerable investment is planned over the next few years to improve many more areas.

Prices for the 2001 season include admission to the Members enclosure at £15. The price for Tattersalls is £10 with OAPs gaining admission for £6 with £5 per car and £4 per occupant for the Silver Ring. Annual Membership was priced at £130 with a discount if purchased before New Year's day. This includes free car parking and reciprocal meetings at several other courses including Epsom, Sandown Park, Windsor, Folkestone and others as well as all meetings at Uttoxeter and Newcastle as an added bonus. If you are planning a group outing you will be entitled to a discount of 20 per cent for parties of 20 or more.

Parties of between 12 and 150 can be entertained in various places around the racecourse and private boxes can cater for up to 200 guests. There are also sites for marquees which can hold 200 guests comfortably. All-inclusive hospitality packages

Artist: **Jacquie Jones** **THE DESPERATE DRIVE** _Courtesy of:_ **The Park Gallery**

are available at £60 - £80 plus VAT per head. There are also numerous bars throughout the course as well as a more formal restaurant, bookings for which can be made by telephoning the racecourse. It is worth noting that all of these facilities are also available for use on non-racedays.

There are no banks on site, but there is a recently refurbished and much improved betting shop located in Tatts. Facilities for children are provided although only at summer meetings. We are pleased to say that course management is currently reviewing facilities for the disabled and some improvements may be forthcoming; currently there is access to all floors of the Grandstand by lift.

I am also pleased to say that a number of sponsorship and marketing opportunities are now available at Brighton. Race sponsors are offered a free box and admission tickets. The number of tickets you receive depends on the amount you give as sponsorship—amounts start from £500 and the more you pay the more you get.

Whether you are a prospective sponsor, a company looking for a venue for corporate hospitality or just a simple punter, Brighton is a fine course and well worth a visit.

Local Favourites

Perhaps it's the sea air that makes so many organisations choose Brighton for their annual conference. The best seafront hotels in Brighton are the **Grand** (01273) 321188 which is quite grand, the **Hilton Brighton Metropole** (01273) 775432, headquarters to many a political conference, the startlingly modern **Thistle Brighton** (01273) 206700, the **Hilton Brighton West Pier** (formerly the Stakis) (01273) 329744, and the **Old Ship** (01273) 329001. Highly recommended by the racecourse management are several restaurants in Brighton itself including **Al Duomo** (01273) 326741 and **Al Forno** (01273) 324905 for fans of Italian cuisine. and **Gars** for Chinese near the Town Hall (01273) 321321. Two restaurants also to note are **Langan's**

Bistro (01273) 606933 and the unpretentious but good **Black Chapati** (01273) 699011. **Whytes** (01273) 776618 is also well worth considering.

The waters of Brighton stretch round the coast and meet with Hove. Here a number of good hotels can be found. One of the best is the **Sackville** (01273) 736292—a pleasant seafront hotel. The **Hungry Monk** (01323) 482178, Jevington, is a restaurant to delight you with a wonderful atmosphere and first rate food. Local recommendations also include **Otello** for Italian (01273) 729774. and for Indian, **Ganges Brasserie** (01273) 728292. Also not far away from Brighton in Kingston near Lewes you are encouraged to try **Juggs** (01273) 472523—a great 15th century pub with good real ales and excellent home made food. **Shelleys** (01273) 472361 is a noted hotel in the High Street.

If you are not content with the seaside offerings in Brighton, then Eastbourne is an elegant and slightly more tranquil alternative. Good value accommodation is plentiful. Examples include the **Bay Lodge Hotel** (01323) 732515 and **Hotel Mandalay** (01323) 729222. However, the star of the show is the impressive **De Vere Grand** (01323) 412345—great for families, expensive but very good. A busy pub to note for its tremendous views is the **Devil's Dyke** at Devil's Dyke on the downs above the town. For some really good food, the **Tottington Manor Hotel Restaurant** (01903) 815757 at Edburton is also worth a visit, as is the extremely comfortable **Hilton Avisford Park Hotel** (01243) 551215 at Walberton—well worth the extra journey for those who enjoy excellent food and sporting facilities.

A final selection that should not be overlooked includes **Amberley Castle** (01798) 831992—medieval style and 20th century comfort. We would also strongly recommend an hotel of real character, **Ockenden Manor** (01444) 416111—a _Travelling the Turf_ favourite. Further north at the delightfully named Pease Pottage, the **Cottesmore Golf & Country Club** (01293) 528256 comes highly recommended.

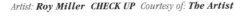
Artist: **Roy Miller** **CHECK UP** _Courtesy of:_ **The Artist**

At Carlisle, **Johnnie Fenwicke-Clennell** is the **Clerk of the Course and Racing Manager**, **Hugh Fitzgerald** the **Executive Chairman** and **Mrs Ann Bliss** the **Administration Director and Secretary**. The course address is **The Grandstand Office, The Racecourse, Durdar Road, Carlisle, Cumbria, CA2 4TS. Tel (01228) 522973. Fax (01228) 591827. e-mail: info@carlisle-races.co.uk web site: www.carlisle-races.co.uk.**

Carlisle is a good 300 miles from the capital. However, it is easy to reach for racegoers from all areas of the country. The M6 is the motorway to follow, exiting at junction 42 and then following the signs two miles to the course. The A69 Carlisle-Newcastle road is the best route from the north east whilst people from areas west of Carlisle should travel on the A595 or the A596. The racecourse is two miles south of the town and the No 66 bus from Carlisle will deposit you at the course. From London, Carlisle bound trains depart from Euston station or alternatively you can jump on a Kings Cross train and change at Newcastle upon Tyne. If you are making the trip by car you will find some 20 acres of grass on which to park your motor. Aviators please note that Carlisle airport is some eight miles away. Helicopters can land on the racecourse provided prior arrangements have been made.

The Cumberland Plate and the Carlisle Bell, two of the course's major races, are steeped in tradition and a delight to attend. Racing at Carlisle takes place every month of the year and an irrigation system has been added to help the going. In 2000 the weekday admission charge to the Club enclosure was £12, while Saturdays, Bank Holidays and evenings were £14, with entry to Tattersalls set at £7. Pensioners and under 21s receive a £3 discount.

Annual Membership is £105, and an additional Lady's Club badge will cost £50. Fourteen reciprocal meetings are also laid on for the Carlisle Member. People under 21 will be glad to know that membership is priced at £50.

Party organisers will be pleased to hear that parties of 10 or more save 20 per cent per badge to the Tattersalls and Club enclosures, plus a free badge. This rises to a 25 per cent discount for groups larger than 45.

Facilities at Carlisle include the highly regarded Club restaurant (please book) and Tattersalls cafeteria as well as the enlarged and welcoming Red Rum Owners and Trainers room and coffee and wine bars. There is also a refurbished bar and restaurant in the old Tote building—the very first Tote in operation, beating Newmarket by 15 minutes! With regard to more private facilities, five rooms are available in which 20 to 100 guests can be entertained at a cost of £80 minimum. Marquees can also be organised and there is a large hall which seats between 250 and 300 people.

Enquiries with regard to on-course catering should be addressed to the secretary, Mrs Ann Bliss. Expect to pay between £18 and £15 for lunch in the restaurant. Romfords (01434) 688 864 also supply the catering for the cafeteria and snack bars. Children are admitted free of charge to the racecourse if accompanied by an adult and there is a free crèche provided for fixtures during the school holidays.

Facilities for disabled racegoers are most considerate at Carlisle with two viewing ramps, specially equipped toilets and easily accessible bars. There is also a trackside car park and picnic area where a levy of £5 per car (£7 on Saturdays, bank holidays and evenings) is requested. There is a betting shop in the Paddock area but no banks are in operation on the course. This friendly racecourse is well positioned between Lakeland and the Borders and those of us seeking a day's racing while touring beautiful countryside will find Carlisle a welcoming port of call.

*Artist: **Martin Williams** GOING TO THE POST Courtesy of: **The Artist***

Local Favourites

In Carlisle itself, one finds a number of possible candidates for a quiet and comfortable night. Firstly, **Cumbria Park** (01228) 522887 is a distinct posibility. **Number Thirty One** (01228) 597080 is a small stylish Victorian town house worthy of note. A restaurant to consider is **No. 10** (01228) 524183. Another guest house of note is **Avondale** (01228) 523012 - excellent value. Secondly, visitors should note the **Cumbrian Hotel** (01228) 531951 in Court Square.

North of Carlisle lies Rockcliffe where a good pub for a snack is the **Crown and Thistle**. The village guards the mouth of the River Eden and is particularly convenient for the A74. Another riverside setting is provided by the extremely pleasant and welcoming **Crosby Lodge Country House** (01228) 573618 at High Crosby. This hotel enjoys a pastoral setting and also has a good restaurant. Returning to Warwick-on-Eden, the **Queen's Arms** (01228) 560699 is another inn of character. Here you will find a restaurant and some comfortable bedrooms. In Talkin, as well as a good golf course, one finds the **Hare and Hounds Inn** (016977) 3456. **Tarn End** at Talkin Tarn (01697) 72340 is a good restaurant which also provides homely accommodation. This is an ideal spot for an early evening stroll to work up a good appetite as the inn is next to a lake and is surrounded by beautiful fells. Another good thought is the **Blacksmiths Arms**—great for bar snacks and some rooms as well.

North of the A69 at Lanercost, the **Abbey Bridge Inn** (016977) 2224 is an unusual pub but a most appealing hostelry in which to savour a winner in the last. However, **Farlam Hall Hotel** (016977) 46234 is definitely the pick of the paddock, a splendid 17th century manor house in gorgeous grounds and a grand restaurant as well—a

really classical performer in every way. A nearby hotel to note is the **Crown** (01228) 561888, a coaching inn with first rate facilities. Last, but certainly not least, for the younger punter planning a racing honeymoon to Carlisle (of which there are surely hundreds!) the **Greenlaw Guest House** (01461) 338361 and the **Welcome Lodge** (01461) 337566 at Gretna Green will provide the required accommodation. The surrounding hostelries and friendly people coupled with a well balanced calendar of sporting fixtures make a visit to Carlisle racecourse a priority for those of you who have not enjoyed the pleasure.

*Artist: **Elizabeth Brookes** DRIVING FINISH Courtesy of: **The Dominion Gallery***

Cartmel offers festival racing with a fun 'shirtsleeve' atmosphere which makes a welcome contrast to some of the country's more 'stiff upper lip' racecourses. It is immensely popular and a thoroughly successful part of Britain's racing scene. The **Clerk of the Course** is **Charles Barnett** and he and the **General Manager, Adrian Mann** can be contacted at **Cartmel Steeplechases Ltd, c/o Aintree Racecourse Co Ltd, Ormskirk Road, Aintree Liverpool L9 5AS. Tel 0151 523 2600 Fax 0151 522 2920.** On racedays contact them at the racecourse itself on **Tel (01539) 536340 Fax (01539) 536004.**

The road to the course meanders through the hills of the Lake District. The most direct routes into the area from the north and south are via the M6, exiting at junction 36 for the A590. From the north east, the A69 is a good bet, whereas the A590 will assist eastbound racegoers. A word of warning, leave plenty of time if travelling by car, especially on bank holidays when traffic can be horrific. By train, the Euston line which stops at Cark in Cartmel from where a link bus runs to the racecourse throughout the day and Grange-over-Sands is your best bet. Parking facilities are separated into two categories: cars parked in the Paddock Parks are charged £5 while the Course Area is free. Helicopters can land here too but only by prior arrangement with the Clerk.

Until the early 1960s racing was held at Cartmel only once a year, on Spring Bank Holiday Monday. Since then it has grown to five days with the addition of an extra meeting in August. The Mondays of the Spring Bank Holiday and the August Bank Holiday provide the main and the most popular meetings. Racegoers come from all over the country to enjoy the racing here. After all, what could be better than to spend a week at Cartmel in May with the non-racedays being spent in the surrounding countryside of the Lake District?

The subscription rate for Annual Membership is £90. This gives the member two badges (a single badge costs £50) and a car pass, plus access to a special viewing area. Demand is always high for these badges and as a result the Members' Enclosure has no Daily Members. The Paddock Enclosure is priced at £10 and the Course, £5, while accompanied children under 16 are admitted free. There are half price entrance charges to the Paddock and the Course for senior citizens. A 20 per cent discount on all admission prices is available for badges purchased 30 days before race meetings. There are continued improvements at the track—a back stairway enables Members to gain easier access to their own vantage point. The new press room can accommodate up to eleven journalists, and a coach park has been added. Despite the changes, including the encouragement of hacks, the Manager's ultimate policy is to foster the pleasant atmosphere and character of the racecourse.

The race meeting however, brings more than horses to this rural setting. A traditional funfair is in attendance and marquees can be provided for parties on request. A new marquee layout for corporate hospitality has recently been added as well as a giant screen on all 5 days of racing. Picnickers are positively encouraged here although there is a catering marquee in the Paddock. Enquiries with regard to on-course catering should be directed to Romfords, The Boundary, Langley, Haydon Bridge, Northumberland, Tel: (01434) 688864. Disabled racegoers have their own viewing area at Cartmel. Other public facilities include telephones (for those all-important bets) and a betting shop in both the Paddock and Course enclosures. Cartmel racecourse is a huge

Artist: **Refna Hamey** **FRIENDS UNTIL THE LAST** *Courtesy of:* **The Artist**

success with large crowds attending any race meeting held there, a real testimonial to good old-fashioned country fair fun. Other racecourses are not so fortunate. A visit in 2001 could be a hot favourite.

Local Favourites

There is no shortage of hotels in this part of the world and a little guidance cannot go amiss. In Cartmel itself, **Aynsome Manor** (015395) 36653 is a super old manor house which makes a good base. The **King's Arms** holds an imposing position in the square and the **Cavendish Arms** (015395) 36240 is thoroughly recommended. **Uplands** (015395) 36248 is a really pleasing restaurant with rooms if you wish to push the boat out. In Cartmel Fell, one finds the absolutely terrific **Mason's Arms** (015395) 68486, always a friendly crowd and some excellent cooking—watch the foreign beers though, they bring on nasty hangovers when mixed with our own brews—just as well it also has bedrooms! In Heversham, the **Blue Bell** (015395) 62018 offers excellent value bar lunches and some accommodation. A little further west in Lowick Green, the **Farmer's Arms** is a pub with similar facilities and an excellent dining room.

Two packs of **Hounds** and a couple of **Hares,** one at Bowland Bridge (015395) 68333 and another at Levens, both with good value bar food. The **Swan** (015395) 31681 at Newby Bridge comes with an enviable reputation and is less than five miles from the racecourse. Two other pleasant establishments with accommodation are the outstanding **Queen's Head** (015394) 32174, Troutbeck, north of Windermere which also yields the **Mortal Man** (015394) 33193 with its particularly friendly welcome and first-class cooking. Bowness-on-Windermere offers two appealing restaurants: the **Gilpin Lodge** (015394) 88818 which has a beautiful situation two miles out of the town—bedrooms here are first class; and **Linthwaite House** (015394) 88600 an hotel with fine cooking. In Windermere, there are some spectacular establishments: **Oragano** (015394) 44954 is a relax-

ing French restaurant—well worth trying. At the **Miller Howe** (015394) 42536 first-class cuisine, breathtaking views and some really special accommodation make this a favourite in the most challenging of fields. Another good runner is **Holbeck Ghyll** (015394) 32375—outstanding menus can be enjoyed here. Further good hotels can be found in and around Underbarrow overlooking the Lyth Valley. In Crook, the **Wild Boar** (015394) 45225 is a comfortable place to stay. Another absolute pearl of an hotel is to be found in Grasmere—**Michael's Nook** (015394) 35496 is delightfully cosy and conjures up exceptional cooking. Grasmere also offers the **White Moss House Hotel** (015394) 35295—another gem. A similarly favourable critique can be made of the **Wordsworth Hotel** (015394) 35592. Cumbria has a whole host of outstanding hotels and what better excuse could one have for visiting than Cartmel Races?

Artist: **Katy Sodeau** ***EARLY IN THE RACE*** *Courtesy of:* **The Artist**

The **General Manager** and **Clerk of the Course** for flat racing at Catterick is **John Gundill**, a well known figure in both British and international racing circles. The winter jumping programme is administered by **IRM Ltd.** and the **Sales and Marketing Manager** is Jeremy Milnes. The address for all correspondence is **The Racecourse, Catterick Bridge, Richmond, North Yorkshire, DL10 7PE. Tel (01748) 811478 Fax (01748) 811082. Web site: www.catterick.com.**

Catterick is very convenient for the north and southbound traveller. The A1 is the route to follow and Catterick lies a short distance from the junction of the A66 (Scotch Corner) on the east side of the Great North Road. Travellers from York should take the A59 west until they reach the A1 and then drive north. From another nearby racecourse town—Thirsk (south east), the A170 and the A61 lead to the A1. By rail the nearest station is at Darlington which is on the speedy line from London's Kings Cross. With regard to parking there are two options. The reserved car park costs £2 a car (or £32 for an annual pass) though on ground adjacent to the racecourse there is free parking for both cars and coaches.

Racing has been taking place at Catterick since 1783 and the course has a full calendar of 27 days from January 1st to December 31st, with a new flat fixture in November. A number of distinguished trainers have yards nearby and consequently many a fair nag has been sent up here in the past. Smaller country courses offer outstanding value for money in terms of sponsorship and promotion, sometimes attracting as much local media coverage as the big tracks. As we have already mentioned, Catterick is well situated and eager to attract commercial support, with Leeds, Bradford, York, Newcastle, Teesside and Manchester fairly close by. It is surprising that more local businessmen have not taken the opportunity to utilise Catterick as a medium for publicity. A quick glance at the Catterick fixture list will indicate that the course holds a good mixture of jump and flat racing with Wednesdays and Saturdays the two most popular days.

In 2000 a joint husband and wife Annual Members badge was good value at £145, while a single badge was £80. Annual Membership also includes eleven reciprocal racedays, as well as nine cricket matches at Headingley and 2 at Scarborough. A price of £12 was asked for joining the Members for a single meeting. Tattersalls was slightly better value at £8, while the Course Enclosure was priced at £2.50. All children under 16 are admitted free when accompanied by an adult. These prices may increase in 2001.

If you want to organise parties then Catterick is quite definitely a place to do it. There is a £2 reduction for Tattersalls if as few as ten people get together and there is also one free pass for every tenth person.

In recent years, Catterick has benefitted from an extensive face lift, including refurbishment of the Parade Ring Bar, the Owners and Trainers Bar, Gods Solution Bar, Dining Room and many of the facilities for jockeys have been improved as well. The old 1926 Grandstand has been extended to provide three private hospitality suites, all with a magnificent view of the course. There are two private luncheon rooms, both of which are extremely comfortable, with space for between 20 and 60 guests to sit down or 80 people to enjoy a more simple buffet and these can be hired at very reasonable rates.

There are a number of experienced personalities involved with the running of the course and they have ambitious plans for the enhancement of racecourse facilities with continual upgrading and expansion projects in the pipeline. If you enjoy your racing in either the height of summer or the depths of winter, don't forget that, in racing parlance, Catterick is an improving type. Catterick has fondly christened itself 'the course with character'—I have no doubt that in this instance the character will show through extremely well. A visit in 2001 is a must.

Local Favourites

With the North Yorkshire moors so close by, Catterick is an ideal place to escape to when a major gamble has gone astray. Alternatively, the dales and fells offer an outstanding number of small hotels and pubs in which to celebrate.

In this area, Middleham stands out as prime racing country with some excellent local establishments. Most notably, the **Millers House Hotel** (01969) 622630 in Middleham which offers quality accommodation and a restaurant of note. Special racing breaks are also on offer here. Also note **Waterford House** (01969) 622090—small but most appealing. The **Foresters Arms** at Carlton (01969) 640272 is a restaurant of note. The **Bridge Inn** (01325) 350106 in Stapleton is not residential, but has a good pub restaurant. The **Black Swan** (01969) 622221 in Middleham is another must for all racegoers. Another training area is Richmond and here the **Castle Tavern** (01748) 823187 should be noted, fine ales and some good home cooking, while the King's Head (01748) 850220 is another worthy favourite. In East Layton nearby, the **Fox Hall Inn** (01325) 718262 is a good value place to stay and the restaurant is also worth a visit. The **Sandpiper** at Leyburn is a good pub, as is the convenient **Farmers Arms** but you must remember these are only a small selection of some 400 public houses to be found in North Yorkshire. Moulton also reveals a really excellent port of call. The **Black Bull Inn** (01325) 377289 has particularly good fish and for loved ones, the carefully restored **Brighton Belle Pullman Car** is ideal for gruesome twosomes. In fact, if you are in the doghouse this establishment is a great place to visit. A short journey south reveals Northallerton and yet more good accommodation in the form of **Porch House** (01609) 779831.

Scotch Corner also provides a convenient hotel which is handy for a number of courses, the **Scotch Corner Hotel** (01748) 850900. An alternative is the **Vintage Hotel** (01748) 824424. Both are only minutes away from the A1. Much of this area is somewhat remote but that is part of its charm. What could be better than a day in the country of North Yorkshire and an evening beside the fire in one of its many friendly hostelries. Thirsk and Ripon may offer alternative suggestions. The **Blue Lion** at East Witton (01969) 624273 is a fine example—good ale and pleasant bedrooms.

Millers House Hotel

This elegant Georgian country house hotel enjoys a quiet and secluded position, set back from the marketplace in the centre of Middleham. The building which dates from 1720 was owned by Hughie Miller - a merchant who became famous as a tipster. Middleham is set in the heart of the Yorkshire Dales and is surrounded by beautiful fells, ancient castles, and picturesque villages. It is the racehorse training centre of the north and countless horses pass the hotel entrance each day, on their way to the nearby moorland gallops.

Owned and managed by Ann and James Lundie, who strive to make each guest feel welcome and relaxed. Their aim is to provide a comfortable, quiet and civilised 'haven' far removed from the hectic technological world, where guests can unwind and enjoy the excellent food, wine and high standards of customer care that the hotel is renowned for.

Middleham is an excellent base from which to enjoy a racing enthusiasts break. There are regular meetings at Cafferick, Thirsk, Ripon, Wetherby and York (all easily accessible). Combine a day at the races with a tour of one of the local training stables and perhaps a morning stroll to the gallops to watch the horses in action. Special racing weekends are organised at the hotel. These start on Friday evening with an informal discussion of the prospects for the next day's racing with the help of a racing journalist. After breakfast on the Saturday there is a chance to watch the horses work out on the gallops and a tour of one of the Stables before being taken to the races. Upon arrival you get a private escorted tour of the course and badges for the members enclosure. Back at the hotel in the evening you are invited to sit down to a luxury banquet dinner with one of the well-known local trainers.

Additional racing breaks for house parties can also be organised to suit race meetings of your choice.

The hotel's reputation for excellent food, fine wine and welcoming atmosphere makes their Gourmet Wine Weekends popular. These are held in early and late season and centre around two fabulous banquet dinners where the food and wine are carefully chosen to complement each other. We also have the services of a professional speaker from the wine trade to introduce the wines and give us guidance on the best way to enjoy them.

For further information about these and other special breaks visit www.hotelwensleydale.com or contact Ann and James at Millers House.

Millers House Hotel
Middleham Wensleydale
North Yorkshire DL8 4NR
Tel: (01969) 622630 Fax: (01969) 623570
e-mail: hotel@millershouse.demon.co.uk
web site: www.hotelwensleydale.com

Hotel Kandinsky

The Hotel Kandinsky, a smart regency building situated near the centre of Cheltenham, has a young feel but it is not just for the young; its also for the young at heart. It is an excellent hotel aimed at both business and leisure guests with reasonable prices and a stylish, comfortable feel.

All the bedrooms have their own sparkle and are warm, clean and inviting. Each bedroom has a telephone with data port facilities plus the special edition of the "magic eye" which will take you down to U-bahn, the private members club. U-bahn offers nineteen-fifties cool style, music and an exclusive private membership including hotel guests. It is a late bar with music: a smart night club.

After a late night dancing in the U-bahn or a meal in the hotel's Cafe Paradiso return to your single, double or suite of rooms complete with six foot bed and comfy Bauhaus inspired furniture and bedspreads.

The Cafe Paradiso at the hotel is a place in which to take in some deeply serious flavours and to eat what you want. The restaurant speciality is pizza freshly prepared in the Brushwood Oven, using simple fresh ingredients. You can choose to eat at the counter or by candlelight depending on your mood and company.

At the Hotel Kandinsky in Cheltenham you are provided with a good base for fine shopping, a day out at the celebrated racecourse or for exploring the many and varied delights of the Cotswolds.

Hotel Kandinsky
Bayshill Road
Montpellier
Cheltenham
Gloucestershire
GL50 3AS
Tel: 01242 527788
Fax: 01242 226412
e mail: info@hotelkandinsky.com
web site: www.hotelkandinsky.com

Cheltenham is a tremendous racecourse and remains the beacon of British racing. In the National Hunt Festival it manages to create an occasion that transcends racing and sport and enters the realms of theatre. If you have never been - you must go - it's a squash but memories from here will last until the grave.

Edward Gillespie is **Managing Director** and **Simon Claisse** is **Clerk of the Course.** They can both be contacted at **Cheltenham Racecourse, Prestbury Park, Cheltenham GL50 4SH. Tel (01242) 513014. Fax (01242) 224227.** For advance bookings for the Festival, ring **(01242) 226226.** Credit cards are welcome. **Email: cheltenham@rht.net. Web site: www.cheltenham.co.uk.**

If you are planning to visit these gorgeous Gloucestershire gallops then you are advised to take the train. The main line service leaves Paddington and arrives at Cheltenham Lansdown where a bus is available to take you to the racecourse. A bus also runs from Cheltenham Spa Station for 2 hours before the first race at all meetings. By car, London is 95 miles away and the course is a mile from Cheltenham's busy town centre. Traffic from the A40 is advised to turn right at the lights near Andoversford which is signposted for Stow on the Wold and aim for Winchcombe. People who prefer the motorway will use the M4 and the M5—the former should be exited at junction 15 and the latter at junction 4 to make the best ground towards Prestbury Park. If you are coming from the north, there are now big improvements which allow you to bypass Evesham. Whichever direction you approach from, you will find AA signs to guide you to the racecourse. There is parking for 14,000 cars—all free except during the Festival, when a parking voucher will cost you £5. For members and coaches parking is free at all times.

Rates of admission vary quite substantially depending on the day, but for the 2000/2001 season prices will vary from £12 to £60 for the Club and £12 to £30 for Tattersalls. For the Courage Enclosure, entrance ranges from £5 to £15. Naturally prices are higher for the National Hunt Festival but you can save money by booking in advance. A Club badge for the Thursday costs £40 until January 1st, £45 until March 1 and £60 on the day. Badges for the Tuesday and Wednesday were £37.50 in advance and £50 up to March 3rd, Tattersalls cost £17 in advance for Tuesday and Wednesday, rising to £20 after March 3rd (£20 rising to £25 for Thursday). A three day badge at £125 is available from January 2nd until January 25th. You can also save in Tattersalls and Courage with advance group bookings. For groups of fifteen and over, booking before March 3rd will be charged at £15 for Tattersalls and £7 for Courage. Advance booking also ensures your admission, which is wise in view of the capacity crowds that attend the Festival. Because of these huge crowds, you are advised, when travelling by car, to arrive early and to listen to the traffic reports on the Festival radio (1584 KHz), a first-class service. Above all, be patient!

The National Hunt Festival with its massive crowds reflects the interest in this superb sporting meeting. Gems in the crown include the Tote Cheltenham Gold Cup, the Queen Mother Champion Chase and the Smurfit Champion Hurdle. Cheltenham offers a feast of racing in an excellent atmosphere and amidst a perfect setting. Other meetings to note include the Murphy's Gold Cup in November, and in December the Tripleprint Gold Cup.

Annual Membership should definitely be considered here. £150 is the asking price plus a £100 enrolment fee for new Members. This includes entry to the National Hunt Festival. Membership excluding the Festival is £50 for enrolment and £75

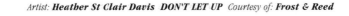

Artist: **Heather St Clair Davis** **DON'T LET UP** *Courtesy of:* **Frost & Reed**

for membership. Seniors (over 65 years) are charged an enrolment fee of £15 and membership at £60 whilst Juniors (under 25 years) are charged a membership fee of £90. Membership lasts for the season (Oct—May).

The course is always superbly well turned out. Facilities include over 100 boxes which are let on an annual basis. However, these can be obtained for a day at a cost of £250 - £500 (except during the National Hunt Festival) accommodating between 12 and 24 persons. Several rooms are also available for private parties numbering between 40 and 200 people. The new Tattersalls Grandstand sports a betting hall, bars, buffets, 700 seats, boxes and a 300-seater tiered panoramic restaurant. There are sites for marquees if required and the ever-expanding metropolis of the tented village at the Festival is a pleasure to be a part of. For people who prefer their own catering, stick to the car parks and organise your own picnics—thoroughly recommended if the weather happens to be good—though this can be a bit of a long shot. There is a good restaurant, the Gold Cup Restaurant for which booking is advised. Tel: (01242) 523203. Other restaurants include the Mandarin and Sea Pigeon, plus a carvery and of course, Barry Copes' excellent seafood bar. The fish and chips in Tatts is a recommended outsider. A new addition to the stable is the L'Escargot Bar behind Tatts. This I imagine, is named after the great chaser rather than the well known French dish. All in all, there are over 90 food outlets during the Festival so you shouldn't go hungry. At smaller meetings there is less choice but the crowds are far smaller and the racecourse itself is more of a pleasure to visit.

Although children are admitted free (except for the Festival) there are no special facilities for them but I understand they are on the agenda for the Course Enclosure. Disabled racegoers are well looked after with special areas overlooking the parade ring and on the lawn in the Club.

Cheltenham thrives on the rivalry between punters from both sides of the Irish Sea who pack the course during the Festival meeting to watch heroes such as Istabraq toy with all comers to win his third Champion Hurdle in a row or Looks Like Trouble foil the expectations of an Irish double by beating Florida Pearl in the Gold Cup. Apart from the lucky 50,000 who are allowed into the course, millions more watch from home and the two elements of sponsorship and television coverage are vital to ensuring this spectacle will continue. We are pleased to report that armchair viewers are assured a front row seat again this year despite the continuing wranglings over the larger issue of media rights involving all courses with the extension of its deal with Channel 4 to cover the Festival. Hats off as well to the Thomas Pink company who quickly moved to take over the sponsorship of the former Murphy's Craic meeting in November. Perhaps they recognised that with many unfortunate punters losing their shirts to the bookies, new business is virtually guaranteed!

*Artist: **David Dent** ISTABRAQ Courtesy of: **The Artist***

The award-winning Cottage in the Wood Hotel and Restaurant enjoys one of the finest settings of any hotel in England. Set high on the Malvern Hills, the views unfold below and stretch for 30 miles to the Cotswold Hills that form the horizon.

John and Sue Pattin who bought the hotel twelve years ago, saw as one of the side benefits the close proximity of Cheltenham Racecourse—"Beats driving down from London" says John—a pilgrimage they used to make frequently.

Apart from Cheltenham which is about half an hour's drive away, within an hour there are a further five racecourses—Worcester, Hereford, Ludlow, Stratford and Warwick. Truly, this is racing country.

The Cottage in the Wood, an AA 3-star country house hotel, offers 20 bedrooms spread across three buildings, each with an individual character of its own. The main house is a late Georgian dower-house, once part of the Blackmore Park Estate owned by the Duke of Gandolfi, which houses the elegant restaurant, lounge and bar together with eight guest bedrooms.

The building giving its name to the hotel is Beech Cottage, once "The Cottage" which now offers four cottagey bedrooms. Dating from around 1650 it has been in its time both a wood-man's cottage and a scrumpy house for walkers on the hills. It's a quiet haven now!

A few yards further on brings you to the Coach House, once cover for the horses and carriages of the house. It must have been a challenge negotiating the drive with a coach and four! It now houses eight bedrooms which, although smaller, offer the finest views of all down the valley to Cheltenham and beyond to Gloucester.

The restaurant offers fine cuisine under the direction of Dominic Pattin (Maria, his eldest sister is General Manager, making it a real family run hotel). It is separately recommended by Egon Ronay and by the AA with the award of two rosettes.

Malvern makes a superb touring base to visit the cathedral cites of Worcester, Hereford and Gloucester. The Forest of Dean, Stratford and Shakespeare country, Cotswolds and the rural charm of timeless Herefordshire and the Welsh Marches all await.

Below the hotel lie the Worcestershire Golf Course and the Three Counties Showground, which has year-round events.

The Cottage in the Wood offers inclusive bargain rates: these are available for two nights or more, seven days of the week virtually year round.

The Cottage in the Wood Hotel and Restaurant
Holywell Road
Malvern Wells
Worcestershire WR14 4LG
Tel: (01684) 575859
Fax: (01684) 560662
e mail: john@cottageinthewood.co.uk
web site: www.cottageinthewood.co.uk

Cheltenham never stages a bad day's racing, though sometimes the weather can be quite extraordinarily bitter. However, this of course, is a natural hazard of the winter game and certainly at Cheltenham one has the blessing of some really first class accommodation and drinking haunts in which to shelter before or after (preferably both) a day at the races. But they do get busy so do try to book well in advance. In the year 2000 as with 1999, the weather was kind to the Festival goers making a visit even more invigorating.

Cheltenham itself owes its growth to the discovery of a mineral spring in 1715. Today, the Pittville Pump Room dispenses the only drinkable alkaline water in Britain which may make a pleasant change from the numerous bottles of whisky, champagne and of course Guinness. The best known hotels in town are the **Queen's** (01242) 514724, scene of many a fine Irish celebration after racing, and the **Cheltenham Park Hotel** (01242) 222021 which is actually two miles out of Cheltenham, set in nine acres of gorgeous grounds. **On The Park** (01242) 518898 is a very civilised town house hotel which also houses a tremendous restaurant (01242) 227713. There are numerous other small hotels and guesthouses too—a quick phone call to the local tourist authority is always a good idea. A charming Georgian hotel is **Prestbury House** (01242) 529533. Some ideas for dinner after racing include **81 Restaurant** (01242) 222466 a good restaurant and also bistro of some distinction. **The Hotel Kandinsky** (01242) 527788 is a newcomer to note from an excellent small stable. **Le Champignon Sauvage** (01242) 573449 is excellent too. Neither establishment is cheap but both provide excellent excuses for a post-race celebration of major proportions. Less expensive dining and an appealing Chinese restaurant can be found at the **Mayflower** (01242) 522426. **Le Petit Blanc** (01242) 266800 is a pleasant brasserie in which to spend a few hours studying the form, as is **The Daffodil** (01242) 700055. Also in the town itself, the **Golden Valley Thistle Hotel** (01242) 232691 is modern but most comfortable. For the Festival you must book well in advance. Some people stay as far away as Bath, Stratford or Hereford while others commute daily to the Festival. Naturally, it is easier to find accommodation outside the March extravaganza but plans should not be made at the last minute if you can possibly avoid it.

It should also be emphasised that although opulence and extravagance are not an uncommon feature of this neck of the woods, cost-conscious visitors are by no means forgotten and some excellent establishments are **Lypiatt House** (01242) 224994, **Prestbury House** (01242) 529533, **Charlton Kings** (01242) 231061 and **Butts Farm** (01242) 524982.

There are also some super restaurants in the better hotels clustered around Cheltenham. In Shurdington, the **Greenway** (01242) 862352 has a lovely rural setting and is a really first class hotel in which to stay. Elsewhere. in nearby Southam, the **Hotel de la Bere** (01242) 237771 is convenient for the racecourse and there are good leisure facilities here while in Bishops Cleeve, the **Cleeveway House** (01242) 672585 is a striking Cotswold building with an outstanding restaurant and some very reasonable accommodation too. Upton St Leonards brings us **Hatton Court** (01452) 617412, an elegant hotel in Cotswold stone with good views over the Severn Valley.

One option when racing at Cheltenham is to head off into the nearby Cotswolds. The Cotswolds are an ideal dumping ground in which to discard one's non-racing partners—a wealth of country houses, galleries and antique shops should keep them quiet. **Wesley House** (01242) 602366 is a delight and **Sudeley Castle** is also particularly good. Some places to catch an hour or two's kip are any one of three hotels located in Broadway. The **Lygon Arms** (01386) 852255 exudes charm and style and the Great Hall which acts as the restaurant is superb—expect a fairly large bill though. The **Dormy House** (01386) 852711 is another excellent hotel/restaurant. The **Broadway Hotel** (01386) 852401 is a beautiful Tudor hotel, complete with minstrels gallery, and nearby **Collin House** (01386) 858354 is excellent—a good each way selection without a doubt. If you are looking for a superbly run pub with an excellent atmosphere try the **Crown and Trumpet** (01386) 853202—it's tremendous. **Olivers** (01386) 854418 is a restaurant for the shortlist. There is also a number of smaller establishments including **Barn House** (01386) 858633, **Windrush House** (01386) 853577 and **The Old Rectory** at Willersey (01386) 853729 - no restaurants but excellent accommodation. A perfect example of a Cotswold manor is the **Buckland Manor** (01386) 852626 in Buckland—once again luxurious rooms accompany an outstanding restaurant. In Upper Slaughter another elegant building, the **Lords of the Manor** (01451) 820243 can be found; superbly comfortable and a fine place for breakfast and dinner. Moreton-in-Marsh, riddled with antique shops, is also the home of the **Manor House Hotel** (01608) 650501—another for your shortlist. Another magnificent hotel is **Lower Slaughter Manor** (01451) 820456 in Lower Slaughter. Supreme comfort and excellent cuisine make this an outstanding favourite in any field. **The Lamb Inn** at Great Rissington (01451) 820388 is also well worth considering. Another tremendous food pub and good for the homesick Irish is the aptly named **Kilkenny Inn**, Kilkenny.

Although many are able to take in all three days of the Festival, some have to make do with a quick visit. Places to stop afterwards include a number of quaint villages which inevitably yield a selection of boozers. In Colesbourne, the **Colesbourne Inn** (01242)870376 is a good stop-off point for a pre-race breakfast or dinner post racing - there's also some good value accomodation. The **Green Dragon** near Cowley is a super place for bar food. Filling bar snacks and some accommodation are also good at the popular **Mill Inn** (01242) 890204 in Withington. A pleasant Whitbread house in Painswick is the **Royal Oak**, a good idea if you're heading for Tetbury. There are a number of worthy hotels to consider in this area. In Tetbury itself one finds the **Snooty Fox Hotel** (01666) 502436 which is a welcoming coaching inn and the **Close** (01666) 502272 in Tetbury is also extremely promising. A little way outside the town one finds one of the area's most outstanding hotels and restaurant, **Calcot Manor** (01666) 890391—tremendous.

Further afield in Malvern Wells, the **Cottage in the Wood** (01684) 575859 offers luxurious accommodation and excellent food and wines. For pub lovers the **Hare and Hounds** in Westonbirt (01666) 880233 is popular with Cheltenham racegoers. People bolting up the M5 may pause for thought as well as a swift one at Twyning where the **Village Inn** is a pleasant village pub. Travellers on the A46 should note the **Mount** at Stanton—more good value food and a fine collection of racing prints. For another place to enjoy good food and pub accommodation try the **Kings Head**, Bledington (01608) 658365 a first class stayer.

There is a number of other very fine hotels to consider. Some of the best include the outstanding **Corse Lawn House Hotel**, Corse Lawn (01452) 780479. This is tremendously well run but inevitably packed for Cheltenham—its restaurant is also excellent and well worth booking months in advance. Further away in Blockley, near Moreton-in-Marsh, **Lower Brook House** (01386) 700286 is a delightful Cotswold inn. Cirencester offers two inns of note; the **Fleece Hotel** (01285) 658507 and the 14th century **King's Head** (01285) 653322. **Stratton House Hotel** (01285) 651761 on the Gloucester Road also has pre-race appeal. Crossing the county to the Forest of Dean and Coleford, try the **Speech House** (01594) 822607—intimately pleasing.

In Ewen, one finds the **Wild Duck Inn** (01285) 770310 a fine inn. Another roost in a welcoming marketplace hotel, the **Bull,** (01285) 712535 can be found in Fairford.

Returning to the Cotswolds, that lovely part of England—various ideas for a recommended Cheltenham stayer include: the **Old Farmhouse Hotel** (01451) 830232 in Lower Swell and in Moreton-in-Marsh, the **Redesdale Arms** (01608) 650308. In Stonehouse, the **Stonehouse Court Hotel** (01453) 825155 is a fine manor house with an excellent reputation, while **Wyck Hill House Hotel** (01451) 31936 in busy Stow on the Wold also fits into the manorial category and the restaurant here is very good. A compliment should also be paid to the popular **Dial House** (01451) 22244, a most pleasant hotel in Bourton on the Water. Continuing our Cotswold tour, the Chipping Campden area is well worth a visit—preferably a long one. The superb **Cotswold House Hotel** (01386) 840330 is a beautiful Regency building where your stay will be both comfortable and relaxing. The restaurant, the **Garden Room** is also good. Two inns to note here include the **Kings Arms** (01386) 840256 and the pleasant **Noel Arms** (01386) 840317. For the lover of Italian food, **Caminetto** (01386) 840330 is a local favourite, whilst just outside Chipping Campden, **Charingworth Manor** (01386) 78555 at Charingworth is an hotel where no expense is spared

in making the guests' stay a memorable one. The **Malt House** (01386) 840295 at Broad Campden is also first class.

Less vaunted, but more reasonably priced post-race stabling can be secured in a number of the pubs that riddle the villages of Gloucestershire. In North Nibley, the **Black Horse** (01453) 546841 is recommended—a friendly, beamed pub with some bedrooms available if you want to make a weekend of it. Blockley offers the **Crown** (01386) 700245 with an excellent array of real ales, bedrooms and good bar food. Some fair bar snacks can be tried in the **Slug and Lettuce** in Cirencester. The **New Inn** (01453) 543659 in Waterley Bottom is also highly recommended. In North Cerney, the **Bathurst Arms** (01285) 831281 offers good bed and breakfast besides being a welcoming and popular pub. In Naunton, the **Black Horse** (01451) 850378 is also charming:—excellent bar food and some accommodation here. The same can be said of the **George** in Winchcombe—a converted Whitbread establishment-and also the **Bakers Arms** at Broad Campden (01386) 840515. People returning to London have a plethora of places to discover. If you wish to break the journey consider Eynsham—here one finds a whole clutch of boozers, the best of which is **Newlands** (01865) 881486 which also boasts a first class restaurant. Yet more pleasant village pubs abound: in Fossebridge, the **Fossebridge** (01285) 720721 is popular and in Ford the **Plough** (01249) 782215 has two bedrooms and is a lively local in which to celebrate.

There are literally hundreds of hostelries in which to reflect on the outcome of the race, and a few not to be missed the **Fox** at Lower Oddington and the **Apple Tree** in Woodmancote—local favourites for a first-class racecourse.

Artist: **David Trundley** **LAST AWAY, CHELTENHAM** *Courtesy of:* **The Artist**

The management at Chepstow is headed by **Managing Director George Francis**, with **David McAllister** as **Clerk of the Course, Peter Horleston as Company Secretary** and **Richard Perry as Commercial Manager.** All enquiries should be made to **Chepstow Racecourse, Chepstow, Monmouthshire NP6 5YH. Tel (01291) 622260 Fax (01291) 627061 e mail: enquiries@chepstow-racecourse.co.uk web site: www.chepstow-racecourse.co.uk.**

Since the opening of the Severn Bridge, now some thirty-odd years ago, Chepstow became much more accessible from the east and London via the M4. The recent opening of the second Severn Crossing now takes the M4 traffic away from Chepstow so there should be few delays on what the course now regards as its private bridge! From the east and south west on the M5 or M4, follow the signs for Chepstow. On the M48, having crossed the 'old' bridge, leave at Junction 2. From the west on the M4 again follow signs for Chepstow M48. Once at the course you will be delighted to hear that all parking is free. Chepstow has a rail station and the racecourse is a mile's canter from the town centre. Bristol Parkway station is a 25 minute drive away and this might be a good bet if you are travelling from London's Paddington station. There is a bus service (Chepstow to Monmouth) which will deposit you outside the course. If a helicopter is more your style then you may land in the middle of the track, opposite the stands. As yet light aircraft are not allowed.

Chepstow racecourse usually hosts a total of 23 days racing—14 meetings over the jumps and 9 on the flat course. Chepstow meetings are all one-day occasions. The year's racing begins in February and there are at least two meetings per month throughout the rest of the year. The course is perhaps best noted for its National Hunt racing, but we should also emphasise the beauty of the setting and the local countryside—an opportunity to visit Chepstow at any time should always be taken, especially when the spirit is somewhat waning. Feature events include the Coral Welsh National, the Rehearsal Chase, the Tote Silver Trophy over jumps and the Golden Daffodil Stakes on the flat.

Chepstow Membership in 2000 cost £155. This included an amazing 27 away days at 16 other courses including Ascot, Ayr, Bangor, Bath Exeter, Goodwood, Ludlow, Newbury, Newton Abbot, Plumpton, Salisbury, Taunton, Uttoxeter, Wincanton, Windsor, and Wolverhampton—an impressive list. The Membership badge is not transferable but a second Member's badge can be transferred. A total of 50 days racing for £155 can't be bad value! A half-year membership is also available at £90 and two badges can be purchased for a total of £180. 2000 daily charges were £15 in Members and £11 in Tatts. The Silver Ring and Centre Course prices were £6 each but are only used on Bank Holiday meetings. It is important to note that prices for the Coral Welsh National are inevitably higher at £22 (Members) and £16 (Tattersalls) and that the two cheaper enclosures are open only

Artist: **Des Murrie** AFTER THE LAST *Courtesy of:* **Osborne Studio Gallery**

on Easter Monday, the Whitsun Bank Holiday, the midsummer Sunday meeting and August Bank Holiday. If you are organising a party then a reduction of £1 per person will be made for parties of 20 or more booked seven days in advance for the Tattersalls or Members Enclosure and the organiser will receive a free ticket. Another generous concession relates to pensioners, with a £3 entrance charge to the course on public holidays and £5 to Tattersalls on other days. At the other end of the age scale a crèche is now available for children up to eleven at £3 per hour from midday onwards.

Chepstow is set in 370 acres of parkland and nestles in the slopes of the Wye Valley. Its facilities include 39 boxes, and nine hospitality suites which can be hired on racedays. £2 million has been spent on the provision of new private boxes and hospitality suites, which cater for 25 to 200 people. Marquees can be arranged for larger functions. The racecourse has three exhibition halls of varying sizes as well as the more exclusive Piercefield Suite. The caterers Letheby & Christopher have varying menus on offer. Enquiries with regard to catering should be made to them on (01242) 523203 (racedays (01291) 625189). The Paddock to the rear of the Grandstand is large and provides the racegoer with a good vantage point. The course also provides a reserved viewing area for wheelchair racegoers. The improvement programme has continued recently with a better crèche facility, a new extension to the Tattersalls' bar, a new passholders and members entrance plus a post-race winner's Reception Room with a £9 million proposed redevelopment scheme under consideration. Chepstow is a charming course in an equally charming setting and is definitely one for the notebook.

Local Favourites

Although not quite on the Welsh side of the border, a quite exceptional hotel is the **Thornbury Castle** (01454) 281182. It is an expensive establishment but has much charm and history as well as comforts that make it all the more appealing. People who wish to stay more locally should consider Chepstow itself where the **Castle View** (01291) 620349, may merit attention. **Jimmy Deans** (01291) 630514 is a pub worth checking out while **Heart of Portugal** (01291) 630404 comes highly recommended. Another to keep in mind is the **Beaufort Hotel** (01291) 624927 which comes recommended by the racecourse management as does the **Piercefield Inn** (01291) 622614, a good pub to note. The **George Hotel** (01291) 625363 adjoins the 16th

century gate and town walls. This is another good spot for a pint and a snack. The **Bridge** has a lovely setting and is worth a visit. The best place to stay if you're a golfer as well as a racing enthusiast is the **Marriott St Pierre Hotel** (01291) 625261. The hotel also offers a whole string of other leisure facilities. Similarly good golf and accommodation can be found at **Celtic Manor** (01633) 413000 near Newport.

The Welsh border country is well known for its beauty. Some particularly good ideas include a visit to Crickhowell for a night at **Gliffaes** (01874) 730371, a friendly hotel, or a visit to the **Bear Hotel** (01873) 810408. Other thoughts include the **Crown** at Whitebrook (01600) 860254—a popular place to stay with an excellent restaurant. Be sure to consider the **Village Green Restaurant** (01600) 860119 in Trellech on your way to Monmouth—there are some good value rooms available here. The **Carpenters Arms** in Shirenewton is a pub of note. In Clearwell, a country inn with bedrooms and restaurant and friendly bars is the **Wyndham Arms** (01594) 833666. The **Clearwell Castle** (01594) 832320 is another popular suggestion—this 18th century edifice is an amazing place to stay especially for lovers of four posters. Remote but very welcoming **Llanwenarth House** (01873) 830289 is a hotel of merit for your consideration. Whilst finally, a well located inn for the Forest of Dean is **Speech House**, Coleford (01594) 822607—some more four posters for the romantic racegoer. Nearby Tintern also offers a few gems: **Parva Farmhouse** (01291) 68941, a restaurant with rooms, is worthy of a pre race inspection and **The Moon and Sixpence** is ideal for a pre or post race tipple.

Artist: **Roy Miller** SILHOUETTES *Courtesy of:* **The Artist**

Chester is one of the most appealing racecourses in Britain. This delightful course is managed by **Charles Barnett** who is both **Chief Executive** and **Clerk of the Course**. and **Lucy Moreau** is **Marketing Manager**. They can be contacted at: **The Racecourse, Chester, Cheshire, CH1 2LY. Tel (01244) 323170 Fax (01244) 344971. Website: www.chester-races.co.uk.**

The racecourse lies to the south east of the town. The M6/M56 motorways serve racegoers from the north and south of the country, exiting at junction 14. Eastbound travellers will find the M62/M6/M56 the clearest route into Chester while A roads abound in the area. The course itself is well signposted by AA and RAC signs and the Chester bypass avoids the busy city centre. Cars and coaches can be parked in the centre of the course and the respective prices are £2 and £5.

The Euston line goes directly to Chester General and there is a bus service from the station to the course on racedays. For those who travel by helicopter there is a landing pad available.

The pattern of racing in 2001 is likely to follow that of 2000. The principal event is the May Festival meeting and the feature races include the Chester Vase, the Capital Bank Dee Stakes, the Shadwell Stud Cheshire Oaks and the Tote Chester Cup. This mini-festival is a true delight for racing enthusiasts. Annual Membership at Chester costs £230. This includes free car parking and free Members entrance for a day at Bangor-on-Dee, Carlisle, Doncaster, Worcester, York, Goodwood and Uttoxeter. Another advantage for the Annual Member is the provision of a special marquee for the May meeting. A really first class idea. A three day badge for the May meeting costs £85 and the daily rate for Tuesday and Thursday is £30. There are limits to capacity for the May Festival meeting and for the County Stand. Advance booking is a necessity for the County Enclosure. Daily Junior badges for racegoers (aged 17 and under) cost £5. Reserved seats for the three days cost an additional £33. Tattersalls charges are £15, and the Dee Stands cost £6 per day. There is

also a charge of £3 for spectators on the open course. Coaches and mini buses can be parked on course for £5 but booking is essential. For the remaining meetings, daily badges cost £20-25 in the County Stand, £12-15 in Tatts, £6-8 in the Dee Stands and £3-4 in the Course Enclosure.

Visitors to the County Stand can view the magnificent panorama of the Roodee, the wide sweep of the River Dee and the Welsh Hills beyond. Children are admitted free to all enclosures except the Members but there are no special facilities for them due to the restricted space. Disabled people have a small reserved stand in the Paddock with a raised level ramp, washroom and a private box facility by the winning post with CCTV. There are betting shops in Tattersalls and the Dee Stands. The racecourse has made a major investment in the new Paddock Pavilion, with new bars and entertainment areas and a new press stand. A new tented facility at every meeting, the Paddock Restaurant, can be pre-booked by ringing the racecourse in advance. The Tatts stand has also been refur-

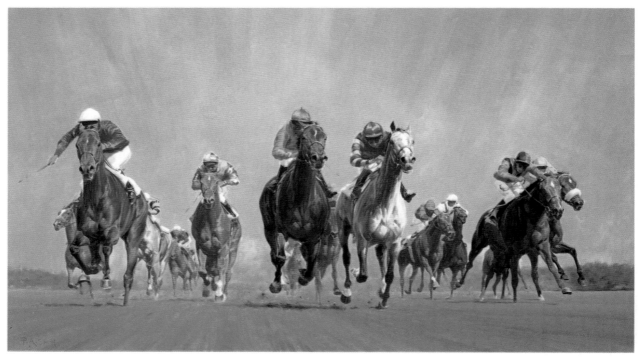

Artist: **Peter Smith** **CHARGE TO THE FINISH** *Courtesy of:* **Frost & Reed**

bished with steppings to the grandstand and a new betting hall with food and bar areas beneath. Chester is an outstanding racecourse in every way and its popularity grows year after year.

Local Favourites

A splendid place to stay is the **Chester Grosvenor** (01244) 324024—the restaurant, **Arkle**, is particularly well thought of. **Broxton Hall** (01829) 782321, and **Thornton Hall** 0151 336 3938 also come highly recommended. Back in Chester, there is an abundance of guesthouses and small hotels so the racegoer on a more limited budget should not worry. Names worth mentioning here are the **Chester Court** (01244) 320779, **Green Gables** (01244) 372243, the **Dene Hotel** (01244) 321165 and the **White Lion** (01928) 722949. Not the cheapest, but still an outstanding favourite, is **Crabwall Manor** (01244) 851666 two miles outside Chester.

Venturing some way north of Chester to the South Wirral and Puddington, one finds the **Craxton Wood Hotel** 0151 339 4717, with a small but selective and very stylish restaurant. People looking for a little luxury when visiting the city should consider one of several hotels. In St Johns Street, **Blossoms** (01244) 323186 is close to the city centre and its many amenities include a good restaurant and two friendly bars. The **Malt Shoppe** and the **Snooty Fox** are both well worth considering. A little farther afield, but still convenient for the city is a splendid

country house hotel, the **Mollington Banastre Hotel** (01244) 851471. There are excellent facilities available here—together with two restaurants—and its own village pub. In Rowton lies another fine country house—the **Rowton Hall Hotel** (01244) 335262—the service here is good and if you don't want to be in the middle of Chester this may well be the answer. South of the city lies the excellent value and secluded **Pheasant Inn** (01829) 70434. A relative newcomer to the Chester field, is the **Chester International Hotel** (01244) 322330. Meanwhile, the **Wild Boar Inn** (01829) 260309 at Beeston has modern facilities and a pleasing setting. The **Park Royal International Hotel** (01925) 730706 does special racing breaks including transport to the racecourse.

In the countryside, there are some fine pubs to note. The **Bickerton Poacher** in Bickerton is an exceptionally busy pub but is good fun too. The **Cock O'Barton** at Barton is quieter. Further south in Whitchurch is **Dearnford Hall** (01948) 662319, providing top class accommodation. In Taporley, the **Swan** (01829) 733838 is a worthy Greenall's pub with a restaurant and some bedrooms if you require them. The **Rising Sun** is also a pub to note here. More of the same can be found in Sutton, north west of Chester at **Sutton Hall**. Finally, a very special hotel can be found at Mold, some twelve miles from Chester. Here, a warm welcome awaits you at **Soughton Hall** (01352) 840811, a stunning hotel in Italianate style with a fine à la carte restaurant. With outstanding hotels and a first class racecourse, a visit to Chester in 2001 simply must be organised.

_____ *The Park Royal International Hotel* _____

The Park Royal International Hotel, Health and Leisure Spa is set in the heart of the Cheshire countryside yet only one minute from junction 10 of the M56 motorway, three minutes from the M6 and twelve minutes from Manchester airport.

Located midway between Aintree, Chester and Haydock racecourses the hotel provides fully air-conditioned conference and banqueting suites for up to 400 guests, 140 deluxe en suite bedrooms, the award-winning AA rosette Harlequin restaurant and comfortable lounges and bars.

You can relax in the superb state of the art health and leisure spa facilities include a 22m swimming pool, sauna, steam room, whirlpool bath, solarium, dance studio and gymnasium. Also available is the Beauty Retreat, with 6 beauty suites including a hydrotherapy bath.

The Park Royal International Hotel is an ideal venue for a short break. Dinner, bed and breakfast rates from £52.50 per person.

The Park Royal International Hotel, Health & Leisure Spa
Stretton Road, Stretton
Warrington, Cheshire WA4 4NS
Tel: (01925) 730706 Fax: (01925) 730740
e mail: hotel@park-royal-int.co.uk
web site: www.parkroyalinthotel.co.uk

The racecourse, owned by Doncaster Metropolitan Borough Council, is managed by International Racecourse Management Ltd. Chief Executive. **John Sanderson is Clerk of the Course**, **General Manager** is **Tim Betteridge** with **Chris Oliver** as the **Office Manager**. Doncaster's exhibition and conference centre is open all year round and information can be obtained by writing to **The Grandstand, Leger Way, Doncaster. DN2 6BB. Tel (01302) 320066/7 Fax (01302) 323271. Website: www.britishracing.com.**

Doncaster racecourse is in South Yorkshire, one mile from the centre of the town itself. The course is within easy reach of motorways and there is a dual carriageway to the course car parks. The A1 and the M1/M18 are good routes from the south and signs now direct racegoers from all motorway approaches. If you are coming from the west then use the A57 and M18 and from the east the M18 and M180. Let the train take the strain from Kings Cross and your journey time will be 85 minutes with a bus from the town to complete the final leg of the journey. Buses from Doncaster (Nos 55, 170 and 171) will drop you 300 metres from the gates—perfect! Helicopters are permitted to land at Doncaster but only by special arrangement so if this is your desired mode of transport then please check with the Office Manager first. Car parking is easy here with space for 3000 cars—all free. There is also a reserved area for Members.

The season at Doncaster consists of 28 day's racing, twenty flat and eight over the sticks. Principal meetings are the St Leger Festival in September and the Worthington Lincoln in March, the Racing Post Trophy in October and the Tote November Handicap. Doncaster has the honour of opening and closing the flat season—a worthy privilege for an excellent racecourse.

Rates of admission for 2000 varied from meeting to meeting and day to day. There was a standard charge of £15 for the Members Enclosure and £9 for the Tattersalls but prices are higher on more prestigious racedays. £4 was the standard charge for the Family Enclosure and again this rose on principal days. For example, charges for St Leger day are £28, £16 and £6 respectively. Annual Membership at Doncaster costs £195. Included in this are 21 reciprocal meetings from Newbury through to Chester and entrance to Yorkshire Cricket Club matches on eleven days. This has to be good value. Dual Membership offers husband and wife a double badge for £295 and Junior Badges are £95. Prices are not expected to change much for 2001. Party discounts are also available and you should contact the racecourse for full details if you are planning a large outing. When you are inviting guests, don't forget to tell them that the course runs a strict dress code of "Jacket and tie, and no jeans allowed" in the Members Enclosure. There's nothing more embarrassing than having a guest turned away because of their attire! Boxes, and there are a total of 70 now, are let on an annual basis. A tented village exists for the St Leger meeting. A £1 million refurbishment programme has recently been completed in the Family Enclosure.

There are numerous bars together with corporate facilities. The Lincoln Restaurant is situated in the Yorkshire Stand and tables are allocated on a first come, first served basis. The Hospitality Club in the St Leger Banqueting Suite is designed to give racegoers a full day at the races in a corporate hospitality

Artist: **Peter Smith** **TOO CLOSE TO CALL** *Courtesy of:* **Frost & Reed**

style without the need for large numbers (a minimum of two people). The caterers are Metro and can be contacted on (01302) 349740.

Doncaster has taken a positive lead in promoting racing as family entertainment and raceday activities include a professionally staffed crèche, children's rides, craft stalls and a selection of raceday music. The Giant Screen is present on major racedays and the course has developed its own corporate entertainment department as well as catering for party bookings. Doncaster is a really friendly well run racecourse and one which in recent years has dramatically improved.

There are a total of 59 racecourses in Britain. Doncaster is the most historic and is fast becoming one of the best with a £30 million transformation planned, incorporating the racecourse and exhibition centre, stabling, bloodstock sales, golf clubhouse and hotel. A visit in 2001 is highly recommended.

Local Favourites

The most historic of Yorkshire racecourses is to be found at Doncaster—perhaps not the most attractive of towns but an excellent racecourse nonetheless. In Doncaster, the **Grand St Leger** (01302) 364111 is extremely comfortable and its restaurant has an imaginative menu. The **Doncaster Moat House** (01302) 799988 is also very appealing. A little south of the town, in Bawtry, stands the **Crown Hotel** (01302) 710341, a pleasant inn in a quiet market square. The **Regent Hotel**

(01302) 364180 and the **Mount Pleasant** (01302) 868219 are shortlisted by people in the know, and the **Rockingham Arms** (01302) 360980 also has a good reputation. Two other hotels to consider are the **Quality Danum Hotel** (01302) 342261 in the town centre—and the **Earl of Doncaster** (01302) 361371, a mere half mile from the racecourse. One final thought for lovers of Indian cooking is the **Aagrah** (01302) 728888, it's well worthwhile.

For people who may want a little more comfort and style there are two hotels that are warmly recommended north of Doncaster. In Wentbridge, the **Wentbridge House Hotel** (01977) 620444 has a pleasant location in the parkland scenery of the Went Valley. **Monk Fryston Hall Hotel** (01977) 682369 is found in the West Riding village of the same name. Pubs to note nearby include the excellent **Inn at Cadeby** and the **Green Tree** at Hatfield Woodhouse (01302) 840305—a few bedrooms

Artist: **Hubert de Watrigant** *UNE BELLE EMPOIGNADE* *Courtesy of:* **Osborne Studio Gallery**

The home of the Derby, Epsom holds a special place in British and world racing. While the accomplishments of jockeys, horses and trainers on other racecourses may fade from view with the passage of time, the connections of the Derby winner become part of history forever. The Aga Khan's success with his redoubtable middle distance horse Sinndar adds to his family's long list of success as winning owners even if the names Oxx and Murtagh are more recent but no less welcome to the Derby's role of honour. Despite this welcome news it is disturbing to hear someone as well travelled as Godolphin's Simon Crisford criticise the atmosphere of Derby Day in comparison with its younger brother the American Derby. Here at Travelling the Turf we were keen supporters of moving the Derby from Wednesday to Saturday and it appears that in the main this has worked well. However, due principally to competition from other sporting events, the whole meeting has not taken centre stage as it should have. Indeed two such excellent races as the Oaks and the Coronation Cup seem to have lost their momentum - which is ironic given they are now an the same card as opposed to being spread over two days. In order to regain the initiative I suspect that this part of the meeting should take place either on the Friday night or possibly the Sunday of the weekend. In addition, if it were practical in a similar way to Silverstone, part of the Downs should be converted to a camp site with funfairs and excitement to get the blood racing. This would certainly grab the attention of the younger racegoer which the racing authorities seem to want to welcome. The course could also be brought to life in a similar way to Cheltenham with racing events, exhibitions, a tented village and bands, bringing the whole of Epsom to the attention of the Nation. I appreciate the calendar is already busy with evening meetings and Sunday fixtures but it is imperative that this weekend is given special attention so it becomes one of the foremost sporting events in the diary let alone the racing calendar.

Andrew Cooper is the **Clerk of the Course** and **Racing Manager** and **Stephen Wallis** is the **General Manager** at Epsom. **Mrs Sue Ellen** is the **Managing Director** and **Jo Dillon** is the **Membership Secretary** who also handles ticket sales. **Tim Darby** is the **Marketing Manager** for United Racecourses and can be reached on **(01372) 461253**. **Laura Southgate** is **Corporate Hospitality Manager** and **Stephen Prior** should be contacted for Sponsorship details. The racecourse can be contacted directly on **tel: (01372) 726311 fax (01372) 748253** but all enquiries are dealt with at Sandown and should be addressed to **United Racecourses, Sandown Park Racecourse, Esher, Surrey KT10 9AJ tel: (01372) 464348 fax: (01372) 470427**. There is a ticket line **tel: (01372) 470047**. **Website: www.epsomderby.co.uk.**

Epsom itself stands on the Surrey Downs of the same name. The mode of transportation depends significantly on the meeting. Derby Day is enormously busy—even helicopters hover in line. However, on other days traffic is less congested. The racecourse is fairly close to the centre of London and people heading from that direction should pursue the A3 south, exiting at the Tolworth junction. Traffic from the west is advised to join the M25 and exit at junction 8 or 9 for the course. The M25, if it is flowing freely, also serves people from the east and the south of the country. The A217 is the best route to observe in order to complete your northbound journey. An excellent idea is to take the train. Lines from the London stations of Waterloo, Charing Cross and Victoria stretch to Epsom. The Downs can be reached from Victoria alone, while Tattenham Corner visitors should

*Artist: **Terence Gilbert** **THE DERBY (TATTENHAM CORNER)** Courtesy of: **The Artist***

take trains from either London Bridge or Charing Cross. If you travel to Epsom by train, buses will take you to the course itself. However, passengers to Tattenham Corner station can enjoy a pleasant walk across the Downs before racing. Many people have picnics here and this seems as ideal a place as any to indulge in your nosebag. Other places in which to have a pre-race snack are the car parks, of which there are many. Charges vary according to your particular setting. Finally, if you are lucky enough to travel by helicopter, you can land here—it's quite a sight I assure you.

There is a range of charges for the various enclosures. Derby Day is unsurprisingly expensive. Admission to the Queens Stand on Derby Day is restricted to Annual Members. Admission to the Club Enclosure costs £40 on Derby Day. Reserved seats cost £18 in advance or £35 (in addition to the club badge) if you just show up on the day. Oaks Day will set you back £40 for Club admission. The more relaxed Lonsdale, Walton and Tattenham enclosures are priced at between £4 and £1, with the Grandstand at between £12 and £20. For both Derby Day and Oaks Day there are discounts for advance bookings. To get a comprehensive listing of the various charges contact the racecourse. Annual Membership in 2000 was priced at £130. A Junior Membership badge was priced at £60. The principal advantage of this membership is that it gives you admission to the Members Enclosure for the Derby—a real bonus. Finally, a number of rooms and private boxes are available. Please ring the racecourse for full details.

There is a restaurant in the Members Enclosure and you should book. A less busy alternative can be found in the Grandstand. The numerous snack bars serve sandwiches but

these are fairly expensive. Disabled facilities have been radically improved at Epsom with ramps, lifts and toilets now provided. A bank can be found behind the Grandstand during Derby week should you blow all your cash early on in the Tote or Coral betting facilities. Also please note that children under 16 are admitted free to all enclosures except the Members on Derby Day. In one of several fairly fundamental changes at the course, the Paddock has been relocated and is now behind the Grandstand. This has ensured that the action has been condensed somewhat, which has to be an improvement.

There has always been, and probably always will be, great debate about The Derby being the ultimate test for three year

Artist: **Peter Smith** *TOP OF THE HILL* *Courtesy of:* **Frost & Reed**

olds and therefore the key pointer to later success at stud. Derby winners still go for very high prices when sold to stud, but are unfortunately now more likely to head for distant places such as Japan than stay at home to improve the domestic breed. The fairness of the descent to Tattenham Corner and the toll it takes on young legs is open to discussion, but there can be no doubt that a Derby winner will always need courage, grit and determination to go with outstanding ability and a turn of foot; attributes that will always be in demand amongst the best bloodstock.

The pedigree of the Derby speaks for itself, and it is the challenge of the distinguished racing and business brains ,as proprietors of Epsom to ensure its development in future years.

In the coming years Epsom should continue to reap the rewards of moving Derby Day to a weekend; despite the howls of protest by the traditionalists, there are clearly no benefits in moving the event back to a time when most people can't attend or watch. From a punter's perspective the new fixture list is firmly, and rightly, committed to weekend racing and the Derby weekend should be the annual highlight of this. In an increasingly busy world, there is always going to be competition for the public's attention - from going to the local DIY to other major sporting events on a Saturday. Can we fly a kite for holding both the Derby and the Oaks on a Sunday to produce the best day's flat racing of the whole year? The weekend action would then start on a Saturday evening with a great carnival party on the Downs with masses of large field handicaps and a super bet to challenge the punters, with lots of entertainment for the whole family and a grand fireworks finale to finish. This would firmly position Epsom and the Derby as the jewel in the crown of British flat racing. Alternatively, as suggested above, an evening or Sunday could be utilised to maximise the impact of the event. It was great to hear that when Sue Ellen, the Managing Director of Epsom, heard of Simon Crisford's complaints she leapt into her car to hear more. Hearing criticisms is one thing, having ideas another, making them work, however, is what counts. It is time for Epsom to deliver.

Local Favourites

People who are staying in this area (rather than in the capital) should note the **Burford Bridge Hotel** (01306) 884561, in Burford Bridge near Dorking—a welcoming hotel beside the A24 and well sited for Epsom Downs. The **White Horse Hotel**, (0870) 4008282 also has great character, though less class. Both of these are ideal for the tourist as they date back centuries. **Partners and Sons** (01306) 882826 is a popular restaurant to sample. Epsom itself contains the **Epsom Downs Hotel** (01372) 740643, a good value and relaxing hotel. In Banstead, a convenient yet unpretentious stayer is the **Heathside** (01737) 353355. Further south in Rusper, an hotel for people who enjoy a little peace and quiet, **Ghyll Manor** (01293) 871571 is a comfortable old manor house.

Turning back towards the racecourse again, the busy town of Reigate is home to the **Cranleigh Hotel** (01737) 223417 and the **Bridge House** (01737) 246801, both unpretentious and good value. The **Whyte Harte** (01883) 743231 in Bletchingly is also a fine place to stay, as is the **Bell** (01883) 743133 in Godstone—ideal for a steak and a drink. **Tutu L'Auberge** (01342 892318 just south of Godstone is also a very pleasant restaurant.

There are numerous pubs to be found in the area—some near, some far. The **Harrow** in Thames Ditton is most obliging as is the **Jolly Farmer** in Weybridge. In Kenley one finds the

Artist: ***D M Dent 1998 DERBY*** *Courtesy of:* ***The Artist***

Artist: **William Newton** *MAQUETTE OF DERBY 2000 TROPHY*
Courtesy of: **Osborne Studio Gallery**

be found in Holmbury St Mary, a really good atmosphere here. In Shere, the **White Horse** is also popular—rightly so—it is charming and offers some excellent home-made food. People who are fond of eating and enjoy the ambience of a good restaurant should try the **Onslow Arms** (01483) 222447 in West Clandon—a classic of its type. The **Bulls Head** is also good here as is the **Jarvis Thatchers Hotel** (01483) 284291, both comfortable and convenient.

The Derby attracts all sorts of people. Gypsies promise you luck but you will still lose your shirt. The Derby is one of the most colourful events of the year and if you want to end it in style visit the village of Nutfield. The hotel here is situated in the former local priory, **Nutfield Priory** (01737) 822066, the perfect place to count your winnings or lick your wounds after a day at the Derby.

Wattenden Arms, an extremely popular pub with some distinguished bar food available. The **Plough** at Blackbrook is also very civilised and the **Plough** (01306) 711793 at Coldharbour offers good food, beer and some accommodation.

If you're contemplating dinner, a local favourite is **Partner's and Sons** (01306) 882826 in Dorking. In Surbiton, **Luca's** 0208 399 2365 is also good—a small restaurant with an ambitious French menu.

An alternative nearby is to be found in Chipstead—the **Ramblers Rest** (01737) 552661 is not cheap but offers a really first class menu, friendly service and a distinguished wine list. Finally, in Hersham the **Dining Room** (01932) 231686 is reported to be excellent, where a friendly atmosphere accompanies bold English cooking

The **Old School House** (01306) 711224 in Ockley should be noted—the well priced menu is extremely appealing. Another pleasant pub to inspect near here is the **Punch Bowl** which has a lovely setting and serves some simple bar snacks as well as having a good dining room. Still in Ockley, **Bryce's** (01306) 627430 is a good pub for decent grub and two other pubs to note while in this area of Surrey include another part of the king's anatomy, on this occasion the **Kings Head**, to

Finally, if your appetite has not been whetted by any of these suggestions (unlikely!), then turn to the Kempton Park and Sandown recommendations where you will see more places to satisfy the Surrey racegoer.

Artist: **William Newton** *GAMBOLLING*
Courtesy of: **Osborne Studio Gallery**

If you are planning a visit to England's delightful West Country then stop off at Exeter racecourse. This pleasant track is in the capable hands of **Mr G Billson, Managing Director, Mr B Soper** as **Raceday Manager** and **Secretary**, and **Mrs Charlotte Faulkner** as **Club Secretary**. The address is **Devon & Exeter Steeplechases Ltd, Exeter Racecourse, Kennford Nr Exeter, EX6 7XS. Tel (01392) 832599. Fax (01392) 833454.**

When travelling to the course it may be as well to stick to the motorways to ensure a speedy route—the M5 feeds from the M4 and the M6. The course is some 190 miles from London and seven miles south west of Exeter. Only 3 miles further down from the end of the M5 motorway the A38 Plymouth road takes you right past the racecourse at the top of Haldon Hill. On arrival at the racecourse there is ample car parking to be found. Essentially this is free, though there is a £2 charge for a special position on the rails. The nearest train station is at Exeter, St Davids, which can be comfortably reached from Paddington. On racedays there is a free bus service to the course from the central bus station in Exeter City Centre

The programme at Exeter features 15 National Hunt meetings, the main race being Gold Cup Day at the end of October. However, racing spans the year here from September to May and lovers of the Devon sun should note the splendid Red Cross Day meeting in early October. Lovers of winter sport should sample the national hunt fixtures, which are seldom affected by seasonal weather. In order to become an Annual Member the sum of £105 is charged for a single badge. This also includes some 23 reciprocal days, although Exeter members certainly have to do some travelling to enjoy them! Daily

rates are £11 for the Members and Tattersalls, Grandstand and Paddock and a really good value £5 for the Silver Ring. Party discounts are available for the Members and Tattersalls—please apply to the course for further details.

The course has hospitality rooms in the new Ansley and Brockman buildings which can hold up to 50 people, while the old Tote has been converted to accommodate a function room for large parties. The Brockman Stand features a new betting hall and owners and trainers bar as well as three new hospitality rooms with spectacular views of the course. The new Paddock now incorporates the winners enclosure and provides much improved views of the pre-saddling enclosure. There is also the Desert Orchid Restaurant, which is capable of seating up to 100

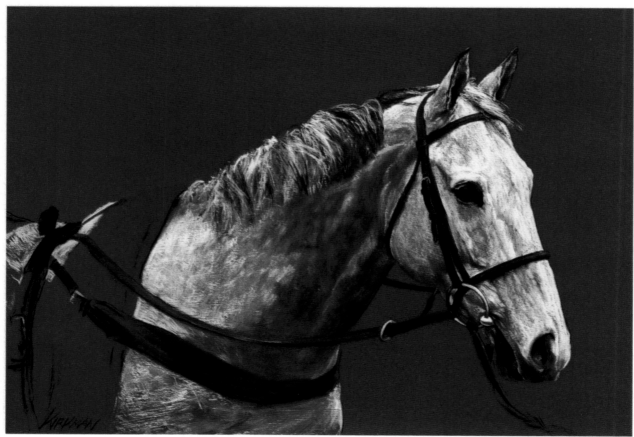

Artist: **Jay Kirkman** **GREY I** *Courtesy of:* **Park Walk Gallery**

people. Booking details are available from Mrs Faulkner (01392) 832599. More elaborate catering can also be arranged through the Catering Division (01392) 832599 and there are facilities for marquees if you wish to have a really good party.

The only drawback to what must be considered to be one of Britain's favourite courses is the lack of facilities for under 16s, although there is an under 5s play area in the old Tote building, and accompanied chilren under 16 are admitted free to the Racecourse. Telephones at the racecourse are located in The Brockman Stand where there is also a betting shop. For the disabled there is a special viewing platform and toilet facilities. This is a wonderful part of the world and a thoroughly pleasant racecourse. A trip is strongly tipped, throughout the year.

Local Favourites

Three miles from the racecourse is the **Lord Haldon** (01392) 832483, a highly commended country house hotel which organises special racing breaks for visitors to Exeter as well as to Newton Abbot. East of the course lies Exeter and here the **Royal Clarence** (01392) 319955 is the pick of the paddock. **Buckerell Lodge** (01392) 221111 and **St Olaves Court** (01392) 217736 also have considerable appeal—both have good restaurants. The **White Hart** (01392) 79897 wins approval from those seeking a characterful inn, **Southgate** (01392) 412812 is also a well thought of establishment.

One thought for golfers and holidaymakers alike is the **Thurlestone Hotel** (01548) 560382 in Thurlestone. A number of these hotels are much quieter in the off season and are therefore that much more appealing, so book up now and take a well earned break.

A good sporting break hotel is the **Manor House** (01647) 440355 at Moretonhampstead. **Woodhayes** (01404) 822237 in Whimple is a real favourite. Both the restaurant and accommodation here are first class. In Diddiscombsleigh, one pub that really should be noted is the welcoming (but somewhat oddly named) **Nobody Inn** (01647) 52394, with good value bedrooms if you like pub accommodation. The bar food and wine here here are good. Close by, the **Huntsman** is a grand alternative. A tremendous pub for a visit after racing is the **Coaching Inn**, Chudleigh—great character and food, whilst on the coast the **Bay Hotel** (01626) 774123 is a comfortable place to stay. Another place to eat is the **Thatch** in Haldon. In North Bovey, the **Ring of Bells** (01647) 40375 is a well known real ale pub with accommodation which is also good value. For those spreading their sightseeing net slightly wider, the **Cridford Inn** (01626) 853694 is also most appealing—an historic inn, offering good food and accommodation—ideal. **Combe House** (01404) 42756, Gittisham, is another outstanding hotel and restaurant, while **Bel Alp House** (01364) 661217 is an excellent country house hotel.

Heading further into Dartmoor there are some really first class hotels. In Chagford, the **Gidleigh Park Hotel** (01647) 432367 is isolated but beautiful and has a first class restaurant. The **Great Tree Hotel** (01647) 432491 is also extremely tranquil while the **Mill End** (01647) 432282 has yet another delightfully quiet setting in the Teign Valley. Finally, some twenty miles from Exeter is Ashburton, which houses the **Holne Chase Hotel** (01364) 631471, a lovely country house hotel where fishing is available and a warm welcome assured.

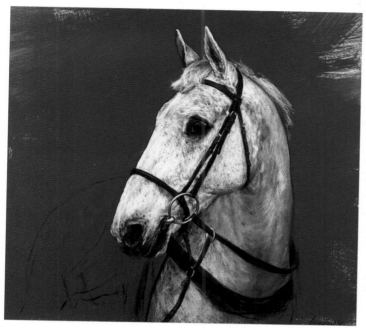

Artist: **Jay Kirkman GREY III** *Courtesy of:* **Park Walk Gallery**

Artist: **Jay Kirkman GREY II** *Courtesy of:* **Park Walk Gallery**

Now this is a racecourse which is well worth a visit. It has a tremendous atmosphere and is great fun. **David Hunter** is **Clerk of the Course** and **Racecourse Manager**, and **Vivien Pope** is the **Company Secretary**. All enquiries should be addressed to **The Racecourse, Fakenham, Norfolk NR21 7NY. Tel (01328) 862388. Fax (01328) 855908. Website: www.fakenhamracecourse.co.uk.**

Fakenham is a great advertisement for racing at the lower end of the spectrum. By and large it appears good value for money and like several similar courses, it often provides a more enjoyable day's racing than its more illustrious competitors.

Fakenham is situated just off the A148 and the town is bypassed to the north making your journey somewhat less tricky. Although the course is well signposted from all directions, London is 125 miles away, King's Lynn 22 miles and Norwich 26 miles. From the north, the A1 and A17 combine to make the most direct route. From the south use the A1065, from the west the A148 and from the east the A1067. Parking facilities at the course are thankfully very good. The main railway station is some 22 miles away at King's Lynn (departing Liverpool Street and King's Cross). Some local bus services do run from the station and the X98 is an express. However, what the area lacks in the way of public transport it makes up for in terms of private facilities. Helicopters may land in the centre of the course.

Despite being a eight-meeting country course, Fakenham has some fairly worthwhile prizes and is well sponsored by local and national firms. Racing highlights are the Prince of Wales Cup, Queen's Cup, David Keith Memorial Chase, Graham Building Supplies Handicap Steeplechase, Stephenson Smart Handicap Steeplechase, plus a point to point and Arab racing. Easter Monday is the major raceday and much recommended. The May meeting is now held on a Sunday.

Badges cost £14 for the Members on Easter and May meetings and £12 on other days. Similarly, Tattersalls prices varied between £10 and £6 on different days. Admission to the Course enclosure costs £5. But please note that Tattersalls and the Course enclosure are combined as one enclosure except on bank holidays and for the May Meeting. If you're local or just keen on Fakenham then you should buy a £100 annual double badge—a worthwhile saving. Annual single badges can be ordered for £75 and a year's membership includes reciprocal days at Huntingdon, Market Rasen, Yarmouth, Southwell, Warwick and Bangor plus one car park badge. Daily badge holders must pay £8 to park in the Members' while public car parking is free. If you're thinking of organising a party to go to Fakenham a 30 per cent discount is available for groups of 30 or more who book in advance, 20 per cent for groups of 20 to 29, and 10 per cent for groups of 10 to 19. If you want to make a real day and night of it, marquees can be hired and all the various trimmings laid on. The Paddock Buffet Restaurant serves good food (there is no need to book) and there is also a members restaurant. The caterers are Event Caterers (01603) 219991 Fax: (01603) 219992.

Artist: **Vic Granger RACING AT FAKENHAM** _Courtesy of:_ **The Artist**

Facilities for the disabled are good here and include their own viewing stand and reserved parking. Children are welcome at Fakenham and are admitted free if under 16 and accompanied by an adult. A new creche is also available for a small charge. There is a Tote betting shop close to the paddock but no bank to replenish your wallet should you be unsuccessful. Fakenham also operates an upmarket caravan/camping site ideally situated for sampling Norfolk's delights, with the added benefit of free entry to race meetings. All in all, Fakenham is a small, rural and friendly racecourse, well run, well supported and recommended to all those who relish travelling the turf.

Local Favourites

Where better to dream of tomorrow's winners than in the serenely peaceful village of Great Snoring? Here, the secluded and personal **Old Rectory** (01328) 820597 is an impressive manor house dating back to 1500. Another outstanding place to stay and eat is to be found at Grimston where **Congham Hall** (01485) 600250 is a delightful country house. The **Fakenham Wine Bar** (01328) 862032 is also a popular haunt, and special mention must be made of the **Old Forge Restaurant** (01328) 878345 at Thursford, which specialises in seafood..And now for a few inspired selections: **Yetmans Restaurant** in Holt (01263) 713320 is reputed to be very good and we are also informed that **Lenwade House Hotel** in Lenwade (01603) 872288 and **Grady's Country House Hotel** in Swaffham (01760) 723355 are delightful. Last, but most definitely not least, the quaintly named Barney houses the highly recommended **Old Brick Kilns** (01328) 878305.

If you decide that a little sea air is in order then the **Jolly Sailors** (01485) 210314 at Brancaster Staithe may be somewhere to visit after racing—a pleasant bar and a fine English menu in the restaurant. A little way from the coast, two locations should be considered. Firstly, in Burnham Market, **Fishes** (01328) 738588 where some superb fish can be enjoyed in an informal atmosphere, and secondly, in Burnham Thorpe, the **Lord Nelson**—an original pub with an excellent drop of Greene King.

In Fakenham, there is **Sculthorpe Mill** (01328) 856161, a converted late 18 century watermill handy for the racecourse, or the **Wensum Lodge Hotel** (01328) 862100, as well as the **Crown** (01328) 710209, a pleasant inn with a restaurant and some accommodation. Moving into Blakeney, you find the **Blakeney Hotel** (01263) 740797 a comfortable family run hotel, while the **Manor Hotel** (01263) 740376 has a marvellous quayside setting. Two pubs to note are the **Kings Arms** and the **White Horse** where excellent bar food is available—ideal for a weekend visit after racing. Just west of here, **Morston Hall**, (01263) 741041 has a good racing name and an excellent reputation. Some way off one finds the **Maltings Hotel** (01263) 588731 near the sea—most appealing. Similarly try the **Hoste Arms** in Burnham Market (01328) 738777, it's a superb inn and makes a fantastic location for a weekend away. Three final places to consider are the **Old Bakehouse** (01328) 820454 in Little Walsingham which offers accommodation, food and a characterful bar. The **White Horse** (01328) 820645 is an inn to note. The **Buckinghamshire Arms** (01263) 732133 in Blickling is also well worth a visit. I am looking forward to my next visit already—one for the diary in 2001.

*Artist: **Heather St Clair Davis** **PIT CREW** Courtesy of: **Frost & Reed***

The **Director of Racing** is **Richard Muddle** and **Clive Stephens** is **Regional Manager.** They can be contacted **c/o Lingfield Park Racecourse, Racecourse Road, Lingfield, Surrey RH7 6PQ** Tel **(01342) 834800** Fax **(01342) 832833.** The **Chief Executive** here is **Graham Parr** and **Claudia Fisher** is the **Sales & Marketing Director.** Web site: **www.folkstone-racecourse.co.uk.**

Located four miles west of Folkestone, Kent's only track is a mere 65 miles from London. Road users from London should leave the M20 at junction 11 where there is a sign directing you to the racecourse and take the A20 towards Lympne, Newingreen and Sellinge. The racecourse is only about one mile from the motorway. From Canterbury the best route is the B2068, the historic Roman 'Stone Street', picking up the AA signs as you go over junction 11. Train users are well catered for—special raceday services depart Charing Cross and Waterloo East (three minutes later) to Westenhanger. The station adjoins the course and is about 100 metres from the main entrance (telephone 0171 928 5100 for details). There is no bus service. Those with helicopters should call the racecourse the day before the meeting to make landing arrangements. Whatever your mode of transport, you will find ample free parking and for those who like to pack a hamper, you can picnic from a car park and watch the racing.

The racecourse has a mixed calendar with about 20 fixtures, the most popular invariably being the aptly named Garden of England Day which takes place in early September and is well worth a visit, as is the United Hunts, the May jumps meeting.

For the 2000/2001 season, Annual Membership is priced at £150. One of the particular benefits of your membership is that it includes ten reciprocal meetings at other tracks. This means that punters can enjoy a taste of flat racing and chasing and hurdling as well as show jumping—ideal for lovers of all manner of equestrian pursuits. Daily rates are £12 for a combined Members and Grandstand admission and £5 per car and £5 per occupant in the Picnic Enclosure. People wishing to organise a party of 20 or more will receive a discount of 20 per cent per person. This should be organised through the racecourse management in advance of the meeting. Children under 16 are admitted free to all areas if accompanied by an adult.

If a picnic sounds like hard work then it may be an idea to sample one of the two restaurants, one of which overlooks the course. Bookings should be made through the racecourse caterers, Letheby & Christopher (01273) 814566. The course has twelve splendid boxes which can seat up to 16 guests and are available for hire on a daily basis. Corporate hospitality rates are from £35 per head. If you are inclined to go for a real bash, then the management will be happy to guide you on the various possibilities available here at Folkestone.

If you wish to place an off-track punt then Tattersalls is where you will find the necessary betting facilities. There is no bank yet at this course and other facilities, including those for disabled, are limited.

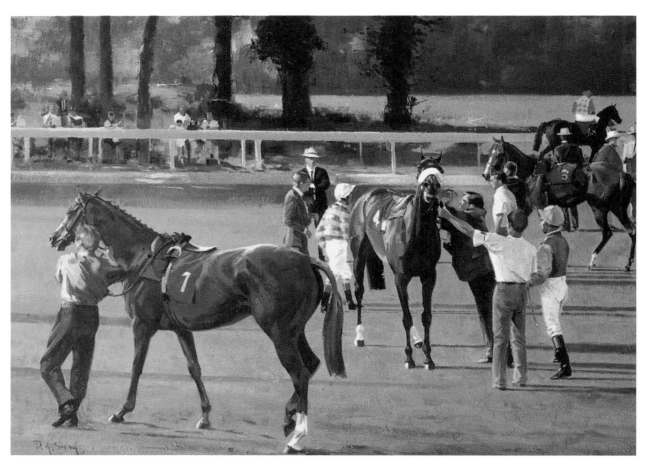

*Artist: **Peter Smith** EVENING MEET - GOING OUT Courtesy of: **Frost & Reed***

There are numerous plans afoot for the continued improvement of Folkestone racecourse. It's interesting to note that the course has only one basic admission charge which allows the punter to enter all areas. This is probably a move that many other courses could consider adopting and well done Folkestone for breaking down the mystery for the new racegoer of having to decide between something called the Silver Ring and Tattersalls!

Local Favourites

A hotel with a watery view is the **Clifton** (01303) 851231 in Folkestone. Reasonably priced accommodation can also be found at the **Belmonte Private Hotel** (01303) 254470. There is a number of restaurants to consider; **Pauls** (01303) 259697 in Bouverie Road is a fine place to spend an evening—the fish and shellfish here are particularly good. **La Tavernetta** (01303) 254955 is another long-standing favourite—Italian cuisine on this occasion. If you are in Hythe and are searching for a good place to stay then the **Hythe Imperial** (01303) 267441 should be the answer. This hotel is particularly comfortable and offers excellent leisure facilities including special golf packages, ideal for those of you who enjoy following the fairways as much as travelling the turf. **Stade Court** (01303) 268263 is less elaborate than its near neighbour but most accommodating and friendly. Sandgate, a little west of Folkestone, offers The **Sandgate Hotel** (01303) 220444, a fine hotel and restaurant.

Dover obviously contains a host of more modest guesthouses where the welcome is guaranteed to be greater than the bill. Potential gems include **Number One** (01304) 202007 and **Walletts Court** (01304) 852424 which is really outstanding. This is definitely one for those who enjoy good service and some style. An excellent restaurant as well. You'll find it at St Margaret's at Cliffe. In Wingham, the **Red Lion** (01227) 720217 offers a good restaurant and some satisfactory, well priced bedrooms.

One of the most appealing things about Kent is the many pubs one can find. In the delightfully named Petts Bottom, the **Duck** (01227) 830354 is a welcoming pub. The aptly named **Flying Horse** in Boughton Aluph (01233) 260914 is a pub to note—some accommodation here. Chilham, a most attractive little village, offers the **White Horse**, an old coaching inn and the **Woolpack** (01227) 730208 where some good accommodation is offered, making it an ideal base for preparing one's excursion to the racecourse. If you can't relax in this village you may as well call it a day! Another pub well worth a visit is the **Five Bells** at Brabourne (01303) 813334 - first class food. The star of the show, in terms of intimate dining, is to be found in Wye, the **Wife of Bath** (01233) 812540. Finally, **Eastwell Manor** (01233) 213000, situated in the gorgeous Eastwell Park, Ashford, is a delightful place with a first class dining room, a front runner in any field. Ideal if you've won a packet on the last at Folkestone.

Artist: **Harry Matthews** **ALL GOING WELL** _Courtesy of:_ **The Artist**

Fontwell Park

There is no more pleasant a course for a day's National Hunt racing than Fontwell Park where **Jonathan Garratt** is the **Chief Executive** and **David McHarg** is the **Clerk of the Course**. They can be contacted on **(01243) 543335. Website: www.fontwellpark.co.uk.**

The racecourse is conveniently situated adjacent to the A27 and the A29 roundabout, midway between Arundel and Chichester. London is 60 miles using the M23 and the A29. The M23 adjoins the M25—that frustratingly one-paced track. The A3 is the best selection to make if one is keen to pursue a trunk road. The trains into this county run from Victoria and the nearest station is at Barnham. There are free buses from the station to the course on racedays so this may be an alternative mode of transport. There is ample car parking available which is provided free. Helicopters may be landed close to the track if you call ahead to make arrangements.

The racecourse staged seventeen National Hunt fixtures in 2000 and fixtures for 2001 are expected to follow a similar pattern. The bank holiday fixture in August which started a few years ago continues to provide some summer sport. The most popular annual event is usually the Spring Bank Holiday meeting in May. There are many Monday and Tuesday meetings at Fontwell Park with a new Sunday meeting in October featuring the Salmon Spray Handicap Hurdle and it may be a good idea to relax for a few days in West Sussex and take in one such meeting. The National Spirit Champion Hurdle Trial in the second half of February often provides a few Cheltenham Pointers.

Entrance to the racecourse is priced at £14 for daily admission to the Members, £10 for the Tattersalls Enclosure and £6 for the Silver Ring, while OAP's can gain entry at £4. All accompanied children under 16 enter free. There are very popular picnic car parks in the Silver Ring and in the centre of the course, if you want to make a real day out of it. An additional charge is made of £4 per car. The Annual Members badge, which includes eleven reciprocal meetings, was priced at £130 in 2000. If you are thinking of organising a party to go to Fontwell races then you can arrange discounted admission prices by booking in advance.

There are 15 private boxes at the course, all recently redecorated, and each can cater for up to 20 guests. There are also larger rooms for up to 100 people and these have also been refurbished; including a new balcony overlooking the paddock.

*Artist: **Claire Eva Burton** BEECH ROAD Courtesy of: **Rosenstiel's***

The racecourse management are happy to assist in organising parties and invite you to drop by anytime to see the facilities.

There is a club restaurant at Fontwell, recently refurbished and extended, and bookings can be made through the racecourse office. There is a new information point and shop in addition to a refurbished annual members, owners and trainers bar and the Kerman Stand provides bars, Tote credit and additional boxes for entertaining. Snack bars can also be found throughout the enclosures with a new fast food outlet in Tattersalls and there is an off-course betting area in the Paddock although no banks. There are lavatories for disabled people positioned in the Silver Ring Enclosure and Tattersalls. If you are blessed with a clear crisp windless day's racing at Fontwell and a couple of fancied flutters oblige you will be pretty close to heaven. Even if they don't you can still anticipate a fine day's racing. A visit to this charming Sussex racecourse is always recommended.

Local Favourites

Where better to begin our gastronomic wander around this most pleasant of English counties than in Storrington where we find **Fleur de Sel** (01903) 742331—a very distinguished restaurant. It is extremely popular and bookings for both lunch and dinner are strongly advised. The **Old Forge** (01903) 743402 is also excellent. Also in Storrington, one can find a really beautifully situated hotel, **Abingworth Hall** (01798) 813636. There is a warm welcome here and the food and wine list are also first class. However, perhaps even more delightful is the outstanding **Little Thakeham** (01903) 744416 with its Lutyens exterior and gardens in the style of Gertrude Jekyll. The hotel and the restaurant are both outstanding.

Another extremely peaceful and relaxing hotel and restaurant double is the **Roundabout Hotel** (01798) 813838 in West Chiltington. If one chooses to visit Arundel, perhaps to view the castle or to browse through some of the delightful antique shops, a particularly relaxing establishment is the **Norfolk Arms** (01903) 882101—a coaching inn for over 200 years and still

welcoming today with the **Butlers Restaurant** (01903) 882222 providing a fine place to dine. There are numerous pubs in Arundel but one to note is the **Swan** (01903) 882314. In addition to bar snacks and a pleasant welcome there is some accommodation here too. A really excellent choice found in Climping is **Bailiffscourt** (01903) 723511—this is the form choice in a truly excellent field. Findon is a pleasing racing village where you will find **Findon Manor** (01903) 872733, a welcoming hotel, and the **Village House** (01903) 873350 where good food can be expected. In the alarmingly named Burpham, The **George and Dragon** (01903) 883131 offers fine fayre to keep the wind up. The aptly named **Black Horse** pub (01243) 551213 in Binstead is ideal to whet the racing appetite. The **Royal Oak** at Walberton (01243) 552865 also offers good food and the **Holly Tree** (01243) 554023 is a pub not to overlook. The **Hilton Avisford Park** (01243) 551215 provides a very comfortable bed for a night or two. In Barnham the **Barnham Hotel** (01243) 552272 is worth a visit.

Not everyone will be able to slumber in Sussex, but any visit should certainly be combined with one of the many splendid pubs that adorn the county. The **Fox** at Charlton is a convenient diversion and the **White Hart** at South Harting is especially handy for Goodwood and Fontwell visitors. Farther afield, the **Black Horse** (01798) 342424 in Byworth is also worth a visit—a comprehensive range of bar snacks and a really cosy restaurant, ideal for a quiet evening after racing. In Petworth, there are a number of places to note. The **Welldiggers** also welcomes; good food and friendly atmosphere combine extremely well. **Soanes** (01798) 343659 is a charming restaurant at which to have a spot of dinner and **Horse Guards Inn** (01798) 342332 is a pub which serves fine meals. The **White Horse Inn** at Sutton (01798) 869221 is also pleasant. In Pulborough, the **Chequers Hotel** (01798) 872486 is a small Queen Anne building where lunch and dinner are both well priced. More expensive, but quite superb, is nearby **Amberley Castle** (01798) 831992 near Arundel. Its outer walls predate racing itself—a fine atmosphere in which to consider the heritage of this sport.

Artist: **Roy Miller IN FLIGHT** *Courtesy of:* **The Artist**

A beautiful 'medieval' manor, Bailiffscourt, standing amid thirty two acres of tranquil Sussex farmland and just two hundred yards from a rare stretch of unspoilt coastline, is situated three miles south of the historic town of Arundel and only a twenty minute drive from Chichester, home of the famous Festival Theatre.

Portsmouth, Southampton and Eastbourne are all within easy driving distance and London is approximately an hour and a half away by car.

This rambling masterpiece and spectacular country house hotel affords individually priced and extravagantly furnished bedrooms—some featuring four poster beds and log fires—each with bathroom en suite, colour television, direct dial telephone and hairdryer.

The award-winning Tapestry restaurant offers fine cuisine and an excellent selection of wines. In the summer, lighter meals may be taken in the walled garden or rose-clad courtyard.

The relaxed and romantic atmosphere does not mean, however, that the corporate entertainer is neglected. Indeed, companies are welcome to this extra special setting for board meetings and conferences—welcome to take over the whole hotel for two or three days as their own country house!

Set in verdant parkland, Bailiffscourt boasts a swimming pool, tennis courts, croquet lawn, golf practice area and helicopter landing pad. You can hack along the beach or ride downland at Arundel, two miles away. Littlehampton provides first class golf courses and windsurfing. Many famous racing 'names' stay here.

Whether you're in pursuit of business or pleasure, Bailiffscourt awaits you.

Bailiffscourt
Climping
West Sussex BN17 5RW
Tel: (01903) 723511 Fax: (01903) 723107
e mail: bailiffscourt@hshotels.co.uk
website: www.hshotels.co.uk

Although some of the storms at the Year 2000 Goodwood were more reminiscent of a thunderous day at Hexham it still managed to dazzle intermittently with some first class racing and entertainment with Giants Causeway looking a particularly good horse when winning the Sussex Stakes. Crimplene also looked to be an exceptional filly and both horses have track records to warm the cockles and muscles of any owner's heart. Ironically, their exploits, stunning as they were, were almost forgotten as much of the talk was focused on Montjeu and Dubai Millennium. As history relates the proposed dual between the two horses never took place, highlighting both the fickle nature of the sport as well as the need for real superstars to catch the imagination of the public and sporting press alike. In its time-honoured way the fixture list will inform us who were the greats of the Millennium year - I suspect it might be quite a fine one - and a number of these were seen at Goodwood.

The management team at Goodwood is headed by **Rod Fabricius,** who acts as **Clerk** and **General Manager, Seamus Buckley** who is **Assistant Clerk, Emma Everest, Hospitality Sales Manager,** and **John Thompson** who is Goodwood's **Racecourse Manager.** They can be contacted at **Goodwood Racecourse, Goodwood House, Chichester, West Sussex PO18 0PS Tel (01243) 755022 Fax (01243) 755025. Web site: www.glorious goodwood.co.uk.**

The racecourse is a 66 mile journey from London. Chichester, the nearest large town, is some five miles away. Chichester railway station is on the Victoria line and there is an efficient bus service from the station to the course on racedays. If you do travel by car from London the journey time is likely to be

an hour and a half. The A29 or the A3 doubled up with the A27 should produce a satisfactory result. The A27, which bypasses Chichester, also serves racegoers from the east and west and has recently been improved. Goodwood has ample parking and this is provided free or at £2 (£5 for the Festival), depending on how far you are prepared to walk. Light aircraft can land at Goodwood Airfield, two miles from the course. Helicopters or taxis can be taken to the course from there. Goodwood racecourse provides a prospectus with some of the best information available so do telephone in advance so you can make your own individual arrangements.

Major races to note are the William Hill Mile at the Glorious Goodwood meeting, the Goodwood Cup, the Vodafone Stewards Cup, the Richmond Stakes and the jewel of the year, the outstanding Sussex Stakes.

The annual membership subscription at Goodwood is £175, admitting the member to the Richmond Enclosure on all Goodwood racedays in the year. The cost however, does not include parking which is extra. Free owners and trainers valet parking is available from the west entrance. Thirty-four reciprocal events are arranged at twenty-one other venues. At the July meeting, daily badges are not on sale to the general public but Members may purchase them at £42 each after 1 June. Entry to the Gordon Enclosure for this meeting costs £18 before the 1st of June and £21 thereafter, while entry to the Public Enclosure costs £6 before June 1st and £7 after. At all other meetings, day badges for the Members are obtainable at £18, with £11 being the price for the Gordon Enclosure and £5 for the Public Enclosure. Members are advised to make reservations for seats for the July meeting. Junior Membership (5-25) can

Artist: **Peter Smith** *JOCKEYS UP, PLEASE Courtesy of:* **Frost & Reed**

be purchased for £80. Parties of 20 or more are entitled to discounts in all enclosures except the Richmond Enclosure.

Tailored packages are available for all your entertainment requirements. Please contact Emma Everest for further details. There are many facilities at Goodwood to suit all tastes and budgets. Enquiries with regard to the catering should be made to Payne & Gunter (01243) 775350. They do a fine job of providing all the ingredients for a good day's racing. The ever-expanding tented village and the superb racing makes for massive crowds at the July fixture, so be warned. Try to arrive at the racecourse in plenty of time, Goodwood always provides a number of worthwhile additional attractions before racing commences.

The third Duke of Richmond organised the first Goodwood race meeting in 1801. It was a friendly competition between himself and other army officers. The event was such a success that in the following year the public was admitted. Thereafter the fame of the location and quality of racing has been so widely acclaimed that racing here has gone from strength to unbridled strength. But Goodwood is also an occasion in the sporting calendar to savour and has been referred to as 'a garden party with racing tacked on'.

Top racing it is too! In addition to this, Goodwood organises various events during the summer meetings which include barbecues, jazz and steel bands, over 65s days and family days—all of which are highly recommended. Other especially laudable points about the course are the excellent children's playground, the lifts and stands for the disabled and numerous betting facilities. There is a Gordon Enclosure crèche facility at Sunday/July/August meetings.

Goodwood has a tremendous setting on the South Downs and certainly the major rebuilding programmes of recent years have improved the course. More is planned and extensive work will be carried out on a new paddock area to include a re-modelled parade ring, underground weighing room and also a new Member's main entrance. A new pavilion concept is also planned along with the creation of a new seafood restaurant. Goodwood is constantly being improved and when coupled with the sport available it makes one of the most glorious amphitheatres in racing.

Goodwood looks forward to celebrating its 200th anniversary in 2002 and has great plans to bring in the double century in fine style. With the makeover of the paddock area completed for the 2001 season and probable further tie-ins between horse racing and the motor racing of the increasingly popular Festival of Speed, Goodwood looks like a firm favourite for the diary in 2001.

Artist: **Constance Halford Thompson** **IMPENDING ENQUIRY** *Courtesy of:* **Osborne Studio Gallery**

Marriott Goodwood Park Hotel & Country Club

Situated within the grounds of historical Goodwood House, ancestral home to the Dukes of Richmond, the Marriott Goodwood Park Hotel & Country Club is surrounded by 12,000 acres of Goodwood Park Estate.

Sympathetically developed, the first class accommodation that distinguishes Marriott hotels provides 94 bedrooms including an elegant four poster and executive rooms.

The award-winning Richmond Room restaurant serves the best of modern English cuisine, and the Goodwood Sports Café Bar is available for more informal meals. The conference facilities can entertain from 10 to 150 delegates and for a uniquely sumptuous setting for a banquet or reception, the State Rooms of Goodwood House itself can be booked for functions linked to your conference.

The leisure facilities offered by the hotel include an indoor, ozone treated swimming pool, spa bath, sauna, steam room, aerobic studio, tennis courts and a fully equipped fitness gym. There is also a health and beauty salon and a solarium.

The 18 hole golf course has for its backdrop beautiful Goodwood House. Clubs and buggies are available for hire and with a retail sports shop, practice ground and professional tuition the player's every need, both practical and aesthetic, is catered for.

Goodwood Racing Breaks are another popular feature of the hotel with the famous racecourse only one mile away and are offered on meetings in May, June, August, and September. The elegant Festival meeting is held each July.

Guests wishing a more peaceful holiday will enjoy exploring the rolling Sussex Downs and a visit to Chichester is not to be missed with its harbour, cathedral and theatre. Arundel Castle is well worth a visit as is the town of Brighton.

Whether you are wanting to improve your golf handicap, visit the races, explore the sights of the South of England or simply unwind from the stress of everyday life, the thoughtful and helpful staff at Marriott Goodwood Park Hotel are waiting to welcome you.

Marriott Goodwood Park Hotel & Country Club
Goodwood
Chichester
West Sussex PO18 0QB
Tel: (01243) 775537
Fax: (01243) 520120
web site: www.marriott.com/marriott/pmegs

There are all manner of good reasons for visiting Goodwood, not least because it is surrounded by some first rate hotels, but make sure you book early as the crowds are enormous. The **Marriott Goodwood Park Hotel** (01243) 775537 is a charming hotel with some delightful rooms, a pleasant restaurant and a friendly welcome that make for a thoroughly worthwhile place to stay. Lovers of golf should make a point of booking here. A visit to nearby Goodwood House should also be fitted in if at all possible. The **Royal Norfolk Hotel** (01243) 826222 in Bognor Regis offers special Goodwood weekly rates. Bognor was incidentally given the addition of Regis after George V recuperated there in 1929. If it was good enough for him, it's good enough for me. The part 16th century **Inglenook** (01243) 262495 is also a worthy consideration in this tricky field.

Goodwood is situated between Midhurst and Chichester. Both towns have a lot to offer. Near Midhurst in Bepton, the **Park House Hotel** (01730) 812880 is a great favourite—thoroughly relaxing and very welcoming. The **Spread Eagle** (01730) 816911 is a first class 18th century inn and certainly one of the best of its type. The accommodation is most comfortable and both lunch and dinner in the restaurant are good. There is a number of excellent pubs in and near to Midhurst and the civilized **Angel** (01730) 812421 offers good value bedrooms and an excellent restaurant, the Cowdray Room. Midhurst really is ideal for lovers of the post-race pub crawl. Restaurants are also in

abundance—**Maxines** (01730) 816271 is well thought of. West of Midhurst is Pulborough, home of the **Chequers Hotel** (01798) 872486, an ideal base for some energetic exploration of the countryside, as is the majestic **Amberley Castle** (01798) 831992 which simply oozes history and class. A genuine favourite in any field.

Travelling south on the A286 and entering Chichester, one is confronted with a number of delights including **Comme Ça** (01243) 788724, a confident nap in any field. Meanwhile, lovers of traditional English food should sample the **Old Cottage Inn** (01243) 773294 in Tangmere. The **Bedford Hotel** (01243) 778000 is a satisfactory place to spend the night. The streets of Chichester are often extremely busy. There are some excellent shops—ideal if you don't wish to attend every day of Glorious Goodwood. At night, the streets have an excellent atmosphere and the cathedral and the Festival Theatre (01243) 781312 are worth a visit. Further west one arrives in Bosham, a delightful village which houses the **Millstream Hotel** (01243) 573234, an attractive small hotel which is a convenient place to stay, especially if you like the coast. In Chilgrove, the **White Horse Inn** (01243) 359219 is excellent—a superb pub and also a fine restaurant not to be missed, the wine list here is breathtaking. In case you take the wrong road out of Chichester and find yourself heading east, do not despair, but head instead for Rustington, where the **Kenmore Guest House** (01903) 784634 will ease the most furrowed brow. Finally, in

Artist: **Terence Gilbert THE FINISH** _Courtesy of:_ **The Artist**

Langrish, near Petersfield, **Langrish House** (01730) 266941 is a little farther afield but is particularly enjoyable.

If, by chance, you anticipate owning or backing a winner, we recommend that you book a table in **Auberge de France** (01428) 651251 in the very pleasant **Lythe Hill Hotel** in Haslemere, a decent French restaurant. Two pleasant pubs can be located by people trekking northwards. In Lickfold, the **Lickfold Inn** (01798) 861285 is a fine Tudor establishment which offers some good value bar snacks and some accommodation. The **Coach and Horses** at Compton (02392) 631228 is a friendly local to try as is the **Anglesey Arms** (01243)773474, a particularly convenient local favourite. Meanwhile the **Three Horseshoes** (01730) 825746 lies just off the B2141 between Chichester and Petersfield and is recommended. The **Elsted Inn** (01730) 813662, Elsted Marsh, also offers some excellent pub grub. For people seeking more liquid refreshment, visit the Chilsdown vineyard. Near Chichester, the Fishbourne Roman Palace is worth a peep while the Weald and Downland Open Air Museum is also something to note. We are grateful to the Goodwood team for suggesting the following places to try: the **Fox Goes Free** (01243) 811461 in Charlton,

the **Hurdlemakers** and the **Tiger** (01323) 423209 in East Dean, and the **Trundle Inn** and the **Selsey Arms** in West Dean. These are recommendations from the horse's mouth so to speak and should definitely be carefully considered when assessing the form. The **Hilton Avisford Park** (01243) 551215, comes with a strong recommendation from the racecourse executive. A great *Travelling the Turf* favourite is **South Lodge Hotel**, Lower Beeding (01403) 891711—a first class hotel and restaurant double and with excellent golf too.

If you have any energy left and the summer sun still shines, one place you should not miss near Plumpton is **Glyndebourne** (01273) 812321—the location of the Glyndebourne Festival (May to mid-August). If you can tie in racing with an evening's opera the contrast will be enormous, but the appeal no less great. **Horsted Place,** Uckfield (01825) 750581 provides a luxurious base, depending, of course, on the state of the following day's betting fund! Golfers will find this hotel particularly appealing. The thought of a day or more at Goodwood fills the heart with joy. A night or two at Horsted Place is icing on a tremendous cake.

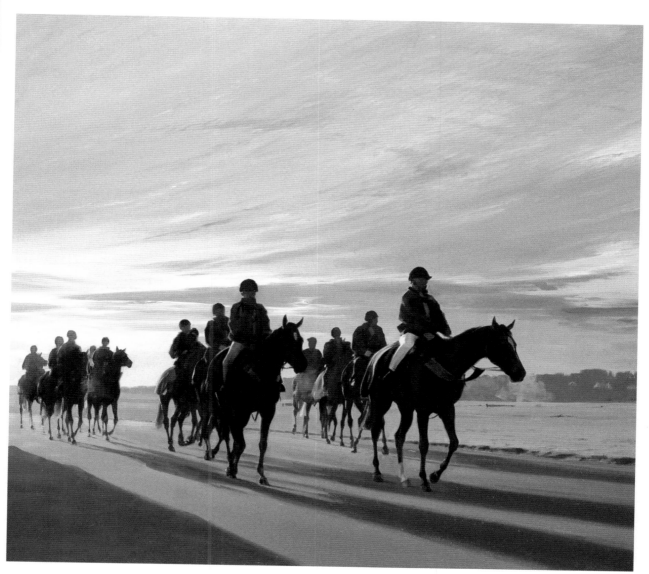

Artist: **Peter Smith MORNING SILHOUETTE** *Courtesy of:* **Frost & Reed**

The people in charge at Hamilton are **Clerk of the Course Hazel Peplinski** and **Chief Executive Morag Gray,** who can both be contacted at **Hamilton Park Racecourse, Bothwell Road, Hamilton, Lanarkshire ML3 0DY. Tel (01698) 283806. Fax: (01698) 286621. Web site: www.hamilton-park.co.uk.**

The course is 10 miles south of Glasgow, in Hamilton, and the track is accessible from Glasgow via the M74, junction 5 or from Edinburgh via the M8, junction 6 and the A723, which runs near the course from east to west. The A776 from East Kilbride may prove an alternative route for eastbound travellers. For punters from the south, the A74 and the M74, junction 5 is an advisable route from Carlisle. Glasgow Central is the city's principal station and trains from London can be caught at Euston. There is a connecting line to Hamilton West which is the course's local station. Another public transport possibility is the free bus service from Motherwell and Hamilton bus and train stations to the course for 2 hours before and after racing, running every 15 minutes. People with light aircraft and helicopters can't land at the course itself but a shuttle service between Heathrow and Glasgow as well as other major cities, could be of some use if you need to make a big plunge and wish to avoid paying tax!

In 2001 there will be 17 days of flat racing at Hamilton Park with plenty of action between March and September, including a Family Night, Ladies Night and Grand National Day. Evening meetings are well worth considering here—ideal for unwinding after a hard day's work in Glasgow. The most popular meeting remains the Saints & Sinners Charity Meeting held in June. I imagine a number of both can be found at such events.

The Annual Membership rates are as follows: a single badge will cost £125 and a double badge (lady and gent) will cost £200 which includes access to the Winning Post Bar and 9 reciprocal days at other racecourses. A more fleeting relationship with Hamilton will cost £12 for a Members badge at a standard race meeting and £15 on a feature day or £8 for the Public Enclosure with a reduced rate if you are a student or a pensioner. The reduced rate for 2000 was £5. Family tickets and discounts on advance bookings are also available.

There are various points that should be noted when considering your trip to Hamilton Park. If you are planning a day out for more than ten people you will receive a discount and this applies to all enclosures. Full details can be obtained from the Secretary but there are private boxes of various sizes and a sponsors' room. Marquees are also available. The caterers at Hamilton are Peppermill Catering and they can be contacted on (01698) 429 310. There are various restaurants—Club dining room, snack bars and a string of drinks bars but, as one might expect, these are fairly busy areas. The Winning Post Bar is an exclusive facility for owners, trainers and Annual Members with a full bar and seafood menu.

The course is compact and the atmosphere is excellent. Those with children under 16 will be pleased to hear about their free admission and the playground. There are some facilities for disabled racegoers which include a snack bar but be warned, there are no banking facilities, although Tote cash and credit facilities are available. So if you intend to make use of the on-course betting shops bring your stake money with you.

There have been some major developments at Hamilton Park in recent years which include the extension of the Grandstand

Artist: **Peter Smith** **WASHING DOWN, HAMILTON PARK** *Courtesy of:* **Frost & Reed**

to accommodate additional boxes. Local people should note that the facilities can be used for conferences and receptions throughout the year. Hamilton Park may not be one of Britain's foremost racecourses but with a situation near to Glasgow the racecourse is extremely popular and to be a part of the throng when your fancy is coming through the field is a happy feeling indeed. Furthermore, it is fair to report that recent years have seen some excellent initiatives developed—may this continue in 2001 and for many years thereafter.

Local Favourites

Within one mile of the course, the **Cricklewood Hotel** (01698) 853 172 is a favourite for eating, drinking and a bed for the night. For the businessman, the **Glasgow Marriott** 0141 226 5577 in Argyle Street offers pleasant cocktail bars and a wealth of leisure facilities. The **Hilton Glasgow** 0141 204 5555 is another high-rise hotel but is well run and comfortable with an excellent restaurant, while the **Hilton Glasgow Grosvenor** 0141 339 8811 is a most impressive hotel with a delightful situation opposite the Botanical Gardens. The **Terrace Restaurant** is well worth visiting. Glasgow offers a variety of attractions and an exquisite Victorian hotel in which to stay is **One Devonshire Gardens** 0141 339 2001, home of a renowned restaurant. Finally, the **Malmasion** 0141 572 1000 is delightfully luxurious and will appeal to those who enjoy contemporary design.

Glasgow has become a veritable Mecca for lovers of fine cuisine with **Rogano** 0141 248 4055 one of its most celebrated. The **Buttery** 0141 221 8188 in Argyle Street, is convenient for the Holiday Inn and an excellent spot for lunch or dinner. Upstairs is expensive and correspondingly elegant while downstairs has a more relaxed air. **D'Arcy's** 0141 226 4309 is also good fun as is the outstanding **Puppet Theatre** 0141 339 8444. A Cantonese restaurant with an extensive menu can be found in Sauchiehall Street—it's called **Loon Fung** 0141 332 1240. **Chimms** (Chinese) and the **Grapevine** on Bothwell Road are also well thought of. **Amber Regent** 0141 331 1655 also provides Chinese cuisine of an award-winning standard. Just around the corner, the **Ubiquitous Chip** 0141 334 5007 is also fancied in

a quite competitive field.

To the west of Glasgow stands **Gleddoch House** (01475) 540711, a distinguished hotel and restaurant. Built on the banks of the Clyde this impressive hotel is particularly charming and golfers will be delighted to hear that there is a nearby course. Golf courses, like pubs, are never far away in Glasgow and its surrounds. Those who like pubs and bars should try **Babbity Bowster** 0141 552 5055.

Returning south of the Clyde, East Kilbride. Two superbly Scottish names to note are the **Hilton East Kilbride** (01355) 236300 and secondly, the **Bruce** (013552) 229771. Both are modern, friendly and relatively convenient for the racecourse. The **Westpoint Hotel** (013552) 36300 is ideal for those who may be on business or who prefer hotels with extensive leisure facilities—the restaurant here is also good. Within a mile of the racecourse is the **Silvertrees Hotel** (01698) 852311. It is family run and well regarded by the local racing fraternity. Finally, seek out **Chapeltoun House** (01560) 482696, one for the notebook in 2001.

Haydock Park is the best all-round racecourse in the north of England, just one of the reasons why it was named Travelling the Turf's *Racecourse of the Year* in both 1998 and 2000. **Lisa Rowe** acts as **Clerk of the Course** and **Racing Manager,** while **Richard Thomas** is **Managing Director** and **Stephen Mansfield** fills the role of **Operations Manager** with **Dean Martin** as the **Sales Manager.** They can be contacted at **Haydock Park Racecourse, Newton-le-Willows, Merseyside WA12 0HQ. Tel (01942) 725963 Fax (01942) 270879.** For further information on racing at Haydock call Talking Pages **0800 600 900** or visit their **web site: www.haydock-park.com.**

Access to the course is off the A49 close to Ashton. The course is superbly served by motorways and the M6 and the M62 converge close by. The new Thelwell viaduct on the M6 has already improved traffic conditions. An additional entrance has also been opened to provide easier access to the Owners and Trainers car park from the A580 end of the racecourse. In order to ensure entry through the western gate, M6 traffic from the north can leave at junction 24 and turn left, then right at the lights—the racecourse is a mile further, on the left. To arrive by train catch the Euston train to Warrington Bank Quay or take the local link to Newton-le-Willows, or catch the 320 bus from Liverpool which will deposit you at the gates. More speedy access can be obtained by using the landing strip or helipad.

The fixture list for 2001 at Haydock should follow that of 2000, which hosted 30 fixtures, with three Friday evening meetings during the summer, a new Saturday evening meeting in August and one Sunday fixture in July. Highlight of the flat season here is always the Old Newton Cup meeting held in early July. For admission to the County Enclosure in 2001 you will pay £17 (£20 on Saturdays and bank holidays). For Tattersalls the prices will be £10 and £12 with £5 and £6 for the Newton Enclosure. On weekends the prices are £12 and £6 respectively. Haydock's Park Suite is a panoramic dining facility that will cost you £56 and a badge must be purchased in advance to confirm your booking. You will however receive

a free racecard. Pensioners are admitted to Tattersalls and the Newton Enclosure at half price, while accompanied children under 16 and those confined to wheelchairs are free. An Annual Badge for the County Stand offers a definite saving. In 2000 a single badge for the year was priced at £190 and £65 for Juniors (under 21). This included a special car pass and twelve reciprocal days racing at twelve different courses. The racecourse also offers discounts in Tattersalls and the Newton Enclosure for parties of 25 or more.

Private facilities at Haydock Park are excellent—they include 32 boxes and six luncheon rooms. The boxes are sited on three floors of the Tommy Whittle Stand, and can accommodate up to 20 people. All boxes are let on a long term basis but a daily waiting list is maintained as several are made available for sub-let every raceday. There is also the Premier Suite from whose glass front you can observe the finishing post, opposite. For larger parties the luncheon rooms can be linked together. The Park Suite can seat 450 people but can be sectioned off to accommodate smaller parties. CCTV and Tote facilities are also

*Artist: **Claire Eva Burton** PHOTO FINISH Courtesy of: **The Artist***

provided. If you wish to use this restaurant, bookings for a table start three months prior to each raceday. A more fun way of catering for a larger party may be to organise a marquee. The Lancaster restaurant in the County Enclosure offers à la carte and tables can be booked in advance by telephoning the sales office.

Improvements continue to be made at this excellent course, with the building of the Centenary Stand which was opened in May 1999 and other renovations costing £3 million. The project provides additional capacity in the County Stand where a new restaurant, Harry's Bistro, has opened in the Premier Suite, extended catering facilities and improved parking. With attendance levels already running at a five-year high at Haydock, this will ensure even more racing fans will be able to enjoy its facilities in comfort in 2001.

Local Favourites

In Lower Peover, the **Bells of Peover** (01565) 722269 has a delightful setting and as well as super bar food the restaurant is recommended. North of the Bells, in Plumley, the **Smoker** (01565) 722338 which has an adjoining restaurant as well as serving excellent bar food can be recommended. The **Dog Inn** (01625) 861421 in Over Peover offers good food and some accommodation. **Ye Olde Parkgate Inn** (01625) 861455 is also good. In Mobberley, the **Bird In Hand** (01565) 873149 is one of the growing band of good food pubs. Other pubs in the area include the extremely welcoming **Fiddle i'th' Bag** at Burtonwood. The **Pickering Arms** at Thelwell is an attractive and friendly village local while in Risley, the **Noggin** is another popular food pub. However, perhaps the most convenient pub

for the racecourse is the **Bay Horse** or even the relaxing **County Inn**. An enticing alternative is the **Bulls Head** (01942) 671621 in Newton-le-Willows where the food, beer and atmosphere are good and, if you wish to make a really early start, bedrooms can be organised. Another likely place for the early bird is the **Posthouse Haydock** at Newton-le-Willows (0870) 4009039 for it stands in parkland fringing the Haydock Park racecourse. For those expectant racegoers travelling from Liverpool on the A580, a **Travelodge** provides a convenient stopover. There is also the **Thistle Haydock** (01942) 272000 which lies near to the course. The **Park Royal International** Hotel (01925) 730706 at Stretton does special racing breaks including transport to the racecourse. Another first class post race retreat is the **Park Hall Hotel** (01257) 452090, well placed and welcoming.

Simply Heathcotes 0161 835 3536 is a good restaurant as is **Brasserie St Pierre** 0161 228 0231 and the **Royal Orchid** 0161 236 5183. Another polished hotel is the **Portland Thistle** Hotel 0161 228 3400, an elegant establishment which also boasts an extremely good leisure centre. The **Le Meridien Victoria and Albert** 0161 832 1188 in a converted 19th century warehouse is first class with a television themed interior. The **Holiday Inn** 0161 236 3333 is also good and the **Crowne Plaza Midland** 0161 23603333 provides top class comfort. Manchester boasts an outstanding array of cosmopolitan cooking. **Yang Sing** 0161 236 2200 in Princess Street is an excellent Chinese restaurant. **Est Est Est** 0161 8339400 at 5 Ridgefield, is also a welcome Italian addition to the field. **Blinkers** 0161 228 2503 is an appropriately named French restaurant, while near the airport **Moss Nook** 0161 437 4778 is the most established restaurant in the area. Some rooms here as well for those wishing to stay.

*Artist: **Henry Kobler** CROWDED START Courtesy of: **Rosentiel's***

Britain, like France has a multitude of charming rustic race-courses and with so much of England being taken up by sprawling urbanisation it is a real pleasure to escape to the country. The shire of Hereford contains many such green fields and within its acres a welcoming picturesque racecourse, Hereford. The team in charge at Hereford are **Clerk of the Course** and **Secretary, John Williams** and **Manager** of the course, **Jason Loosemore**. They can be contacted at **The Racecourse, Roman Road, Hereford HR4 9QU** or **Shepherds Meadow, Lane Head, Eaton Bishop, Hereford HR2 9UA. Tel: (01981) 250436** or **Fax: (01981) 250192. Web site: www.hereford-racecourse.co.uk.**

Hereford racecourse is clearly signposted and there are good roads on the northern outskirts of the city. Indeed, the whole area is bordered by several major roads from the Midlands, South Wales and the south west. From the north, the racecourse can be reached via the A49 from Leominster and the A4110. The main southern approach roads are the A49 and the A495. The A438 through Hereford itself passes close to the racecourse and there's also an approach on the A4103 from Worcester. London is approximately 120 miles away and if you are travelling to Hereford by train then Paddington station is the one from which to make your departure. The station is a mile from the course and a taxi will be required from there unless you wish to take a short stroll. Should you be fairly busy and/or well off then subject to prior arrangement helicopters are welcome. If you decide to take the motor, two large free car parks await you, one of which is a picnic style car park with a complete view of all the racing. Please note however, that the entrance for the Course Enclosure is off the A49, whilst the Tattersalls entrance can be found off the A4103.

The racecourse held 17 National Hunt meetings in 2000. The bank holiday fixture in April is the most popular and there is also a splendid alternative to the Grand National. As the Clerk of the Course points out, most of the racing here is bread and butter stuff but there are often large fields and racing is competitive. The course also has a Boxing Day feature in addition to the existing three bank holiday meetings. Admission to the Members Enclosure is £13 and £10 for Tattersalls and the Course costs £5. There is no Annual Membership here. Discounts are available for Tattersalls for larger groups and you should contact the racecourse for further details.

Boxes are available to hire on a daily basis and differ in size catering for up to 40 guests. There is a larger room which will take up to 150 guests or marquees can be erected if you wish for an even bigger party. There is also a restaurant in the Course Enclosure where there is no need to book. Various packages are on offer here from the caterers, Hughes of Welshpool (01432) 353135. The usual snack bars are dotted around the course for those who only need a quick bite. If you wish to take your children racing and they are under 16 they are admitted free. Disabled racegoers will be pleased to note that access is easy from Tattersalls and there is also a special viewing area. There is a betting shop in Tattersalls as well as a new Owners and Trainers bar.

Artist: **Jay Kirkman** **LEADING UP** *Courtesy of:* **Park Walk Gallery**

Hereford is one of those delightful out of the way county towns where the pace of life is slightly slower than average. The horses may also be of lesser speed than those seen at Ascot or Cheltenham but racing is still competitive here and should you wish for a peaceful day out, there are few finer courses at which to spend the day. There are few places in England which are truly away from it all. Hereford is one of those places—try to visit it in 2001.

Local Favourites

For those who wish to really soak up the racecourse atmosphere, a five minute walk from the aforementioned track brings one to the doorstep of the **Starting Gate Inn** (01432) 274853 which is attached to the extremely convenient **Travel Inn** (01432) 274853. The **Green Dragon** (01432) 272506 and the **Three Counties Hotel** (01432) 299955, dating from 1850, are also safe bets (always a dangerous claim to make). Pubs to try amidst the Malvern Hills include the splendid and highly recommended **Bunch of Carrots** (01432) 870237 at Hampton Bishop, a leading riverside pub about three miles from the course. The **Butchers Arms** (01432) 860281 at Woolhope, a half-timbered building which offers good bar food, a restaurant and some pleasing accommodation. Nearby, in Fownhope, the **Green Man** (01432) 860243 is a popular local fancy with excellent food and good pub accommodation. The **Ancient Camp Inn** (01981) 250449 in Ruckhall is a first rate stayer as is the **Olde Salutation** (01544) 318443 in Weobley. To the north through Leominster lies Kimbolton where you'll find the **Lower Bache Guest House** (01568) 750304 offering charming accommodation, first class food and wonderful views. In Ledbury the timbered **Feathers** (01531) 635266 is appealing. The **Hope End** (01531) 633616, at Hope End, is also peaceful with a fine restaurant. Another Ledbury thought is **Ye Olde Talbot** (01531) 632963 which has a beautiful exterior as well as a friendly interior. Northwest of Ledbury in Bishops Frome, you come across the **Green Dragon** (01885) 490607 whose good beer,

filling bar food and traditional atmosphere make for a perfect post-race rendezvous.

The county of Herefordshire, characterised by brown and white faced cows, is stunning, with the countryside approaching the Welsh border of particular note. In this direction, the **Lord Nelson** (01981) 22208 at Bishopstone has a good restaurant and bar food. In Eardisland, the **White Swan** is a good stop-off point for people travelling north, while at Whitney-on-Wye, the **Rhydspence** (01497) 831262 offers superb bar meals and some accommodation—a must for a long weekend if booked well in advance. Venturing back through England, one finds the **Broad Oak**, Eastway, an excellent place for a post-race supper. Where else? At Sellack, try the **Lough Pool** (no rooms here though). Our trip comes full circle at delightful Ross-on-Wye where some outstanding hotels can be found. The **Chase** (01989) 763161 is a charmingly personal Victorian hotel and **Pengethley Manor** (01989) 730211 a little outside the town, is also a marvellous hotel with a super restaurant. Finally, **Pheasants** (01989) 565751 is a restaurant with rooms to note. It provides another excuse for visiting this gorgeous area.

*Artist: **Malcolm Coward** **SOD IT** Courtesy of: **Sally Mitchell Fine Arts***

Clerk of the Course, Secretary and Manager at this delightful course are all roles which are admirably carried out by **Charles Enderby,** who can be contacted at **The Racecourse Office, The Riding, Hexham, Northumberland. Tel (01434) 606881. Fax (01434) 605814** and **Mrs Linda Clements** who handles all **Sponsorship** and would be delighted to show prospective clients around Tel **(01434) 609643.** Web site: **www.hexham-racecourse.co.uk.**

Hexham lies 20 miles from Newcastle, about 35 miles from Carlisle and some 300 miles from the bustle of Trafalgar Square. The course itself is a mile south of the market town of Hexham, sandwiched between the B6305 and the B6306. The road from Newcastle to Carlisle, the A69, is convenient for joining either of these two minor roads. The Newcastle western bypass should speed up your journey considerably if you are using the A1. If you are northbound on the A1 and have a little extra time in which to make your journey, leave the A1 at its junction with the A68 and follow the road through the Durham hills—stunning. The M6 and the A69 are the most direct routes for those travelling from Carlisle and the west of the country, although the A686 through the Gilderdale Forest is an appealing alternative. There are bus and train stations in Hexham. Newcastle is on the main Kings Cross—Edinburgh route and the journey time is swift. A connecting train can be caught from Newcastle to Hexham. There is a free bus from the train and bus stations to the racecourse on racedays. The majority of racegoers however, seem to drive to the course where there are acres of free parking and Members have a reserved area. There is also plenty of room in this charming, peaceful setting to land your noisy helicopter but please notify the course prior to your arrival.

To take advantage of the better weather, Hexham now stages a couple of summer jumping fixtures in June as part of its 14 fixture annual programme. The biggest day of the year is a local derby for point to pointers in the form of the Heart of All England Maiden Hunter Chase. In 2001 admission charges will be £12 for Members and £8 for Tattersalls. OAPs are allowed in to Tatts for only £6 and children 16 and under are free. If you wish to enroll as an Annual Member in the Hexham Race Club, the price will be £75 for a single and £110 for a double badge. This is excellent value as it includes car parking close to the stands at Hexham, as well as 17 reciprocal meetings at nearby Carlisle, Newcastle, and Kelso as well as Perth, Catterick, Bangor, Ripon, Hamilton, Ayr and Haydock. For people wishing to organise parties, there is a 20 per cent reduction for groups of 15 or more in both enclosures and a free bottle of whisky for the organisers of parties over 50.

The racecourse has just completed a major expansion programme which has seen the completion of the new Ramshaw Stand, which provides excellent facilities in the Members when the weather is less than kind. There is a new Members' Bar on the ground floor and you can enjoy the carvery and a drink in the Curlew Room on the first floor. The stand has a lift and therefore can accommodate the needs of disabled people. There are also three new private boxes on the top floor which can cater for up to 30 sponsor's or private guests. Larger parties can be accommodated by using a large adjoining room, or for parties of up to 180 people, the Henderson Room in the connecting stand may be used. The new stand has extensive Tote facilities and many television monitors. Recent improvements have also been carried out to provide a new Tote betting shop with a bar.

Artist: **Dennis C Kirtley** EXPLORATION *Courtesy of:* **The Artist**

Prices and specifications for catering can be found out by contacting the excellent local caterers—Romfords (01434) 688864. Disabled people can enjoy a superb view of racing from their own special car park which can be entered next to owners/trainers gate at the west end of the stands.

This is one of the most scenic of England's National Hunt racecourses and has one of the finest views of any course in Britain. With its new stand, a watering system to ensure good going and a fixture list that takes advantage of the summer weather, Hexham is a sure bet for a visit in 2001.

Local Favourites

Hexham is a delightful market town and is ideally situated for touring the world heritage site of Hadrian's Wall and the Northumberland National Park with its hundreds of square miles of rugged beauty.

Just north of Hexham at Chollerford the **George Hotel** (01434) 681611 is a famous hostelry that is right on the river North Tyne. Just to the south of Hexham is the **Lord Crewe Arms** (01434) 675251, hidden deep in the valley of the Derwent River in Blanchland, a delightful place whose setting has gone unchanged for centuries. Just a few miles down the river Tyne lies Corbridge, another picturesque village with some interesting shops. Here the **Black Bull** is a popular meeting place and the busy **Corbridge Tandoori** (01434) 633676 is a good bet for an evening meal. Similarly, the Valley (01434) 633434 is another winner. If you wish to stay in the village, the **Angel Inn** (01434) 632119 has pleasant bedrooms and good food, while just outside Corbridge the Ramblers country House (01434) 632424 is a great choice for food.

Back in Hexham itself, the **Beaumont Hotel** (01434) 602331 overlooks the Abbey grounds and is a convenient place to stay for the racegoer. A pub of note is the **Tap & Spile** which has excellent real ales. Almost opposite, on the other side of the road from Hexham racecourse is **Danielle's Bistro** (01434) 601122. A good bet for Italian is **La Famiglia** (01434) 601700 tucked away on St Mary's Chare. For Indian cuisine don't pass by **Diwan-E-Am** (01434) 603191 on Hexham's main street and the bistro at the **Royal Hotel** (01434) 602270 is a restaurant with real merit. Just south of the racecourse the **Dipton Mill** pub is perfectly placed for a drink and lunch before racing. Excellent home-made food and real ale made in its own brewery.

In Wall, a few miles up the North Tyne, the **Hadrian Hotel** (01434) 681232 offers a reasonably priced bed for the night as well as some excellent food. Across the river at Newbrough, **Newbrough Lodge** (01434) 674545 is a fine country house with rooms, while in the village of Great Whittington the **Queens Head** can be highly recommended. Also not far away is **The Rat** at Anick, where you are sure to receive a warm welcome.

A final thought is **Slaley Hall** (01434) 673350 a five star hotel with excellent leisure facilities and a championship golf course. If you prefer a pleasant pub, the recently refurbished **Travellers Rest** on the same road is an ideal place to end your day after a visit to one of Britain's most picturesque racecourses.

*Artist: **Adrian Dent** UNDER ORDERS Courtesy of: **The Artist***

The **Clerk of the Course**, **Hugo Bevan** and the **Manager, Jim Allen**, can be contacted at the **Racecourse Office, Brampton, Huntingdon, Cambridgeshire PE18 8NN. Tel (01480) 453373. Fax (01480) 455275. Website: www.huntingdonracing.co.uk.**

The course lies just outside Brampton, conveniently positioned for travellers from the south (London is 60 miles away) and also from the north as it is a mile to the east of the A1, just off the A14, the A1/M11 road link, which takes you right past the course. The nearest railway station is just outside Huntingdon, two miles away. It's on the main 125 line and a very short journey from Kings Cross. There is no direct bus service from the station to the racecourse but there is a bus to Brampton, one and a quarter miles from Huntingdon, and taxis are easy to find.

They only race over the sticks at Huntingdon, but a full 18 day fixture list is on offer. The most popular tend to be Easter Monday and Boxing Day which always guarantee large crowds. Highlights include the Sidney Banks Memorial Hurdle and the Peterborough Chase, which carries a prize of £35,000 and often produces excellent fields.

Huntingdon Racecourse which is presided over by Hugo the Huntingdon Hound, a 7 foot high mascot, has free parking for cars and coaches, and if a picnic is the order of the day there is no charge for parking adjacent to the rails. The charge for Double Membership was £230 in 2000 whereas a single badge cost £125. Junior Membership (16-24) was available at £60. There was a £15 charge for a Daily Member's badge whilst the entrance charge for Tatts was £10 and the cost for the popular Course Enclosure picnic car park was £5, although these prices

may increase in 2001. The management offer a 20 per cent discount for parties of 15 or more in Tattersalls. The Tattersall's bars have recently been refurbished with some new outlets for snacks added and Gifford's Bar now affords views of the course, parade ring and new winner's enclosure. Various boxes on the course provide for parties of all sizes, with prices ranging from £250 to £650 plus VAT. The course has six viewing boxes, which can accommodate between 12 and 24 people and have an unrivalled view of the track. The latest innovation, at prices starting from £500, are trackside chalets which can seat up to 75 people. The Centenary Rooms can seat up to 60, with an individual Tote point and bar and a large private viewing area. The Waterloo Room can hold up to 100 and is very popular with social clubs and works outings.

It is encouraging to note that the boxes are taken by companies from all over the country and not merely local concerns. Marquees can also be arranged for larger parties of 50 or more. The course management allows children under 16 to be admitted free of charge and on its bank holiday fixtures provides a variety of children's entertainments and crèche facilities.

The racegoer is able to lunch in either the Members or the recently refurbished Tattersalls restaurants. Booking is advisable for the former. There is a new 170 seat members restaurant and now also have two large bar areas. The caterers are Letheby & Christopher and they can be contacted on (01638) 662750. A selection of snacks is available from the bars which are scattered through the Grandstand and in the Course Enclosure. There are public telephones on the course but there is no bank, which makes life frustrating if you spot a likely winner and you've blown all your cash! The course's off-track betting shop

Artist: **Jonathan Trowell** WINTER GAME *Courtesy of:* **The Artist**

is, however, a retreat for the hardened punter who wants to keep in touch with racing around the country and escape the outrageous odds that some bookmakers lay when taking money for races elsewhere. This is a friendly unpretentious racetrack which offers competitive racing. Huntingdon is steadily being improved and is definitely worthy of a visit in 2001.

Local Favourites

Huntingdon has grown dramatically through the 90s and the millennium see no respite in this growth. The town's foremost hotel is the **Old Bridge** (01480) 452681, a popular meeting place where one can enjoy a drink, a quiet lunch, a more comprehensive dinner in the fine restaurant or if you have travelled some distance, a room for the night. You should be well satisfied on all counts. An alternative suggestion is the **George** (01480) 432444, another popular bar with satisfactory accommodation. The Swallow (01954) 230919 is a relatively recent addition but has a good range of facilities. The **Stukeleys Country Hotel** (01480) 456927 is five minutes from the course. The bar is always busy and the bar snack menu and restaurant offer a variety of meals.

In Fen Drayton, the **Three Tuns** (01954) 230242 is another pleasant drinking establishment—very popular with people in the know throughout Cambridgeshire. The **Lion Hotel** (01480) 810313 at Buckden, just off the A1 south of Huntingdon is a 15th century coaching house offering a friendly, personal welcome. The George (01480) 810307 is also well regarded. In Arrington, the **Hardwicke Arms** (01223) 208802 is a super little pub with some excellent rooms. Another nearby hall which doubles as an hotel has a particularly appropriate name, **Slepe Hall** (01480) 463122 (pronounced as in a long snooze!) in St Ives. Needingworth near by has the **Pike and Eel** (01480) 463336—exceptionally cosy, offering comfortable accommodation and views of the River Ouse with boats mooring in front of the inn. The **Old Ferry Boat** at Holywell (01480) 463227 is also good. Fine food and accommodation to consider. A good pub restaurant is sheltered within the **Pheasant** (01832) 710241 at Keyston, and if you prefer a bar snack

then you will not be disappointed, it is excellent. For people who are unable to sample these various offerings and need to journey home up the A1 a pint at the **Bell** (0733) 241066 at Stilton may be an idea—a splendid hotel with an excellent restaurant as well as a comfortable bar. Nearby, The **Loch Fyne Oyster Bar** in Elton (01832) 280298 is an informal seafood restaurant to consider. Those going south should perhaps try one of three pubs near to the A1. Firstly the **Leeds Arms** (01480) 880283 at Eltisley which is a particularly welcoming establishment offering some good food and accommodation. The **Eight Bells** in the pleasant village of Abbotsley is also worth a stop and finally, the **White Horse** (01480) 474453 at Eaton Socon is a part 13th century inn with a pleasant restaurant, good atmosphere and also some bedrooms. Two other first class pubs with restaurants to note are the **Three Horseshoes** in Madingley (01954) 210221 and the excellent **Anchor** at Sutton Gault (01353) 778537—first class food and some bedrooms. The perfect place to celebrate having plundered the bookies. The Haydock (01780) 782223 remains a very convenient stop off point for the A1 and offers a good restaurant, bedrooms and a pleasant bar for barsnacks. Finally a Travelling the Turf favourite: The **Falcon** at Fotheringhay (01832) 226254 is a tremendous food pub.

Artist: **Jo Taylor** **THE STEEPLECHASE** *Courtesy of:* **Osborne Studio Gallery**

Tillmouth Park

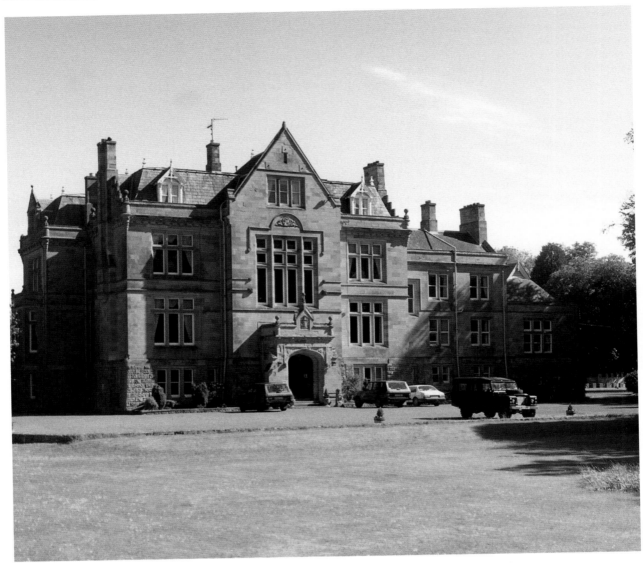

Built in 1882 by the famous architect Charles Barry, using stones from nearby Twizel Castle, Tillmouth typifies a more leisured age. A secluded mansion, set in fifteen acres of mature parkland and gardens, you'll feel yourself relax into its atmosphere of a bygone age.

All of the fourteen en suite bedrooms are generous in size and individually furnished to the highest standard. The spacious public rooms are furnished with the same attention to detail and open log fires create a relaxing ambience.

Tillmouth Park is an ideal centre for country pursuits - fishing, shooting, riding and of course, golf. Spring fishing packages can be arranged on the river Tweed with all the fisherman's requirements catered for. There is also an abundance of excel-

lent shooting in the Borders within 30 minute's drive of the hotel. Berwick-upon-Tweed and the Hirsel at Coldstream are just two excellent golf courses nearby. There are many stately homes to visit such as Floors Castle, Manderston and Paxton. Ruined abbeys, Flodden Field and Holy Island are all within easy reach. Kelso Racecourse is only 15 minutes drive away.

The Library Dining Room offers contemporary British cuisine presented by Head Chef Martin Furlong and his brigade. To match the award winning food there is an extensive wine list and comprehensive range of malt whiskies. The Park Bistro also offers excellent cuisine in an informal setting.

You can be assured of a warm welcome in the Borders when you visit Tillmouth Park.

Tillmouth Park Hotel
Cornhill-On-Tweed
Northumberland
TD12 4UU
Tel: (01890) 882255
Fax: (01890) 882540
web site: www.tillmouthpark.co.uk

This friendly course is exceptionally well administered by **Richard Landale** who is the **Managing Director** and **Secretary** and is the person to contact for further information at the following address: **c/o Sale & Partners, 18-20 Glendale Road, Wooler, Northumberland NE71 6DW. Tel (01668) 281611. Fax (01668) 281113.** The **Clerk of the Course** is **Jonnie Fenwicke-Clennell.** Web site www.kelso-races.co.uk.

Kelso is easy to find and the course lies to the north of the town itself, off the A6089 and the A699. The journey from London is 320 miles. The A1(M) is the best route to take and the A697 or the A698 both lead to spectacular routes through the Borders and Northumberland. From the west take the M6 to junction 44, from here the A7 and the A698 are the best roads to choose. From Edinburgh the A68 and the A698 is the combination to follow. Both the Edinburgh and Newcastle bypasses have now been completed and Kelso itself now has a new bypass road, so make sure you don't go whizzing by in haste.

There are other options for your journey, but the car has to be the best bet. The nearest railway station is in Berwick, 22 miles away on the Kings Cross line. There are no buses to the course from the station, but the racecourse can arrange transportation. Aviators are also diverted to nearby Winfield but helicopters are now welcomed. It seems fairly obvious then, that some form of motor transportation is in order and there is, after all, the incentive of free parking. What's more, there is no reserved area for Members—first come, first served. Special disabled parking can also be arranged in advance.

Kelso are extremely able at finding sponsorship for their races and with good prize money on offer competitive fields are almost always assured. Of course the going is all important and a new irrigation system should help ground conditions in the Spring and Autumn. With a good spread of fixtures in 2001, Kelso should be able to maintain its outstanding record of attracting people to a course which has no large close centres to draw from. Basically, it's very well served by local people because it provides excellent value in a welcoming atmosphere.

Admission prices are in line with most country courses. £12 is the midweek price for admission to the Members (£15 on Saturdays) £7 for the Tattersalls Enclosure or £4 if you happen to be an OAP. Annual Membership, which includes a private bar/viewing room and 25 reciprocal days, costs £170 for a double badge, £90 for a single and £65 for OAPs. A generous discount of up £2 per ticket is offered to pre-booked parties. As far as corporate hospitality is concerned, Kelso offers the new Younger Grandstand with five boxes, four to accommodate up to 25 people and one that will hold 45. There is also the Dukes Room (50 people), the Hamilton and Tweedie rooms (70 people), the Doody Room (20 people) and three viewing boxes. Please apply to the Secretary. Prices start from £100. Marquees can be erected and will hold up to 850 guests. The catering is provided by two local firms and a very high standard of home cooked delicious food is available at tremendous value—breakfast £2.50, lunch £7.50. Taking tea in the restaurant next to the parade ring is a particularly delightful way to pass the last race or two and a new bar, The Buchanan Room has opened in Tattersalls.

The course is well stocked with the standard items expected of a racecourse and children under 16 are admitted free. Although there is no bank, the Secretary will usually cash cheques and there is a betting shop in the Tattersalls Enclosure, together with a new Tote building in which to spend your money! There are WCs and viewing ramps for the disabled. More unusually there is a golf course in the middle of the course, and a Sunday market throughout the year.

Kelso is one of the most welcoming racecourses in the country and is also one of the best run and many others could learn from the management here. We wish all involved a successful 2001.

Local Favourites

We choose to start our journey at a real favourite, **The Roxburghe Hotel and Golf Course** (01573) 450331—formerly Sunlaws House, a hotel of distinction. You will find this hotel just south of Kelso at Heiton. The hotel is beautifully furnished and the restaurant first rate. The hotel is a great favourite and a trip to Kelso followed by a visit here is about as good as it gets. If you enjoy Golf or Salmon fishing then this is the jewel for you. Further north, in Kelso itself - an extremely pleasant market town - one finds the **Ednam House Hotel** (01573) 224168. The Tweedside setting has obvious appeal for anglers, but the hotel is also convenient for the racecourse. Another place to visit is the **Queens Head Hotel** (01573) 224636—the bar snacks here are good, as indeed they are at the **Cross Keys Hotel** (01573) 223303 in Kelso's town square. Kelso is a pleasant border town and there are a number of pleasant shops for non racing friends to visit.

Rain or shine, Melrose is a charming border town and **Burts Hotel** (01896) 822285 is the one to note—good bar meals and more formal meals as well as good accommodation. **Dunfermline House** (01896) 822148 is a splendid guesthouse close to Melrose Abbey. **Bon Accord** (01896) 822645 in Market Square is worth more than a little consideration. A little further south, in St Boswells, two hotels should also be noted. Firstly, the most hospitable **Buccleuch Arms** (01835) 822243 and also the highly recommended **Dryburgh Abbey** (01835) 822261. The **Collingwood Arms** (01890) 882424 in Cornhill, The **Besom Inn** at Coldstream (01890) 882391 and the **Tankerville Arms** (01668) 281581 in Wooler also come highly recommended by those in the know.

Well warmed up, you may decide to brave the elements and visit Gattonside. Here, the **Hoebridge Inn** (01896) 823082 is appealing. Trekking north towards the uplands, one arrives in Lauder. Here, the **Black Bull** (01578) 712208 is a pleasant, modernised Georgian coaching inn. Eddleston offers the excellent **Horseshoe Inn**. Again a fair distance from Kelso, one finds Ettrickbridge. Here, **Ettrickshaws** (01750) 52229 is well worth the journey—good value hospitality and some extremely imaginative set menus. The **Phillipburn House Hotel** (01750) 20747 is also a pleasant place in which to stay. The **Wheatsheaf** (01890) 860257 in Swinton is also a good choice. Finally, the **Tillmouth Park Hotel** (01890) 882255 boasts nine miles of excellent salmon fishing on the river Tweed and also organises packages for racegoers—a cosy hospitable hotel ideal for anyone travelling from the south.

Kempton Park has come on leaps and bounds during the past few years and serves London and South East admirably. The announcement of another racecourse for the London area is as welcome as it was unexpected. The capital has several excellent courses and a bit of competition to keep them all on their toes is no bad thing.

The **General Manager, Julian Thick**, and the **Secretary, Beverley Frith** can be contacted at **Kempton Park Racecourse, Staines Road East, Sunbury-on-Thames TW16 5AQ. Tel (01932) 782292 Fax (01932) 782044.** Information on corporate hospitality is available from **Laura Southgate** and sponsorship enquiries should be directed to **Stephen Prior.** Marketing enquiries are dealt with by **Tim Darby** at Sandown Park racecourse on **(01372) 461253.** Web site: www.kempton.co.uk.

The racecourse is situated some 15 miles from central London and is well served by the motorway links. The M25 and the M3 make the trip in from the country especially good. For the popular evening meetings, however, one should consider the rush hour build-up. The A316 and the A308 will take you over the Thames to within a stone's throw of the racecourse. The A308 via Hampton Court is the best road from the south. For train travellers, there is an excellent service direct to the course from Waterloo. For those travelling by bus, there is a bus stop outside the racecourse gates and buses can be taken from Staines and Kingston. The main car park lies adjacent to the Grandstand and costs £2, while free parking can be found in the Silver Ring car park and in the centre of the course. If you wish to arrive by helicopter, that's fine, but light aircraft are not welcomed. Helicopters are requested to land between the dovecote and the lake—but phone in advance and notify the course.

Kempton provides some superb racing throughout the year and the highlight is, without doubt, the Christmas Festival, including the Pertemps King George VI Steeplechase on Boxing Day. The post-Christmas euphoria always makes for a jovial atmosphere. You can guarantee the King George will provide a memorable spectacle. June features the Gala Evening with bands, barbecues, a funfair and fireworks. Purists may argue that this is far from what racing is really all about, but Kempton is booming, the racing is of a very competitive standard and if you go along I will bet you a fiver straight you'll have a great time.

There was a total of 26 meetings here in 2000, with racing on the flat and over the jumps. This should also be largely the case in 2001. An excellent selection of races can be seen and the rates for Daily Membership last year were as follows. On Premium days, a charge of £17 was levied, which rose to £29 for Classic days such as the King George and dropped to £15 on Feature days. Junior Members (17-21 years) prices were £10 on Premium Days and £8 on Feature Days. No discounts were offered on Classic days. You could, however, save some money on badges if they were booked in advance, which took a fiver off a badge for big meetings. You would have to book at least a week in advance especially for Premier and Classic days. Entrance to the Paddock Enclosure in 2000 was priced at £13 (£15 on Boxing Day) while the Silver Ring cost you £5 (£10 on Boxing Day). Accompanied children under 16 are admitted free to all enclosures. Annual Membership in 2000 cost £185 for a full (both flat and jump meetings) single membership which included a free label for the Members' car park. For those 17-21 years old this dropped to £90. A single membership for National Hunt racing only stood at £105, while a similar arrangement for the flat was £125. Reciprocal arrangements were made

*Artist: **Roy Miller** COMING IN AT KEMPTON Courtesy of: **The Artist***

for admission by members at Goodwood, Taunton, Lingfield, Newbury, Newton Abbot, Epsom and Sandown. A special rate of admission is offered to parties of 12 or more, and discounts are available on purchases of more than one member's badge at certain meetings.

The facilities at Kempton are excellent and boxes, suites and conference areas can all be organised. The private boxes are let annually, but they do become available on some days and there are usually one or two up for grabs and on quieter days they represent excellent value. They also have balconies overlooking the racecourse and its very attractive grounds. Certainly as far as venues for entertaining go these boxes take some beating. The boxes can seat twelve people for lunch or about 20 for a less formal buffet. Each box has closed circuit television, private bar facilities and a number of other perks. Prices for these rooms range from £550 to £650, the location being the deciding factor. The management generally know whether boxes are free two to three weeks in advance. This may not leave much time to organise a party, but for those who do not need to plan too far in advance it is a first class idea.

Lunch is available in the new Jubilee Restaurant from £69 per person. If you wish to have lunch before racing, contact Pam Lewis on (01372) 463072. More modest refreshments and nourishment can be found in numerous snack bars, particularly on the ground floor of the new Grandstand which is also home to the Sporting Index Sports Bar. Finally, one may enjoy a picnic in the course enclosure car parks, should this be your form of nourishment.

Facilities for children include a playground in the centre of the course and a crèche. Good amenities for disabled people including a viewing ramp can also be found. Owners are made particularly welcome with discounts on lunch and a very welcome bottle of bubbly for the successful owners.

It is the attention to detail of small things such as these that saw Kempton rewarded with the Travelling the Turf Racecourse of the Year award for 1999. Good quality racing is to be found here year-round and perhaps it is the proximity to London that has ensured its success.

It could be this very factor that will provide Kempton, along with its metropolitan neighbours Sandown and Epsom, with a challenge for the future. In a few years time, London will have its first new racecourse in many years with the building of the newly licensed London City Racecourse at Fairlop Waters in Redbridge. Few racecourses have the luxury of being able to plan their facilities and layout from a clean slate and make it really punter-friendly from day one. The new £40 million floodlit track, accessible to seven million Londoners, with over 30 fixtures, will no doubt present major competition to the existing courses and set a new standard of what people expect when they go racing. Kempton does an excellent job now, but let's hope the powers that be take note and meet the competition head on in 2002.

*Artist: **John Atkins** PULLING UP Courtesy of: **The Artist***

Racing at either Sandown or Kempton offers a great variety of enticing possibilities for culinary refreshment. Those journeying back to the capital should also find that many of the following suggestions make convenient and relaxing stop-offs.

In Esher, **Good Earth** (01372) 462489 offers a good Chinese menu, while lovers of South East Asian fayre will enjoy **La Orient** (01372) 466628. In East Molesey, one finds an extremely popular French restaurant, **Le Chien Qui Fume** 0208 979 7150.

Pubs conveniently placed for Sandown include the **Albert Arms** and the **Cricketers**. Alternatively for Kempton try the **Kings Head** in Shepperton, or the **Three Horseshoes** in Laleham. If you are staying in the area, then there are a number of possibilities to consider. In Weybridge, the **Oatlands Park Hotel** (01932) 847242 is an ever improving favourite. A well appointed alternative is the **Ship Thistle Hotel** (01932) 848364, while **Casa Romana** (01932) 843470 is an exciting Italian affair. Alternatively, another place for your post-race nosebag is to be found in Woking, at the reasonably priced **Wheatsheaf** (014837) 73047. Leisure lovers and golfers should note the outstanding country house hotel, **Selsdon Park** 0208 657 8811 in Sanderstead, a thoroughly delightful establishment. A smaller but extremely refined establishment is the **Angel Posting House and Livery** (01483) 564555 in Guildford. Excellent cuisine combines well with all the comforts one could wish for—a real find.

In Cobham we might consider three options. The **Woodlands Park Hotel** (01372) 843933, at Stoke D'Abernon, **Quattro** (01932) 863973 a very favourable Italian restaurant or if one just wants a post-race pint, the **Cricketers**. In Ripley, south west of Cobham, another restaurant beckons, **Michels'** (01483) 224777—outstanding French cuisine. Finally, the **Hilton Cobham** (01932) 864471 in Cobham is a large, well run concern from the internationally acclaimed stable of the same name.

Turning to London, there is a whole mass of outstanding restaurants, some cheap and cheerful, others cheerful until the bill comes! Outside the capital, however, a number of establishments might be thought of. In Richmond, one finds all manner of good eating places and pubs, and two good hotels as well. There are numerous boozers to sample on route but a little gem with excellent food is the **White Horse** off Sheen Lane in Richmond, ideal for postrace fayre. The **Petersham** 0208 940 7471 is ideal and has a very good restaurant and the **Richmond Gate** 0208 940 0061 which is a worthwhile port of call and has been warmly recommended of late. Richmond itself has good shopping and a range of restaurants and pubs to suit all tastes and budgets. Down by the Thames, the appropriately named **River Terrace** 0208 332 2524 not only offers the 'Old Father' but also provides first rate cooking. In Egham one should note several establishments. The **Eclipse** is an ideal place for a drink (should be nearer Sandown, I suppose), the **Olive Grove** (01784) 439494 is a good restaurant to note, while **Great Fosters** (01784) 433822 is an interesting building which houses a good hotel—obviously better value than Central London offerings. The **Runnymede** (01784) 436171 is more modern but is a popular visiting spot for the many who travel this way. In Staines, the **Swan** is a fine public house as is the **Harrow** in Compton, south of Guildford—note the racing prints here. In Sunbury-on-Thames, the **Castle** (019327) 83647 is a pleasant French restaurant and Shepperton is also handy for the racecourse where the **Warren Lodge** (01932) 242972 is a good place to stay—its terrace overlooks the Thames. The **Anchor Hotel** (01932) 221618 is another worthy candidate—pleasant bars and bedrooms and not too pricey. One of the largest hotels in the area is the

Shepperton Moat House (01932) 241404, less intimate than some by virtue of its size, but a worthy recommendation just the same. The **Thames Court** (01932) 221957 in Surbiton is another spot to note. This restaurant offers French cuisine while the bar has a variety of sandwiches and cold meats—excellent. Surbiton also offers the **Warwick Guesthouse** 0208 399 5837 for excellent value accommodation. Also note **Chez Max** 0208 399 2365, an enjoyable restaurant in which to dine. Alternatively, **Le Petit Max** 0208 977 0236 is a good place to visit after an evening at Kempton, or Sandown for that matter, as is the appropriately named **Luca** 0208 3992365 on Maple Road.

Racegoers who enjoy cricket should seek out the **Swan** in Claygate in summer as it doubles as the local cricket pavilion—excellent bar food as well.

If you are coming back through London, the following tips should cover most options. The **Kings Arms**, Hampton Court is a good pub for a pint either before or after racing and we also recommend the **Imperial Arms** 0207 736 9179 run by racing enthusiasts. It serves first class food and excellent wine and beer—a real favourite. An outstanding hotel offering style and comfort can be found on Wimbledon Common, **Cannizaro House** 0208 879 1464. This sumptuous Georgian mansion is an elegant but friendly hotel in which to stay. There are also a variety of pubs and restaurants in Wimbledon, all great fun. If you want to celebrate in style but don't wish to return to the better known West End eating haunts, try the popular **Riva** 0208 748 0434 in Barnes, the **Blue Elephant** 0207 386 7005 in Fulham Broadway—excellent Thai food—or the **River Café** 0207 381 6217, Hammersmith, for unbeatable new-wave Italian cuisine. **The Canteen** 0207 351 7330 in Chelsea Harbour is also superb.

Restaurants closer to the racecourse which are well thought of include **Sonny's** 0208 748 0393 in Barnes, **Crowthers** 0208 876 6372, and **Monsieur Max** 0208 979 5546.

Artist: **Claire Eva Burton** **THE FINISH** *Courtesy of:* **The Artist**

Oatlands Park Hotel

This luxurious hotel is conveniently situated in Weybridge, just a thirty minute train journey from London and within easy access of both Heathrow and Gatwick airports. Set in its own acres of parkland and surrounded by the beautiful Surrey countryside it is the perfect location for business and pleasure alike. Traditional style and charm are combined with modern luxuries to make your stay here a memorable one.

Many of the bedrooms enjoy delightful views over the extensive grounds and the Broadwater Lake. All rooms are tastefully designed to a high standard of comfort and decor and range from superior to the larger deluxe rooms and suites. All have direct dial telephone, tea and coffee making facilities, a trouser press and satellite televisions.

Dining in the elegant Broadwater Restaurant is a pleasure not to be missed. Guests are invited to choose from a creative à la carte menu which caters for all tastes and incorporates only the finest ingredients.

The Oatlands Park is the perfect venue for both board meetings and conferences, with the highly skilled management team ensuring that the whole event runs smoothly and efficiently.

Dinner dances can be arranged for up to 220 guests, or perhaps visitors would like to attend one of the themed evenings - whether the choice is a Henry VIII banquet or even a 'Night at the Races'.

For racegoers the hotel could not be more conveniently situated being close to many famous racecourses - Kempton Park, Sandown, Ascot and Epsom. The hotel can arrange many activities ranging from laser clay pigeon shooting to corporate golf days on its own 9 hole course.

For the less energetic a quiet stroll around the beautiful gardens is the perfect way to relax or perhaps you might enjoy a friendly game of croquet or boules.

Oatlands Park Hotel
Oatlands Drive
Weybridge
Surrey
KT13 9HB
Tel: (01932) 847242
Fax: (01932) 842252
www.oatlandsparkhotel.co.uk

The **Clerk of the Course** is **Captain Nick Lees** while **Company Secretary** and **Manager** is **Russell Parrott**. They can be contacted at **The Racecourse, Oadby, Leicester, LE2 4AL. Tel: (0116) 271 6515. Fax: (0116) 271 1746.**

Leicester racecourse is in Oadby, two miles south east of Leicester on the A6 Market Harborough Road. Both the M1, exit junction 21, and the M69 might prove useful in reaching the track. From the west and Birmingham (40 miles away) take the M6 exiting at junction 2 and follow the M69 to the M1. Try to use the B5418 and avoid Leicester's one-way system at all costs. Southbound travellers will find the A46 and the M1 the best routes while the A6 and the M1 are possibilities for the northbound racegoer. People making the journey from Newmarket might wish to use the A47 turn off before Leicester, through Evington. The Southern District Distributor Road links the M1 (junction 21) with the A6 at the entrance to the course. Trains run from St Pancras to Leicester, a journey of about an hour and a half. A bus service runs from the station on racedays and there is a regular service from Leicester City to the track. The ample parking facilities are provided free of charge here and if you have a helicopter, you can land it in the centre of the course.

Leicester enjoys a full year of flat and National Hunt. There are no Annual Members but in 2001 Daily Members will pay £15 for a badge, and those in Tattersalls £11. Rates include a free card and parking. Discounts are offered on parties of 20 or more booked in advance into Tattersalls. £28 admits a car and four occupants to the Picnic Car Park. Accompanied children under 16 years old are admitted free.

Dramatic changes have taken place at Leicester during the past few years. The old Tattersalls and Silver Ring grandstands have been replaced by a new Tatts stand with a betting hall on the ground floor and a restaurant upstairs which is open for banqueting on non-racedays. At the top of the grandstand the Fernie Room has been refurbished and is available for daily lettings, as is the Barleythorpe Seafood restaurant. These complement the Belvoir Bar in the Club Enclosure where boxes can accommodate 12-14 for a sit-down meal or 20 for a buffet, and three double boxes that will take 30 to 40 people quite comfortably. The accommodation is equipped with closed circuit television and private Tote betting facilities. Marquees can be erected in the Paddock area if required.

Artist: **Barrie Linklater PARADE RING POTENTIAL** Courtesy of: **Patterson Gallery**

In the new grandstand, the Conference Centre can accommodate anything from a theatre style meeting for up to 400 people down to a private party for 50. For bookings contact Mr Buckle on (0116) 271 9840

The caterers, Drewetts, can be contacted on (01788) 544171 and will be able to assist with menus. There is a playground for children, and viewing stands in the Members for disabled people. There are public telephones in all enclosures and a Ladbrokes betting shop in Tattersalls but there are no banks at the racecourse.

Leicester is a well situated racecourse and it is excellent to report the developments that have taken place—one to bear in mind when scanning the 2001 racing calendar!

Local Favourites

If you wish to stay in the city then one suggestion is that you plump for one of the larger hotels in the city centre. The **Holiday Inn Leicester** (0116) 2531161 is particularly modern but has swimming pools and that sort of thing to make up for the situation. Less modern, Victorian actually, is the **Grand** (0116) 255 5599—note here a particularly good coffee shop and some welcoming bars. The **Hilton Leicester** (0116) 2630066 is another to be considered. **The Hilton** (0116) 2630066 and the **Belmont Hotel** (0116) 254 4773 also come highly recommended by Leicester Racecourse themselves. Among the vast number of guesthouses and B&Bs in the area, **Leigh Court** (01886) 832275 and the **Scotia Hotel** (0116) 254 9200 stand out from the crowd.

In Rothley, the **Rothley Court** (0116) 237 4141 is a manor house with a super setting and restaurant. **The Limes** (0116) 2302531 also has a good local reputation. In Quorn itself, the **Quorn Country Hotel** (01509) 415050 blends together a combination of traditional hospitality and modern amenities. There are a number of appealing pubs to be found in and around Charnwood and one of them is the **Carrington Arms** (01664) 840228, Ashby Folville—good bar food here. A longer

trip for a hotel of merit is the **Johnscliffe Hotel** in Newtown Linford (01530) 242228. South of the city in Whetstone, the **Old Vicarage** (0116) 277 1195 is a pleasant restaurant close to Leicester. The **Three Swans** (01858) 466644 at Market Harborough is another comfortable and highly recommended establishment. In Old Dalby, the **Crown Inn** (01664) 823134 dates from the 17th century and is a lovely place for a pint and a fireside chat—there's also a fairly handy restaurant. A hotel of note is the **Harboro Hotel** (01664) 60121. The restaurant here is also worth a visit. Alternative accommodation can be found in the **George** (01664) 62112, an extremely comfortable and well looked after inn which is strongly recommended. The **Rose and Crown** in Hose is a popular pub with tremendous character and some good food. In Braunston, as opposed to Branston, The **Old Plough** (01572) 722714 is also very welcoming, while on the way to Oakham, the **Noel Arms** at Langham is also recommended—a good restaurant here (01572) 722931. Two supremely popular pubs are the **Bell** at East Langton (01858) 545567 and the **Berwicke Arms,** Hallaton, (01858) 89217, both renowned for really first rate food. Finally, the remotely set **Old Barn** (01858) 545215 offers good food in the evenings and some pleasant accommodation.

First class is a description one should also apply to the area's leading hotel, **Hambleton Hall** (01572) 756991. The grounds lead down to Rutland Water and the bedrooms are superb. The highlight of the house is the restaurant—outstanding. Less grand, but no less welcoming accommodation can be found at the **Finch's Arms** (01572) 756575 which serves fine food and in Oakham's market place—the **George**, a good place for a drink, as is the **Nevill Arms**, Medbourne (01858) 565288—some accommodation as well —and the **Marquess Of Exeter** at Lydington (01572) 822477. The adjoining hotel has a good restaurant and accommodation. A worthy addition to the well stocked Oakham stable is the **Whipper-In Hotel** (01572) 756971. The bedrooms here have great individual charm and the restaurant is excellent. A final thought for lovers of over- the-top quality, try **Stapleford Park** (01572) 787522—a really fine choice if you've got a winning jackpot ticket.

Artist: **Margaret Moore NECK AND NECK** _Courtesy of:_ **Osborne Studio Gallery**

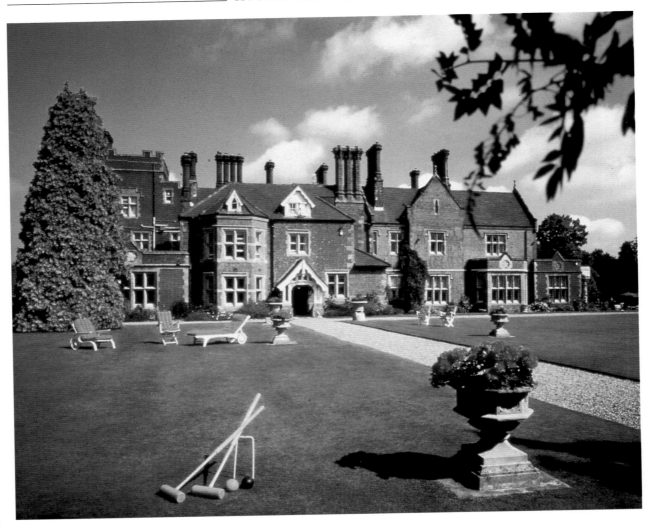

One of the most exclusive hotels in England, set in 135 acres of private parkland, Alexander House reflects a bygone era when English country house living was a most sought after ideal. In the ambience created by its stunning decor, tasteful furnishing and splendid works of art, Alexander House successfully combines tradition with all the modern-day comforts and facilities

The oldest part of the present house, facing the south lawn, was once a farmhouse, dating from the 17th century. A stone dated 1608 survives in the boundary wall and is thought to be a lintel from an earlier building on the site. Some of England's most important families have made Alexander House their home, including poet Percy Bysshe Shelley and William Campbell, Governor of the Bank of England.

Today Alexander House has 15 exclusive bedrooms and a wealth of public and meeting rooms. The hotel has a range of amenities for those who enjoy the outdoors including croquet, clock golf and tennis courts on site, as well as golf, fishing, clay pigeon shooting, archery, riding and off-road driving further afield.

Superb table d'hôte and à la carte meals are served in Alexander's Restaurant which is renowned for its delicious classic English and French cuisine, rare wines and vintage ports. The menus emphasise the goodness of fresh natural foods carefully prepared and artistically presented.

Located close to Turners Hill and East Grinstead in the West Sussex countryside, there is a host of places of interest to visit including the Natural Trust properties at Wakefield, Hever Castle, Sir Winston Churchill's Chartwell, the operas at Glyndebourne and, for those travelling the turf, the course at Lingfield Park is close by with the courses at Goodwood, Fontwell Park, Brighton and Plumpton not too far away.

Alexander House
Turners Hill
West Sussex RH10 4QD
Tel: (01342) 714914
Fax: (01342) 717328
e mail: info@alexanderhouse.co.uk
web site: www.alexanderhouse.co.uk

The Clerk of the Course is Fergus Cameron who can be contacted at Racecourse Road, Lingfield, Surrey RH7 6PQ. Tel (01342) 834800. Fax (01342) 832833. The Regional Manager here is Clive Stephens and the Marketing Director is Claudia Fisher. Website: www.lingfieldpark.co.uk.

Lingfield is easily accessible from London which is only 21 miles away. The M25 and the A22 are the best routes to follow from the capital. The racecourse itself is on the B2029. The A22 is the best route for northbound travellers, exiting for the course at Newchapel. Westbound travellers should take the A264 while those heading east should pursue the M25 and the A22, exiting at junction 6. On arrival, there is a choice of car parks with parking for 7,000 cars. The public car park is free.

The Members in the centre of the course is more convenient but a charge of £3 is levied if space is reserved in advance. If you don't want to take the car then a train from Victoria or London Bridge to Lingfield Station is a convenient option (with combined rail and race tickets available) and a short walk will see you to the racecourse gates. For more local requirements, the 429 bus from East Grinstead to Godstone will take you via the track. If speed is of the essence then helicopters are free to land in the centre of the course provided you make the arrangements in advance.

There are a staggering 72 meetings, offering both flat and jump racing on the grass track and all-weather course. These include some really worthwhile evening racing. The most popular event of the year is the excellent Classic trials meeting in May, featuring the Derby Trial, and the Oaks Trial. The Churchill stakes on the All Weather Track in November is also popular. The rates for entrance to Lingfield in 2000 were £15 for the Club and £10 for the Family enclosure. Children under 16 who are accompanied by an adult are admitted free but there is a maximum of two children per adult. Prices rise to £16 and £12 respectively on Stakes day and Silver Trophy day, and to £18 and £13 on Derby Trial day. Discounts are available for groups of 20 to 40, with further reductions for groups of over 40. Annual Members in 2000 were charged £160. This included reciprocal dates at Epsom, Folkestone, Brighton, Sandown, Windsor, Goodwood and Hickstead as well as social membership of the Lingfield Park golf club.

Lingfield Park is an excellent and popular place at which to entertain as the facilities are good. Boxes for 12-350 guests are available. Private boxes all have racecourse videos as does the Eclipse Suite. For people who want a far bigger function, the Garden Room in the Pavilion in the Members Enclosure can accommodate from 20 to 350 people. There are four restaurants—the Derby Restaurant in Tattersalls, the Trackside Carvery, the Brasserie in the Members & the new Champagne & Seafood Restaurant. You could also try the User Friendly bar in Tattersalls. Both the Members and Grandstand Enclosures have betting shops as well as Tote facilities. There is a play area for children and a crèche for 3 to 7 year olds. There are special viewing areas and lavatories for disabled people as well as car parks and it is good to see the course making an effort here. As

Artist: **Claire Eva Burton** CHESTNUT - GREEN SILKS *Courtesy of:* **The Artist**

yet there is no bank at the track—so come prepared if you like a flutter. The Ladbrokes betting shop is located in Tattersalls. All-weather racing is already beginning to show its merits in keeping the industry moving. Some may say that it fails to attract top racehorses—but what about the US? With the principal races in the Breeders Cup on dirt, it would be great if a really prestigious race could be held on Britain's all-weather to catch the imagination more in this country. With its new management in place we wish Lingfield good fortune for 2001.

Local Favourites

Lingfield Park is surrounded by good hostelries. Sampling a different one after each meeting of the year would not be impossible. Some notable examples are the **Hare & Hounds** (01342) 832351 in Lingfield and the **Castle Inn** (01892) 870247 in the delightful village of Chiddingstone. Other suggestions in the locality include the **Crown** (01892) 864742 at Groombridge—a pleasantly situated old inn with some fine ales, a restaurant and some bedrooms if needs be. **The Bottle House** (01892) 870306 and the **Spotted Dog** (01892) 870253 in Penhurst are also firm favourites, as is the **Royal Oak** at Dormansland—ideal for a pint or two. In Edenbridge. **Honours Mill** (01732) 866757 is a handy place to enjoy good food and wine—be sure to book - and **Haxted Mill** (01732) 862914 is also worth investigating. Another one to try is **Goldhill Mill** (01732) 851626 a really outstanding B&B—no restaurant though. Another good restaurant to consider is the **Old Lodge** at Limpsfield (01883) 712996. This establishment is not cheap but it is extremely well thought of. Also note **La Bonne Auberge** (01342) 892318 in South Godstone where superb French cooking can be enjoyed in elegant surroundings.

If you are keen to stay nearby, then several ideas spring to mind. Firstly, the **Copthorne Effingham Park** (01342) 714971 in the village of Copthorne has much appeal, (good restaurant and leisure facilities), while in Tonbridge, the **Rose and Crown** (01732) 357966 in Tonbridge High Street is also a satisfactory port of call. To the south, in Royal Tunbridge Wells, the **Royal**

Wells Inn (01892) 511188 is excellent value and a super place to stay—the restaurant is also worth a visit. On Mount Ephraim, the **Spa Hotel** (01892) 520331 boasts outstanding facilities and a commendable restaurant. One should also consider **Thackerays House** (01892) 511921, which not only boasts an outstanding menu but also has a divine wine list. What better place to end up after a successful day's sport? Well, **Gravetye Manor** (01342) 810567, is an outstanding hotel and restaurant double and **Ashdown Park** (01342) 824988 offers relaxation and excellent cuisine. Other less grand, but worthy recommendations in East Grinstead include the **Jarvis Felbridge Hotel** (01342) 326992, the **Woodbury House** (01342) 313657, and the **Cranfield Lodge Hotel** (01342) 321251, which are all well worth a visit. In a similar vein, nearby Hartfield offers **Bolebrook Watermill** (01892) 770425—exceptional value and very charming. Racegoers who thirst after sheer luxury will appreciate **Alexander House** (01342) 714914, located at Turners Hill—not terribly close to the racecourse but well worth a detour. Finally a pub to note: the excellent **George & Dragon** at Speldhurst—a fine friendly boozer to count ones ill-gotten gains.

Artist: **David Dent** *RACING Courtesy of:* **The Artist**

The **Clerk of the Course** and **Secretary** at Ludlow is **Bob Davies**. He can be contacted at **Shepherds Meadow, Eaton Bishop, Lane Head, Hereford HR2 9UA. Tel (01981) 250052 Fax (01981) 250192.** Alternatively, on racedays **Tel (01584) 856221** or **Fax (01584) 856217. Web site www.ludlow-racecourse.co.uk**

The racecourse is situated in beautiful Shropshire countryside yet the course is easily accessible from major routes. The track is two miles north-west of Ludlow. The favoured routes are the A49 via Shrewsbury from the north or through Hereford from the south. Racegoers from areas west of Ludlow should follow the A4113. Travellers from the east of the country should aim to reach the A44 from Worcester and then make the best use of the A49. Anyone wishing to circumnavigate the town should use the Ludlow bypass. There are both rail and bus stations in Ludlow and the Midland Red runs from Hereford to Shrewsbury on the A49. The railway station is small but the line can be joined from Newport which in turn is on a direct route from Paddington or from Euston, via Shrewsbury. There is ample free parking should you decide to drive. Cars can be parked alongside the course in the spring and autumn although this is restricted during the winter months. Helicopters can also land at Ludlow providing you ask permission first.

The racecourse now stages 15 meetings, all National Hunt, and the principal of these is the Charity Meeting in April—in 2000 this was in aid of the Cancer Unit Trust at Royal Shrewsbury Hospital. Major races include the Forbra Gold Cup in March and the Prince of Wales Amateur Riders' Handicap Chase in December. All of the fixtures, bar one on May Bank Holiday, take place during the week—no doubt to the delight of the local farming community. However, the ordinary mortal should not be put off midweek racing—and certainly Ludlow is a pleasant and friendly racecourse to visit.

Annual Membership in 2000 was priced at £125 with 22 reciprocal meetings and a Single Day Guest voucher. Juniors (under 21s) are entitled to a reduced rate which in 2000 was £75. Daily admission charges are £15 for the Members, £10 for Tatts and £5 for the Course Ring. Senior Citizens have the concession of a £2 refreshment voucher for use in Tattersalls and discounts are available for groups of 12 or more. Disabled people in wheelchairs are allowed into the Members at the same price as Tattersalls. Charges are expected to remain the same in 2001.

The Members building, the Clive Pavilion, provides bar and restaurant facilities for Annual Members, owners and trainers. Non-raceday functions for up to 500 people can also be accommodated. There are two spacious rooms available for entertaining parties of between 25 and 35. Marquees can be arranged at the racecourse if you are planning a large party. The marquees can cater for groups from 30 to 350. The cost of an 'all-in' party is approximately £40 per person, including racecard, lunch and admission. The course caterers are Hughes of Welshpool who can be contacted on (01938) 553366. Hughes also deal with all functions on non-racedays. In addition to the new restaurant, snacks are available from Tattersalls and Members. A 3 year programme has just been completed with improvements being made to all the bends, and the fences, plus a reservoir and watering system has been installed. The Course bar was refurbished a few years ago and new Tote facilities were installed, as well as more seating. There are also plans to improve the Tattersalls Enclosure in May 2001 by providing a new roof over the stand and moving the

Artist: **Malcolm Coward HURDLE RACE** _Courtesy of:_ **Sally Mitchell Fine Arts**

Racecourse Betting Shop providing access from the Tattersalls Bar.

Children are welcome here and they will be entertained by the free bouncy castle at late spring meetings. For those even younger there is now a mother and baby room for Course patrons. The disabled racegoer is provided with a viewing ramp and ground floor toilet facilities. Tote credit facilities are available in the Members. The racecourse betting shop is now run by the Tote and if you are a punter with a fancy at another course, then the licensed betting office in Tatts allows you to punt on that cert. Ludlow is to be applauded for its commitment to provide modern facilities in all areas. It benefits from its splendid scenic location and delights in a peace that is seldom found in Britain. A good reason for visiting Shropshire, and where better place to start than the racecourse.

Local Favourites

A number of fine establishments can be found in Ludlow. **Overton Grange** (01584) 873500 is an Edwardian manor offering excellent cuisine. The 16th century **Feathers Hotel** (01584) 875261 is extremely popular and offers a good restaurant. More moderately priced accommodation is found at **No 28** (01584) 876996 and **Cecil** (01584) 872442. Two pubs to note are the **Bull** and the **Church**, both providing a great atmosphere for a pre or post-race rendezvous. Another hotel in which to spoil yourself is **Dinham Hall** (01584) 876464 which has a first class restaurant and comfortable rooms. A restaurant for those who delight in excellent food is the **Merchant House** (01584) 875438—but do book. The **Unicorn** (01584) 873555 is a pub worthy of note here, with some accommodation too. Two other thoughts for good food are the well named **Oaks** (01584) 872325 and **The Courtyard** (01584) 878080.

Just over the border in Wales, the **Radnorshire Arms Hotel** (01544) 267406 at Presteigne is steeped in history—a favourite of Elizabeth I who lived here once. East of Ludlow at Abberley,

along the A443, the **Elms Hotel** (01299) 896666 is another hotel with an impressive history and thoughtful service. To the south in Leominster, the racegoer will find a haven of peace and hospitality at **Withenfield Guest House** (01568) 612011. We also recommend the **Marsh Country Hotel** (01568) 613952—a delightful timbered house with a really fine restaurant—definitely one for the shortlist.

In the curiously named Hopton Wafers, the **Crown Inn** (01299) 270372 is a popular pub which provides an excellent bar menu and restaurant. In Clun, the **Sun Inn** (01588) 640277 is a 15th century listed building which also has good value accommodation and bar snacks. Thirteen miles south of Shrewsbury is Church Stretton, home of the **Denehurst Hotel** (01694) 722699 and in nearby All Stretton you'll find the **Stretton Hall Hotel** (01694) 723224—ideal if you want peace and quiet in a traditional style. Before leaving the area consider The **Roebuck Inn** in Brimfield, whose restaurant (01584) 711230 is first class. Clearly, a visit to Ludlow is in order for national hunt enthusiasts. If you haven't been, try to go in 2001, it's a really pleasant course.

*Artist: **Terence Gilbert** AT THE START Courtesy of: **The Artist***

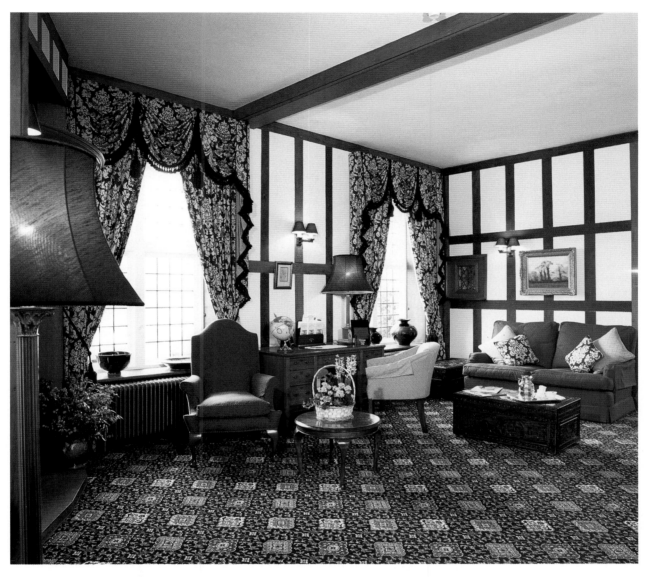

A warm welcome awaits you from the heart of Shropshire, relax in luxury and enjoy an unhurried way of life, long forgotten in the quickening pace of today's world.

Slumber within our sumptuous individually designed bedrooms and relax in our spacious traditional lounges with blazing log fires and unrivalled views over the beautiful Shropshire countryside. For guests wishing to wine and dine our "Les Marches" restaurant has been recognised for excellence in cuisine and service, it's listed in all the major guides and has international accolades expected in a restaurant of this calibre. Every item on our carefully composed menus has been selected for seasonal freshness and complementary flavours. Our award winning cellars carry an extensive list covering the traditional wine regions of Europe and those of the new world.

Racegoers are ideally placed at Overton Grange, during the week Ludlow's National Hunt meetings beckon, but for weekends, Wolverhampton, Worcester, and Hereford are all within easy reach and Cheltenham, Stratford and Warwick are all within striking distance.

An ideal location to console or to celebrate after a day's racing.

Overton Grange Hotel
Ludlow
Shropshire
SY8 4AD
Tel: 01584 873500
Fax: 01584 873524

Major Charles Moore acts as **Clerk of the Course** and **Pip Adams** is the **Racecourse Manager** at this pleasant Lincolnshire course. **Stephen Bakin** is **Head Groundsman** and **Victoria Nicholson** is the **Sales/Marketing Assistant.** All the members of this team can be contacted at: **The Racecourse, Legsby Road, Market Rasen, Lincs. LN8 3EA Tel (01673) 843434. Fax (01673) 844532. web site: www.marketrasenraces.co.uk e mail: marketrasen@rht.net**

The racecourse is some twelve miles north east of the county town of Lincoln, just off the A46, midway between Lincoln and Grimsby. The course is adjacent to the A631 on the eastern edge of the town approximately 150 miles from London. The A1 is the closest major road to the course and this, coupled with the A46, is the best route from the south. From the north, use a combination of the M62, M18 and M180 link to the A15, then the A631 at Caenby Corner. Those travelling by train should note that Market Rasen is on the Newark to Cleethorpes line. Change at Newark if you are coming from Kings Cross. The station is approximately ten minutes walk from the course. Should you travel by car you will find ample free parking. Market Rasen is also the place to take your helicopter. During the war the course was requisitioned and used as an anti-aircraft headquarters. Fear not, you are unlikely to be shot down.

The racing pattern in 2000 included 18 meetings plus two point-to-points and a day's Arab Racing. The course's most popular occasions are traditionally their Easter Monday and Boxing Day meetings, the most popular races being the Lincolnshire National held on Boxing Day, and the Handicap 'Chase and Hurdle staged at the summer meeting in July. The rates for admission in 2000 were £15, £10 and £5 for the Members', Tattersalls and Silver Ring respectively. A Jubilee Club for pensioners gives reduced admission to Tatts and the Silver Ring. If you are planning on taking a party of people, special rates are available depending on the numbers—15 or more is the usual figure. Contact the Secretary for terms. Annual Members are charged £130 for a single subscription while £225 is the price for a husband and wife dual membership. This entitles members to exclusive facilities together with 23 reciprocal dates at other courses all over the country.

There are facilities for all sorts of parties and they vary in number, price and location. The Club Enclosure's private boxes - recently upgraded and refurbished - have been increased to an impressive 17, seven on annual lets and nine corporate rooms let on a daily basis. The County Room can take parties of up to 100 people, or smaller groups if desired. and the Brocklesby Suite can cater for parties of up to 300. There is also a pay and play golf course which can be made available for corporate entertainment or as part of conference activities. Bookings should be made through the Commercial Manager and the price will be around £395. The caterers can be contacted through the racecourse and provide a selection of meals in a choice of bars and restaurants. Alternatively, you may wish to take a picnic and there are two designated picnic areas. In 2000 the charge for entrance to these areas was £4 per car and £5 per adult occupant. In addition improved facilities include a new winners enclosure and pre-parade ring.

If you are disabled there is a special viewing area and two specially adapted lavatories. At the weekend and Bank Holiday

Artist: **Malcolm Coward** _AFTER THE RACE_ _Courtesy of:_ **Sally Mitchell Fine Arts**

meetings a fully supervised crèche is provided on the first floor of the Silver Ring Stand. For older children, there is a recently refurbished playground. All accompanied children under 16 are admitted free of charge. Annual and Daily Members can take advantage of the dining room in the Brocklesby Suite which offers lunch and views of the course. There is also a recently renovated Members Bar and the Red Rum Bar in Tattersalls. Bookings for the restaurant may be made direct with the caterers, Craven Gilpin 0113 287 6387.

Lincolnshire remains one of England's most unspoiled counties and if you are looking for a new racecourse to visit in 2001 Market Rasen would make a fine choice.

Local Favourites

Steeped in history, with narrow cobbled streets, Lincoln is filled with antique and craft shops. Lovers of history should visit the cathedral which holds one of the original copies of the Magna Carta. An appealing place to eat is the **Wig and Mitre** (01522) 537482 on the appropriately named Steep Hill. There are a large number of hotels to be found in the city. The **Posthouse Lincoln** (0870) 4009052 is modern but has pleasant views and is comfortable. More convenient and with a city centre setting is the **White Hart Hotel** (01522) 526222 a particular pleasing establishment. **The Courtyard by Marriott** (01522) 544244 is also well worth noting. Extremely comfortable but less expensive accommodation can be found in the **Moor Lodge Hotel** (01522) 791366, Branston, a little way outside the city. Lincoln also offers the outstanding, particularly from a price point of view, **D'Isney Place Hotel** (01522) 538881. The **Jews House** (01522) 524851 is an inspired French restaurant. Those wishing to stay close to the racecourse should note the **Limes Hotel** (01673) 842357, Market Rasen, for good accommodation, food and service. The town also boasts a friendly and popular restaurant to consider, **Jossals** (01673) 843948. **Kenwick Park** (01507) 608806 in Louth is further afield but worth considering. In the opposite direction is the **Village** (01427) 788309 where the comfort and attention may make it your last stop! The convenient **Admiral**

Rodney (01507) 523131 and the **Petwood House Hotel** (01526) 352411 offer special racing packages—check with the hotel for details. The **Washingborough Hall Hotel** (01522) 790340 is also one to note for those who like a little extra luxury.

Those merely looking for a pub for a pre-race pint, or post-race celebration are directed to the **White Swan** which is thoroughly recommended. To the revamped **Chase** or the excellent **Red Lion**. A more than comfortable bed for the night can be found at the **Waveney Guest House** (01673) 843236 and **Beechwood Guest House** (01673) 844043. The **Black Horse** (01507) 343646 at Donnington on Bain is a good all-round performer. Less convenient is Woodhall Spa, but this town should be visited not for racing but for some excellent golf. The **Golf Hotel** (01526) 53535 and the Edwardian **Dower House Hotel** (01526) 52588 are both good. Two pubs relatively near to the racecourse are the **Chicken** at Binbrook with good bar food, and the **Nickerson Arms** at Rothwell, also remote but worth finding just the same. One final thought, consider a trip to Stamford and a night at the **George** (01780) 55171. This really is one of our leading recommendations—a must for all lovers of fine hotels.

Artist: **Heather St Claire Davis** **FAST WORKOUT** *Courtesy of:* **Frost & Reed**

The **Manager** and **Clerk of the Course** at Musselburgh is Bill Farnsworth and he can be reached on **0131 665 2859 Fax 0131 653 2083.** Enquiries about Corporate Hospitality can also be addressed to him on the above number. **e mail: info@musselburgh-racecourse.co.uk Web site: www.musselburgh-racecourse.co.uk.**

The racecourse stands proudly around the historic golf course of Musselburgh links which in turn lies on the Firth of Forth. Its situation, six miles east of Scotland's capital city, is some 350 miles north of its English counterpart. The major routes to be considered are the M8 and the City bypass from the west and the A1 and A198 from the east. The A7, A68 and A702 should be used for people coming from the south. The Musselburgh bypass (A1) is now in operation and traffic for the racecourse is much improved as a result.

Edinburgh's main railway station, Waverley, is on the excellent Intercity 125 line and Kings Cross is little more than three and a half hours away. The nearest station to the course is Musselburgh East and on racedays a courtesy bus from here will take you to the course. Check with the racecourse to find out which trains it meets. If you decide to drive you will be pleased to hear there is an excellent choice of areas in which to park your car and these are all free. Coaches are also welcome. If you are an aviator and happen to be passing in your helicopter, approach the course (by prior arrangement) from the north and land in an area adjacent to the car park.

There are two enclosures, the Members which costs £12 for a day badge and the Grandstand and Paddock where a fee of £8 is charged for entry unless you happen to be an OAP or unemployed—in which case there is a £4 levy. Accompanied children under 16 years are allowed in free and entertainment is provided for them at some meetings. £130 is charged for a year's membership with £90 being asked for an additional badge, while National Hunt season membership is available at £60. Membership includes reserved parking and reciprocal meetings at ten other courses. The 2000 fixture list was spread throughout the year with both flat racing and meetings over the jumps. There were three evening meetings during the summer, two Saturday fixtures and one on Sunday in September.

Sponsors' rooms are available for hire in the Queen's Stand, where you can entertain in style. Local companies can sponsor fences and hurdles as well as the races themselves. A hospitality complex opened a few years ago comprising 6 private boxes for groups of up to 24, a large ground floor room for parties of between 60 and 100 and a new lads canteen. The first floor Grandstand has been refurbished and there is now a Members Restaurant overlooking the racecourse. On the ground floor of the Grandstand, the Pinkie Bar has also been redone, with snacks available to patrons here.

There are a number of snack bars throughout the course and one restaurant, the Club. If you are keen to know more with regard to the racecourse catering, your initial contact should be Bill Farnsworth on 0131 665 2859.

November 1999 saw the start of a £1 million development to include a new weigh-in room; owners, trainers and members

Artist: **Peter Smith** **THREE ABREAST** *Courtesy of:* **Frost & Reed**

entrance; on-course betting shop, public food and bar outlet, plus a Tote Credit facility.

As you would expect, there are public telephones, and viewing ramps, loos and some bars for the disabled racegoers. No banking facilities are available, but if you have a particular fancy then the Tote run an on-course shop. A pleasant racecourse which is well worth a visit when looking for a few winners in 2001.

Local Favourites

Outside Edinburgh, a simply outstanding hotel should be visited if at all possible. It has the class of a Derby winner and a history and character as rich as the Grand National—**Greywalls** (01620) 842144. Overlooking Muirfield, this superb hotel and restaurant is thoroughly recommended. Gullane also reveals an excellent restaurant **La Potinière** (01620) 843214—which is small, cosy, refined and enormously popular. You really must plan ahead and book if you want a table here, but it's well worth it. Golfing enthusiasts will vouch for the fact that guesthouses of ambience abound—the **Golfers Inn** (01620) 843259 is but one example. South of Gullane in Gifford, the **Tweeddale Arms** (01620) 810240 makes a good base—ideal for exploring the East Lothian coast. Remaining outside the city, one finds Howgate and the **Old Howgate Inn** (01968) 674244, a splendid pub for food as is the **Horseshoes Inn** at Eddleston a little south of Howgate. Nearby the **Cringletie House Hotel** (01721) 730233 is an extremely welcoming hotel—comfortable too. The restaurant is also very good. Returning north to Penicuik, one finds another fine pub with a separate restaurant and some bedrooms, **Habbies Howe** (01968) 676969. In Haddington the **Waterside Bistro** (01620) 835674 comes highly recommended, and **Maitlandfield House** (01620) 826513 provides a comfortable base.

There is a whole host of restaurants outside Edinburgh. Pride of place goes to the **Champany Inn** (01506) 834532 in Linlithgow where the steaks are said to be among the finest in Britain. The **Lauriston Farm Restaurant** 0131 312 7071 is another where a slight detour will reap tasty dividends. Another within easy shooting distance is **The Cockatoo** on Old Craighill Road 0131 660 1211. A restaurant within a hotel can be found in Uphall—**Houstoun House** (01506) 853831 is a charming place in which to stay with a delightful restaurant. Finally, mention should be made of the **Cramond Inn** 0131 336 2035 at Cramond, a pleasant place to spend an evening.

In Edinburgh itself the **Caledonian Hotel** 0131 225 2433 is grand, superbly comfortable and the **Pompadour** restaurant is really something to cherish and the **George Hotel** 0131 225 1251 is first class. The **Balmoral Hotel** 0131 5562414 on Princes Street is a luxurious experience and houses two outstanding restaurants in **Number One** and **Hadrian's**. Less traditional is the **Sheraton Grand Hotel**, one of the racecourse's major sponsors, 0131 229 9131, which stands opposite the Usher Hall. As you will imagine there is a whole range of hotels in Edinburgh and it is a delightful city to visit. **Channings** 0131 315 2226 is a townhouse hotel to savour.

*Artist: **Peter Smith** **SHARP WORK** Courtesy of: **Frost & Reed***

The **Managing Director** at Newbury is **Mark Kershaw** and he can be contacted at **The Racecourse, Newbury, Berkshire RG14 7NZ. Tel (01635) 40015. Fax (01635) 528354.** The **Hon Sir David Sieff** is Newbury's Chairman. **Website: www.newbury-racecourse.co.uk.**

Travellers from the east and London should use the M4 (junction 12) and complete their journey on the A4. Eastbound racegoers should also use the M4 (junction 13), while those from the south and north converge on the A34, causing chaos and terrible queues which must be circumvented if possible. However, the new bypass which is now open is helping to alleviate the situation and there are new signs directing traffic to the racecourse. One good thing—there is plenty of excellent parking once you finally do arrive! It's entirely free except for the Southmead car park at £2 and in the picnic car park where there is a £6 charge on Hennessy Day and £4 on all other days, plus £4 per adult.

A new and good idea for all meetings is to take advantage of the train. On production of your rail ticket you get £2 off entry to Members, except on Hennessy Day. Finally, if anybody wishes to jet in there is a landing strip at the racecourse, situated in the centre of the track. Please contact the Secretary for details.

With 28 days of racing both on the flat and over the jumps the Newbury racegoer is blessed with some outstanding fixtures. Races such as the Tote Gold Trophy, the Lane's End Greenham Stakes, the Juddmonte Lockinge Stakes, the Geoffrey

Freer Stakes, the Vodafone Horris Hill Stakes, the Perpetual St Simon Stakes, the Dubai Duty Free International Raceday and the Hennessy Gold Cup make racing at Newbury a delight. With so many top races on the flat and over the jumps, it's not surprising that the course is popular.

Despite the quality of racing, Double Membership was well priced at £380 in 2000 which included one non-transferable badge and one transferable badge. Single Members are charged £190. Junior Membership is £80 (18-25 year olds). A car park badge is also provided together with 29 reciprocal meetings at some excellent racecourses. In 2000 a National Hunt only membership was introduced, available at a cost of £95, an excellent deal for fans of the jumping game. Daily admission to the Club Enclosure costs between £15-26 depending on the meeting. Tattersalls will be priced at between £8 and £12 and the Silver Ring, Geoffrey Freer Stand and picnic car park at £4-6. Parties are encouraged and 20 per cent discounts are offered to groups of twelve or more except in the Members. Credit card bookings are also accepted.

The Newbury racegoer is able to enjoy an excellent view of the racecourse from most areas. The Members Restaurant can accommodate 220 people. The Moët e Chandon Champagne Bar has moved to the Hampshire Stand and offers a complete sports information service as part of the facilities. The Manton Club Room, on the top floor of the Hampshire Stand, offers a bar, restaurant, TV and betting facilities to Annual Members. The new Grandstand which replaces the old Tattersalls Grandstand

Artist: **Claire Eva Burton THE 1997 HENNESSY GOLD CUP** *Courtesy of:* **Rosenstiel's**

will be open for the 2001 season and package prices start from £25 to include admission, a 2 course meal and a seat for the day. If you do have any catering enquiries, telephone Mark Atkinson, the Catering Manager, at Sodexho (01635) 521081. Facilities for larger parties (up to 1,000) can also be arranged. Corporate entertaining facilities at Newbury are now first class and boxes and function rooms of various sizes can be reserved. Naturally, costs will vary dramatically but contact the racecourse and you are sure to be well taken care of. There are many other snack bars in all the enclosures and the restaurants and bars are open two hours before the first race. Children under 17 are admitted free into all enclosures. Younger punters may wish to make use of the Rocking Horse Nursery, which takes up to eight year olds. The fully staffed crèche is open on non-racedays as well as racedays. The idea of encouraging families to go racing is a good one and can only be of benefit for the track and hopefully the sport in general.

The racecourse provides good viewing facilities together with lavatories for the disabled. Telephones are available but surprisingly no bank has yet set up shop despite repeated requests from Newbury's management. Indeed, there have been many demands made on the Newbury Executive in recent years. By and large, they have done well and the racecourse is now one of the very best in the country. Some of the character may have been lost but this has been replaced by an amphitheatre for racing that exudes class. There are other smaller and more thoughtful examples of Newbury's efforts too. Each owner is invited for a drink and given a complimentary video should their horse win or be placed. This may seem almost trivial but owners put a lot into the sport and such little touches are appreciated.

In the years since *Travelling the Turf* was first published Newbury has achieved a great deal. It has responded to the many demands made upon it by the present day punter, offering good facilities and top class racing.

In spite of all this praise, however, there are still many areas that can be improved to make going racing the first class experience that everyone expects. Running a racecourse means operating a service business and management should pay heed to the fact that the paying public now expects and demands levels of service, and a customer-friendly approach, or it will take its leisure money elsewhere.

Newbury has always been an immensely popular racecourse and has in the past decade consistently improved its facilities and is continuing to do so in a thoroughly impressive way. The most timely hallmark in this transition is the opening of the new stand and with a very reasonable price for the package mentioned above the idea should be a certain success. It nestles in an area where racing has a strong following, is handy for London and racing's second 'city' Lambourn. It therefore need not worry as much as other courses about proposed changes to the fixture list which will jeopardise some key race nights and consequent gate receipts. The move from Saturday nights to Sundays is, in our opinion, thoroughly foolish. Yes, build up the Sunday fixture list but not at the expense of Saturday night when racecourses such as Newbury can be seen to best advantage. A visit in 2001, as ever, is definitely recommended.

Artist: **Heather St Clair Davis** **THE APPRENTICE** *Courtesy of:* **Frost & Reed**

Newbury racecourse is ideally situated well away from the capital but conveniently placed for folk from Hampshire, Oxfordshire, Berkshire and other ritzy shires of the south. In Newbury itself the **Chequers Hotel** (01635) 38000 is most convenient while at Stroud Green, the **Plough on the Green** offers a superb garden, covered barbecue area and an excellent bar. Just 500 yards opposite the main car park entrance and five minutes walk across Stroud Green it is very popular on racedays with racegoers in the know.

Farther afield, a hotel certainly worth an inspection is **Jarvis Elcot Park Hotel & Country Club** (01488) 658100, a Georgian mansion set in 16 acres of parkland overlooking the Kennet Valley. The restaurant is good here and some attractive two-day breaks are available.

Slightly farther afield is Hungerford and within its compass are some first class places to visit. The **Bear** at Hungerford (01488) 682512 is probably the best place to stay. It is a 13th century inn with an excellent welcome. If you are looking for something to eat then the set lunches are recommended while the evening menu is also good. An alternative eating place to the Bear is an extremely pleasant pub the **John O'Gaunt** (01488) 683535—a tremendous meeting place before and after racing. There are a number of bedrooms too. **Marshgate Cottage** (01488) 682307 also provides a more than comfortable bed for the night. Hungerford itself is riddled with antique shops and to many it may well be worth a visit on this score alone.

On to Pangbourne, and an old favourite, the **Copper Inn** (01189) 842244, which is thoroughly recommended. The **White Hart Inn** at Hampstead Marshall (01488) 658201 has also shown good form—good food and pleasant bedrooms. Another outstanding inn is located in Yattendon: the **Royal Oak** (01635) 201325. Once again, a splendid all-round performer—simple homely bars, a decent fire, cosy bedrooms and a really excellent restaurant. In Goring, the **John Barleycorn** and the **Miller of Mansfield** are fun pubs, ideal for a post-race celebration. Both offer simple accommodation and good bar food. The **Leatherne Bottel** (01491) 872667 offers a pleasant riverside setting in which to imbibe—a good restaurant as well. Across the Thames and into Streatley more lavish accommodation can be found at the **Swan Diplomat** (01491) 878800. An outstanding restaurant accompanies the hotel which also boasts fine leisure facilities.

Towards Wallingford, at Moulsford, lies the glorious Thames-side retreat, the **Beetle and Wedge** (01491) 651381. The restaurant here is outstanding. A real must. In Aldworth, the **Bell** (01635) 578272 is a really cosy pub in which to take shelter. Heading towards the rolling Berkshire Downs and the Ilsleys, a number of pubs can be found. In East Ilsley, the **Crown and Horns** (01635) 281545 deserves a particular mention—not least for its excellent collection of sporting prints and racing photographs, with accommodation available too. Racing enthusiasts will also enjoy the **Hare & Hounds** (01488) 71386 at Lambourn—a well trained landlord! The **Stag** is another decent pub, while in nearby West Ilsley the **Harrow** (01635) 281260 is pleasant and offers good home cooking. The **Sun in the Wood** (01635) 42377 also offers good food. Finally, for the real galloping gourmets, a trip to Great Milton will yield the majestic **Le Manoir aux Quat' Saisons** (01844) 278881. This is a restaurant with rooms of international acclaim. You will need a decent winner to meet the bill here but it is well worth it.

A pub with excellent food is the **Dundas Arms** (01488) 658263 at Kintbury. The restaurant has pride of place here

but if you are looking for a place to stay this may be your solution. The bedrooms are located in a converted stable block. In Chieveley, the **Blue Boar Inn** (01635) 248236 is handy for the M4, junction 13. In a secluded downs setting, its thatched exterior hides some splendid bar food and excellent ales. Accommodation is also available here. Another pub with an extremely popular restaurant and some comfortable bedrooms is the **Five Bells** at Wickham (01488) 38242. The answer has to be to take Friday off—go racing—eat a good lunch and in the evening nestle down in a quiet pub ready for racing on Saturday. If you do, note the **Winterbourne Arms** (01635) 248200—a pub with good food.

Other ideas? Well, in Stanford Dingley the **Old Boot** (01189) 744292 is worth a visit while the **Bull** (01189) 744409 here is a grand pub, a definite if you have won on the last. If you're travelling on the A4, as many people will, one place to pull over at is the **Rising Sun**, Woolhampton—really first class beer, good bar snacks and if you are feeling a little more peckish there is a separate restaurant. In Kingsclere, a particularly strong racing influence in the village and a rather good pub as well is the **Crown Inn** (01635) 298956.

If you get round even half of the above for goodness sake don't drive home! To that end, a few more excellent hotels. In Hurstbourne Tarrant, **Esseborne Manor** (01264) 736444 is outstanding—once again a tremendous restaurant, a warmly recommended all rounder. People heading south might wish to stay at Silchester. The **Romans Hotel** (01189) 700421 could be the answer—well priced and very comfortable.

Between Newbury and Ascot, in Shinfield one finds **L'Ortolan** (01189) 883783. The chef has an outstanding reputation and style, and high quality cuisine is quite categorically odds on. In Pingewood, the **Kirtons Hotel & Country Club** (01189) 500885 does a special racegoers package which offers good value. Nearer to Newbury, at Old Burghclere, the **Dew Pond** (01635) 278408 is well worth considering.

Newbury is one of the south's growth areas and new hotels to add to your list include **The Vineyard** (01635) 528770 in Stockcross, the **Newbury Manor Hotel** (01635) 528838 and the **Hilton Newbury Centre** (01635) 529000 in the town itself and the recently refurbished **Queens Hotel** (01635) 44518 only 2 minutes from the racecourse. The Hilton is owned by Ladbrokes and will inevitably be developing weekend breaks to tie in with the racing at Newbury. The **Donnington Valley Hotel and Golf Course** (01635) 551199 is also one for your shortlist. The **Hilton Newbury North** (01635) 247010 is also worth considering.

Outside the town, but within a decent stone's throw, one finds the **Regency Park Hotel** (01635) 871555 another first class candidate for a visit, as is a hotel that has been warmly recommended by one of our readers—the **Hinds Head Hotel** (01189) 712194 in Aldermaston. It sounds tremendous and reminds me to ask readers to let us know of any good information they might have. As all punters know, it is useful to have a little inside knowledge!

We hope you plunder a bounty or two while racing at Newbury in 2001. Very few racecourses offer as much and these local favourites also make up a select field. Whether you are popping in for a pint or two before or after racing, or organising a weekend away from it all, Berkshire offers no end of distractions.

The Vineyard at Stockcross

Just a stone's throw from Newbury Racecourse, The Vineyard is the perfect place for celebrating a successful day's racing or, indeed, any other occasion demanding simply the very best food and wine in unique and memorable surroundings.

The 'classical French cuisine with a modern British twist', is matched by one of the widest and most innovative global wine lists featuring many bottles, rarely, if ever, seen in the UK, including a number from the renowned Peter Michael Winery.

Individually designed bedrooms and suites are complemented by a stimulating collection of paintings and sculptures. The Vineyard Spa, with its superb beauty treatment suites, provides the perfect environment in which to relax.

The Vineyard at Stockcross
Newbury
Berkshire
RG20 8JU
Tel: (01635) 528770
Fax: (01635) 528398
web site: www.the-vineyard.co.uk

Donnington Valley Hotel

Within close proximity of Newbury Racecourse, Donnington Valley Hotel is an individually designed 4 star hotel offering uncompromising quality and personal service. The newly refurbished 'Wine Press' restaurant offers a choice of both modern and traditional dishes in relaxed surroundings. The food is complemented by a large selection of over 350 wines, including those from the Peter Michael Winery in California.

The hotel is surrounded by its own superb 18 hole, 71 par golf course with a Grade II listed Victorian clubhouse offering visitors exceptional facilities.

Donnington Valley Hotel and Golf Club
Old Oxford Road
Donnington
Newbury
Berkshire
RG14 3AG
Tel: (01635) 551199
Fax: (01635) 551123
web site: www.donningtonvalley.co.uk

Major David McAllister is **Clerk of the Course** and he, together with **Chairman, Stan Clarke CBE,** and **General Manager, Grant Knowles** can be contacted at **Newcastle Racecourse, High Gosforth Park, Newcastle upon Tyne NE3 5HP. Tel 0191 236 2020. Fax 0191 236 7761. Web site www.newcastleracecourse.co.uk. E mail: info@newcastleracecourse.co.uk.**

Those who are making the trip to Newcastle from the south should remember that the city can be bypassed by following the A1. The racecourse is in High Gosforth Park, which can be accessed by taking the junction signposted Wideopen. The same applies to those travelling from the north. From the east, use the A19 and A1056. The Western bypass has cut about twenty minutes from the journey around the city. The journey from Newcastle's Tyneside to London's Thameside is a good 280 miles and one mode of transport to use is the electrified Great North Eastern Railway service from Kings Cross. The course is a further four miles or so from Newcastle's Central Station—a fifteen minute taxi journey. The Metro, Newcastle's underground, can be taken to South Gosforth, Regent Centre or Four Lane Ends, and on racedays a free bus service operates between these stations and the course, two hours prior to the first race and for one hour after the last. Quicker transportation can be found by using the nearby airport or, if prior notice is given, you may land a helicopter. There is ample parking, all free of charge, with areas for Annual Members and disabled guests.

There are now 30 flat and national hunt fixtures throughout the year at Gosforth Park and the highlight of the season is the new three-day Northumberland Plate Festival in late June which runs from Thursday to Saturday and includes a Friday evening meeting. Saturday sees the £130,000 Northumberland Plate, a handicap over two miles which always attracts large fields. Highlights of the National Hunt season are the Fighting Fifth Hurdle and the Tote Northern National, one of the warm-up races for the Grand National.

Members Club Enclosure badges cost £15 increasing to £25 at the Plate meeting. Good value are Tattersalls at £10 (£12 for Plate Day) or the Silver Ring at £5 at all times. There is a concession for advance-booked parties of 15 or more, with a £2 discount for OAPs and disabled people. Annual Membership is £250 for a double badge and £165 for a single. These prices include a car park badge and numerous reciprocal meetings across the country as well as free admission to Uttoxeter and Brighton races.

The facilities at the course include privately leased boxes and rooms for hire and areas for marquees should you have something a little more adventurous in mind. The Members' Enclosure comprises restaurants, a carvery, bars and a food take-away counter, with a separate restaurant for owners and trainers. The Silver Ring and Tattersalls both have large grandstands, long bars, toilets, betting shops, Tote, food take-away counters and access to a Family Foodhall. Numerous snack bars are available for you while you sup the Newky Brown.

Annual and Daily Members have benefited from the many improvements at the course. The refurbished Members' Grandstand has twelve hospitality boxes, with an Annual Members restaurant/bar and a Daily Members Bar and Carvery take-away counter, also Tote and betting shops are available.

 Artist: **Philip Toon FINAL ADJUSTMENTS** *Courtesy of:* **The Artist**

Children under 16, with an adult, are admitted free to all enclosures. At weekend and Bank Holiday meetings entertainments are arranged for them—including Punch & Judy shows, funfair rides, face painting etc.

Since Gosforth Park has been taken over, there has been a £4 million renovation programme to date. Moving the Winners Enclosure to the front of the stands has been a major benefit for all racegoers. The reinstatement of the first furlong on the picturesque Mile—over which the Blaydon Race is now run is also a plus for the course. The reintroduction of the Blaydon Races in August is an obvious and appealing marketing concept. Make no mistake, this is a racecourse on the up. One to visit in 2001.

Local Favourites

The busy city of Newcastle lies close to the racecourse, but at the same time, Scotland, the Lake District and North Yorkshire are all within striking distance. In the Tyne Valley a Country House to consider is **Newbrough Lodge** (01434) 674545. A pleasant place to stay in Longhorsley is the **Linden Hall Hotel** (01670) 516611—it has a delightful setting in 300 acres of parkland, with the added attraction of an 18 hole golf course. The **Granby** (01665) 570228 in Longframlington, further north, is an ideal pub for a weekend in the country. Also out of town is the **Plough Inn** (01661) 853555—a pub with a restaurant, and **Horton Grange** (01661) 860686, located five miles from the course. The restaurant here is excellent.

Two comfortable hotels are the **Holiday Inn** in Seaton Burn 0191 236 5432 with good leisure facilities—ideal for business people—and the **Swallow Gosforth Park Hotel** 0191 236 4111. This is an excellent, modern hotel where the **Brandling** restaurant offers nouvelle cuisine. Both are convenient for the racecourse, the latter being right next door. In town The **Copthorne Newcastle** 0191 222 0333 and the **Vermont** Hotels 0191 233 1010 are excellent, as is **Malmaison** 0191 245 5000 a little further along the Quayside, overlooking the River Tyne.

Newcastle also has a variety of fabulous restaurants. The **Fisherman's Lodge** in Jesmond Dene 0191 281 3281 is a super restaurant while on the quayside **Uno's** 0191 261 5264 is very popular. Lovers of Chinese food are spoilt for choice on Stowell Street. Sample any of the following; the **Mandarin** 0191 261 7881, the **King Neptune** 0191 261 6657, the **Royal Circle** 0191 261 2300 and the **Palace Garden** 0191 232 3117; and for lovers of Indian cuisine, **Sachins** 0191 261 9035, serves up a tasty treat and **Vujon** 0191 2210601 is a must. Arguably Newcastle's finest restaurant is **21 Queen Street** 0191 222 0755 on Princes Wharf virtually beneath the Tyne Bridge. Round the corner, **Treacle Moon** 0191 232 5537 is also very good and **Est Est Est** 0191 260 2291 caters for lovers of Italian cuisine.

Some great pubs of note include the **Crown Posada**, and **Kinnears**, part of the Theatre Royal on Grey Street. Also on Grey Street, the **Metropolitan** 0191 2302306 is a great restaurant for lunch or supper. Also, the **Shiremoor House Farm** 0191 257 6302 pub and restaurant, which is noted for its beer range. Lovers of nightlife must check out the Quayside—for atmosphere it's hard to beat.

Take a blend of period architectural styles. Add the reputation of one of the finest hotels and widely acclaimed restaurants in the UK. Stir gently through years of private ownership and garnish with 21st Century leisure opportunities. Then serve large helpings of the Hintlesham Hall house of hospitality, nestling in its own Suffolk estate about 45 minutes from Newmarket.

The distinctive Georgian facade masks the Hall's Elizabethan origins which become obvious from the tranquil rear gardens. There, in the adjacent park and renowned herb garden, you would hardly know that the Hall's own 18 hole championship golf course is alongside or that the Orangery is a modern health and fitness boutique with state-of-the-art equipment, excellent instruction and specialist treatments. Saunas, steam and spa are in the Clubhouse along with alternative dining opportunities.

Minutes from Ipswich's Inter City rail station and from the A12 and A14 (to Newmarket), Hintlesham Hall is close to many of Suffolk's 16th Century wool villages: A treasure trove for antique hunters, this lovely corner of England also offers The Heritage Coast, Constable Country, a wealth of period properties and easy access to London, Cambridge and The Midlands.

Hintlesham Hall
Hintlesham
Nr Ipswich
Suffolk IP8 3NS
Tel: (01473) 652334
Fax: (01473) 652463
e mail: reservations@hintlesham-hall.co.uk
web site: www.hintlesham-hall.co.uk

The town of Newmarket seems to breathe racing and it is blessed with two of the finest courses in Britain. The Guineas meeting 2000 witnessed the opening of the Millennium Stand at Newmarket by Her Majesty The Queen. Although corporate entertaining facilities are top notch there was considerable disaffection from many of Newmarket's annual members who considered they had fared badly by comparison. It is difficult to know exactly how the annual members are regarded in the pecking order when compared with the corporate visitor. On the one hand a good lump of cash comes in one block. On the other the price per admission is considerably higher. Any diplomat would suggest that both are equally significant and if we accept this it appears that Newmarket needs to offer the annual member a few sweeteners.

One thing that is for certain is the quality of the racing on offer at Newmarket which remains excellent and with the Rowley Mile and the July Course the Newmarket visitor has two courses offering a feast of top quality horse racing.

Newmarket certainly has an energetic team and Chairman Peter Player will surely win back the the confidence and cash of annual members. In essence racing on the Rowley Mile is extraordinary with the horses thundering at you from the heath, passing the bushes and flashing by the stands. Both Newmarket courses host excellent race days and the Champions meeting as well as the Guineas weekend offer particularly fine racing. This is a racecourse that has a fascinating history and a great future so a visit in 2001 is thoroughly recommended. The management team here is headed by **Nick Lees** the **Clerk of the Course** and **Director of Racing**, and by the new **Managing Director, Lisa Rowe.** They are ably assisted by **Gaynor Haxby** as **Commercial Manager** and **Christian Mitchell** as **Operations Manager** who can be contacted at **Westfield House, Camridge Road, Newmarket, Suffolk CB8 0TG**. Tel **(01638) 663482 Fax (01638) 663044** or at **The Racecourse, Rowley Mile**. **Tel (01638) 662762**. The **July Racecourse** telephone number is **(01638) 662752 and the booking hotline** is **(01638) 675500.** Membership enquiries are dealt with on **(01638) 675555**You can also visit Newmarket via the Internet at **www.newmarketracecourses.co.uk.**

Crowds flock to Newmarket for their many popular meetings, so an early start is recommended. From London it is a mere 60 mile sprint up the M11—exit junction 9 for the new dual carriageway A11, leaving it at Six Mile Bottom and thence to Newmarket. The A14 links Felixstowe with the M1 and M6, and the A1 will assist both northbound and southbound visitors. Racegoers on busy days should note the back exit via Exning onto the A14, thus avoiding the particularly heavy going. From Norwich and the east, the A11 is the obvious route, while from Bury St Edmunds the A45 can be useful. There are numerous car parks on the Heath for both cars and coaches.

If travelling by train, start at Liverpool Street. Buses meet the trains in Cambridge and ensure prompt delivery to the races. A further innovation is the introduction of a separate free bus service to the course from the station and Newmarket High Street. The CAA have given their permission for use of the July landing strip when there is racing on the July course, although craft must not land or take off over the racecourse buildings. The Rowley Mile strip can also be used.

Major races include the two Classics, the Sagitta 1000 and 2000 Guineas. Special entertainment is usually laid on including bands and special children's facilities and an enormous shopping mall—and of course, first class racing. Other highlights include the Cesarewitch, the Cambridgeshire, the Craven Stakes, the Cheveley Park Stakes, the Middle Park, and the Dewhurst.

Artist: **Martin Williams UNDER THE TREES, NEWMARKET** *Courtesy of:* **Osborne Studio Gallery**

The ambience of the two Newmarket courses—the Rowley Mile and the July Racecourse—is totally different with the former featuring racing in spring and autumn in a highly professional manner and the latter creating an excellent atmosphere in beautiful surroundings for the more relaxed summer meetings. Attending one of the popular evening meetings on the July Course is a tremendous way to relax and forget your troubles.

In 2001, membership rates will be £250 for an Annual Members badge with a £50 joining fee which will include free admission and car parking at 35 meetings starting with the Craven Meeting in April and ending with the Final Meeting in October, and there are also 4 reciprocal day's racing at Cheltenham, Goodwood, Doncaster and Sandown Park. For Juniors (16-25), a badge is well priced at £100 with a £15 joining fee. Inaugural membership requires an additional fee of £35 for senior members and £10 for juniors. Daily prices vary. On the 1000 and 2000 Guineas days and the Dubai Champion Stakes Day Members Badges cost around £30. Other feature days are priced at £25 with all other days at the £18 mark. Admission to the Grandstand is £12 on ordinary days, rising to £15 on the four big days. Of note is the fact that the Tattersalls facilities on the Rowley Mile now offer some of the best value racing entertainment in Britain. The Silver Ring enclosure has a similar system—£5 and £4 being the respective asking prices. Parties of 20 or more are offered a 20 per cent discount if arranged in advance with the racecourse. Children under 16 years are admitted free and there is a creche which is open on all days on the July course and for some fixtures held on

the Rowley mile. A fully equipped playground is available throughout the season.

Of course during the building of the new stand on the Rowley Mile Course, the facilities for corporate entertaining were moved to the July Course. On the July Course, the oak panelled Queens Room and the Jockey Club Dining Room are also available for hire. As the entertainment facilities are so comprehensive it is advisable to contact the racecourse. The racecourse caterers Letheby & Christopher, (01638) 662750 are also happy to assist with any catering requirements. The old thatched bar on the July Course has been replaced by the splendid Dante Bar and will soon be complemented by a refurbished and adjoining new Members Bar. The new Ocean Swell Bar has also been a great success.

Telephones are available as well as extra betting facilities. Disabled people have lavatories, escalators help the elderly and overall, everyone from junior to senior is well catered for. Newmarket offers two well run racecourses. They differ dramatically—the Rowley Mile exudes history while the July Course is one of the most picturesque in the country.

Newmarket is the capital of British Racing and a trip around the town to the gallops, museum, National Stud and all manner of friendly boozers will reveal this spirit. The racecourse needs to be a beacon of this excellence - after all this is where so many of the great tussles took place in those early days, on the Rowley Mile.

Swynford Paddocks

Swynford Paddocks Hotel & Restaurant
Swynford Paddocks is an elegant eighteenth century country house hotel nestling in idyllic countryside with racehorses grazing its pastures. Situated just outside Newmarket, and only six miles from the ancient university city of Cambridge, the hotel is reached easily from both the A11 and A14.

The hotel's 15 bedrooms, each with views of the surrounding countryside, are individually decorated to the highest standards. The intimate panelled restaurant is renowned for its first-class cuisine and features an imaginative menu which changes regularly to take advantage of fresh seasonal fayre.

The hotel's relaxing atmosphere, tranquil surroundings and ample parking make it an ideal venue for all forms of corporate entertainment. The extensive and attractive grounds form an ideal backdrop for any event, while a luxury marquee can accommodate up to 180 guests.

Swynford Paddocks Hotel & Restaurant,
Six Mile Bottom, Newmarket, Suffolk CB8 0UE
Tel: (01638) 570234
Fax: (01638) 570283
web site: www.swynfordpaddocks.com
e mail: sales@swynfordpaddocks.com

SWYNFORD PADDOCKS
HOTEL AND RESTAURANT

Swynford Paddocks Stud
Whether it's a racehorse enjoying a break before resuming its career, convalescence after surgery or a yearling or juvenile embarking on a pre-sales or pre-training regime, we cater for their every need.

A modern dedicated foaling unit allows us to take in expectant mares through to delivery, as well as mares scheduled to be covered. Stallion selection and mare compatibility, timings and budgets, the welfare of mares and foals - we can assist you in your quest for future winners.

For further information please contact the Stud Manager on (01638) 570232, or the hotel.

Nestled within seven acres of garden and woodland, Ravenwood Hall offers tranquillity and seclusion but is merely a few miles from Newmarket. An impressive Tudor building, the Hall, with its striking elaborate oak carving and wall paintings, dates back to 1530 and the turbulent reign of Henry VIII. Having survived this fascinating period of English history, it has now become one of England's finer country house hotels. The 14 comfortable bedrooms have private bathrooms and are furnished with antiques reflecting the Hall's historic tradition.

For the racing enthusiast Ravenwood could not be better situated as it is so close to the historic town of Newmarket. Transport to and from the races can be arranged if required.

The Hall is also perfectly positioned to visit the historic University city of Cambridge, with its wealth of beautiful colleges, fascinating traditions and architecture. Punting on the River Cam makes a perfect summer afternoon, while the world famous Fitzwilliam Museum is well worth a long visit.

The famous medieval wool towns of Lavenham and Long Melford, with their wealth of timbered houses and antique shops, are just waiting to be explored whilst the bustling market town of Bury St Edmunds offers many historic attractions.

For the avid golfer there are two well kept courses nearby. Fishing and riding can both be arranged whilst hotel proprietor,

Craig Jarvis is a keen point-to-point rider who regularly takes guests to local meets and takes pride in organising a splendid day's hunting or driven shooting by prior arrangement. Many pleasurable hours can also be spent using the hotel's leisure facilities including a hard tennis court, a croquet lawn, and a heated swimming pool. There are also plenty of woodland walks in the countryside surrounding the Hall.

On returning from your day's pursuits, relax beside a blazing inglenook fire enjoying a cream tea in winter or recline by the heated swimming pool sipping a refreshing drink in summer.

Finish the day off in the impressive restaurant which retains its carved timbers and huge inglenook fireplace from Tudor Times. This makes for a cosy and intimate atmosphere in which to enjoy the delights of the kitchen served with traditional courtesy.

With home preserved fruits and vegetables, and with meats and fish smoked on the premises, the Head Chef, Annete Beasant uses the abundant seasonal foods locally produced, with flair and imagination. All this combines into a menu which is both adventurous and classical, featuring many long-forgotten English recipes.

For a less formal setting, hearty bar meals are also served in the cosy informality of The Bar.

Ravenwood Hall Country Hotel & Restaurant
Rougham, Bury St Edmunds
Suffolk IP30 9JA
Tel: (01359) 270345
Fax: (01359) 270788
e mail: enquiries@ravenwoodhall.co.uk
web site: www.ravenwoodhall.co.uk

For centuries the Black Lion has commanded its glorious position overlooking the Green in Long Melford under the imposing gaze of the church. Since at least 1661 guests have enjoyed its fine hospitality and the hotel has received wide acclaim for its superb food and splendid accommodation. Recognised by all major guides, the Black Lion is enjoyed by visitors and locals alike. It has recently undergone a major refurbishment and is the latest in a small group of historic hotels and restaurants in Suffolk which includes Ravenwood Hall near Bury St Edmunds and Tuddenham Mill near Newmarket.

Classically influenced, mouthwatering dishes are freshly made to order using fresh locally grown Suffolk produce seasoned with herbs cultivated in the garden. The Black Lion offers a wide choice of fixed price menus and a full à la carte menu to stimulate your tastebuds. Just the thing after a hard day at the races. The menu changes regularly to reflect seasonal dishes to be accompanied by fine wines.

After your meal retire to the comfort of the lounge or pass through the French windows into the walled courtyard garden beyond. Just the place to unwind after dinner or whilst studying the Racing Post after a hearty country breakfast. If you still have the energy then you will find bookcases offering reading matter on every conceivable subject and games to while away the time on rainy days.

And so to bed. The hotel's ten light and airy en-suite bedrooms are beautifully furnished with antiques. All rooms overlook the village green out over the gates and turrets of Melford Hall and have colour televisions, direct dial telephones and generous hospitality trays. If you are lucky you could be sleeping in one of the two four poster beds or luxuriating in an antique brass bedstead or even a mahogany half tester in the bridal suite. Several of the rooms are suitable for families and well behaved children are very welcome. Dogs are accepted by appointment.

Long Melford is famous for quaint architecture and a wealth of antique shops. A stone's throw away are two 15th century manor houses: Kentwell Hall lovingly restored to its medieval splendour, and National Trust Melford Hall, the family seat of the Hyde-Parkers, who are still in residence. Other places of interest nearby include the wool village of Lavenham, historic Bury St Edmunds, Sudbury, the birthplace of Thomas Gainsborough, the university city of Cambridge, Newmarket, the home of British racing, and Constable country.

A veritable home from home. You can be assured of a warm welcome at the Black Lion in Long Melford.

Black Lion Hotel & Restaurant
Church Walk
The Green
Long Melford
Suffolk, CO10 9DN
Tel: (01787) 312356
Fax: (01787) 374557
web site: www.ravenwoodhall.co.uk

Icannot recommend a visit to Newmarket more highly. If you want to stay in style and don't mind a short drive, **Swynford Paddocks** (01638) 570234 is ideal. This outstanding hotel located in Six Mile Bottom has elegant bedrooms and an excellent restaurant. Closer to home, the High Street of Newmarket offers a number of places to stay. The **Rutland Arms** (01638) 664251 and the **White Hart** (01638) 663051 opposite the Jockey Club are both comfortable and convenient, while on the Bury Road, the **Bedford Lodge** (01638) 663175 is a popular racing location. Bar snacks in all the above hotels are good and dining is also available. Lovers of Chinese food should earmark **The Fountain**—pricey but good. A less extravagant, although still highly recommended establishment is **Hill Farmhouse** (01638) 730253 which can be found to the south of the racecourse in Kirtling. A modern, but well located hotel is the **Heath Court** (01638) 667171—ideal for early morning gallops. Brasserie 22 (01638) 660646 in the High Street is also worthy of note. There are many outstanding hotels in East Anglia. One thinks of **Le Maison Talbooth** (01206) 322367 in Dedham near Colchester (note the outstanding Talbooth restaurant—really first class). In Woodbridge, **Seckford Hall** (01394) 385678 is a supremely comfortable country house hotel, while closer to Newmarket in Bury St Edmunds, the **Angel** (01284) 753926 is a fine house with a first class restaurant. Another to note here is the **Priory** (01284) 706101. **Ravenwood Hall** (01359) 271542 at Rougham Green is also well placed for visiting racegoers and a warm welcome is assured. Further south in Broxted, the **Whitehall** (01279) 850603 is another appealing manor with a splendid restaurant. The **Great House** (01787) 247431 at Lavenham should not be forgotten either with delicious French and English cooking. Meanwhile at Hintlesham, one finds **Hintlesham Hall** (01473) 852334—a classic stayer with a golf course and some excellent cuisine.

Lovers of pub food will also be spoilt. In Dullingham, the **Kings Head** (01634) 842709 is a friendly, extremely busy racing pub with an excellent restaurant. In nearby Woodditton, another popular pub is the **Three Blackbirds** (01638) 730811, a mere five minute's drive from the Rowley Mile racecourse. Other excellent establishments include two **Red Lions** - one at Icklingham (01638) 717802 and one at Hinxton (01799) 530601 - good food at both. The **Star** at Lidgate (01638) 500275 is also a good choice and the racing fraternity is particularly keen on the **Old Plough** at Ashley. Another real favourite is the excellent **Affleck Arms** at Dalham (01638 500306).

Two Cambridge hotels often used for Newmarket meetings are the **University Arms** (01223) 351241 and the **Garden House** (01223) 259988. The one overlooks Parkers Piece and the other the River Cam—both are excellent. Cambridge is also the

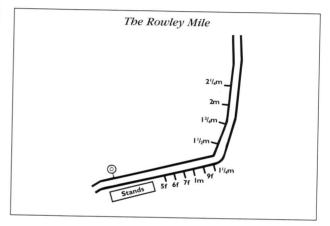

The Rowley Mile

2¼m
2m
1¾m
1½m
1¼m
5f 6f 7f 1m 9f
Stands

*Artist: **John Atkins** NEWMARKET Courtesy of: **The Artist***

perfect town in which to leave the person who may find a day or a week at the races a trifle tedious. Two excellent restaurants to note in the city are **Midsummer House** (01223) 369299 on Midsummer Common or **22 Chesterton Road** (01223) 351880—ideal for pre-sales, or post-racing discussions.

Other restaurants to consider include **Bradfield House** (01284) 386301 at Bradfield Combust—excellent English cooking, but do note the restaurant closes for lunch on Saturday—some rooms here as well. The **Hole in the Wall** (01223) 812282 in Wilbraham is a fine restaurant, but please remember to book in advance. Also in Bury St Edmunds is the **Butterfly** (01284) 760884, with a modern, continental feel, and in nearby Ixworth **Theobalds Restaurant** (01359) 31707 is there for discovering, open fire and all. North of Newmarket one finds the superb cathedral at Ely. In the same town the **Lamb** (01353) 663574 is comfortable while the **Old Fire Engine** (01353) 662582 produces some outstanding food—well worth the trip. If Chinese cooking is your style then try the **Peking Duck** (01353) 662063. Another good hotel near Ely is the aptly named **Fenlands Lodge** (01353) 667047, which is comfortable and the restaurant is also good. In Glemsford, a restaurant to shortlist is **Barretts** (01787) 281573—excellent sauces and a fine wine list. **Stocks Restaurant** (01223) 811202 in Botisham also comes warmly recommended by a man in the know.

In case you have time between racing and opening time, or whatever you happen to be awaiting in Newmarket, we would strongly recommend you visit the National Horseracing Museum, a well thought-out establishment which owes much to the support of Britain's best known owners. The High Street reveals all manner of interesting shops—saddlers, tailors, bookshops and galleries.

With the fabulous array of weekend meetings as well as midweek occasions we will endeavour to recommend some pleasant inns, or pubs with rooms nearby. In Kennett, north of Newmarket, the **Bell** (01638) 750286 is an idea, while to the south, in Kirtling, the **Queens Head** (01638) 731737 will not disappoint; it is a delightful 16th century building and offers excellent food. Further afield in Lavenham, the **Swan** (01787) 247477 is a delightful 14th century inn which also boasts a first-class restaurant. A free house which is a delight to visit

is the **Angel** at Lavenham (01787) 247388—good food and some accommodation—ideal. While in Long Melford, four establishments are worth considering: firstly, the excellent **Black Lion** (01787) 312356 is highly recommended and secondly, the **Bull** (01787) 378494. **Chimneys** (01787) 379806 is a restaurant with an excellent reputation and Scutchers (01787) 310200 makes up a magnificent four timer. **Alfonso's** (01787) 280372 in Cavendish is a splendid Italian restaurant opposite the village green. Returning towards Newmarket, the **Bell** (01638) 717272 at Mildenhall is a fine all-rounder and is pretty good value. Also consider the **Green Man** at Six Mile Bottom (01638) 570373; it is owned by a very keen racing man and by all accounts an evening here offers that happy combination of quality fayre and good company.

One final thought for the racing enthusiast who also enjoys golf and has a taste for style and elegance—try **Hanbury Manor** (01920) 487722. It is a fair distance from Newmarket but is outstanding in every way. A place to spoil your non-racing partner!

Racing at Newmarket is to be recommended. From the bustling betting shop to the early morning gallops, from a smoke filled boozer to wide open heath, this is quintessentially a racing town and if you are looking for a day or two away in 2000, Newmarket is a worthy favourite.

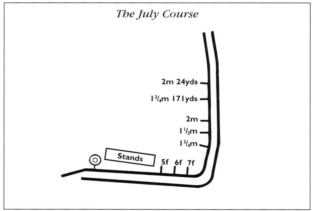

The July Course

2m 24yds

1³/₄m 171yds

2m

1¹/₂m

1³/₄m

Stands   5f 6f 7f

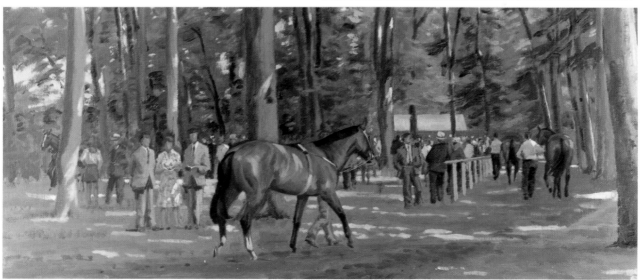

*Artist: **Neil Cawthorne** JULY COURSE Courtesy of: **The Artist***

The course is managed by **Pat Masterson** and he will be able to provide details of all the goings on at Newton Abbot. The **Clerk of the Course** is **R D Farrant** and all enquiries should be directed to **The Racecourse, Kingsteignton Road, Newton Abbot. Tel (01626) 353235, Fax (01626) 336972. Website: www.newton-abbot-races.co.uk.**

The racecourse is easily accessible via the M5, joined by the M4 and M6. The course is located just off the A380 which joins the M5. If you are journeying from Cornwall then a number of A roads are convenient. The A38 from Plymouth and the A30 via Okehampton are two obvious selections. It is as well to try to time your journey well because the M5 can get ridiculously one-paced on occasions. Despite the rural setting, the public transport services are good. Trains depart from Paddington and a bus can then be taken from the local station to the racecourse. Helicopters are welcomed at the course and car parking is free unless you wish to park beside the course rails.

The feature races in a busy fixture list of National Hunt racing include the Claude Whitley Memorial Cup Steeplechase and William Hill Hurdle, both £8000 added races in November, along with the Langstone Cliff Hotel Steeplechase and Thurlestone Hotel Hurdle on Boxing Day. The course holds an abundance of meetings in August and has just added some summer jumping to its calendar.

Newton Abbot is one of the few racecourses for which there is no Members Enclosure. The two enclosures are the Paddock for which a charge of £11 applies and £5 for the Course Enclosure. Despite the absence of a Members Enclosure, a season ticket can be obtained for £120 which includes 36 reciprocal meetings. People who are holidaying in groups and local people should note the following discount rates. Essentially, if you get ten or more people together you will save £2 per head on admission into the Tattersalls Enclosure if you book in advance. The course has a good selection of sponsors and they generally make use of the private function rooms. Eleven private boxes are also available for hire, some by the day, The Teign Suite has recently been extended and there is also a large sponsors' suite which can accommodate up to 250. However, if you wish to organise a substantial party, do telephone the course to check on availability. An alternative if these rooms are unavailable is to have a marquee in Tattersalls. It is clear, however, that the course really relies on the passing racegoer and they will be pleased to hear that picnics can be enjoyed at the racecourse—a charge of £1.50 is made for cars parked alongside the rails. If self-catering sounds too much like hard work, then there is the new Terrace Restaurant which overlooks the winning post, along with a self-service carvery and more modest snacks in the bars. Any prior enquiries with regard to catering should be made to the racecourse or alternatively, addressed to the racecourse's caterers Partyfare Ltd. (01626) 331285 or (01404) 43035. Although children are admitted free, there are no special play areas for them. There are three public telephones and disabled people have the benefit of a viewing ramp and a lift in the Grandstand and the Teign Suite.

For those racing fans looking for a long weekend in the country, this is a fabulous answer. The racecourse is extremely welcoming and the standard of racing is not bad. There are also many splendid hostelries nearby in which to spend your ill-gotten gains.

*Artist: **Margaret Barrett** MUD SLINGERS Courtesy of: **The Artist***

Local Favourites

In Newton Abbot, the **Queens Hotel** (01626) 363133 welcomes visitors before and after racing, as does the excellent **Langstone Cliff Hotel** (01626) 865155. A reasonably priced alternative is the **Lamora Guest House** (01626) 65627. There is also the **Passage House Hotel** (01626) 55515—modern but extremely welcoming—and the **Two Mile Oak** (01803) 812411—really filling bar snacks. One such pub in Kingsteignton is the excellent **Old Rydon Inn** (01626) 54626. Another king this time in Kingskerswell, **Pitt House** (01803) 873374 is a good restaurant in a 15th century thatched dower-house.

If you have the chance, visit Dartmouth, where the **Carved Angel** (01803) 832465 is the finest restaurant in the area. Another excellent port of call in this delightful naval town is the **Royal Castle** (01803) 833033. All along the coast one finds nooks and crannies to explore and eventually one arrives at the larger resorts of Paignton, Torbay and Torquay. In Staverton both **Kingston House** (01803) 762235 and the **Sea Trout Inn** (01803) 762274 are worth visiting.

There are all manner of activities to be found in Torquay and having played golf, fished or even after a trip to the races one place to visit is **Remy's** (01803) 292359, ideal for dinner. Further round the coast one comes to Teignmouth and the extremely welcoming **Bay Hotel** (01626) 774123. No less excellent is **Thomas Luny House** (01626) 772976, an award-winning, yet relatively inexpensive guesthouse. For people not wishing to visit the coast there are a number of excellent and secluded places to sample. A quiet country inn in which to spend a night is the **Rock Inn** (01364) 661305 in Haytor Vale. In nearby Haytor, the **Bel Alp House** (01364) 661217 is an extremely welcoming country house hotel to consider, as is the excellent **Leusdon Lodge** (01364) 631304 in Poundsgate. In Ashburton, the **Holne Chase Hotel** (01364) 631471 is a superb place to stay and it also has a fine restaurant.

There are seven public houses by the name of **Church House** within a small radius. One you should certainly visit is located in Rattery (01364) 642220—a welcoming place for a drink and substantial bar snacks. Another is in **Torbryan** (01803) 812372—typically cosy. Nearer to Newton Abbot is Woodland and the superb **Rising Sun**. The **Hare and Hounds** (01626) 873119 at Kingskerswell has a good carvery the **Barn Owl** (01803) 872130—is extremely friendly and has bedrooms—the **Chasers Arms** (01626) 873119 at Stokeinteignhead is also recommended.

*Artist: **John Atkins** **LOOSE HORSE** Courtesy of: **The Artist***

Buckland-Tout-Saints is a small luxury country house hotel situated in one of the most idyllic locations in the United Kingdom. Set in spectacular gardens and woodlands in the heart of the beautiful South Hams area of South Devon, close to the Kingsbridge Estuary, the hotel occupies an impressive grade two listed manor house built in 1690 which was turned into a hotel in 1956 and then extensively renovated in 1999.

Deluxe rooms and luxury suites, many with fabulous views, exceptional French and English cuisine, fine wines and friendly and caring staff, help to create the very special Buckland ambience. The peaceful surroundings enjoyed by private guests also make Buckland-Tout-Saints an ideal venue for exclusive conferences, corporate entertainment and board meetings. Private dinner parties and weddings (several rooms are licensed for civil ceremonies) can also be arranged, and it is a secure environment for confidential meetings. Whether you are organising an event for two or two hundred people, helpful staff and elegant facilities combine to create the best possible solution to meet your specific requirements.

The hotel has a helicopter-landing site and will arrange helicopter transportation to meet your requirements. There is also a hotel minibus for your convenience. Less then two miles from Kingsbridge, several well known golf courses and the famous sailing centres of Dartmouth and Salcombe lie within a ten mile radius. Golfing, sailing, fishing and shooting, together with many other activities, can be arranged by request. The wilds of Dartmoor, Dartington Glassworks, numerous quaint fishing ports and several National Trust properties are nearby.

Buckland-Tout-Saints Hotel & Restaurant
Goveton
Kingsbridge
Devon
TQ7 2DS
Tel: 01548 853055
Fax: 01548 856261
e mail: buckland@tout-saints. co.uk

Nottingham is run by the **Racecourse Manager, Sally Westcott**, ably assisted by **Secretary**, **Ann Whelbourne** and **Events & Leisure co-ordinator, Nina Daly** (the friendliest team in the Midlands—so they tell us!) **Clerk of the Course** is **Major Charles Moore**. The team can be contacted at **Nottingham Racecourse, Colwick Park, Colwick Road, Nottingham NG2 4BE. Tel (01159) 580620. Fax (01159) 584515. E mail: nottingham@rht.net. Web site: www.nottinghamracecourse.co.uk.**

The course lies east of the city off the B686 Colwick road. The M1 offers good going but does suffer from the odd tailback. Southbound travellers should exit at junction 25 and follow the A52 to pick up the A6011 at West Bridgford. From there follow the brown tourist signs and the Park & Ride racecourse signs. The A46 from Leicester is an alternative although renowned for one-paced lorries. From the A46, follow the A606 and the A612. The nearest railway station is in the city, two miles from the course (trains leave London from St Pancras). Buses (Nos 20 and 21) leave the city centre every 15 minutes. If you do take the wheels, you will be pleased to hear that all parking is free. Helicopters may land in the centre of the course by prior arrangement with the management.

Nottingham used to be a dual purpose course, but a couple of years ago switched to flat racing only. Even so Annual Members get to enjoy about 20 fixtures between March and October with a number of reciprocal days at other racecourses and Nottinghamshire County Cricket. The summer Saturday and evening fixtures of free entertainment have proved to be very popular—demonstrating that when racecourses do offer

an extra something it certainly pays off.

In 2000, entrance to the Members Enclosure in the Centenary Stand was £15, the Grandstand in Tattersalls £10 and the Silver Ring £5. Annual Membership costs £145 or £270 for a married couple, including parking and use of the Centenary Stand and Enclosure. A Junior badge for those 16-24 years old costs £80 and Jubilee Club Membership is available to anyone over the age of 65. For a lifetime joining fee of £5, discounted admission is available into the Silver Ring (£3) and Tattersalls (£7) at all fixtures. All annual badges entitle the bearer to a free racecard as well as discounts on admission for their guests, a real incentive to join that should be taken up by other courses. Nottingham also offers discounts for those who pay for their annual membership early. Children under 16 are admitted free if accompanied by an adult.

The Grandstand has also been refurbished. Recent innovations include a new Sheriff of Nottingham foodcourt, a significantly enhanced Member's Restaurant, a new Tattersalls Bar on the first floor with access directly onto the Steppings and a Champagne and Seafood bar. There is also a lift to all floors in the Grandstand. The private boxes have capacities of between twelve and eighty people. Packages are available to include badges, bar, Bucks Fizz and a meal—contact the racecourse for further information. There is space for a marquee which will take up to 500 guests. The restaurant has been moved to the top floor of the Grandstand and has the best view in the house. It is advisable to book—particularly for window seats! The caterers, Letheby and Christopher can be contacted via

Artist: **Claire Eva Burton** *WALKING OUT Courtesy of:* **The Artist**

the racecourse office (0115) 9580620. If you are going to Nottingham for the first time, please note that a dress code is in effect in the Members and patrons are requested not to wear denim, T-shirts or shorts (ties and polo neck shirts preferred).

Nottingham also provides more than adequate extra facilities. Children have an adventure playground in addition to the playground in the Silver Ring. Disabled people have a viewing stand and a lift in the Centenary Stand and pay telephones abound. Should you wish to book Nottingham's facilities on a non-raceday, the racecourse has developed a worthy Conference Centre providing conference and exhibition facilities. Another positive step at a thoroughly positive racecourse. Nottingham's management have a great enthusiasm for the sport. We wish them all well in 2001.

Local Favourites

The better hotels in the city are essentially extremely modern affairs. The **Holiday Inn** (0115) 950 0600 is close to the course and does mean you can avoid the city centre, although all the city facilities are accessible. The **Forte Crest** (0115) 947 0131 is a 13-storey hotel which boasts panoramic views of the city. Alternatively, the **Rutland Square** (0115) 941 1114 should not be ignored. The **Nottingham Moat House** (0115) 935 9988 is another up to date hotel. The **Hilton Hotels** (0115) 934 9700 have recently opened in Nottingham following a year long refurbishment programme offering city centre location (2 miles from the racecourse) with leisure facilities. Outside the city, one hotel geared to the businessman's requirements is the **Posthouse Nottingham/Derby** (0870) 400 9062 which has good facilities and is extremely convenient for the M1 (junction 25). **Alter Ego** (0115) 959 8253 is convenient for the racecourse (a three mile drive). Other restaurants to consider include the excellent **Sonny's** (0115) 947 3041, and **Higoi** (0115) 942 3379 an excellent Japanese restaurant. **Saagar** (0115) 963 2014 is a particularly good Indian restaurant and **Harts Restaurant** (0115) 9110666 is definitely worth investigation.

Outside the town, one place definitely to visit is the outstanding public house in Old Dalby, the **Crown** (01664) 823134. If you're a real ale fan then this is the pub for you and the pub

food in this gorgeous converted farmhouse is excellent. Highly recommended by those at the racecourse is the **Peacock** at Redmile Belvoir. The **Martins Arms** in Colston Bassett (01949) 81361 also warrants attention—good food and accomodation here. There is also a restaurant in which you can dine in the evenings. Although it is a bit of a trek, **Stapleford Park** (01572) 787522 just outside Melton Mowbray is excellent. Although expensive, this 16th century marvel is worth every penny for a luxurious stay and good food. The **Priest House** (01232) 810649 has a delightful setting and is handy for the M1. In Plumtree, **Perkins** (0115) 937 3695 offers a tempting menu off the blackboard and this makes for an ideal post-racing spot. Another quiet pub in which to reflect on the day to come, or just gone by, is the **Star** at West Leake. The **Victoria** at Beeston will appeal to real ale aficionados and **Risley Hall** (0115) 939 9000 is an appealing hotel. The **White House** has a fine setting, overlooking the waters of the River Soar and the **White Lady** (01623) 797447 in Newstead Abbey is a restaurant worth paying a visit. In Castle Donington, the **Cross Keys** (01332) 812214 has good food and a cosy atmosphere and the **Priest House on the River** (01332) 810649 has a delightful river setting. Finally, the **Royal Horseshoes** in Waltham-on-the-Wolds is a pleasant village pub with above average accommodation—ideal for lovers of England's countryside.

Artist: **Brian Stanley** THE WINNER *Courtesy of:* **The Artist**

This friendly course is run by **Sam Morshead** as **General Manager** and **Clerk of the Course** while **Lucy Normile** is **Secretary** and **Treasurer.** They can be found at **Perth Racecourse, Scone Palace Park, Perth PH2 6BB. Tel (01738) 551597 Fax (01738) 553021 web site: www.perth-races.co.uk**

Although Perth is Britain's most northerly racecourse, some 450 miles from London, it is fairly accessible from all quarters of the country. When you reach Perth by car watch out for new Tourist Board signs for Scone Palace which will conveniently take you to the racecourse itself. Edinburgh is 44 miles away and the M90 can be taken from Edinburgh via the Forth Bridge, making your way through the Ochil Hills and past Loch Leven—a wonderful drive. The A9 struggles through the beautiful Perthshire countryside via Aviemore, Blair Atholl, Pitlochry and Blairgowrie. Even the train picks out numerous beauty spots as it shunts north from Edinburgh and the distant Kings Cross in London, and there is a free bus service to the course from Perth town centre. Helicopters may be landed by prior arrangement while aircraft should be landed at Scone aerodrome some two miles away. Car parking at the racecourse is plentiful and free.

The wooded parkland of Scone Palace is the setting for this superbly picturesque course. The fixture list is well designed and all the meetings are run over two or three days. The sponsorship at the course is particularly good and this, coupled with the general popularity of the course, ensures some good fields. Meetings take place in late April, mid May and early June, with a new Sunday fixture at the end of June, mid August and September, although these fixtures have yet to be confirmed. The main race of the year is the £20,000 City of Perth Golf

Handicap run on the June Sunday. The April Festival is still the flagship meeting.

The rates for the various enclosures are as follows: Members £15, £8 for the Paddock Enclosure, with pensioners and students at £4, and a mere £2 for the Course Enclosure. The Annual Membership subscription for 2000 was set at £85 for a single badge with a £145 charge for a double badge and £45 for a Junior Membership. There are discounts of £2 per person for clans of 15 strong or more which applies to Tattersalls only. This enclosure has been enlarged to allow people to get nearer the last fence and hurdle and an additional uncovered viewing area has been put up in the same area. All enclosures have excellent views of the course and its sweeping wooded turns. However, if you're one of those people who hate to be parted from your car then centre course parking is an option at a price of £5 - good value for picnic lovers

The Grandstand is delightfully compact and allows for a superb atmosphere as the well backed favourite strides by. Private boxes which will accommodate between 20 and 30 people can be arranged with the General Manager, with full catering facilities to fit the required budget. There is now an excellent stand for corporate hospitality and private parties which can cater for parties from 16 to 50, all with private viewing facilities. There are restaurants in all the enclosures and the course caterers are Sodexho Prestige. There are telephones at the course and viewing ramps for the disabled. Special facilities for children are now provided during the August holiday fixture.

A new owners and trainers bar was recently added as well as a new parade ring with winner's enclosure. The old saddling

Artist: **Margaret Barrett** **SAFELY OVER** *Courtesy of:* **The Artist**

boxes have been renovated to create three new hospitality boxes and new saddling boxes and pre-parade ring have been built. Improved facilities in the centre of the course now offer snack & bar facilities & an improved Tote area. Furthermore, there is a new Member's Bar, and a renovated Club Bar plus a new weighroom complex is planned for 2001. Perth may be Britain's most northerly track but it is also one of the country's most attractive—it's no small wonder that Perth has been voted the best small course in the North four times in the past eight years.

Local Favourites

In Perth, the **Hunting Tower** (01738) 583771 is a comfortable place in which to stay. Excellent value accommodation is plentiful in Perth with **Clark Kimberley** (01738) 637406 and the **Clunie Guest House** (01738) 623625 providing comfort and style and the **New County Hotel** (01738) 623355 in Perth is worth a look in. **Let's Eat Again** (01738) 633771 in George Street is a seafood restaurant to note and **Let's Eat** (01738) 643377 is also good; and for a taste of Italy try **Puccini's Ristorante Italiano** (01738) 626000. The **Hilton Perth** (01738) 628281 is extremely well run and worthy of attention. **Kingfauns Castle** (01738) 620777, a renowned 17th century castle, is also first class. An hotel exceptionally close to the racecourse is **Murrayshall Country House** (01738) 551171 in New Scone. The hotel offers a fine restaurant and a championship golf course and comes thoroughly recommended. An alternative idea is to visit Auchterhouse where the **Old Mansion House** (01382) 320366 provides an outstanding hotel-restaurant double. People making use of the A94 should note Alyth and here the **Lands of Loyal Hotel** (01828) 633151 is a pleasant and reasonably priced country house hotel in which to stay. Eastwards, one finds Blairgowrie, home of a wonderful golf course, Rosemount. South of the town in Kinclaven by Stanley, the **Ballathie House** (01250) 883268 has another gorgeous Tayside setting. Another outstanding hotel to consider is **Dalmunzie House** (01250) 885224, family run and welcoming—cottages are also available

in the grounds for those who prefer the more independent life.

Another majestic place is, of course, **Gleneagles Hotel** (01764) 662231. Not only are there superb golf courses but the hotel exudes class—a first rate establishment in every way. More modest but still friendly accomodation can be found at the **Glenfarg Hotel** (01577) 830241. En route to England, try Cleish near Kinross, where **Nivingston House** (01577) 850216 offers an inviting restaurant and some comfortable accommodation. We should also alert you to two outstanding establishments, one at Dunblane, the other at Dunkeld. **Cromlix House** (01786) 822125 is superb and the restaurant is one of Scotland's finest. **Kinnaird House** (01796) 482440 is another hotel and restaurant that oozes class and is a great place to celebrate if the right horse wins—note the excellent game fishing here. Another hotel to please game fishermen is the **Hilton Dunkeld House Hotel** (01350) 727771 with a delightful riverside setting for this welcoming establishment. Just outside Perth, **Dupplin Castle** (01738) 623224 is family run, extremely welcoming and thoroughly relaxing. Ideal after a tight finish in the last.

*Artist: **John Atkins** **ALL TO PLAY FOR** Courtesy of: **The Artist***

Plumpton is a well run friendly racecourse within easy striking distance of London. **Patrick Davis** is **Chief Executive** of the racecourse, **Clerk of the Course** is **David McHarg** and **Mrs Lorna Bromley-Martin** is **Marketing and Hospitality Manager**. They can be contacted at the racecourse offices on **(01273) 890383 fax: (01273) 891557. Web site: www.plumptonracecourse.co.uk**

Plumpton lies approximately 50 miles from London, midway between Haywards Heath and Lewes. The M23 is the best route south but after this, the motorist is left with various A and B roads. The A23, the A273 and the B2112 seem the best routes to punt on. From Brighton and the south coast, the A27 Lewes road coupled with the A273 should oblige. The course lies in the village of Plumpton Green. The quaint name of this village reflects its unspoilt character but the quiet is occasionally broken by the sound of the train. This is good news for racegoers though, as the station lies beside the course. The best idea is to catch the Victoria-Hastings train to Plumpton Station. There is also a free bus service from Brighton Railway station to Plumpton on racedays. If you can't spare the time to train it, helicopters are able to land at the racecourse. For parking there is no charge, unless you venture into the centre of the course with a picnic in mind, in which case, it will cost £6 admission per person which includes the car. Plumpton racecourse hosts 16 days racing per year from September through April and, as with many of the smaller National Hunt courses, the Easter meetings prove to be the most popular.

The price for entry into Plumpton's Members Enclosure is £14, the Tattersalls Enclosure is £10 and the Silver Ring is £6. Children under 16 are admitted free of charge. If you wish to join as an annual member at Plumpton the cost is £125. You will also be entitled to many reciprocal days of equestrian sport at other racecourses and venues. Parties of 20 or more people receive a 10% discount in any enclosure if booked in advance.

For people wishing to do some entertaining, Plumpton racecourse may have the answer. Bookings for private boxes for groups of 10-40 guests are available and should be made through the racecourse office. Box Rental is from £120 per meeting. Additional facilities accommodating up to 70 guests are also available and marquee sites are ideally located for entertainment of larger parties. For all catering requirements contact Appetence Food & Wine Ltd on (01273) 401777.

The popular Members Restaurant overlooks the course and tables can be booked in advance with the caterers or by contacting the racecourse office. In addition, fast food outlets and bars are available throughout the various enclosures.

This delightful course does provide good entertainment and we are delighted to hear of its continuing improvements. If you have not visited Plumpton before, we would warmly recommend a midweek winter afternoon where exciting racing in a pleasant atmosphere is assured.

Local Favourites

We start at a pinnacle of excellence, some way north of Plumpton—**Gravetye Manor** (01342) 810567 in Gravetye, south of East Grinstead. Another top hotel can be found at Cuckfield, **Ockendon Manor** (01444) 416111—the building is 16th century and the traditional open fires and panelling add immense charm to the excellent facilities. The restaurant is also particularly well

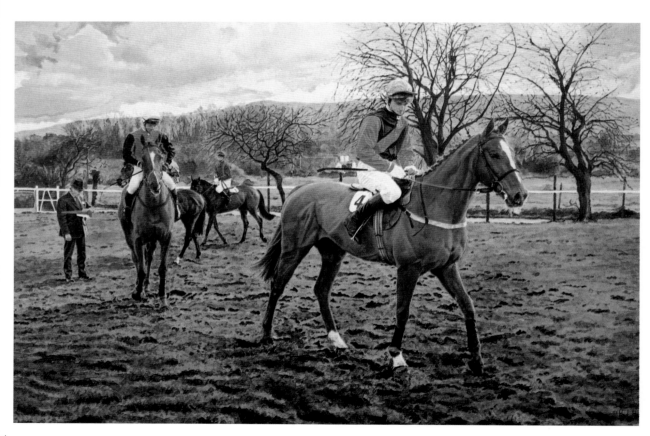

Artist: **Paul Hart** *AT THE START, PLUMPTON Courtesy of:* **The Artist**

thought of. Ashdown Forest has some delightful scenery and an excellent base from which to explore is the **Chequers Inn** (01342) 823333 at Forest Row. In Lower Beeding, **South Lodge** (01403) 891711 is an attractive restaurant and boasts some excellent accommodation within. For lovers of luxury, a final recommendation here is for **Horsted Place** (01825) 750581 near Uckfield, where both the rooms and the restaurant are of a standard seldom equalled.

Much further south, one arrives in the extremely pleasant Sussex town of Lewes. Here one finds an hotel engulfed by a roaming creeper—**Shelleys** (01273) 472361. There is a number of restaurants in Lewes. **Pailin** (01273) 473906 is a fine one where imaginative cooking ensures delightful eating. Staying in this part of the world need not cost a fortune and for the avid bargain hunters **Millers** (01273) 475631 should fit the bill. In Ditchling, the **Bull** (01273) 843147 is a pleasant coaching inn. While restaurants come and go, pubs generally stand their ground. In Fulking, the **Shepherd and Dog** is a pleasant small country pub and the bar snacks here are excellent. Closer to the racecourse at Clayton, the **Jack and Jill** is also a friendly place while the **Rainbow Arms** in Cooksbridge is welcoming and provides good bar snacks too. Another pub with a good restaurant is aptly named the **Stewards Enquiry** on the Lewes Road near Ringmer. The **Highlands** in Uckfield is another establishment patronised by those in search of good fare. Not too far away we find Chiddingly's the **Six Bells**—most appealing with old beams and excellent snacks as well as some good beers. In Horsted Keynes, try the **Green Man** or the excellent

Gardners Arms at Ardingly, more excellent snacks in an ancient and traditional free house. Another fairly convenient stop could be made at the **Hare and Hounds**, a pleasant village pub east of Uckfield. Racegoers who like country pubs with charm, should try **Juggs** in Kingston. Rustic to the core, it is a country pub for a country course. Finally, a selection of pubs in Plumpton Green that come recommended by those who run the course - the aptly named **Winning Post**, **The Fountain** and **The Plough**. In Plumpton itself the **Half Moon** also comes highly recommended. Just a few to consider when planning your racing in 2001.

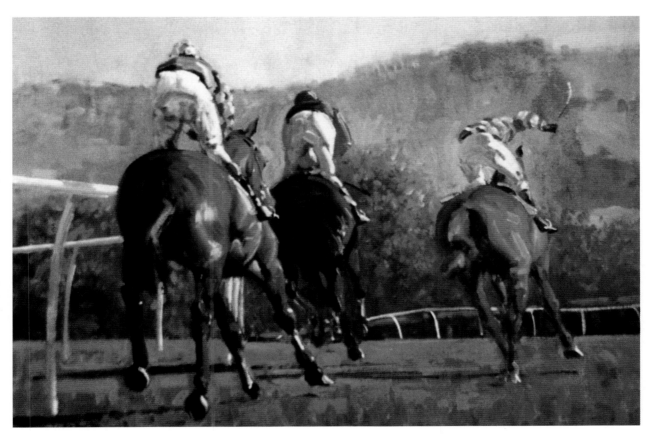

*Artist: **Malcolm Coward** BOTTOMS UP, PLUMPTON Courtesy of: **Sally Mitchell Fine Arts***

A lot of hard work goes into making Pontefract one of the most popular racecourses in the north of England. The man in charge of this most progressive of courses is **Norman Gundill**, who acts as **Clerk, Manager** and **Secretary**. He can be contacted at **The Racecourse, Pontefract Park, Pontefract. Tel (01977) 702210** (racedays only) or at **33 Ropergate, Pontefract WF8 1LE. Tel (01977) 703224 Fax (01977) 600577. Web site: www.pontefract.races.co.uk.**

The course is marvellously situated for motorway access, the entrance being only half a mile from junction 32 of the M62, making it an excellent location for racegoers from almost all areas of the country. Leeds lies nine miles west of Pontefract and the A1 and M1 and M18 are all within ten miles of the course. Although there are plenty of busy rail stations nearby - Doncaster, York and Leeds - Pontefract is not on a main line station, so this is probably a course where one should take the car. There are vast car parking areas and all parking is free, other than the Special Reserve Park, where a charge of £10 is levied. Buses are an option too, with those from Pontefract and Leeds passing the gates. If you are in a particular hurry, there are ample open playing fields in the park in which to place one's helicopter. You must check with the Secretary first though, just in case some other activity is taking place.

A few years ago the Paddock section of the Main Stand was extended and a new Dalby Stand with 8 private boxes and a new champagne bar was built, greatly adding to the amenities at the course and there is now a new Tote facility which will serve the Third Ring. The course was granted an additional evening meeting in June and two more Sundays, in addition to the already popular Sunday fixture in August. Charges for 2000 were £14 for a daily membership, £9 for entrance to the Paddock, £4 for the Silver Ring and £2.50 for the Third Ring. The best value, however, is the Third Ring car park which cost £5 per car and includes up to four people. If you wish to become an Annual Member the adult single badge is priced at £105, whilst a husband and wife team can be members for the very reasonable sum of £140. The prices for 2001 will probably stay the same.

Annual Members are also entitled to reciprocal meetings at Thirsk, Doncaster, Haydock Park, Beverley, Newcastle, Market Rasen, Nottingham and Catterick. The racecourse executive is also to be applauded for reciprocal meetings at a variety of Yorkshire County Cricket Club venues including Headingley and Sheffield. The course also offers special discounts for parties in all racecourse enclosures. Contact the Secretary for further details.

For those wishing to entertain guests at Pontefract, although the Club Chalet has been made into a bar for Owners and Trainers and is no longer available for private parties, the Private Room in the Main Stand looks directly out over the course and larger parties can be accommodated in the Entertainment Suite. The private boxes in the Dalby Stand certainly appear good value. The stand was built on the site of the old Club entrance and Champagne Bar. Each box seats up to 20 and the stand itself faces down the finishing straight, overlooks the horsewalk and has views over the Parade Ring—a superb place at which to make the most of a day's racing. Charges vary so it is best to contact the racecourse for details. Pontefract would certainly

Artist: **Margaret Barrett** **TURNING FOR HOME** *Courtesy of:* **The Artist**

be a tremendous place to have a company summer party with a difference. Catering arrangements should be made directly with the racecourse caterers, Craven Gilpin & Sons (0113) 2876387.

Snack bars can be found throughout the course and more substantial food can be had in the Club and Paddock restaurants. Finally, should you wish to have a picnic, the place to go is the Third Ring car park on the stands side. Both the stands serving the Silver Ring and the Third Ring are being refurbished. There is a special playground for the youngsters in the Third Ring and, if under 16, they will be admitted free when accompanied by an adult. A fully supervised crèche operates in the Third Ring at holiday meetings at Easter and August and at evening meetings. Another good reason to go racing at this friendly, well run racecourse.

Local Favourites

Pontefract is ideally placed for venturing further north, and one place that should be visited is Ilkley—a little distant but well worth the trek. Here, **Rombalds** (01943) 603201 is a really excellent place to stay—home comforts and a warm Yorkshire welcome are the order of the day. What's more, if you happen to wake up a little hungry on Sunday morning after an evening at Pontefract, fear not, their Edwardian breakfast is an absolute monster and should keep the largest of wolves from the door. Ilkley is cluttered with some delightful antique shops. The **Box Tree** (01943) 608484 is a celebrated restaurant to note. The **Grove** (01943) 600298 is also well thought of. Closer to the course, Leeds has a few good fancies (see Wetherby).

Returning to more local spots, one should consider some places in which to have an ale or two. In Ledsham, the **Chequers** (01977) 683135 is an enormously popular free house, resplen-

dent with oak beams and open fires. In Ledston's Main Street, one finds an equine establishment, the **White Horse** and another warm welcome and fire, so I understand. The **Greyhound** in Saxton is also a pleasing Yorkshire hostelry. In Wentbridge, the **Wentbridge House Hotel** (01977) 620444 is a glorious, early 18th century hotel, very cosy and well appointed, standing in 15 acres of grounds. The restaurant here is well thought of, a fine place to visit prior to the racecourse and perfect for a post race celebration. Another historic and worthy entry to the Pontefract shortlist is found at Monk Fryston. Here, **Monk Fryston Hall** (01977) 682369 has pleasant interiors and formal gardens as well as a more modern wing. **Rogerthorpe Manor Country House Hotel** in nearby Badsworth (01977) 643839 comes personally recommended by the racecourse management, making it a fine place to stay when visiting Pontefract in 2001.

Artist: **Claire Eva Burton** **FIRST TO THE POST** *Courtesy of:* **Rosenstiel's**

The team in charge at Redcar is headed by the **Chairman, Peter Hill-Walker**, ably assisted by **Mr J E Gundill, Clerk of the Course and General Manager.** They can be contacted at **Redcar Racecourse, Redcar, Cleveland TS10 2BY. Tel (01642) 484068 Fax (01642) 488272. Website: www.redcarracing.co.uk.** International Racecourse Management are also part of the impressive executive structure. Together they form as fine a team as you will find in racing and continuing improvements at the racecourse are evidence of this.

Redcar racecourse is located in the south of this coastal town to the north east of the Yorkshire Moors. Redcar is accessible by road from the A19 dual carriageway, which passes within 15 minutes of the racecourse (via the Parkway). The A19 links to the south with the A1 at Dishforth and to the north at Newcastle. Travellers from the east will find the A67 and the A66 routes the most direct into Redcar and the racecourse. The nearest railway station, Redcar Central Station, is in the town itself, a distance of approximately half a mile from the track—a ten minute walk at the most! A fast train service runs from Kings Cross to Darlington where you can catch the local train to Redcar. The bus station is a mere 150 yard hike from the Grandstand—perfect. There are ample free parking facilities with three major areas for cars and coaches.

The principal racing days here include the Spring Bank Holiday Monday with other days in June, July, August and September. Two of the feature races are the Zetland Gold Cup, which will be worth some £20,000 in prize money, and also the £100,000 Two Year Old Trophy which is the focal point of Redcar's racing calendar.

Annual Membership in 2000 was priced at £100 and £42 for Juniors (under 25). The charge for Joint Membership. was £150. Annual Membership includes a car pass for each meeting plus the use of a private room, bar, catering and Tote kiosk. The use of a private bar is an excellent concept and one which all the racecourses should adopt for their annual patrons. The daily admissions for the Members, Tattersalls and the Course were priced at £14, £10 and £3 respectively. OAP's receive discounted admission in Tattersalls of £5 and only £1.50 for the Course enclosure. The racecourse offers a discount to parties of 12 or more, reducing the daily prices to £10 for the Club, £5.50 for Tattersalls and £2 for the Course and one free ticket is included with pre-booked groups of 20 tickets. The stand facilities are excellent and the colourful flower beds form a cheerful feature—all further indications of the management's eagerness to please.

The course will be happy to provide information with regard to boxes, conference suites and rooms for smaller gatherings. The Paddock Rooms have added a new dimension to Redcar's facilities as a fully self-contained entertainment centre with magnificent spectating facilities and suites to cater for between 35 and 140. A major refurbishment has been carried out during the past few years, completely renovating the facilities which now include the Crow's Nest viewing restaurant with full table service, while the Voltigeur restaurant has a carvery. The Classic Suite provides great corporate hospitality and caters for up to 120 guests. The four luxurious executive boxes cater for 8-12 guests (Silver Service) or 15 + if Buffet-style menu. In 1999 a new Winning Enclosure bar was added as well as a food hall for Tatts patrons. For those whose punting instincts are stronger

Artist: **Terence Gilbert** *THE FINISH* *Courtesy of:* **The Artist**

than their hunger or thirst, the new state-of-the-art Tote Betting shop will serve admirably. Catering is handled by Romfords (01642) 478024 or (01434) 688864.

Children are admitted free if under the age of 16 (excluding Redcar's Family Funday in August where a minimal charge will be made) and accompanied and there is a playground provided. Other facilities include a viewing ramp for the disabled opposite the winning post, and lavatories for the disabled in all enclosures. Although there are no special banking facilities, public telephones are available for any necessary credit punts and there is a Tote betting shop. Go and visit and try one of the Tote's new bets in 2001.

Local Favourites

The north east of England may not enjoy the most illustrious of reputations elsewhere, but in this case ignorance is not bliss. Few who venture this far north are in any hurry to leave. In Crathorne, near Yarm, there is an extremely fine hotel the **Crathorne Hall Hotel** (01642) 700398. The hotel enjoys a splendid setting and it is thoroughly welcoming—a good choice. In Yarm itself, **Santoro** (01642) 781305 is a good Italian restaurant to note. At Staddle Bridge, **The Tontine** (01609) 882671 is a truly delightful hotel run by the McCoy brothers with a genuine 1930s feel. It is also home to **McCoy's Bistro.** In Stockton-on-Tees, the **Swallow Hotel** (01642) 679721 boasts extremely comfortable accommodation and is high on the list of visiting business people. **Romanby Court** (01609) 774918 is a fine restaurant to consider in Northallerton, **Solberge Hall** (01609) 779191 is also good.

If the bustle of the city centre hotels is not to your liking then you may care to try the **Grinkle Park Hotel** in Loftus

(01287) 640515—the parkland setting of this Victorian hotel is especially attractive. Alternatively, why not sample the luxurious **Ayton Hall** (01642) 723595 in Great Ayton. **Manor House Farm** (01642) 722384 is somewhat smaller and can be found at Ingleby Greenhow. Farther afield in Goathland, the **Mallyan Spout Hotel** (01947) 896486 is recommended. The **Endeavour** in Staithes (01947) 840825 is a really splendid restaurant.

There are several pubs to note in the area and one such establishment is the **Ship** at Saltburn-by-the-Sea, splendid seafood, snacks and good views—well worth a trip out. Farther west in Egglescliffe, the **Blue Bell** (01642) 780358 has good food as well as fine views of the River Tees. A little further afield the **Horse Shoe** at Egton Bridge (01947) 895245 has a lovely setting and good value bedrooms and a similar description can be applied to the **Duke of Wellington** (01287) 660351 in Danby. A peaceful atmosphere in which to peruse your Racing Post and consider the day ahead at Redcar races.

Artist: **John Atkins** *HEAD ON* *Courtesy of:* **The Artist**

The authorities are headed by **Michael Hutchinson** who acts as **Managing Director** and is assisted by **Clerk of the Course, James Hutchinson.** They can be contacted at 77 **North Street, Ripon, North Yorkshire HG4 1DS. Tel (01765) 602156 Fax (01765) 690018.**

The most obvious way to get to Ripon is by car for there is no train station at the town itself, and while trains do stop at Harrogate the nearest major station is at York, which is some 23 miles away. If you do wish to travel by train then the King's Cross line is the one to board. London itself lies 200 miles away and the best way of reaching the racecourse from the south is to use the A1/A1(M). The course is two miles east of Ripon, off the B6265, which in turn is just four miles from the A1. The A61 from Leeds and Harrogate is a useful road from the south and this, together with the A19, will assist racegoers from the north east. Similar access is provided by the A61 from Thirsk for those travelling from the east. A new bypass to the east of the city takes you directly to the course. There are ample parking areas at the racecourse and this is provided free. If people are hurrying to the course then helicopters are a welcome option provided you give prior warning.

The spring and summer months play host to Ripon's race meetings and August is particularly crowded with excellent fixtures. The William Hill Great St Wilfrid Handicap (£37,500) is the feature race whilst many a good entry is attracted by the Champion Two Year Old Trophy (£20,000). Lovers of summer sports who enrol as Members of Ripon will also be offered a taste of another splendid summer game—cricket. Annual Members are given nine days' complimentary Yorkshire cricket, as well as reciprocal meetings at Newcastle, Haydock, Doncaster,

Redcar, Catterick, Market Rasen, Hexham and Pontefract. Membership for husband and wife is £135, a single badge £90 and a junior (under 21) is required to pay a £60 subscription. If you are able to justify only the occasional visit to Ripon then daily badges cost £14 in the Club, £9 in Tattersalls, and £4 and £3 in the Silver Ring and Course Enclosures. Children under 16 are admitted free as long as they are accompanied.

Various group discounts are available for Tattersalls and the Silver Ring, starting with parties of 20 or more and becoming more generous as the numbers increase. A 50 per cent discount is given to parties which can scramble together 250 people. If you are looking for an afternoon with slightly more than the average entry badge allows, then a range of boxes is available for hire, catering for between 25 and 100 people. If you require precise details, contact the course as they have an excellent printed brochure. These offer good value but don't forget to sort out the catering at the same time. For bigger parties a marquee area is available in the Paddock, but there is not too much room and if you are organising a bigger event, there is also a location available in the car park adjacent to the Paddock. Taking a car and four passengers into the course enclosure for £10 offers excellent value.

There are restaurants and snack bars in all enclosures—parts of the Members' and Tattersalls stands have been rebuilt, increasing and improving the facilities available while new railings around the Parade Ring create a smart appearance and give added protection for both horses and people. As an added attraction, music lovers will enjoy a variety of music from Ripon's award-winning re-creation of a Victorian bandstand. Ripon was the first course to have a children's playground and

Artist: **Margaret Barrett** *FINAL BURST Courtesy of:* **The Artist**

there are now two—one on either side of the course—marvellous. Other details to note are that there are telephones in the Paddock, Silver Ring and Course enclosures. Disabled racegoers are well catered for in all rings with reserved car parking. There are William Hill operated betting shops in all Rings. Those of you who have not visited Ripon should give it a try. It is fondly called the 'Garden Racecourse' and is one of the most pleasing in the country.

Local Favourites

Ripon has much to offer to the sightseer—notably Fountains Abbey, Ripon Cathedral, Newby Hall and the recently re-opened canal. Ripon's leading hotel the **Ripon Spa** (01765) 602172 is a particularly racing orientated abode, while the **Unicorn** (01765) 602202 is a traditional coaching inn. Less glamorous, but quite agreeable accommodation can also be had at the **Crescent Lodge Guest House** (01765) 602331. One pub within sight of the course **The Blackamoor Inn** comes highly recommended. The **Old Deanery** (01765) 603518 is a charming restaurant with rooms, which is particularly well fancied.

In Markington the **Hob Green Hotel** (01423) 770031 is another extremely restful place to stay with award winning gardens and excellent food. Great character and some good accommodation can be found in the **Sportsman's Arms** (01423) 711306 in Wath-in-Nidderdale. If you love the country, stay here—it's a charming setting and the food is also first class as is the **Yorke Arms** (01423) 755243 at Ramsgill. The **Rose Manor Hotel** (01423) 322245 is also well thought of and can be found in Boroughbridge as can the **Crown** (01423) 322 328.

Harrogate will also make a good base while you visit Yorkshire. An 18th century building with an extremely attractive setting is a fair description of the splendid **Studley Hotel** (01423) 560425 where a good restaurant is complemented by comfortable accommodation. **Rudding Park** (01423) 871350 will apeal to golfers as well as racegoers. The value of staying in Harrogate is that firstly one can leave one's non-racing partner in a delightful town in which to browse and secondly, in the evening, one has a number of restaurants to visit. The **Drum and Monkey** (01423) 502650 is good, downstairs—a bustling bar and superb food, upstairs a more formal and extremely popular dining room. **The Bistro** (01423) 530708 is also good. Racing devotees may wish to visit **Grundy's** (01423) 502610.

For people who have to rush home the same day then a few options before you set sail. In Staveley, the **Royal Oak** (01423) 340267 is a welcoming country pub with good food while in Roecliffe, the **Crown** (01423) 322578 is another great little pub. Other public houses handy for the A1 include the **Olde Punch Bowl** in Marton cum Grafton and the **Ship at Aldborough**—note the Roman connection here. The **Sawley Arms** in Sawley is highly recommended for meals. A final tip before we leave this area—**The George** at Wormald Green (01765) 677214, is sure to impress if price is no object. Racing at Ripon can be competitive and will need a clear head. A trip in 2001 is recommended.

Artist: **John Atkins** **PULLING UP** *Courtesy of:* **The Artist**

Salisbury is an enchanting racecourse and keen racegoers should definitely make the effort to attend a meeting here in 2000. **Ian Renton** runs Salisbury as the **Clerk of the Course**. He can be contacted at **Salisbury Racecourse, Netherhampton, Wiltshire SP2 8PN** or on **(01722) 326461/327327 Fax (01722) 412710. Web site: www.salisburyracecourse.co.uk.**

The racecourse is located three and a half miles south west of Salisbury on the A3094. The best plan is to aim for the town and from there you should follow the signs to the racecourse. The A360 is the best route from the north. For people heading from the east or the west of the country the A30 is ideal. Other modes of transport to be considered are the train/bus double. The first leg is the Waterloo-Salisbury line which should be coupled with a courtesy bus from Salisbury station to the racecourse. If you wish to use the helicopter then there is no problem—as long as you telephone the management in advance. There are excellent car parking facilities at the course which are provided free of charge.

In 2001, racing will likely follow the same format as in 2000 with the major meeting again being the Bibury Meeting which takes place in late June. The feature race on the card is the Champagne Stakes worth £15,000. Other major races of the season are the Upavon Fillies Stakes (£25,000) in August and the Dick Poole Stakes (£12,000) in September.

There are two evening meetings and two Sunday meetings when there is entertainment for the children and jazz bands and barbecues add a certain spice to some competitive racing. Additionally, the Sunday meeting in May is well worth a visit when plenty of entertainment is laid on for all the family to accompany an excellent programme of racing.

Admission prices may increase slightly in 2001 but last year the visitor was asked £15 for the Members, £10 for Tattersalls and £5 for the Course Enclosure. Children are admitted free, if accompanied. If you wish to become an Annual Member the rate is £110. However, in addition you receive a car pass and eleven reciprocal meetings plus, of course, the prestige of belonging to the oldest known racing club still in existence — the Bibury.

If you wish to organise a party at Salisbury, and it's a special place to have one—discounts are available, subject to numbers on advance bookings. Private hospitality boxes located above the Members Bar and the new Festival Stand accommodate between 12 and 40 guests. These are available for daily hire from £600 per day or on an annual basis. Daily sublets can be arranged, depending on the day and the box required. However, it is always worth contacting the racecourse for availability or cancellations. The best idea however, may be to organise a marquee or chalet located adjacent to the parade ring and the winning post catering for up to 300 guests. Salisbury runs its own Bibury Club Catering Company and provides an excellent food service to the recently refurbished Members Restaurant where advance booking is essential. There is also a snack bar located in the Bibury Suite if you fancy something less substantial and a seafood bar in the refurbished Paddock Bar. On the drinking front, Members can enjoy the Wessex Bar, while in Tattersalls a temporary Pavilion Bar is erected to cater for the larger crowds in July and August. Disabled people are given the opportunity to enjoy racing by virtue of a raised viewing area—situated in the Members Enclosure. A Tote betting shop is located in Tattersalls and telephones are available. An evening or afternoon at Salisbury is thoroughly recommended.

Artist: **Brian Halton** **SETTLE** _Courtesy of:_ **The Artist**

Local Favourites

Hampshire, Dorset and Wiltshire are home to an enticing array of country pubs. Here is a quick listing of some of the various contenders: the **Compasses** (01722) 714318 in Lower Chicksgrove has bar snacks and a traditional atmosphere as well as a separate restaurant and cosy rooms if required. Another pub-restaurant ideal for informal post-race nosh is the **Black Dog** (01722) 716344 in Chilmark. The **Black Horse** (01722) 716251 in Teffont Magna has super food and pleasing accommodation. The same can be said of a critter—the **Fox Inn** (01258) 880328, a lovely village pub. In Broad Chalke, the **Queen's Head** (01722) 780344 is a good stayer and in another gorgeous village, Fonthill Bishop, the **King's Arms** is a picturesque alternative, while the **Victoria and Albert** in Netherhampton is very convenient so too is the **Barford Inn** at Barford St Martin (01722) 742242. The list goes on and on. If you love the country and it's traditionally copious cuisine, then this is an area for you. Two local tips worth following are the **Pembroke Arms** at Wilton and **Cricket Field Cottage** (01722) 322595. Both also offer good accommodation. We then come across a couple of tools. Before you take offence, relax—merely a reference to two other excellent pubs in the vicinity, the **Malet Arms** in Newton Toney, and the **Silver Plough** (01722) 712266 in Pitton, a tremendous hostelry with a restaurant. A good pub to stay in is the **Barford** (01722) 742242—good value and good food.

Then there's Salisbury. A charming city and the county town of Wiltshire. The rivers Avon, Bourne, Wylye and Nadder converge here. Many people visit the area to see the cathedral or shop in the market and the town is a busy and thriving focal point. The **Rose and Crown** (01722) 399955 has a lovely setting on the banks of the River Avon, overlooking the cathedral. The **Old Bell Inn** (01722) 327958 also has pleasing bedrooms and two lovely four posters and the bar is a civilised meeting place.

The **White Hart** (01722) 327476 has great character and is an ideal choice before racing at the Bibury Club. **Milford Hall** (01722) 417411 is also reported to be of an excellent standard. If you are in search of a pub then the **Haunch of Venison** (01722) 322024 exudes character and provides good food while the Tudor **King's Arms** (01722) 327629 offers good value accommodation. The **Coach and Horses** (01722) 336254 also offers good food. Outside the town, a really super pub to note is the **Fox and Goose** at Coombe Bissett—well worth a post-race pint.

Some distance from Salisbury, but a definite must if you have time, is the **Sign of the Angel** (01249) 730230 at Lacock—also a possibility for Newbury. Marlborough offers the splendid **Ivy House Hotel** (01672) 515333 which is thoroughly recommended. Closer to the racecourse, try **Howard's House Hotel** (01722) 716392—a real gem of a place—an ideal port of call for those of you wishing to break the journey before racing at Salisbury.

Artist: **Katy Sodeau** **ROUNDING THE BEND** *Courtesy of:* **The Artist**

Richard Evans is a fine journalist and the team at Sandown and United Racecourses generally must have been devastated when he wrote his Valentine's Day message in *The Daily Telegraph*: "Not every course can reach the heights achieved by York and Cheltenham. But courses, large and small, can improve given the right leadership. Ascot and Brighton are recent examples while Mark Kershaw is doing his best to revive Newbury. Sadly, Sandown gives the impression of being in decline."

These words were the result of some serious failings in the management of certain sponsorships and were probably fair comment. However, Sandown like Newbury last year has probably had a blip and like Newbury must bounce back. It is after all one of the very best racecourses in Britain. Any comments to this effect either favourable or unfavourable from any visitor in 2001 would be most interesting to read.

At Sandown, **Steve Brice** is the **General Manager** while **Andrew Cooper** is the **Group Racing Manager** for United Racecourses Ltd, and **Tim Darby** is **Marketing Manager Tel (01372) 461253.** If you wish to contact them, write to **Sandown Park Racecourse, Esher, Surrey KT10 9AJ. Tel (01372) 463072 Fax (01372) 465205. Web site: www.sandown.co.uk** There is also a bookings hotline on **(01372) 470047.**

The racecourse is a mere 15 miles from the centre of London in the suburb of Esher. The best route from the capital is to take the A3 out of central London itself. The A308 and the A309 are trunk roads that run nearby, and the racecourse itself lies off the A307, the Portsmouth Road. Racegoers from London are strongly recommended to use the Esher—Waterloo / Clapham Junction line as it passes the course. If you live closer to the course, buses from Kingston, Guildford and Staines all go to

Esher and stop in the High Street. Assuming that you are in a car, you will find free parking off the Portsmouth Road. Parking in the Members car park carries a charge of £2. If time is of the essence you can take a helicopter and land on the golf course in the centre of the track—but please check beforehand. Golf is of course suspended on racedays.

Fixtures for 2001 are expected to remain at 26 with meetings both on the flat and over the jumps - with the famous mixed meeting on Whitbread Gold Cup Day, when the combination of the Thresher Classic Trial and the Whitbread produces arguably the most exciting day's racing of the year. Other highlights at Sandown are the Sunderlands Imperial Cup, the Agfa Diamond Chase and the Coral-Eclipse Stakes on the flat—the first major clash of the generations each summer.

Classic Days in 2000 warranted charges of £30 (Club) £16 (Club Junior) £20 (Grandstand) and £6 (Park). On Premium Days, the charges were a bit lower—£18, £14, £13 and £5. On feature days, the Club is £17 and the Grandstand is £11 with Juniors charged at £12 and the Park at £5. If you book ahead for Classic and Premium Days you can save some money on all of these rates. Annual Membership now runs from October to September, and is £230 per year, £110 for Juniors. You can also get a Jump Membership only at £100 or Flat only for £145. Finally, if it is your intention to organise a party to Sandown then contact the course for the full range of discounts or add-ons available.

The 36 boxes at Sandown are let on an annual basis. However, you may be lucky enough to sublet one of these and should phone the Club Secretary to see what is available. Numerous

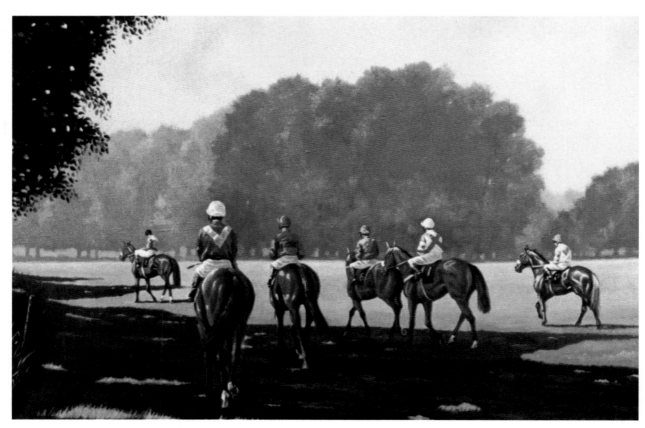

Artist: **Philip Toon** **COOL IN THE SHADE** *Courtesy of:* **The Artist**

private rooms are also available to rent and marquee sites can be organised. The caterers here are Ring & Brymer who can be contacted on (01372) 465292. The Members Restaurant, located at the top of the Members Grandstand, will set you back approximately £30 for lunch and you are advised to book. As well as the Tack and Saddle restaurant in the Grandstand, costing approximately £6.50 per head, there are all manner of snack bars at the course but these can be rather pricey. The Country Bar is now open for exclusive use by Annual Members, Owners and Trainers. You may prefer to take your own picnic to enjoy in the car parks. Unless, of course, you are an owner and can enjoy the Winning Owners Room near the Winners Enclosure where winning owners can watch a video replay of their race. It is often said that sponsorship and entertaining go hand in hand. Sandown has some excellent ways of entertaining guests, and during the warmer weather it has a Summer Pavilion next to the pre-parade rings and winners enclosures that offers some excellent packages for groups of 20 or more guests - from £95 plus VAT per head upwards. The tariff includes members badge, wine, a three course meal, racecards etc. for each guest. A great way to spend a summer afternoon or evening.

The course improvements continue and over the past year both the weighing room and the owners and trainers bar have been renovated and refurbished. A Tote betting shop has been installed for both Tatts and Members.

There is now a family picnic area in the Park Enclosure. Children under 16 are admitted free to the course and are well catered for at Sandown with a large playground. A crèche has now been opened providing first class facilities free for young children. Similarly, facilities for the disabled here are excellent with specially equipped toilets, viewing areas, reserved parking and access ramps to all areas.

Sandown has an excellent record in producing a really high standard of racing across its fixture list. Owners report it to be one of the most accommodating in the country as do trainers. With punters and patrons having similarly positive beliefs it is little wonder that Sandown is considered by many to be their favourite racecourse. The start of the millennium may have shown some problems; we feel confident that these will be ironed out and the course will ride high again. We wish them well in the year 2001, and beyond.

Artist: **John Atkins** _UP THE HILL AT SANDOWN_ _Courtesy of:_ **The Artist**

Artist: **John Atkins** **SANDOWN PARK** *Courtesy of:* **The Artist**

Because of Sandown's proximity to London, many racegoers will inevitably be heading back to the capital after a day at the track so it is difficult to know where to start a selection of hotels and restaurants. For those who want luxury and have the money to spend, **Blakes Hotel** 0207 370 6701 in South Kensington is quite superb as is the renowned **Browns Hotel** 0207 493 6020. That bastion of old-fashioned English values, **Claridge's** 0207 629 8860 on Brook Street needs no introduction - its discreet luxury and elegance are quite unsurpassed. Park Lane delivers a number of excellent hotels. The **Dorchester** 0207 629 8888 has recently been totally refurbished and is crying out for a pre-race inspection. The **Grosvenor House** 0207 499 6363 is another impressive hotel and a star performer for the Forte stable. The **Four Seasons Hotel** 0207 499 0888 and the **Hyatt Carlton Tower** 0207 235 1234 are two other thoroughbreds with outstanding restaurants as well. If the above are slightly out of the range of the impoverished racegoer, then it goes without saying that London provides a veritable multitude of accommodation at vastly varying rates. One highly recommended establishment that combines comfort and value is the **Aston Court Hotel** 0207 602 9954.

So far, the emphasis has been on central London. A bit farther south on Wimbledon Common, **Cannizaro House** 0208 879 1464 is a delight, a true country house overlooking the common and superbly appointed throughout. Staying south of the river, **Prima Donna** 0207 223 9737 in Battersea is a hot favourite—delicious Italian food and very good value. **Mi Piache** (01372) 462200 and **Le Petit Pierrot** at Claygate are both newcomers to the Sandown field but they're

convenient and good if you are seeking a port of call.

What of those who prefer to stay in the Esher area to sample the local delights? The **Dining Room** (01932) 231686 at Hersham serves good English food, whilst the **Hilton Cobham** (01932) 864471 in nearby Cobham has excellent facilities such as saunas and whirlpool baths. If you are lucky enough to fly to Sandown by helicopter, then you will be pleased to know that your chopper is also welcome here. Elsewhere, in Coatham the **Woodlands Park Hotel** (01372) 843933 is an improving type and an excellent choice for visitors to Sandown. Slightly farther afield, in Weybridge, the **Warbeck House Hotel** (01932) 848764 is unpretentious but recommended. The **Oatlands Park Hotel** (01932) 847242 is a strong local fancy and a recent upgrading makes it a handy favourite. **Casa Romana** (01932) 843470 is an excellent Italian to note. **Good Earth** (01372) 462489 is an extremely handy and first rate Chinese restaurant. Less convenient, but outstanding cuisine can also be found at **Michels**, Ripley (01483) 224777—excellent.

Finally, Sandown, Kempton and Epsom are not only joined by their association with United Racecourses, but also by very close proximity to one another. So, if you are still fishing for more ideas and suggestions of where to eat or stay, then either the Kempton or Epsom section should provide all you require. One place that comes highly recommended by the racecourse management and handy for all three is the **Petersham Hotel** in Richmond 0208 940 7471. The restaurant here is also really first class.

Artist: **John Atkins** **SANDOWN PARK, PULLING UP** *Courtesy of:* **The Artist**

Gatton Manor Hotel, Golf & Country Club is set in 250 acres of parkland in the heart of the beautiful Surrey countryside and boasts a well established 18 hole, par 72 championship length golf course of 6653 yards. The whole course has immense character incorporating the natural waters of the River Arun. It has the advantage of three starting points at the first, fourth and tenth and veers over undulating ground through the peace and tranquillity of woods, with fourteen scenic water holes.

The enjoyable and interesting course is designed to challenge every golfer and has arguably the best finishing hole in the south. Firstly you are faced with a tee shot over water to the sloping fairway. Your second shot has to carry a stream some 50 yards from the middle of the green. The green itself is bunkered from left to right and is enclosed round the back with an interesting selection of fir trees.

Golf is certainly not all that Gatton Manor has to offer. The golfer, in his leisure moments, or indeed the non-golfer, can enjoy the benefits of the purpose-built gymnasium and health club which houses all the latest equipment, saunas, jacuzzi and solarium. Take a leisurely walk around the estate, and see many of the specimen trees and shrubs from the magnificent hybrid rhododendrons to the exotic magnolias and vast tulip tree.

The estate also teems with wildlife and the keen observer can see such birds as kingfisher, greenfinch and yellowhammer, whilst animals such as otter, and roe deer are to be seen in their natural habitat. Other outdoor activities available include tennis, bowls and coarse fishing. Alternatively guests can relax in the oak-beamed Golf Bar.

The attractive manor was built in 1728 and has been tastefully decorated to a high standard providing eighteen hotel rooms, all of which have en suite facilities. Adjoining the manor house is the delightful two-tiered dining room, residents' lounge, and private conference suites.

Gatton Manor Hotel, Golf & Country Club
Standon Lane
Ockley
nr Dorking
Surrey, RH5 5PQ
Tel: (01306) 627555
Fax: (01306) 627713
e mail: gattonmanor@enterprise.net

Sedgefield

The team in charge here are **Chairman Bob Bowden, Clerk of the Course, James Hutchinson** and **Manager** and **Secretary, Alan Brown,** who can be contacted at **The Bungalow**, Sedgefield Racecourse, Sedgefield, Stockton on Tees TS21 2HW Tel (race-days only) (01740) 620366 Office (01740) 621925 Fax (01740) 620663.

The racecourse is approachable from Middlesbrough and the east via the A177, while the A1(M) makes the racecourse easily accessible for both northbound and southbound travellers, just follow the brown tourist signs to the course. For racegoers from the larger conurbations to the southwest the M62 and the A1(M) provide good routes. Despite its proximity to the Great North Road, the track has a remote and quiet setting. Major train routes run to the centre of Darlington some 250 miles from London. The closest rail stations are at Stockton-on-Tees (nine miles away), Durham (twelve miles) and Darlington itself. There is ample free parking for a variety of vehicles, although there is a charge of £2 in the Paddock car park. Helicopters are also able to land at Sedgefield, but do please call in advance.

Sedgefield is the only course in County Durham and prides itself on being known as 'The Friendly Course'. There were 22 national hunt fixtures on offer in 2000 including 3 summer jumping meetings and the fixture list is likely to remain relatively unchanged. The course's major race each year is the Durham National Handicap Steeplechase and it should be noted that the management here have managed to attract excellent sponsorship support to boost the prizes.

The course has only two enclosures: a combined Paddock and Tattersalls area which is reasonably priced at £10 (OAPs £5) and the Course Enclosure which is equally good value at £3. The course also offers special party rates with a 50 per cent discount for groups of 40 or more in the Paddock. Children under 16 are admitted free in both enclosures.

During recent years the racecourse management has spent over a million pounds on improvements to the track, stabling and public amenities. A new weighing room, incorporating two entertainment suites with viewing balconies overlooking the parade ring and winners enclosure have been added, as well as a renovated public bar. A new pavilion has recently been built to house a bar, snack bar, restaurant and private boxes with new Tote facilities. There are now ten private boxes, the six additional ones situated in the new pavilion. All have excellent views of the winning post. Two sponsors suites are available for hire, the first seats up to 100 while the smaller one seats up to 40. The caterers are Ramside Event Catering who can be contacted on 0191 236 4148. Good value lunches are available at Sedgefield in the Pavilion Restaurant which seats 100. There are various snack bars to keep the hunger pangs at bay as well as two restaurants, offering both à la carte and table d'hôte dining.

There are two special Family Evenings which is splendid to report. This type of entertainment is excellent and if recent research is to be believed, this is the area with the most growth potential. The disabled racegoer has special ramps to ensure a pleasant day. An on-course betting office is in existence as well as telephones, although no banking facilities are available. Sedgefield is well supported by the local community and visitors from further afield are encouraged to visit this unspoilt, well run racecourse which has been significantly refurbished

*Artist: **Klaus Philipp** STEEPLECHASER Courtesy of: **The Artist***

Sedgefield

in recent years. A visit in 2001 should certainly be put in the diary.

Local Favourites

Sedgefield is surrounded by a number of good hotels and a visit in 2001 is well recommended. **Blackwell Grange** (01325) 509955 in Darlington is also one to note. An excellent Italian restaurant is **Sardis** (01325) 461222—which, given the quality, is well priced. Heading north we find **Headlam Hall** (01325) 730238—a worthy selection—whilst the **Dog** (01325) 312152 is a possibility for a pre-race pint. **Redworth Hall Hotel & Country Club** (01388) 772442 is a fine hotel—a good restaurant here as well. **Ramside Hall** 0191 3865282 outside Durham is also handy. A good golf course for those who enjoy this sport.

Stapleton offers the **Hilton White Horse Hotel** (01325) 382121—not grand but comfortable and convenient. For an excellent post-race nosebag try the **Black Bull Inn** (01325) 377289 in Moulton. It's a mile and a half off the A1 at Scotch Corner and is one of the most celebrated fish restaurants in the country. In Rushyford, three miles from the course, one finds the **Swallow Eden Arms Hotel** (01388) 720541 which receives promising reports from locals in the know. On the doorstep of the racecourse itself, the **Dun Cow** (01740) 620894 will provide for your every reasonable need! The **George** at Piercebridge (01325) 374576 has a magnificent setting and offers good food and some accommodation.

Over in the city of Durham the cathedral is awe - inspiring and the castle is also worth a look. If you are going to stay here, then the better hotels include the stylish **Royal County** 0191

3866821 which overlooks the River Wear and the **Three Tuns** 0191 386 4326. If you like a good restaurant try **Bistro 21** in Aykley Heads 0191 384 4354 it's a real gem. In Coatham Mundeville - a 15 minute drive from Sedgefield - between Darlington and Newton Aycliffe, one finds a hot favourite—**Hall Garth Golf and Country Club** (01325) 300400, a well appointed 16th century mansion—thoroughly recommended.

There are two places nearer the course that should also be considered in your each-way plans. Firstly, **Hardwick Hall** (01740) 620253, which lies one mile west of the town making it most convenient for early morning race enthusiasts. Secondly, the **Nags Head** (01740) 620234, an extremely friendly pub which offers good bar snacks as well as having a separate restaurant. A good idea for a pre-race rendezvous when travelling the turf in 2001.

*Artist: **Neil Cawthorne** UPS AND DOWNS Courtesy of: **The Artist***

The **Clerk of the Course** at Southwell is **Michael Prosser,** the **Operations Manager** is **Amanda Boby,** the **Commercial Manager** is **Pat Mitchell,** the **Estate Manager** is **David Williams** and **Sales and Marketing Manager** is **Adam Gray.** They can be contacted at the **Southwell Racecourse, Rolleston, Newark NG25 OTS. Tel (01636) 814481. Fax (01636) 812271. Website: www.southwell-racecourse.co.uk.**

The racecourse itself has a splendidly scenic setting. A Midlands track, it is situated just outside the Nottinghamshire village of Rolleston some five miles from Newark and within access of various motorway routes. Westminster Abbey is some 138 miles away and the A1 is the most direct route to follow. Northbound travellers should exit for the racecourse on the A6065 and then pursue the A617. The A46, which runs from east to west, serves racegoers from those points of the compass. The A617 should be used by travellers from the north west and is convenient owing largely to its connection with the M1, junction 29. Drivers should also note the new Newark bypass. If you do not wish to travel by car, then the train is a cert. In fact, Rolleston's station is one of the most convenient racecourse stations in the land. Nottingham is on London's St Pancras line and from here one can catch a train to nearby Rolleston. Some of the Mansfield/Newark buses also stop in Rolleston a quarter of a mile from the course. As one would expect with such a rural track, there are plenty of parking areas in the fields around which are free. Helicopters may land in the centre of the course, subject to prior agreement.

As a result of its all-weather track, Southwell has experienced a whole new lease of life. The 2001 fixture list will follow a broadly similar pattern to 2000. Admission to the course is £14 for Daily Members and £8 for Tattersalls. OAP's may get in to Tatts for £6 if they are members of the Diamond Club into which there is a £2.50 administration charge. The cost of Annual Membership at Southwell is £190 for a single and £280 for a married couple. Membership includes parking, reciprocal meetings and the use of the Queen Mother's Restaurant, Paddock viewing balcony and Members Bar and Restaurant. The racecourse offers attractive discounts to Tattersalls according to the size of your party—contact the racecourse management for details. For groups of 30—50 there is a £1 discount rising to £1.50 for groups of 50 or more. These discounts are restricted to Tattersalls only.

This year will see the completion of new Corporate Hospitality suites at Southwell, which will be able to accommodate parties of up to 50 people. Each will overlook the track and adjoin the Members Suite. The present members area will be extended substantially to take care of the course's growing membership and those wishing to dine in the Queen Mother restaurant. When it is complete, the Members Suite will be able to host up to 450 people.

Other details to be noted when considering a day's outing at Southwell—children under 16 are admitted free if they are accompanied by an adult. If the racing does not grip them then they will be delighted to hear that there is a supervised play area available at a small cost of £1 per child. There are two telephones in the Tote hall and one in the Members Bar and Weighing Room. Facilities for the disabled are good. Both floors are purpose built with lavatories, a lift and viewing platform. There is a Tote and Ladbrokes betting shop in the Grandstand too.

Artist: **Katy Sodeau** *CIRCLING BEFORE THE START* *Courtesy of:* **The Artist**

This is a developing racecourse with a constant eye to the future. It boasts a small motel with an 18 hole golf course and all manner of other facilities. The development of the golf course emphasises well the endeavour to offer racegoers a facility over and above the racecourse itself. There are also American-style training barns. With a constant eye ahead, RAM Racecourses Ltd are reconditioning this essentially rural track. They are experts in the art and we wish them well. All-weather racing does a huge amount for the sport—congratulations to all involved.

Local Favourites

The **Saracen's Head Hotel** (01636) 812701 is the ideal starting point for visitors to Southwell racecourse. The inn dates from the 16th century and its Stuart heritage is displayed in many paintings. Southwell also boasts **Upton Fields House** (01636) 812303 an excellent bed & breakfast establishment. Somewhat further afield, **The George** (01780) 750750 at Stamford is a magnificent old coaching inn whilst the **Cavendish** (01246) 582311 occupies a superb setting in the grounds of Chatsworth and has a fine restaurant with venison a speciality. In Stamford, a super old market town, note the **Lord Burghley**—a lively pub renowned for its fine ales. Other places to stay include the **Bull and Swan Inn** (01780) 63558 and the **Crown Hotel** (01780) 63136—both are marvellous old inns and make for a pleasant place to stay. For those heading south, the **Ram Jam Inn** (01780) 410776 on the A1 at Stretton is convenient and well recommended as a good stopping place. The **Black Swan** (016360) 626474, is a really good restaurant in Beckingham. The **Square & Compass** in Normanton on Trent is a good pub to remember, as is the handy **Red Lion** in Thurgaton.

The **French Horn** at Upton, is certainly worth visiting for its good value, quality pub food and is especially convenient for Rolleston and the racecourse. In Maplebeck, a little further north, the **Beehive** village pub is worth a visit despite or perhaps because it is a little out of the way in the Nottinghamshire countryside. Travelling in the same direction, the medieval village of Laxton offers the hospitable **Moorgate Farmhouse**

(01777) 870274 and the **Dovecote** is a friendly place to visit. In Marston, the **Thorold Arms**, convenient for A1 travellers and for **Marston Hall**, offers a particularly good drop of ale and nice bar meals. In Bottesford, due north of Belvoir Castle, one finds an excellent and intimate restaurant—the **Peacock** at Redmile (01949) 842554. Other than Belvoir Castle itself, Newstead Abbey is a sight worth seeing, home of the poet, the sixth Lord Byron, housing numerous personal articles; the gardens too are ideal for a diversion for the less than enthusiastic racing partner. Golfers might care to note the **Belton Woods** (01476) 593200—a large hotel with good leisure facilities. **Harry's Place** (01476) 561780 at Great Gonerby is top of the handicap in the restaurant stakes—first class. Four miles further north you find **Barkston House** (01400) 50555 in Barkston, a charming restaurant with rooms. South of Southwell at Lowdham, the **Springfield Inn** (01602) 663387 is a comfortable place in which to stay, as is **Langar Hall** (01949) 60559 in Langar whilst Southwell's **Racecourse Hotel** (01636) 814481 is excellent value. The **Full Moon Inn**, just one mile from the racecourse is also a newcomer of note. Finally, we recommend a local favourite; the **Old Forge** at Southwell (01636) 812809. Bed and Breakfast may be had at **Racecourse Farm** (01636) 812176, a five minute walk from the course.

*Artist: **H Matthews KICK BACK** Courtesy of: **The Artist***

Racecourse Manager and Clerk of the Course at Stratford is Mr Stephen Lambert. He can be contacted via The Racecourse, Luddington Road, Stratford upon Avon. CV37 9SE. Tel (01789) 267949 /269411 Fax (01789) 415850. Website: www.stratfordracecourse.net.

Stratford is fairly easy to reach from all directions and the racecourse lies one mile south west of the town. Access is via the M40 (Warwick turn off) from the north. From other directions, the M5, M42 and M6 are all within a half hour's drive of the course. The new Stratford bypass is handy and there are AA signs to the racecourse to further assist on racedays. If you wish to travel by train from London then you should aim for Stratford-upon-Avon from Euston, changing at Coventry, or Paddington changing at Leamington Spa. There is no bus directly from the station to the course but buses from the town heading to Evesham do pass the entrance to Luddington Road. There is ample parking at Stratford with a large free car park. A charge of £2 is made for cars parking in the main car park in the centre of the course from which you can access the new exit route from the racecourse. Members park separately. There are also good facilities for coaches but limited scope for helicopters, so please arrange with the racecourse in advance.

In 2000 there were 14 fixtures, including the popular Monday in March which coincides with the Cheltenham festival, drawing a good crowd; and a Sunday meeting in July. The major fixture remains the Horse and Hound Cup Final Championship Hunters Steeplechase which is now a two day festival. In 2000, Annual Membership badges cost £100 with an extra £7 required for an annual car park badge. Daily Membership is now £15. Entrance to Tattersalls is £10, whereas the Course Enclosure costs £4. If you are planning a party, 15 is the minimum required for a 20 per cent reduction. For further details, contact the Manager. Children under 16 are welcomed at no charge.

There is a new hospitality room at Stratford and the course does have plenty of facilities in the way of boxes, conference areas and function rooms. The Avon Suite is specifically designed for corporate hospitality, catering for up to 90 people. Requests for these facilities should be directed to the racecourse management. The outside caterers are Jenkinson Caterers Ltd who can be contacted on (01785) 252247. The course has several bars which have recently been refurbished and provide snacks. The Paddock Suite Restaurant has also undergone a £350,000 refurbishment and is available for bookings.

The new grandstand provides comfortable and improved facilities. Members now have a champagne/ seafood bar, tea room, Tote, and William Hill betting shop, while Tatts patrons benefit from a new snack bar, Tote, betting shop and bar. There is also a large box on the second floor for corporate entertainment. There are some amenities for disabled racegoers for whom a small stand is provided, with excellent viewing. Telephones are located in the Members Enclosure and Tattersalls but there is no bank at the course so bring plenty of readies with you.

Stratford racecourse is a good track. The M40 extension makes the trip far speedier for many visitors and this will hopefully boost attendances. There are all manner of reasons for going racing: a day in the fresh air, a rendezvous with friends, a tilt at the ring or, if you are lucky, to watch your own horse run. Stratford does not profess to being Britain's foremost

Artist: **Malcolm Coward** *RIDING A FINISH* *Courtesy of:* **Sally Mitchell Fine Arts**

racecourse but it provides good racing in a convenient location and a visit should be considered in 2001.

Local Favourites

The first production of *A Midsummer Night's Dream* apparently took place in the grounds of **Alveston Manor** (01789) 204581. The house retains much of its Elizabethan charm and is a relaxing place to stay. A Georgian hotel convenient for the theatre is **Stratford House** (01789) 268288, less expensive and with an excellent restaurant. On the Warwick road the **Welcombe Hotel** (01789) 295252 is also well thought of, boasting 18 holes of golf, some delightful rooms and a first class restaurant. Pride of place goes to **Ettington Park** (01789) 450123 in nearby Alderminster. The hotel is magnificent, the bedrooms are charmingly furnished and the bars and library comfortable and relaxing. In Ettington itself, the **Chase Hotel** (01789) 740000 is good value with an excellent restaurant. Among the wealth of

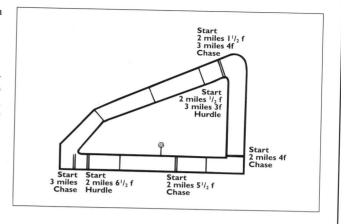

guesthouses that form an equally important part of Stratford's accommodation industry, **Broad Marston Manor** (01789) 720252 is recommended. Another hotel of acclaim outside Stratford-upon-Avon—the **Billesley Manor** (01789) 279955, is a fine gabled manor house. Those seeking fine fare might consider **Liaison** (01789) 293400 or **The Opposition** (01789) 269980. The **Boathouse** (01789) 297733 has a pleasant riverside setting.

People who prefer a day out without an overnight stay might wish to sample any one of a number of pubs. In Wellesbourne, the **King's Head** (01789) 840206 is good for lunch and **Charlecotte Park**, a superb Elizabethan mansion, lies close by and can be viewed between April and October. The **Charlecote Pheasant** (01789) 279954 is a good hotel to visit. The **Butcher's Arms** at Priors Hardwick, more of a restaurant than a pub, is handy for the A41 while the A34 reveals the **White Hart** (01789) 450205 at Newbold-on-Stour, an excellent place to have a bar snack. In Oxhill, the **Peacock** is an extremely hospitable village pub as is the **Royal Oak** in Whatcote. Traditionalists will enjoy the **King's Head** (01789) 488242 at Aston Cantlow, another tremendously atmospheric pub. In Wilmcote, the **Swan House** is also splendid with an excellent and varied menu. If you are keen to enjoy the Cotswolds after the Stratford steeds then a reasonably priced and extremely relaxing hotel to visit is the **Three Ways House** (01386) 438429 at Mickleton—the restaurant is also quietly civilised with a fine wine list. In Chipping Campden, two establishments worthy of note are the **Cotswold House Hotel** (01386) 840330 and its restaurant and the **Noel Arms** (01386) 840317. Finally, close by at Charingworth, **Charingworth Manor** (01386) 593555 provides accommodation and service of the highest standard, while the **Houndshill** (01789) 740267 is a pleasant inn on the A422 and an ideal place to stay.

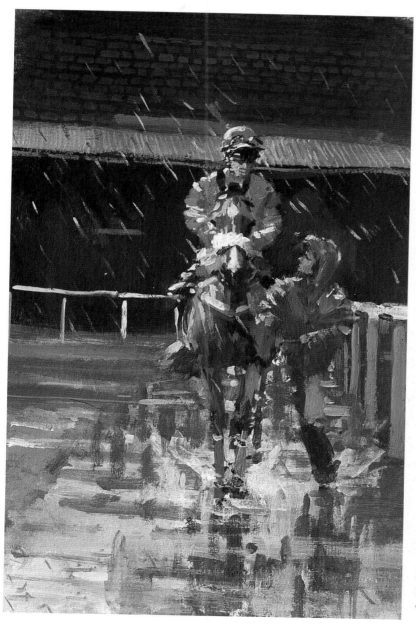

*Artist: **David Trundley** SLANTING DOWN Courtesy of: **The Artist***

Michael Trickey, the well known West Country point-to-point trainer and hunter judge, who regularly judges at the Dublin and Great Yorkshire shows, is **Clerk of the Course**. He and **John Hills**, the **Manager** and **Secretary**, can both be contacted via the course at **Orchard Portman, Taunton, Somerset TA3 7BL. Tel (01823) 337172 Fax (01823) 325881. Website: www.tauntonracecourse.co.uk.** Few racecourse managers are so genuinely enthusiastic about the task in hand, and we warmly recommend a visit if you are exploring the south west in 2001.

Taunton is 100 minutes from London on a fast train with a direct service from Plymouth and has good connections from the North and Midlands. The course is situated close to the M5, 50 minutes south of the M4 intersection, while the A303 is fast achieving near motorway status as a major trunk route giving access from the south coast. Why not travel the day before racing and spend the night in a local hostelry? Buy your day badge and a plentiful supply of Tote vouchers in advance from the racecourse secretary and you won't need to worry about living it up overnight in the Cider County. Our punter could also settle comfortably into a Pullman seat on the Paddington train secure in the knowledge that his Day badge will be £12, Paddock £10 or Course £6. Cars are free—unless they go onto the centre of the course as the base for a family picnic or portable grandstand, in which case have £3 handy.

Those who know Taunton well are delighted by the new pre-Parade Ring and Winners Enclosure which has been returned to the Parade Ring. Together they give the dedicated punter a much improved view of the horses before and after the race.

When the weather is wet and the wind keen, the Saddle Room on the ground floor of the Paddock Stand is an ideal place to have tea, coffee and a snack while you put your feet up and study the form. Catering is now 'in-house' at Taunton and very popular it is too! You can choose from the 'Racegoers Special' - a two or three-course quick service lunch in the Orchard Restaurant, or you can really indulge yourself and book a table in the restaurant with a birds-eye view of the course. The latter will cost you £36.50 for an all day table with a three course lunch, afternoon tea, complimentary racecard and tea and coffee service throughout the day. Admission is also included at a special discounted rate. These tables are popular though, so please book early. There is also a first-class Owners and Trainers Bar which is situated next to the Parade Ring and enjoys a fine view of the course.

You may enjoy your day at Taunton so much that you decide to become an Annual Member. 2001 prices are likely to be £90 for a single membership and £150 double for a Gentleman and Lady. This will give you 13 days racing at Taunton plus another 14 at other courses around the country including Newbury, Cheltenham, Chepstow and Wincanton.

The course betting shop is run by Peter Jolliffe. This and the Tote betting shops are in Tattersalls, together with two public telephones for credit punters. The course has reserved a prime viewing area next to the restaurant for the disabled, and all the public parts of the course help accommodate their needs. Manager John Hills is a man who clearly loves his racing—if you love yours, take a trip to Taunton and you won't be disappointed.

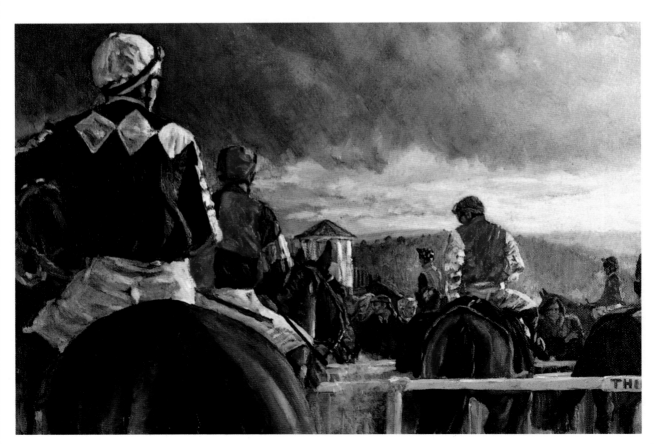

Artist: **David Dent** *COME RAIN OR SHINE Courtesy of:* **Howard Manning**

Local Favourites

In the town itself, the **Castle Hotel** (01823) 272671 on Castle Green is excellent in every way. One mile outside the town at Bishop's Hull lies the outstanding (and outstandingly reasonable) **Meryan House Hotel** (01823) 337445. Also south of the town is **Rumwell Manor Hotel** (01823) 461902 a quietly elegant hotel set in five acres of parkland. The city centre is changing nearly every day but restaurants are a little thin on the ground although **Porters Wine Bar** (01823) 256688 is an enjoyable establishment. Some of the many pubs in the area are obviously good places to meet for a post-race beverage. In Staple Fitzpaine, close to the racecourse, the **Greyhound** (01823) 480227 is a splendid little pub serving an excellent pint and good bar snacks. It also has an adjoining restaurant, a fine place for post-race dinner. The **Volunteer** at Seavington St Michael is a good place both for its cooking and for that extraordinary stuff, Scrumpy. Another good value food pub is the **Square and Compass** (01823) 480467 in Ashill. The **Rose and Crown** at East Lyng is also good. Breaking momentarily from the pub scene, it is well worth seeking out **Farthings Country House Hotel** (01823) 480664 at Hatch Beauchamp—an attractive Georgian house convenient for the racecourse. **Nightingales** (01823) 480806 is a well thought of restaurant to consider here. The **Mount Somerset** (01823) 44250 is also well worth a pre race inspection.

Many people racing at Taunton are locals just out for a quick day's sport. If, however, you have made a bit of an effort to go to Taunton races, then one great place to reward yourself is the **Kingfishers Catch** (01823) 432394 at Bishops Lydeard on the A358 (more a restaurant than a pub) en route to the splendid Dunster Castle. A hotel which affords great comfort is **Langley House** (01984) 623318, near Wiveliscombe on the A361. With sofas, an array of fresh flowers and some splendid views, one really feels the closeness of the countryside. For an informal stay and personal attention, this cannot be beaten—an excellent restaurant here as well. We finish with two splendid pubs. The **Rising Sun** (01823) 490436 in the very appropriately named Knapp especially for those who enjoy fish, and the **Rose and Crown** (01823) 490296 at Stoke St Gregory—an outstanding establishment and very welcoming (some good value rooms here - ask for the cottage rooms). Further north in Nether Stowey lies the **Apple Tree Hotel** (01278) 733238—highly recommended. Take a trip this year to the south west—it's a delightful part of the country.

*Artist: **David Trundley** TAUNTON EVENING MEETING Courtesy of: **The Artist***

Situated in the North Yorkshire town of Asenby you will find the delightfully different Crab Manor. Since it was opened back in July 1990, this hotel has provided a whirlwind tour of some of the World's most famous hotels - but without stepping onto a single aeroplane or grappling with the tiniest bit of jet-lag. Crab Manor is where grown-ups can step into their dreams.

The reason this is possible is because the converted Georgian House, set in beautiful gardens and grounds, is a collection of rooms fashioned, complete with antiques and artifacts, on unique different luxury hotels from around the world, transporting guests into a fantasy of exotic faraway places. The whistle stop tour takes in Le Manoir, Oxford; Sandy Lane, Barbados; La Mamounia, Marrakech; Turnberry, Scotland; Cipriani Palace, Venice; Mount Nelson, Cape Town; Waldorf Astoria, New York - or the luxury rooms with special extras are Sharrow Bay,

Ullswater; Le Touessroc, Mauritius; Raffles, Singapore; and Bird Island, Seychelles.

Alongside the Manor is the Crab & Lobster restaurant, an Aladdin's cave of a place (which has racing, and all sorts, of mementos from years gone by) that has had food critics singing its praises since its opening. As you probably guessed from the name the restaurant has a magnificent collection of fish dishes from which to choose. From the humble Cod & Chips through to Lobster Thermidor there is something to suit everybody's taste.

For the racing enthusiast Crab Manor is handily placed for all the courses in Yorkshire but is set half way between Thirsk and Ripon, making it a perfect stopover whilst visiting some of the more northerly courses. So for that extra special night away the Crab Manor has to be high on anybody's list.

Crab Manor
Asenby
Thirsk
North Yorkshire
YO7 3QL
Tel: (01845) 577286
Fax: (01845) 577109
e mail: reservations@crabandlobster.co.uk

Mr Christopher Tetley acts as **Clerk of the Course, Manager and Secretary,** and **Gaynor Garrity** is **Sponsorship and Marketing Manager.** Both can be contacted at **Thirsk Racecourse, Station Road, Thirsk, North Yorkshire YO7 1Ql. Tel (01845) 522276 Fax (01845) 525353. Web site: www.thirskracecourse.net E mail: info@thirskraces.fastnet.co.uk**

The racecourse is situated just off the A61 west of Thirsk. The best route for travellers from the south is to use the A1/A1M northbound and then follow the A61, or the A19 if journeying from York. Southbound drivers should also use the A1, or alternatively the A61 or A19. If travelling from the east, the A170 is convenient whilst eastbound journeyers should take the M62 and the A1 north. There is ample car parking to be found on arriving. If you wish to travel by train, the Kings Cross line is pretty swift and Thirsk station is a mere six furlongs away from the station, although you will need to change en route. Buses to Thirsk will take you to within a quick canter of the track but there are no special race buses. One other point that should be noted is that there are facilities for helicopters if you're lucky enough to have one. In the past one frequently heard of jockeys missing races due to delays on the A1. The road is clearer now but make sure you set off in good time just to be sure.

With so many weekend fixtures and an evening fixture, the Thirsk racegoer is thoroughly spoilt. The 2001 Guineas Trial is the oldest Classic trial in the country. The Thirsk Hunt Cup day is also good value. There were some thirteen racing days held during 2000 with the meetings in April, May and August perennially the most popular.

There are three enclosures at Thirsk: the Members, Tattersalls and the Family Ring. In 2000, prices were £14, £9 and £3. Party bookings are encouraged and various arrangements and discounts can be agreed with the course. This largely depends on your ability to gather troops to the fray. Basically, the more the merrier. However, these party terms do not apply to the Members Enclosure. In 2000, Membership cost £90, whilst Associate Membership cost £150—this apparently means a man, plus another member of the family—family is not defined! Annual Members are also entitled to a 10 per cent discount in selected local restaurants. Juniors are welcomed and the Annual Membership subscription is good value at £40. Your membership also entitles you to nine reciprocal meetings and eleven days courtesy of Yorkshire Cricket Club—what a bargain! Cars can be parked beside the course in the Family Ring on all days.

The racecourse rests at the foot of the Hambleton Hills and has an excellent setting, subject naturally to the weather. There are several snack bars around the course and a more substantial restaurant can be found in the Members Stand. The Grimthorpe Hall in Tattersalls, combines bars, a tea bar, fast food outlets and Tote facilities. Bookings for lunch should be made through Craven Gilpin & Sons in Leeds (0113) 287 6387. Bars in both the Members and Tattersalls have also been improved and the Manton Suite has new hospitality facilities available: tables for 10 or larger parties can be reserved in advance at an all inclusive price. If you wish to have a picnic then the racecourse welcomes this and if you want to order a viewing box this can also be arranged—there is a choice of five and they can hold from ten to twenty people. For large functions there is an ideal

Artist: **Peter Smith** *COMING IN AFTER THE LAST RACE, EVENING* *Courtesy of:* **Frost & Reed**

place near the Paddock for a marquee and a new function room for Members overlooking the lawns and Parade Ring which opened in Spring 2000. This will cater for two parties of 50, one of 100, or individual tables which can be reserved for the full day. Again, arrangements and bookings can be made through the racecourse. This is a friendly racecourse in a beautiful part of England—well worth a visit.

Local Favourites

In Thirsk itself, the **Golden Fleece** (01845) 523108 is a convenient place to stay. The hotel is an old coaching inn and it faces onto a cobbled market square. Just outside the town is the small but cosy **Sheppard's** (01845) 523655. **The Angel** at Topcliffe (01845) 577237 is another to consider. Climbing into the Hambleton Hills one arrives at Helmsley. Here, there is a number of good hotels, pubs and another scenic market place. This is an ideal base for exploring the nearby Dales and two sights that should definitely be seen are the ruins of Rievaulx and Byland Abbey. The **Black Swan** (01439) 770466 is extremely comfortable with a fine restaurant. A similar accolade befits the **Feathers** (01439) 770275.

Another good spot is the **Fauconberg Arms** (01347) 868214 in Coxwold, a first class pub popular locally (always a good sign) with some good bedrooms. In Harome the **Pheasant** (01439) 771241, a pleasant hotel, provides good accommodation in relaxing surroundings and **The Star Inn** (01439) 770397 is also excellent. In Kirkbymoorside, the **George & Dragon** (01751) 433334 is excellent for a bar snack and some cosy bedrooms make it an ideal place to stay.

The **Plough Inn** (01751) 4731515 in Fadmoor is first class. Other good restaurants can be found near Northallerton. In nearby Staddle Bridge, an outstanding restaurant is **McCoys Bistro** (01609) 882671. An evening here will be one to remember. In Pickhill, the appropriately named **Nags Head Inn** (01845) 567391 is a favourite—good food and some pleasant accommodation. The **Bay Horse** in Rainton and the **Fox and Hounds** in

Carthorpe are also very popular. Another interesting alternative is the excellent **Solberge Hall** (01609) 779191 in Newby Wiske, a really appealing place with delightful views of the moors. A little further afield, but extremely conveniently situated for the A1 is the **Crown Hotel** (01423) 322328 in Boroughbridge. Those who enjoy a really first class inn should sample the delights of the **Worsley Arms Hotel** at Hovingham (01653) 628234—an excellent establishment.

Other selections in this excellent field—all within five miles of the course—include the **Crab and Lobster** (01845) 577286 at Asenby—extremely popular and rightly so—make sure you get there early. Crab Manor, contactable on the same number is a really fun hotel—order a brochure and you will see why! The **Carpenters Arms** (01845) 537369 at Felixkirk and the **Whitestonecliffe Inn** (01845) 597271 in Sutton under Whitestonecliffe are also good. Slightly further afield, in Kilburn, is the **Forresters Arms** (01347) 868386. Kilburn is the home of the famous 'Mouse Man' furniture maker. Finally, we come to the **George and Dragon**, Melmerby, (01765) 640303. This is a small inn located between Thirsk and Ripon—ideally placed for two of Yorkshire's excellent racetracks.

*Artist: **Jacquie Jones** TURNING FOR HOME Courtesy of: **The Artist***

The Worsley Arms Hotel

The Worsley Arms Hotel is an attractive stone built Georgian Inn in the heart of Hovingham, one of Yorkshires most beautiful villages.

Built in 1841 the hotel was the idea of Sir William Worsley, the first Baronet. His intention was to provide accommodation for travellers who were attending the nearby Hovingham Spa. Unfortunately the mile and a half treck down a dust lane proved unacceptable and the Spa failed.

Across the village green from the Worsley Arms sits Hovingham Hall, designed and built in 1760 by Thomas Worsley. The hall is the home of Sir Marcus Worsley, the fifth Baronet, and is the birthplace of his sister, Her Royal Highness The Duchess of Kent.

The Worsley Arms is currently operated by Anthony and Sally Finn. Together with the hard working team they create a relaxed atmosphere for you to enjoy.

Meals may be taken in the Restaurant or in the less formal Cricketers Bar. Which ever you choose be prepared for the wine list, which is renowned for both its range and value for money. For those with an interest in wine, ask to visit the cellar where an interesting selection of 'bin ends' can be found.

When the sun shines you can enjoy afternoon tea or a light snack in the beautiful walled garden or in winter in front of a log fire in one of the spacious lounges.

The bedrooms, each with private bathroom, are individually and tastefully decorated, providing every comfort with extensive modern facilities.

The village is on the edge of a designated Area of Outstanding Natural Beauty; national parks are on the doorstep, the nearby Yorkshire Dales and the North York Moors. The area is rich in romantic and historic sites—the ruined abbeys of Rievaulx and Fountains, the castles of Helmsley and Pickering, the stately homes of Castle Howard, Duncombe Park and, of course, Hovingham Hall. Leisure pursuits abound as the hotel is ideally placed for quality racing, golfing (the championship courses of Ganton and Fulford are within half an hour's drive), shooting and walking.

The Worsley Arms Hotel
Hovingham
York
YO6 4LA
Tel: (01653) 628234
Fax: (01653) 628130

Chris Palmer leads the Towcester team as **Managing Director,** and **Hugo Bevan** is **Clerk of the Course**. Contact can be made by writing to **Towcester Racecourse, Easton Neston, Towcester, Northants NN12 7HS. Tel (01327) 353414 Fax (01327) 358534. Web site: www.towcester-racecourse.co.uk.**

The racecourse itself is situated one mile south east of the town of Towcester which lies at the intersection of the A43 and the A5. Although the course itself has a tranquil setting, the M1 is only a few miles away. People travelling from both the north and south should get on to the M1 and exit at junction 15a. The A43 towards Oxford should be followed for some six miles until the junction with the A5. From the town centre, follow the signs for the racecourse.

The major train routes leave Euston and racegoers are advised to go either to Milton Keynes or Northampton. The former is some eleven miles away and the latter nine. Bus services run from Northampton but only as far as Towcester, half a mile short of the racecourse. A better bet would be to take a helicopter, but make arrangements with the racecourse staff beforehand. There is ample free parking space which is ideal for picnics and there is a roped off area for Members parking.

In 2000 there was a total of 17 fixtures, including one Sunday meeting. The bank holiday meetings at Easter and in early May are always popular—6000 racegoers wisely decided to spend last Easter Monday at Towcester and evening meetings also bring out the locals in droves. The course provides lots of entertainment for evening, Easter and bank holiday meetings and this is obviously paying dividends.

Day badges will be £14 for the Members, £10 for Tattersalls and £6 for the Course Enclosure. People lucky enough to justify getting the most out of an Annual Membership will pay £145 single or £135 each double (no junior rates). OAPs will pay £11 for a day badge for the Members and £7 for Tattersalls.

The £1 million redevelopment of the Grace Stand includes a 150 seater restaurant and six private boxes with lifts to all floors for the disabled. If you are wishing to take a party racing then do contact the racecourse for discounts which are given on group bookings of 20 or more. If you prefer more exclusive comfort then the Members Lawn has a newly erected Paddock Pavilion, which can cater for groups from 20 to 250. For smaller groups there is the Old Press Box or the Stewards Tower. Alternatively you could have a marquee beside the Grace Stand or hire one of the range of corporate hospitality boxes.

The racecourse has the standard telephone and betting facilities in Tattersalls but there are no banking facilities available. Towcester has much to commend it, not least its marvellous setting. It is surely one of the most charming country courses in Britain. It is no surprise that many rate this unassuming course as one of the country's most appealing. A visit for 2001 is an absolute priority.

Local Favourites

If you should wish to make a weekend trip to Towcester then the following hotels are to be noted. In Northampton, the **Northampton Moat House** (01604) 739988 is good. Another to remember is the **Swallow Hotel** (01604) 768700. The hotel is

Artist: **Heather St Clair Davis FULL OF PROMISE** *Courtesy of:* **Frost & Reed**

modern in design but luxurious and the leisure facilities are good. The Racecourse has links with the **Hilton Northampton Hotel** (01604) 700666 and the **Saracen's Head** (01327) 350414 in Towcester itself and if you mention you are visiting for the races you can get a special rate. Also, opposite the racecourse is **The Folly** which has recently been refurbished and offers quality food.

The **Farthingstone Hotel, Golf & Leisure Centre** (01327) 361291 is well placed for the racecourse and is very comfortable. The **Plough** (01327) 350738, on the road out of Towcester, is well worth a post-race quickie and the **Brave Old Oak** is also worth your attention. In Stoke Bruerne a canal-side stop-off reveals the **Boat Inn** (01604) 862428. The pub itself has a fairly modern interior but the welcome is genuine as is the restaurant—a sound each-way chance. **Bruerne's Lock** (01604) 863654 with its canal—side setting is also reported to be good.

Only six miles from Towcester lies Roade. The aptly named **Roadehouse Restaurant** (01604) 863372 has a pleasant situation in the village which is only two miles from junction 15 of the motorway. There are rooms here as well. In Horton, the **French Partridge** (01604) 870033 is an outstanding restaurant. After a cold afternoon's racing, there could be nothing better than sitting down to some quite superb game—a really first class idea. The **Vine House Restaurant** (01327) 811267 at Paulerspury also offers excellent cooking and some pleasing bedrooms, definitely one for the Towcester visitor. In Weedon, the **Crossroads** (01327) 340354 is convenient for the M1, junction 16, and is also extremely pleasant. (Breakfasts and coffees are served to non-residents). There are a number of pubs which have appeal:

in Akeley, the **Bull and Butcher** (01280) 860257 is friendly and offers superb steaks, in Brackley Hatch, the **Green Man** may be inspected, whilst Potterspury offers the **Old Talbot**. North of Towcester, the **Red Lion** (01604) 770223 at East Haddon offers good bar food, good beer and some pleasant accommodation. For those keen on having an outstanding weekend, two somewhat distant thoughts. **Hartwell House** (01296) 747444 is the first—seeing is believing—a classic country house hotel located near Aylesbury. Alternatively, Woburn is a pleasant town where **Woburn Abbey** warrants a look, whilst other places to visit include the **Bedford Arms** (01525) 290441, an elegant inn and **Paris House** (01525) 290692—a marvellous restaurant with racing connections. Finally, The **Bell** is a pleasant place to enjoy a pint and bar snack.

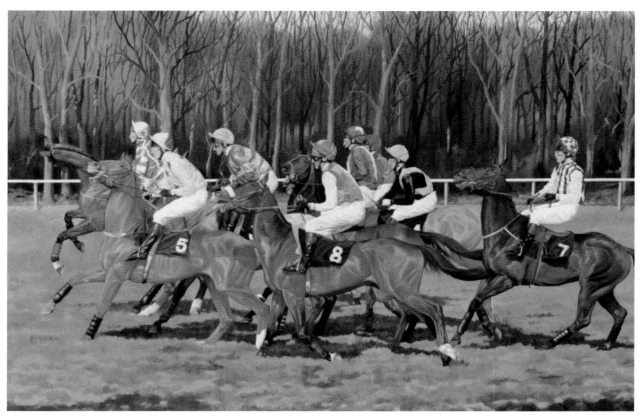

*Artist: **Philip Toon** OVER EAGER Courtesy of: **The Artist***

At Uttoxeter, **Rod Street** is the **Managing Director** and his seconds-in-command are **Louise Aspinall James Morley,** and **Lisa Needham.** Clerk of the Course is **David McAllister. Lynda Fletcher** and **Esther Hartas** are **Customer Services Assistants.** Uttoxeter also has another extremely valuable asset in their 'hands on' **Chairman, Stan Clarke CBE.** All may be contacted at **The Racecourse, Wood Lane, Uttoxeter, Staffordshire ST14 8BD. Tel (01889) 562561 Fax (01889) 562786. E mail: info@uttoxeterracecourse.co.uk. Web site: www.uttoxeterracecourse.co.uk.**

Uttoxeter is conveniently situated in the heart of the Midlands, equidistant between Stoke-on-Trent and Derby, just off the new A50, which has made the course even more accessible, London is 135 miles away to the south east. The course is a short hop from the town centre, just off the B5017 and is clearly signposted from the A50, A515 and A518. From the north or south of the country, the M6 is the motorway to aim for. Exit at junction 14 and then use the Stafford ring road or take junction 15 and follow the signs for the A50 to Derby. The new M40/M42 link is also a possibility if you do not wish to tackle the M1/M6 combination. All parking at the course is free and there is plenty available.

For those who prefer to travel by train, Uttoxeter Railway Station is right next door—you can walk off the platform straight onto the racecourse. Frequent Intercity services from Birmingham, Glasgow, Liverpool and Manchester run to Derby and Stoke-on-Trent, both of which run regular connecting trains to Uttoxeter. A direct service also operates from Crewe. By air, helicopters may land (by prior arrangement with the management) at the course itself, whilst light aircraft may use Tatenhill Airfield at Needwood, 7 miles from the racecourse. Telephone Tatenhill Aviation on (01283) 575283.

Uttoxeter enjoys an attendance of up to 15,000 on busy days and is surely a shining example of what can be achieved in all-round excellence at the races. Uttoxeter has been named "Best Regional Racecourse" for nine out of ten years, as well as the most "Owner Friendly". Prize money will be over £1,000,000 and this has played a large part in attracting the best horses for competitive jump racing. Uttoxeter now has two pattern races and the BBC covers the February and March meetings—another worthy tribute, along with Channel 4 coverage in January, May and December.

Admission prices at Uttoxeter for 2001 are £15 for the Members Enclosure, £11 for Tattersalls and £5 for the Centre course (a great place to picnic or bring your own barbecue, with a point-to-point atmosphere). On Midlands National day in March, Club and Tattersall prices rise to £25 and £15 respectively for the £160,000 added event. There are discounts for pensioners and under 16s are admitted free when accompanied by an adult. Annual Membership is excellent value at £160 for a single badge or £240 for a double badge. Juniors pay just £75. As well as 22 days at Uttoxeter, membership includes 23 reciprocal fixtures at other courses. Also included are all fixtures at Uttoxeter's sister courses, Newcastle and Brighton, as well as Fairyhouse, which all adds up to a staggering 100 days! Outstanding racing value for the enthusiast. Tickets and annual membership can now be purchased online from Uttoxeter's website.

Uttoxeter is an ideal place for corporate hospitality and the immaculate facilities at the progressive racecourse provide a setting in which companies can entertain in either a formal or informal manner. 65 rooms and boxes are available for parties of between 15 and 1000 guests. The latest addition to the hospitality facilities are

Artist: **Peter Smith** **FIRST HURDLE - THE BACKSTRAIGHT** *Courtesy of:* **Frost & Reed**

5 new corporate hospitality boxes built in 2000, overlooking the parade ring and winner's enclosure.

The Members restaurant, the Platinum Suite, has been recently refurbished to the highest standards and tables may be reserved in advance and retained throughout the meeting. Tables may also be reserved in Hoops Champagne and Seafood bar, adjacent to the Paddock.

At major meetings and on bank holidays, youngsters can enjoy a funfair and quad bikes—an excellent way to distract the kids. There are three public telephone boxes and reserved parking on the rails for disabled racegoers as well as a viewing platform and loos.

This is a thoroughly well-run and friendly racecourse offering fine facilities—a visit in 2001 should be a high priority.

Local Favourites

South of Stoke, in Stone, the **Crown** (01785) 813535 is an 18th century coaching inn set in lovely gardens which offers a pleasant restaurant. **Granvilles** (01785) 816658 is also a wine bar and restaurant to consider. Note **Callow Hall** (01335) 300900—a tranquil retreat. There are many pubs hidden away in these parts and invariably they have superb views. A place worth taking some trouble to find is the **Old Beams** (01538) 308254 at Waterhouses. This is a tremendous restaurant which has character and charm as well as some excellent food and pleasant bedrooms—thoroughly recommended.

In Uttoxeter itself, the **White Hart** (01889) 562437 is an historic coaching inn and the bar here makes a good place to meet if you are planning to see friends before the races. Another good inn is

Ye Olde Dog and Partridge (01283) 813030 in Tutbury. The building dates from the 15th century and the bars here are typical of this kind of inn, welcoming and refreshing. The **Mill House** (0116) 2536421 is a delightful alternative to consider. Perhaps an even more enchanting place to stay can be found in Rolleston-on-Dove. Here, the **Brookhouse Inn** (01283) 814188 has charming bars, a good restaurant and extremely pleasing bedrooms. Another superb hotel and restaurant double can be found close to here; the **Dovecliffe Hall** (01283) 531818 at Stretton. If you are seeking somewhere relatively inexpensive try the **Crown** (01283) 840227 in Abbots Bromley. **The Beeches**, in Doveridge (01889) 590288 is an excellent farmhouse-style establishment offering cosy accommodation and superb meals. Finally, the **Blacksmiths Arms** (01889) 562178 in Marchington offers innovative and realistically priced cuisine in rustic country-pub surroundings and is a favourite with the management of this first rate racecourse.

*Artist: **Paul Hart** FINAL RACE Courtesy of: **The Artist***

Hugo Bevan, Clerk of the Course and Christian Leech, Racecourse Manager can be contacted at Warwick Racecourse, Hampton Street, Warwick CV34 6HN. Tel (01926) 491553. Fax (01926) 403223. Web site: www.warwickracecourse.co.uk.

Warwick racecourse lies close to the junction of the A46 and the A41 and is convenient for the M1, M5 and M6, a mere eight miles from Stratford (which should be avoided in the summer) and 20 miles from Birmingham—following the M6—M42 (junction 2), thence on the A41. The A46 via Leamington Spa from the north and via Stratford from the south is most convenient. Travellers from the south and west might join the A46 from the A422, (Anne Hathaway's cottage marks the appropriate junction). Road travellers should also note the new M40 link as junction 15 is only two miles from the racecourse, making it extremely handy for Londoners and those from the south east.

The somewhat difficult train journey from London has been improved and there is now an hourly service direct from London to Warwick and Leamington. The station is a 20 minute walk from the racecourse. There is free parking for 3000 cars and there is also parking in the Members car park, but you will be charged £5 as a non-member for the privilege. Coaches are also welcome here with space for 100 altogether. Helicopters may land in the centre of the track at Warwick by arrangement but as for light aircraft, they are somewhat unwelcomingly sent to Coventry.

Racing in 2000 included both flat racing and National Hunt meetings, as well as one mixed fixture in March, one of the few on this side of the Irish Sea. Annual Membership rates for 2000 were £120 for a full badge and £75 for a National Hunt badge. Juniors (16 to 24) are charged £50 but please also note an extra £10 is asked for a car park badge if required. A Half Yearly Membership may be purchased from June 1st at a cost of £60. In addition to racing at Warwick, full Members are entitled to reciprocal arrangements at ten other courses. Each member is also given two vouchers which admit guests to the Club during the year. The Daily Club badge in 2000 was £15, Tattersalls (Grandstand and Paddock) £11 and £5 for the Course Enclosure. Warwick has undertaken an extensive £3 million refurbishment of the Members and Tattersalls grandstands, to include greater viewing, dining and betting facilities for punters, the results of which will be evident in 2001. Accompanied children under 16 are admitted free. Discounts on a sliding scale are given for parties of 20 or more in Tattersalls, if booked in advance.

Boxes in the Paddock Suite are available on a daily basis and enjoy spectacular views as well as from the balcony over the Paddock and racecourse. The elegant Castle Suite accommodates 60 for lunch or dinner and 80 for a buffet meal whilst the Chandler Suite, situated on the ground floor of the Members Enclosure, has a private viewing stand. The suite may be divided into three rooms if required. The Spartan Missile Room is opposite the winning post, offering entertaining views of the betting ring too. There are snack bars in all enclosures and two restaurants: the Paddock Bar and recently refurbished Members Bar. Booking is advisable on major racedays and can be done by telephoning the course caterers, Amadeus on 0121 767 2543. The Council Room in Tatts has also been refurbished and more upgrading is planned over the next few years. An exclusive Owners and Trainers room is also available.

Artist: **Malcolm Coward COMING IN AT WARWICK** *Courtesy of:* **Sally Mitchell Fine Arts**

A crèche is provided for all Saturday fixtures and bank holiday fixtures. Disabled people are accommodated by means of a raised stand, ramps and lavatories in the Members Enclosure. There are no banks on site at Warwick so come prepared as there is a betting shop in Tattersalls and the Course Enclosure (open Saturdays and bank holidays only).

While it is fair to say that no Midlands course is a major sporting venue, several provide excellent entertainment. Furthermore, Members here can enjoy a variety of racing at under £5 a head and to my mind that represents very good value.

Local Favourites

If you are staying nearby, a number of hotels stand out. A well thought of hotel is the **Hilton Warwick** (01926) 499555, most convenient for the A46 and the M40. By contrast, the **Old Fourpenny Shop** (01926) 491360 is small but appealing. The **Glebe** (01926) 624218 in Barford has good leisure facilities—an interesting option. We have also had a tip from one of Britain's foremost jockeys—the **Woodhouse Hotel** in Princethorpe (01926) 632131. **Walton Hall** (01789) 842424 is also a very good local hotel with a good restaurant, and we're told by a reliable source that **Henrietta's** (01926) 642212 in Kineton is excellent. Another popular local watering hole is the **Racehorse** in Stratford Road. Kenilworth has two fancied restaurants **Simpsons** (01926) 864567 and the **Restaurant Bosquet** (01926) 852463, while Charlecote offers the **Charlecote Pheasant** (01789) 470333–a pleasant hotel for a weekend away. Another original establishment, the **Case is Altered** in Five Ways is delightful (no youngsters though). However, children are welcomed at another fine establishment, the **Bulls Head** at Wootton Wanen.

Further north in Henley-in-Arden a friendly place to stay is the **Ardencote Manor House** (01926) 843111, a country house with views over the Warwickshire countryside. In Sutton Coldfield, **New Hall** 0121 378 2442 offers a stylish haven in the oldest moated manor house in England while The Belfry (01675) 470301 just outside Sutton Coldfield, provides sumptuous comfort. Alternatively try the **Hilton Birmingham Metropole** 0121 780 4242 or, as a contrast, splendid Tudor **Yew Trees**—superb character and a very high standard. The bedrooms are cheerful and the bars are an extremely good place to meet before dining in the Oakwood Restaurant. Perhaps the most outstanding place to visit in the area is **Mallory Court** (01926) 330214. Situated in Bishops Tachbrook, south of Leamington Spa, this is a picture of elegance. Bedrooms are sumptuous, while the restaurant provides exquisite French cooking. In the Parade of Leamington Spa itself, one finds a more modest, but no less welcoming hotel, the **Regent** (01926) 427231, a restaurant here of note as well. We trust one of the above appeals whilst visiting Warwick in 2001.

Wetherby

Wetherby is an extremely popular racecourse and there is no doubt this is a well run course, as most of the Yorkshire tracks are. It has an informal atmosphere but provides an excellent standard of racing. **Christopher Tetley** is **Clerk of the Course, James Sanderson** is the **Manager** and **Melissa Green** is in charge of **Sales & Marketing.** They can be contacted through **Wetherby Steeplechase Committee Ltd., The Racecourse, York Road, Wetherby, West Yorkshire LS22 5EJ. Tel (01937) 582035. Fax (01937) 580565. E mail: info@wetherbyracing.co.uk.**

The course is one of the most accessible in the country, being close to the A1 and thereby providing an excellent route for both north and southbound vehicles. Wetherby is 200 miles from London and close to Leeds, Harrogate and York. York is about 13 miles from the racecourse and buses run there from outside the railway station. The B1224 is the most direct route from York. The M62 runs from the west of the country and it connects with the new A1/M1 link road, which finishes about 5 miles south of Wetherby. There is a railway station in Harrogate about nine miles away and a bus station in Wetherby which is one and a half miles from the course. The 770 runs from Leeds City Bus Station to Wetherby Bus Station every half hour from Monday to Saturday. Car parking is ample and is provided free of charge.

Sixteen fixtures are due to be scheduled next season, including one Sunday meeting in November. A number of local Yorkshire trainers send good horses to Wetherby and a generally high standard of racing can be expected. The crowd is both vocal and knowledgeable and this generates a superb atmosphere coupled with the traditionally hearty voices of a Yorkshire crowd—always entertaining for southerners!

Annual Membership is good value at £130. Joint Membership for married couples is also well priced at £210. Daily Membership rates are £15, Tattersalls £9 rising to £16 and £15 respectively, on high days and the popular Course Enclosure is £3, reduced to £1.50 for pensioners. Cars are admitted to the centre of course for £12 (including up to 4 adults). Children under 16 are admitted free if accompanied by an adult.

In 1995 the new Saddling-up Enclosure, Weighing Room and Administration Complex was built at a cost of £375,000. In addition, the Wetherby Millennium Stand opened in December 1999. Built at a cost of £4.2 million this development forms the new Member's Stand and offers 20 corporate hospitality boxes as well as state-of-the-art facilities and surroundings such as 3 new bars, a restaurant with a Parade Ring view and raised viewing for 500. Other facilities include a children's playground in the Course Enclosure, and viewing facilities close to the winning post for disabled people. There is no racecourse bank but there are public telephones and a betting shop which is located in the Paddock Enclosure.

All in all, Wetherby is a friendly racecourse. It is one of the top jumping tracks in the north and the only one of the nine Yorkshire courses devoted entirely to National Hunt racing. Although probably still not for everyone, summer jumping seems to be catching on with many trainers and owners keeping their top of the ground horses for racing at this time of the year. We can't think of a better place to hold one than Wetherby. Provided the ground was not too firm and the entries held up it would be sure to attract an immense crowd. Whatever the going or weather, I can always recommend a day at Wetherby where racing over the sticks is at its best. Be sure to visit in 2001.

Artist: **Klaus Philipp** **AFTER THE RACE** *Courtesy of:* **The Artist**

Local Favourites

In West Yorkshire, there are relatively few hotels but several pubs. However, Leeds makes up for the lack of hotels elsewhere and a selection includes the **Hilton Leeds City** (0113) 244 2000, which is modern and comfortable. A more traditional, 1930s hotel is the **Le Meridien Queen's** (0113) 243 1323 in the city square. There are many good restaurants in Leeds but one with a definite pedigree is **Sang Sang** (0113) 246 8664. **42 The Calls** (0113) 244 0099 is a marvellously novel and good value weekend haunt to consider if in these parts. It also demonstrates what can be done with derelict buildings. Furthermore, **Brasserie Forty Four** (0113) 234 3232 is an excellent place in which to enjoy dinner and **Pool Court at 42** (0113) 244 4242 makes this a trio of excellence to challenge any. A winner in the last at nearby Wetherby and dinner in any of these would satisfy the most discerning of punters. An alternative, however, is **Oulton Hall** (0113) 282 1000, a classy performer with good leisure facilities from the DeVere stable. Two other hotels of note in Leeds are the **Leeds Marriott** (0113) 2366366 and the **Leeds Crowne Plaza** (0113) 2442200, both of which provide top-class, if pricey, accommodation. Other good restaurants include **Rascasse** (0113) 244 6611 and **Leodis** (0113) 242 1010 both with excellent fayre and settings.

If you can escape the city, then run to Harewood where the best known landmark in the village is Harewood House. Open from April to October, the gardens, collections of Chippendale furniture and superb English works of art are all fascinating. Here the **Harewood Arms** (0113) 288 6566 is ideally placed and reasonable. Good public houses nearby are the **Windmill** in Linton and the **White Swan** (01937) 832217 at Wighill, a marvellous country boozer with a fine collection of racing prints—a pleasant restaurant as well. Whilst we are in the vicinity of Linton, **Wood Hall** (01937) 587271 is quite outstanding. This is a converted Georgian manor which has excellent amenities. **Linton Springs** (01937) 585353 is also well regarded. A good guest house is **Prospect House** (01937) 582428—offering a pleasant welcome to the weary (or exuberant) traveller. **David Wooleys** (01943) 864002 is a good restaurant to consider.

There are two hotels convenient for the racecourse, The **Bridge Inn** at Walshford (01937) 580115 and the **Jarvis Wetherby Hotel** (01937) 583881.

Much of the countryside in Yorkshire is full of mystery, none more haunting than that surrounding the former home of Emily and Charlotte Bronte. A pub that dates back to well before the birth of the sisters can be found at Bardsey, the **Bingley Arms**, a mere four miles from Wetherby—the perfect place to celebrate an historic win at the races.

*Artist: **Brian Stanley** **THERE'S A FALLER** Courtesy of: **The Artist***

Lamb Inn

The Lamb Inn at Hindon, a fine 17th century Inn, is situated in picturesque Hindon, a Wiltshire village between Shaftesbury and Salisbury. It is noted for its friendly welcome and traditional atmosphere.

The oldest part of the building boasts a distinguished history as an historic Coaching Inn supplying fresh horses for traffic travelling between London and the West Country. Each of the fourteen attractively decorated en suite bedrooms is equipped with television and telephone. The Lamb is open all year round and can cater for meetings, conferences and weddings.

The restaurant always prides itself in the preparation of the finest local vegetable and game produce. Fresh seafood is supplied daily en-route to London from the various Cornish ports. The bar with its welcoming log fires and relaxing ambience tempts visitors with a variety of fine local and guest cask-conditioned ales. There is an imaginative and extensive bar menu, offering both hot and cold food at lunch time and in the evening.

Cora Scott continues the tradition of previous patrons of the Lamb in their enthusiastic involvement in both the Flat and National Hunt racing scenes. The Lamb at Hindon, is conveniently placed for both Wincanton and Salisbury racecourses with Taunton and Bath being slightly further afield. In addition other outdoor activities, including riding, hunting, shooting and fishing are all easily arranged and there are several fine golf courses in the local area.

Being located in the gateway to the West Country you have an abundance of places to visit including the New Forest, Stonehenge, Longleat Safari Park, Thruxton Race Track, and the towns of Salisbury, Warminster and Wincanton, so whatever the reason for your visit you will find The Lamb Inn the ideal venue.

The Lamb Inn
Hindon
Sailsbury
Wiltshire
SP3 6DP
Tel: (01747) 820573
Fax: (01747) 820605

Wincanton is a very worthwhile establishment to visit and win or lose you will surely enjoy a good day out. **Ian Renton, Clerk of the Course**, and **Madeleine White, Assistant Manager/Marketing Executive** have the enviable task of running this most popular of jumping courses. They can be contacted at **The Racecourse, Wincanton, Somerset BA9 8BJ. Tel (01963) 32344. Fax (01963) 34668. Web site: www.wincntonracecourse.co.uk.**

The course itself lies just off the A303 bypass, on the B3081 and like many racecourses on racedays is signposted by AA signposts and local directional signs. If you are travelling from London, some 110 miles away, then the M4 and the M3 both trek in that westward direction. Equally satisfactory is the old A4. Wincanton itself lies on the A303. Travellers north and south should note the A357 and the A37 respectively. A public bus service winds its way to Wincanton, but the nearest railway stations are at Templecombe on the Waterloo line seven miles away, where a free coach service will meet the London Waterloo train, or at Castle Cary on the Paddington route. There is a taxi service from both stations but taxis at the latter need to be ordered in advance. Large car parks are available and there is no charge for parking. Finally, helicopters may land in the centre of the course by prior arrangement.

On your arrival there will inevitably be some fairly competitive racing. The Boxing Day meeting, including the Mid Season Chase and the Lord Stalbridge Gold Cup is the most popular. Other leading races include the Jim Ford Challenge Cup and the Axminster 100 Kingwell Hurdle in late February and the Tanglefoot Elite Hurdle and Badger Chase in November. These races often attract excellent horses and local trainers use them as 'prep' events for more prestigious races later in the year.

In the 2000/01 season visits to Wincanton will cost £15 for Members, £10 for Tatts and £5 for the Course Enclosure. The price of an Annual Members Badge is £120, with a £5 discount if you join before the end of November. A car pass is also thrown in which gives you preferential parking plus reciprocal days racing at various tracks around the country including Ascot, Salisbury, Newbury, Taunton, Exeter, Bath, Sandown, Cheltenham, Kempton and Doncaster with a voucher book scheme. For those aged between 17 and 22 Junior Annual Membership is available at £60 and the Junior Club costs £7.50, although this is not available on Boxing Day. If one wishes to gather a group of friends together then a 15-20 per cent discount applies for parties in excess of ten and if you are taking a really substantial number then further discounts can be arranged. Bigger parties of 30 to 120 may wish to make use of the private rooms available. Companies or individuals wishing to take advantage of these facilities should contact the racecourse.

You may well be surprised at the excellent value you can receive entertaining at the races. The course has seven boxes which are let either daily or annually. Sited on the top floor they offer splendid views of the course. Another plan for a party at the races is to arrange for your own marquee—an area near the parade ring is ideal. If you like the idea of lunching whilst you fill out your bets, then the Members Restaurant overlooks the Paddock and should serve you well—bookings can be made through the course office. The three course lunch will cost from around £18.50. The Stalbridge Bar and the Tattersalls Bar have both been refurbished and there is a new Tote Members betting shop. The racecourse caterers are Parkers Catering at Milborne Port (01963) 250368. Alternatively, there are the snack bars and a picnic area in the refurbished Course Enclosure.

*Artist: **Philip Toon** BETWEEN THE SHOWERS Courtesy of: **The Artist***

Car parking on the course costs £5 plus £5 for each occupant. This is a great way to get the best out of racing, particularly for newcomers to the sport.

16s and under are admitted free with children's entertainment and a crèche available at the Easter Monday and October Sunday meetings. There are plenty of telephones and disabled viewing in the Hatherleigh Stand and Tattersalls. Special discounts can be made in advance for disabled people on written application to the course. Wincanton offers exciting and competitive racing with welcoming staff who will ensure you have a happy and—hopefully, a successful day at the races.

Local Favourites

Wincanton is a first rate jumping track to visit and the following establishments may help stave off a winter chill after a day at the races. An excellent pub to try is the **Unicorn Inn** (01963) 32324 in Bayford, which has a pleasant atmosphere, good bar snacks and a number of bedrooms. In Hindon, one finds the **Lamb** (01747) 89573 with some good bar food and comfortable accommodation. As the road diverges one has the choice of Warminster or Mere. In Mere you should visit the **Old Ship** (01747) 860258 which has a pleasant bar with appetizing snacks. The town also houses the highly recommended **Chetcombe House Hotel** (01747) 860219 and the **Talbot Hotel** (01747) 860427. In Warminster you have an excellent proposition in the form of **Bishopstrow House** (01985) 212312, an outstanding Georgian mansion. The hotel is a delight and the restaurant is excellent. In Shepton Mallet, **Blostin's** (01749) 343648 enjoys an extremely good following, while **Bowlish House** (01749) 342022 is much recommended for a pleasant evening after a successful day at Wincanton races. Some accommodation here and also at **Brottens Lodge** (01749) 880352—a first rate restaurant. At Evercreech the **Pecking Mill** (01749) 830336 offers good food and some bedrooms. Nearer to Wincanton, several places should be mentioned. Bruton

offers **Truffles** (01749) 812255, a restaurant of note. Two **Bulls** now, one in Brewham, the other in Hardway—good bar food here. And nearby Stourton proves a worthy diversion with a Palladian mansion and superb gardens. The **Spread Eagle** (01747) 840587 is the local to note and it has some accommodation if required. In Bourtons, neighbouring Wincanton, the **Hunters Lodge Inn** is popular with racegoers. Wincanton itself offers the charming and good value **Lower Church Farm** (01963) 32307, while in Holbrook, the **Holbrook House** (01963) 32377 is an ideal place to stay. Not quite so convenient—but appealing—is **Bonds** (01963) 350464 in Castle Cary, which has delightful bedrooms and a fine restaurant. The **George** (01963) 350761 in the marketplace is also good. South of Wincanton in the village of Barwick, **Little Barwick House** (01935) 23902 is most accommodating and offers an outstanding dinner, the specialities being fish and game. Nearby, a handy pub for the A30 is the **Queen's Head** (01963) 250314, at Milborne Port, which has excellent value accommodation and some good bar snacks. Our final thought for racegoers considering a visit to Wincanton is the outstanding **Charlton House** (01749) 342008 a superb Georgian house which reveals an outstanding hotel and restaurant double.

Artist: **Heather St Clair Davis STAND, DAMN IT!** _Courtesy of:_ **Frost & Reed**

Holbrook House Hotel

HOLBROOK HOUSE HOTEL, WINCANTON, SOM.

RICHARD ADSHEAD 1974

Peace and tranquillity are the hallmarks of this lovely Georgian house set amidst seventeen acres of beautiful parkland gardens, just off the A303 near Wincanton. Holbrook provides a perfect setting in which to explore the delightful surrounding countryside of Somerset, Wiltshire and Dorset, and is just minutes from Wincanton Racecourse.

The history of Holbrook dates back to Saxon times, with the earliest records of a property on site having been drawn up during the reign of Edward III and has many famous connections down the centuries.

The house has recently undergone a major refurbishment - bedrooms are spacious and elegant, lounges and public rooms are inviting with roaring log fires in the winter and pleasant views of the attractive surrounds. The award winning Restaurant's relaxed atmosphere and imaginative cuisine is worthy of its 2 AA Rosettes, complemented by a well stocked cellar.

The newly opened Health Spa will delight those wishing to be pampered, equipped with state of the art gym, sauna, steam rooms, and indoor pool, or perhaps indulge in a massage or facial in the Beauty Treatment Rooms and Hairdressing Salon.

Other activities within the grounds include tennis, croquet and our heated outdoor pool, or simply enjoy a stroll around the Holbrook nature trail.

Seating 200 people, the new function and conference suite provides the latest business facilities and is perfect for wedding receptions, private banqueting and corporate meetings.

Many guests keep returning to Holbrook House over the years and have found it the perfect retreat in which to relax, unwind and be totally pampered. If you are going racing in the south west of England or simply wishing to find a welcoming hotel, Holbrook House is the perfect setting.

Holbrook House Hotel
Wincanton
Somerset
BA9 8B5
Tel: (01963) 32377
Fax: (01963) 32681

Windsor is a busy racecourse, renowned for its midsummer evening races. The **Clerk of the Course** at Windsor is **Fraser Garritty** and he can be reached on **(01753) 865234**. The **General Manager, Clive Stephens** can be contacted at the racecourse office, **Royal Windsor Races, The Racecourse, Windsor, Berkshire SL4 5JJ. Tel (01753) 865234/864726 Fax (01753) 830156. Web site: www.windsorracing.co.uk.**

The racecourse is on the A308 between Windsor and Maidenhead. West and eastbound traffic on the M4 should leave the motorway at junction 6. The M3 traffic from the south should leave the motorway at interchange 3 and follow the A332 to Windsor. Travellers from the north and the east will find a combination of the M25, M4 and the A308 the best route. For those who might prefer a slight change from the normal mode of transportation, why not travel by river bus. The summer shuttle boat service operates from Barry Avenue Promenade close to Windsor Bridge in the town centre and takes racegoers to the racecourse jetty, close to the Paddock. The journey takes about ten minutes and there is a bar on board. For further information contact French Brothers (01753) 862933/851900. There are frequent rail services from Waterloo and Paddington to Windsor and Eton (Riverside) and Windsor and Eton (Central) respectively, both two miles away. The Green Line bus terminus is one mile from the course. The car parking facilities cost £1, £1.50 and £2 and coaches just £5. On another plane, helicopter landing facilities are available but permission should be sought in advance.

In 2000 Windsor restricted itself to Flat racing–a pity but it seems this is in the best interests of the course. Most racing here is run on Monday evenings with an August bank holiday and Saturday evening meeting as well. These occasions are enormously popular with owners and this assures good support from some of the country's leading stables which in turn guarantees huge crowds. A simple formula and a great success! These evenings often precede the year's major flat meetings and serve as an excellent aperitif for the week's principal attractions. What better way to spend a summer evening? However, the traffic out of London is usually so congested that an early start is strongly advised.

In 2000 Annual Membership Badges for Royal Windsor Race Club were priced at £140 each. Daily badges are £16 for the Club, £11 for the Tattersalls and Paddock Enclosure and £4 for the Silver Ring. The course encourages advance bookings for the Tattersalls Stand and Paddock, for which discounts are offered for parties and groups. A similar deal is available for the Silver Ring where the discount is £1. The executive also encourages the reservation of the Churchill Suite and private boxes in the Royal Windsor Grandstand and Paddock Pavilion, overlooking the finishing straight. Lunch and dinner can be reserved by contacting the course caterers, Letheby & Christopher (01753) 832552. The potential for company and business entertainment is particularly interesting when one considers the evening meetings. Corporate hospitality is organised by the racecourse office. It is also worth noting that

Artist: **Claire Eva Burton** **UNDER ORDERS** Courtesy of: **The Artist**

children under 16 are admitted free and there are public telephones available but no banks are in attendance as yet. Disabled people are well looked after with a special viewing stand and reserved paddock viewing. Admission for wheelchair users is free of charge, which is excellent.

All in all Windsor has great appeal. The new Royal Windsor Stand, housing the Castle Restaurant and viewing boxes, is an excellent addition. We hope the investment is richly rewarded in the years to come.

Local Favourites

If you do wish to stay in the area then a hotel that is worthy of recommendation is **Fredrick's** (01628) 635934 on Shoppenhangers Road—the bedrooms are comfortable and the restaurant excellent. The menu changes frequently and one is treated to some splendidly imaginative cooking. A similarly outstanding hotel and restaurant double is to be found along the Windsor road—it is an absolute pearl and its name is **Oakley Court** (01753) 609988. All manner of facilities are complemented by excellent service, gracious surroundings and beautiful grounds. The restaurant, the **Oak Leaf Room,** is another great pleasure. For people who do not wish such extravagance then **Sir Christopher Wren's House Hotel** (01753) 861354 is excellent—the **Stroks Restaurant** has a splendid setting and is definitely one to sample. A further example of good fare and good value service is **Melrose House** (01753) 865328.

In Eton, on the High Street to be precise, the **Christopher Hotel** (01753) 852359 has comfortable bedrooms and a palatable selection of real ales. This is also a good base for exploring the antique shops of Eton if this happens to be to your liking. The **Eton Wine Bar** (01753) 854921 is also very good. Returning to Windsor, a number of suggestions arise. There are several excellent establishments that nestle beneath the magnificent castle, the **Castle** (01753) 851011 being a particularly notable example. Another well known landmark in Marlow is the **Compleat Angler** (01628) 484444. Its setting on the Thames

is renowned as one of the most superb spots. The **Valaisan** restaurant is also outstanding and visitors can enjoy marvellous views of the river. In Taplow a superb hotel is **Taplow House** (01628) 670056—excellent comfort and once again an elegant formal restaurant—the **Tulip Tree**. Lovers of truly excellent cooking should consider **L'Ortolan** (01189) 883783 in Shinfield, it's excellent. Similarly The **Waterside Inn** (01628) 620691 is, on its day, up there with the best - some pleasant rooms here as well. Also consider **Cliveden** (01628) 668561 an incredible hotel with a restaurant, **Waldo's**, for those who came up trumps with a good win.

People looking for a less formal evening meal should consider the **Walnut Tree** in Farly, and in Cookham the **Royal Exchange** is also well worth a trip. Also in Cookham, the **Bel and Dragon** (01628) 521263 in the High Street is good—there is a fine restaurant to be found here. **Alfonso's** (01628) 525775 is also a fine restaurant to visit. Elsewhere in Cookham, lovers of oriental cuisine should seek out the **Peking Inn** (01628) 520900—where booking is advisable. **The Inn on the Green** in Cookham Dean is also to be noted. The **Long Barn** in Cippenham, also offers good food and great character. In Dorney, the **Palmer Arms** (01628) 666612 is also excellent, serving really tremendous bar meals.

Artist: **Margaret Moore** *ANYBODY'S RACE* *Courtesy of:* **Osborne Studio Gallery**

Racing has been revolutionised at Wolverhampton. The complex now calls itself Dunstall Park Centre, and enquiries should be addressed to the **Clerk of the Course Michael Prosser at Dunstall Park Centre, Gorsebrook Road, Wolverhampton WV6 0PE Tel (01902) 421421 Fax (01902) 421621. E mail: dunstall@parkuk.freeserve.co.uk. Web site: www.wolverhampton-racecourse.co.uk.**

The course lies some 16 miles north west of Birmingham, close to Tettenhall, and the area is well served by motorways. Lancastrians should follow the M6 to junction 12 and thereafter the A449. Racegoers from the south west should pursue the M5 to the M6 and on to the M54 to junction 2 followed by the A449, whilst Welshmen should aim for Wellington and the M54. London racegoers will find the M1 and the M6 most useful. The course is approximately 130 miles distant. The nearest railway station is in Wolverhampton—take the train from Euston and then grab a taxi for the five minute journey to the course. There is a bus station in the town centre and buses run to the course. Free parking is provided for cars with 2000 spaces and plenty of room for coaches. Helicopters can land at the course but please contact the racecourse management in advance.

Fixtures for 2001 should continue at a similar pattern to previous years, with around 50 meetings. As the only floodlit racecourse in Great Britain, regular Saturday evening racing makes for a superb night out, and there is a continuing growth of restaurants and style of dining to cater for the increasing popularity. 2000 saw the successful return of 2 summer jumping fixtures - no floodlights needed! Full Annual Membership of the Club Enclosure at £150 is excellent value. Access to the Club Enclosure is for Annual Subscribers, day members, owners,

trainers, executive box holders and invited guests. The 400 seater tiered viewing restaurant offers panoramic views of the racetrack for all racegoers with a courier betting service available at each table. Admission to the racecourse is £8 and on selected dates £10 for all areas other than the Club Enclosure which is £15 and on selected dates £20. Pensioners may apply to join the Diamond Club at the really good value price of £2.50, which allows a discount of £2 off either Tattersalls or Member's enclosures. For Saturday evening meetings there is a choice of three restaurants which all offer various deals including your entry, racecard, three course meal and dancing until midnight. In 2000 prices started at £25 in the Ringside, £32.90 for the tiered Zongalero Viewing Restaurant, and £39.95 in the Member's Restaurant. Some special themed evenings are planned, and entrance prices may vary accordingly, so please check in advance. Discounts are also offered for parties of over 40 on Tattersalls entrance, while there are two free places available in the Ringside Restaurant for parties with up to or over 41 guests.

The eight private boxes accommodate parties of 16—64 seated and up to 80 for buffets and are let on a daily basis. Larger function suites are also available for corporate and private hire. Packages are tailored to include hire of box, a four course silver service meal, access to the Owners and Members lounge, admission charge and car parking. A courier betting service is also available on request. The popular Fashion Festival is run in conjunction with the prestigious Weatherby Dash sprint in August. Contact the course for a fixture booklet with a list of themes.

Wolverhampton is an amazing achievement. Some £15.7 million has been invested to create an all-weather track, turf

Artist: **John Lewis Fitzgerald** *FINAL FURLONG* *Courtesy of:* **Solomon & Whitehead**

course, floodlights, a new Grandstand, boxes and a 400 seater restaurant on the top floor. Not to mention a 54 bedroomed Holiday Inn Hotel.

Local Favourites

The most obvious recommendation is the **Holiday Inn Garden Court Hotel** at Dunstall Park (01902) 713313. The 54 rooms are all en suite with TV, telephone, tea and coffee making facilities. Accommodation starts at £84 per night b&b for two and is specially tailored for the punter, being linked to the main grandstand and with the Racing Channel and SiS in every bedroom. The hotel also boasts a relaxing bar and bistro, and disabled facilities—a fitness room is available for use by hotel guests. The **Mount** (01902) 752055 is also well worth a pre or post race inspection

One of the best known leisure centres in the country is situated at Wishaw: the **Belfry** (01675) 470301—a whole host of pursuits can be enjoyed here aside from golf. The hotel's restaurants promise nouvelle cuisine as well as English fare. Alternatively, you may wish to visit the **Moor Hall Hotel**, Sutton Coldfield 0121 3083751 which also has strong associations with the nearby golf course and is a most welcoming place to stay. Another Hall also can be found at Sutton Coldfield, **New Hall** 0121 378 2442. This is an outstanding establishment with an inspiring setting and a fine restaurant—just two good reasons for staying there. If any or all of the above are full then another good place to try is the **Standbridge Hotel** 0121 3543007.

In Birmingham, one finds some very large hotels. The **Hyatt Regency** 0121 643 1234 is extremely good and has a distinguished restaurant—**Number 282.** Similarly, the **Holiday Inn** 0121 631 2000 offers excellent leisure facilities. If you get a

yen for Chinese food, the **Queens Cantonese** restaurant (01902) 713399 in Queen Street, Wolverhampton comes highly recommended. For a taste of something different the same applies to a local pub with Tex Mex food, the **Bentlands Pub** (01902) 843654 which is in Suckling Green Lane, Codsall, Wolverhampton or the **Barley Mow** who specialise in Yorkies. For a taste of Italy, **Cataldos** restaurant (01902) 838090 comes highly recommended.

Chaddesley Corbett also offers an establishment of distinction in **Brockencote Hall** (01562) 777876. The house, restaurant and grounds are all worth a pre-race inspection: combined they make up a great favourite. Finally, on the hotel front, another sporting hotel with great appeal is **Patshall Park** (01902) 700100, where the accent is on an excellent golf course. To complete our section on a rather bizarre note, visit the **Crooked House** (01384) 238583 an unusual establishment with good food. The **Mill House** 0121 459 5800 in Kings Norton is small but exceptional. One final trip to consider is to Worfield and the **Old Vicarage** (01746) 716497—a delightful setting and good food.

The people in charge of the course at Worcester are **John Baker**, the **Manager**, and **Hugo Bevan**, the **Clerk of the Course**. Administration and corporate hospitality are the preserve of **Christine Draper** and **Administration Assistant** is Kerry Sexty. The course address is: **Grandstand Road, Worcester WR1 3EJ. Tel (01905) 25364. Fax (01905) 617563.** The telephone number for racedays only is **(01905) 21338. Website: www.worcester-racecourse.co.uk.**

To reach the racecourse, which lies some 120 miles west of London and 20 miles from Birmingham, one might use any one of the following routes. From the west, the M5 (junction 6) and thence the A449 and the A38 provide a winning combination. The course itself rests between Broadheath and Herwick. The A58 from Birmingham provides a smooth route for racegoers from the West Midlands. The M5 (junction 7) is another route which benefits from the A38. From the Cotswolds, the A44 is a pleasant trek—the A443 is a help here. People who consider this to be the age of the train, can use it via the Paddington line. Get off at Worcester Foregate St. If the proverbial flying horse is preferred to the so-called iron horse, then phone the manager in advance who will inform you where to land your chopper. Car parking is free, except for picnic parking where a £3 charge is made.

The 2001 season should enjoy a fixture list similar to that of 2000, with 15 meetings, around 10 of which are summer fixtures, with some excellent evening and Wednesday afternoon meetings. A wet and windy Wednesday at Worcester may not immediately appeal but even when the elements prove uncooperative a day out can still be well worthwhile. Annual Membership is now available but please check with the

racecourse for rates. Members Daily Badges in 2000 were priced at £14, entrance to Tattersalls £10 and the Silver Ring £5. OAPs are entitled to Centre Course tickets at £3. Something also worth noting is a discount for parties of twelve or more when prices of £10.40, £8 and £4.40 are available for Members, Tattersalls and the Centre Course respectively. You should book in advance to obtain these prices and you may pay by credit card. Badges can be purchased from the Manager's office but must be paid for at least seven days in advance.

What sounds great fun are the riverboats moored behind the grandstand for parties from 30 to 200. The Worcester management team are clearly refusing to give in to the ravages of the Severn, and are instead harnessing its beauty for their own ends. For landlubbers there are the usual boxes and a superb sponsors' room capable of holding up to 120 people. Punters please note that the Croft Suite also has a restaurant for which reservations can be made, on (01905) 25970. A marquee has now been erected on a permanent basis next to the Paddock and this can accommodate an extra 60 hospitality guests. It is clear that there is plenty of scope for all sorts of additional entertainment and this is reflected in the fact that the racecourse has the support of numerous sponsors.

Other advantages of coming to Worcester are that children are admitted free before their 16th birthday. In addition, there are children's facilities during the summer. Disabled people have special viewing facilities and there is a lift to the Members restaurant. Telephones can be found adjacent to the grandstand where the course betting shop is also located. Make no mistake, this is a delightful racetrack—its facilities are good and a day's racing here is to be thoroughly recommended.

Artist: **Heather St Clair Davis** DUEL _Courtesy of:_ **Frost & Reed**

Local Favourites

The ancient cathedral city of Worcester, which is delightfully peaceful, also has some excellent antique shops and a variety of hotels and restaurants should you be anticipating a large gamble coming off. The **Giffard Hotel** (01905) 726262, overlooking the cathedral's precincts, is modern while **Brown's** (01905) 26263 is a splendidly converted corn mill, ideal for lunch and dinner and situated beside the cricket ground. Returning Cathedral-wards, a thirsty fellow should find the **Farriers Arms,** a traditional public house, and the **Cardinals Hat** (01905) 22423 on Friar Street for equally good refreshment. A converted glove factory makes for another noteworthy hotel, with good accommodation and a fine restaurant, called **Fownes** (01905) 613151. **Il Pescatore** (01905) 21444 is a good Italian restaurant to look out for. Still in Worcester, **The Star Hotel** (01905) 24308 is recommended by the racecourse management, as is **Ostlers** restaurant (01905) 612300 at The Moors in Worcester.

Outside the city itself, amid the fruit trees and the whiff of hops, one finds a feast of delights, starting with the racecourse. In Colwall, the **Colwall Park Hotel** (01684) 40206 stands in front of the old National Hunt course and is a tremendous place to stay. The hotel offers English cooking and the Edwardian dining room is backed up by an extensive bar menu. Some lovely places can be found in and around Great Malvern. In Malvern Wells, the **Croque-en-Bouche** (01684) 565612 is one of the country's finest dining places. Alternatively, visit the **Cottage in the Wood Hotel** (01684) 575859. A really wonderful place to stay, it also has a highly regarded restaurant which is open to non-residents. One commendable hotel in Malvern is the **Foley Arms** (01684) 73397, a charming Georgian edifice in which to slumber. Another great place to stay with a good restaurant is the **Elms Hotel** (01299) 896666 in Abberley. Where next? Try Bromsgrove and **Grafton Manor** (01527) 579007 where

tradition and luxury combine to make yours a delightful stay. Less glamourous but still comfortable is the **Phepson Guest House** (01905) 69205 in Himbleton. Whilst in Droitwich Spa, the **Chateau Impney** (01905) 774411 is yet another good idea for those of you seeking refined stabling when visiting these parts.

In Wyre Piddle, the **Anchor** (01386) 552799 is a grand pub cum restaurant. The **Talbot** (01886) 821235 at Knightwick is also a tremendous inn with good value accommodation. Followers of the Archers might care to make a pilgrimage to the **Old Bull**, Inkberrow whilst those looking for some good pub food should visit the **Bear and Ragged Staff** (01886) 833399 in Bransford or The **Bell** at Pensax (01299) 896677. And don't forget Ombersley, where the **Kings Arms** (01905) 620315, the **Crown and Sandys Arms** (01905) 620252 provide good food and warm hospitality. A fitting double for visitors to Worcester racecourse.

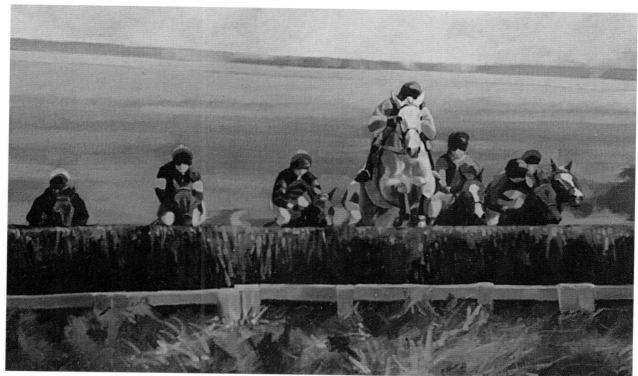

Artist: **Alison Wilson** *THE GREY IN THE LEAD* Courtesy of: ***The Artist***

Those in charge at Yarmouth are **David Henson** who is **Clerk of the Course** and **David Thompson** as **Racecourse Manager**. They can be contacted at **The Racecourse, Jellicoe Road, Great Yarmouth NR30 4AU. Tel (01493) 842527. Fax (01493) 843254.**

The journey to Yarmouth by road has now been made much faster by the opening of the southern bypass around Norwich and by the many new sections of dual carriageway on the A11 and A47. From London, the following treble is advised—the M11, A11 and A47. The A12 via Colchester, Ipswich and Lowestoft however, will certainly prove a more stimulating option. Were you to make a seafront promenade the night before, please note that a bus runs regularly from the seafront to the racecourse. Furthermore, the local bus routes run from each of the town's holiday centres. The nearest railway station is in Yarmouth itself and although no bus runs directly from here, the track is only a leisurely 30 minute walk away but is also only 5 minutes away from the main road where the bus runs. London racegoers should use the Liverpool Street line. Back on the roads, the A47 via Norwich serves the racegoer travelling from the north and west of the country. There is plenty of room for car parking, for which there is a £2 charge. Limited space is reserved for coaches if pre-booked with the course management.

Average attendance here is around 3500 and meetings in 2001 will hopefully follow the same pattern as last year with 17 fixtures including four evenings and one Sunday, the highlight being the three-day September meeting. The great Mtoto won his first race here and some superb two year olds make the short trip from Newmarket for their racecourse debut. If you only want the odd day's racing here a daily membership is the ticket and £13.50 is the asking price. If you wish to be closer to the bookmakers then Tattersalls is the answer and this cost £9 in 2000. Alternatively, the Silver/Family Enclosure will cost you £5 for the day. Admission to the September Festival is £14, £9.50 and £5, respectively. An Annual Members' badge cost £130 in 2000 and the racecourse now also does a joint annual membership for £235. Membership includes a car park sticker and reciprocal meetings at Huntingdon, Fakenham and Nottingham. Discounts are also available, a party of 20 or more being admitted at a reduced rate into Tattersalls.

The racecourse is eager to combine business with leisure and there are four hospitality boxes and 2 large new marquees, ideal for corporate entertainment. The boxes can be hired on a per person basis with prices starting from £16; catering costs are additional. All the boxes are fitted with closed circuit television screens and are located in the centre of the course. Should you wish to arrange for a private room or even a marquee, then contact the racecourse. Smaller and more discreet festivities can be organised through the Club restaurant, while the more rushed may get snacks from numerous points around the track. Those under 16 years are admitted free if accompanied by an adult. Indeed, Yarmouth is focusing its attention on families. There are playgrounds, sideshows, a bouncy castle, train rides and extra sideshows arranged for evening and Sunday fixtures. One point you should remember is that there is no bank, so have enough readies to hand. If you wish to bet at the on-course betting shops, you'll find them in Tattersalls and the Silver Ring. There are facilities for disabled people in all enclosures. British resorts are increasingly having to compete with exotic holiday spots abroad. They need to offer the visitor a good time. One such offering is a day at the races and in this respect the local Yarmouth community are well served. We wish them a bumper season in 2001.

Local Favourites

A traditional seaside hotel is the **Imperial** (01493) 851113, an ideal meeting place prior to the races. A strong local recommendation comes for the **Furzedown** (01493) 844138—another popular haunt of racegoers. Two local favourites noted by the racecourse management include the **Burlington** (01493) 844568 and the **Star** (01493) 842294. They are certainly worth a pre-race inspection, The **Regency Dolphin** (01493) 855070 is also well thought of. Two fine restaurants are **Friends Bistro** (01493) 852538 and **Seafood Restaurant** (01493) 856009 on the North Quay. The latter is fairly pricey but is a great favourite of the Newmarket trainers. In Gorleston-on-Sea the **Pier Hotel** (01493) 662631 has spectacular views along the river, harbour-mouth and across the glorious sandy beach out to sea—ideal when visiting Great Yarmouth. East of the town, in South Walsham, one finds a very English mansion, **South Walsham Hall** (01603) 270378. The hotel is beautifully situated for the Norfolk Broads. Back in nearby Gorleston-on-Sea The **Cliff Hotel** (01493) 662179 is also a good bet.

Norwich itself is a delightful city, over 1000 years old. The better hotels are **Swallow Sprowston Manor** (01603) 410871, **Dunston Hall Hotel Golf and Country Club** (01508) 470444 (good leisure facilities here) and the **Maids Head Hotel** (01603) 761111, a 13th century building ideally situated near the cathedral. If you enjoy good fish then **Greens** (01603) 623733 is excellent, while splendid Italian cuisine can be found at **Marco's** (01603) 624044. Norwich is something of a gastronomer's paradise. Other restaurants for consideration include the best in the field, **Adlards** (01603) 633522 and **By Appointment** (01603) 630730—handy for the impressive cathedral and castle. Three stayers of merit outside the town include the **Petersfield** (01692) 630745 at Horning, the **Kingfisher** (01692) 581974 at Stalham and **Church Farm Hotel and Country Club** (01493) 780251 at Burgh Castle. If you are wishing to journey further westwards then try the **Park Farm** (01603) 810264 in Hethersett. Good facilities and restaurant make this a most appealing place to stay. A number of good boozers can be found either on the coast or amongst the Norfolk Broads. Lovers of real ale should try the **Fur and Feather** (01603) 720003 at Woodbastwick, it is excellent. In Hickling, the **Pleasure Boat Inn** (01493) 393378 has a charming waterside setting as has the **Eels Foot** in Ormesby St Michael—both of these serve good food. In appropriately named Horsey, the **Nelson's Head** is a pleasant coastal pub, while at Winterton-on-Sea, the **Fisherman's Return** (01493) 393305 has some comfortable bedrooms and also does good bar food—ideal for escaping the throngs when racing at Yarmouth.

York

York is an extremely complete racecourse. It may not host the thrills and spills of the winter game but its calendar of spring and summer fare is sumptuous. This racecourse, is like Cheltenham, if you haven't visited you haven't lived! If this is the scenario in your racing life, try and put matters straight in 2001.

The man in charge here is the extremely capable **John Smith** who acts as **Clerk, Manager** and **Secretary**. He can be contacted at **The Racecourse, York YO23 1EX. Tel (01904) 620911 Fax (01904) 611071. Web site: www.yorkracecourse.co.uk.**

The course is located a mile outside the centre of the beautiful cathedral city which lies some 200 miles from London. York railway station is a mile from the racecourse and is on the Kings Cross line (London to York in as little as 106 minutes). There are frequent buses to complete the journey to the track, only five minutes ride away. A combination of the A64 and the A1036 is the answer for visitors from south, east and west, or you could try the new M1/A1 link (signed as M1) while from the north, the A19 and York Ring Road help you avoid the busy city centre. There are numerous car parks which are well organised and free. One way of avoiding the traffic is to come by helicopter and land at the course—I don't suppose you will find a long queue in the skies over York. Landing facilities for light aircraft also exist close to the course, at Rufforth. Full details are available from the racecourse office.

Particularly valuable races include the Dante Stakes, the Tattersalls Musidora Stakes and the Merewood Homes Yorkshire Cup run in May—the platform for racing of the highest calibre including two Classic trials. In August, the Tote Ebor Festival includes some of the most impressive racing of the year with the Aston Upthorpe Yorkshire Oaks and the Scottish Equitable

Gimcrack as well as the Group One Juddmonte International. The overriding popularity and good feeling of the summer meeting is superb but less crowded fixtures can be enjoyed in June, July, September and October. In all, the course offers a total of 15 day's racing with over £3 million in prize money.

Daily charges for 2001 have yet to be finalised but for the August meeting in 2000 were £40, £20, £6 and £4 for the Members, Tattersalls, Silver Ring and Course Enclosures, respectively. On other days Members were charged £20, with Tatts at £10 but there were small extra charges in the County Stand and Tattersalls for the May Meeting and Saturday fixtures where the Silver Ring is £5 and the Course Enclosure is £3. There is a generous saving on three day badges for the May, August and October meetings and further details of these are available from the racecourse—'phenomenal value' I'm assured! A new 24 hour credit card hotline for badge orders over £30 has been set up on (0345) 585642. Senior citizens are given discounts in the Silver Ring and Course enclosures—an excellent policy. There is a waiting list for Senior County Stand annual membership, but for those fortunate enough to obtain it, there are reciprocal arrangements included with daily membership at Haydock, Newcastle, Doncaster and Chester and with Yorkshire County Cricket Club! Party organisers should also note that the racecourse offers concessions for all meetings except the August Festival but including Saturday fixtures.

With the Knavesmire Stand and the remodelling of existing facilities, York is almost unrivalled in the choice of quality facilities for private entertaining. Subject to availability, quality 'dining with viewing' suites are available for parties of between 4 and 400. The Dante Suite (200 guests); Knavesmire Boxes (20, 40 and 50 guests) and Melrose Boxes (16, 30 and 40) are outstanding. A complete gamut of restaurants and bars features

Artist: **Roy Miller** PHOTO FINISH *Courtesy of:* **The Artist**

Mount Royale Hotel

The hotel is the result of the tasteful blending of two beautiful William IV detached houses. The Mount Royale is owned and run by Richard and Christine Oxtoby and their son Stuart and daughter Sarah. Stuart has recently taken over as Managing Director. The Oxtoby's have spent a good deal of effort on restoring the former glory of these buildings and their efforts have been well rewarded.

Any traveller having an interest in English history must surely rate the fascinating city of York at least alongside London. The capital of the north and second city of the realm, it began its long and fascinating life around AD71 as a fortress to protect the Roman 9th legion. The marauding Vikings gave the city its name, derived from Jorvik or Yorvik. This period of history has been magnificently captured in the Jorvik Viking Centre, one of the most entertaining museums in the country.

The minster or cathedral is the largest medieval structure in Britain. There has been a minster on the site since the 7th century. The present one is the fourth and was started about 1220, taking 250 years to complete. The city is still protected by ancient city walls, guarded by defensive bastions, working portcullis and barbican at the Walmgate bar.

Wander around the Micklegate bar, where traitors' severed heads were displayed or visit the National Rail Museum.

Staying in York involves mixing with some of the most fascinating sights in the world. Relaxing afterwards in the intimate cocktail bar of the Mount Royale, or enjoying a delicious meal in the restaurant overlooking the delightful garden, enhances the whole experience. Enjoying the gracious beauty of the hotel, the style and antiquity of much of the furnishings, or slipping into the secluded heated swimming pool is the perfect way to pamper the body as well as the mind.

The hotel is ideal for the small conference or private party, and is only a short drive from the rolling Yorkshire Dales. The perfect base, offering peace and tranquillity in the heart of this wonderful city.

Mount Royale Hotel
The Mount
York, YO24 1GU
Tel: (01904) 628856
Fax: (01904) 611171
e mail: reservations@mountroyale.co.uk
web site: www.mountroyale.co.uk

the famous Gimcrack Room and the 'dine with view' Ebor Restaurant (advance booking only) in the new stand where the all-in admission, gourmet luncheon and Grandstand viewing seat package offers real value. Enquiries should be addressed to Craven and Gilpin at the racecourse, (01904) 638971. The Silver Ring and the Course Enclosure have numerous places to feed and sup. John Smith is keen to attract families to race meetings so there is a free 'colts and fillies' crèche in operation at meetings held during the school holidays. Incidentally, champagne enthusiasts should note that the York racecourse offers a different brand on sale at each meeting at a bargain price on the refurbished Champagne Terrace. Prices start from below £20—only Ascot sells more champagne than York.

There is no doubt that York is one of the most successful and best run racecourses in the country. It is thoughtfully managed and immensely popular. Witness the shop facilities, information service and disabled facilities. The racecourse has managed to combine the new stands with the more traditional features really well. The course really tries to take care of the owners and trainers who provide the product too—they now have a club of their own on the first floor of the Melrose Stand and there is now a new winning connections and sponsors room. Visitors should try to see the museum (4th floor, main grandstand) which superbly illustrates the rich history of the Knavesmire turf. The Knavesmire has a glorious past but it also has a sparkling future. The August Festival is one of the most popular in the calendar. Some say that the north is starved of top class racing—those who proclaim this have surely never visited York. To miss the August Festival is surely to miss one of the highlights of the sporting summer, and it must be remembered that there are a number of less expensive enclosures.

There is no doubt that a visit to the Knavesmire is a great experience, but just getting to the major meetings and back home again can be a bit harrowing. York typifies the increasing traffic problems facing the racegoer, and is not unique in this regard – just the thought of getting to Chester, Cheltenham, Ascot or any one of the metropolitan courses is almost enough to bite the bullet and stay in front of the telly at home. Apart from those relatively few jockeys, trainers and owners who have only to call up the 'chopper' or 'plane to wing onto the turf, the growing number of racecourses who successfully attract the crowds face serious problems getting people in and out. Instead of just telling people to leave as early as possible, perhaps a few 'park and ride' schemes could be devised to alleviate this problem. Racecourse managers should take a serious look at their own situation and do a bit of planning so that the punter's first and last experience of his racing day is not spoilt by endless queues of cars.

Dean Court

In its unrivalled position in the shadow of York Minster, the Dean Court offers you the best in comfort, fine food and personal service. The majority of rooms have been refurbished recently including newly created deluxe and superior rooms, each of which has a feature bed, an excellent bathroom and many little extras.

You may wish for a chauffeur driven limousine or champagne hamper for your day at the races (although hampers are not permitted in the racecourse enclosure). These arrangements can be made by the hotel's professional staff all of whom will ensure your visit to York races is a memorable one—perhaps a racing certainty!

Dean Court Hotel
Duncombe Place
York
YO1 2EF
Tel: (01904) 625082
Fax: (01904) 620305
e mail: sales@deancourt-york.co.uk

York City has so much to offer—the racecourse, the castle, the minster and its many quaint streets which now house some super shops. The Shambles is perhaps the best known of these—a delightful warren with tiny lanes running into each other. More recent additions to the city include the Yorkshire Museum, the Jorvik Viking Museum and the National Railway Museum. For racing fanatics looking for a suitable place to 'ditch' loved ones whilst at the course, York is without doubt the most complete choice.

The city's hotels really capture the imagination. However, in order to make the most of the visit, rooms should be booked well in advance. The city's leading establishment is **Middlethorpe Hall** (01904) 641241 which is set in superb grounds and overlooks the racecourse and has an excellent restaurant. Another first class hotel is found within two beautifully kept William IV houses, the **Mount Royale** (01904) 628856. One of the highlights here is the charming dining room which overlooks beautiful gardens. This hotel is a real favourite and is strongly recommended. Another listed building is the excellent **Judges Lodging** (01904) 638733—superbly stylish—and do visit the 18th century wine cellars which now house an exquisite cocktail bar. For a prime position opposite the Minster, the **Dean Court Hotel** (01904) 625082 is the one to opt for—very comfortable too. The city straddles the Ouse and a most modern hotel which overlooks the river is the **York Moat House** (01904) 459988. Two further additions to the Yorkshire stable are the huge and modern **Post House Hotel** (0870) 4009085 and the **Grange Hotel** (01904) 644744 in Clifton. The latter boasts an excellent restaurant within its Regency walls. Its newly refurbished seafood restaurant has a racing 'cyclorama' which has to be seen. A view of the Tote-Ebor start can be gained from the **Swallow Hotel** (01904) 701000. Also in York is the **Royal York** (01904) 653681 a gigantic but elegant edifice right next to the station. **Arndale** (01904) 702424 offers excellent accommodation but sadly does not have a restaurant.

York has something to offer every taste and pocket, and those planning a flutter well beyond their means may wish to save a little on their accommodation. If so, they should try the still excellent but relatively modestly priced **Hudsons Hotel** (01904) 621267, the **Town House** (01904) 636171 or the equally relaxing **Grasmead House Hotel** (01904) 629996.

Restaurants in York are not as strong as the hotels but pay special attention to **Barbers Restaurant** (01904) 627929, an established vegetarian restaurant. An excellent venue for a pre-race brunch or post-race tea is the famous **Bettys** in the centre of York—renowned for its truly moreish cream cakes. Two other distinguished restaurants are **Melton's** (01904) 634341 and **19 Grape Lane** (01904) 636366 which offers outstanding English cooking.

York is unsurprisingly riddled with pubs. The **Black Swan** (01904) 625236 on Peaseholme Green offers a lively atmosphere and some good value bedrooms. For a riverside setting try the **Kings Arms.** There are number of pubs beside the Ouse which appeal and for a more central location try the **York Arms** in Petergate. Real ale lovers will enjoy the **Tap and Spile** (01904) 656158 in Petersgate, while shoppers can enjoy some refreshment in the **Olde Starre** (01904) 623063 in Stonegate. **Aldwark Manor** (01347) 838146 at Alne near Easingwold is well worth considering for those wishing to stay outside York itself. Further north at Helmsley, the **Feversham Arms** (01439) 770766 offers elegant accommodation and excellent lunches. A trip to Malton can never go amiss, after all this is one of Britain's

major racing towns. There are numerous pubs of note here, the **Kings Head** is especially of note and the **Green Man** (01653) 600370 is a good place to stay. The **Talbot** (01653) 694031 and **Greenacres County** (01653) 693623 are also well worth shortlisting. If passing through Hovingham, meanwhile, do not overlook the **Worsley Arms Hotel** (01653) 628234, another great favourite, and secluded Nunnington contains the well known **Ryedale Lodge.** (01439) 748246. Little more than a brisk gallop away at Low Catton, lies the comfortable **Derwent Lodge** (01759) 371468. A pub to note here is the inappropriately named **Gold Cup** (01759) 371354. The **St Vincent Arms** (01904) 608349 in Sutton Upon Derwent is a good boozer and the **Three Hares** (01937) 832128 in Bilborough is also one to note— excellent food here—a strong fancy. The **Ship Inn** (01904) 905609 at Acaster Malbis has good food and good value accommodation. Finally, the **Dawnay Arms** (01347) 848345 is a recommended stayer after the last.

The **Crown** (01423) 322328 at Boroughbridge is another racing favourite, and rightly so, drawing racegoers from all the Yorkshire courses. **Jarvis International Hotel** (01904) 670222, is also well positioned for the many who choose to visit the Knavesmire. Heading off towards Beverley, an inn of great character is the **Feathers,** Pocklington (01759) 303155 — an ideal choice if your trip is on a more restricted budget. The **Londesborough Arms** in Market Weighton (01430) 872214 is another extremely welcoming establishment to add to the shortlist. A first class racing haunt which offers a friendly welcome and good food is the **Bay Horse** (01423) 770230 at Burnt Yates—a bit of a drive but well worth the effort. Another is the **Boars Head** (01423) 771888—a particularly smart establishment. In the picturesque town of Harrogate, the **Majestic Hotel** (01423) 700300 provides a welcome watering hole for racegoers. There are many people who visit York for the races but it has many other attractions, so do try to book in advance. A combination of racing at York, coupled with a stay in delightful York City itself or the neighbouring countryside is, as ever, warmly recommended.

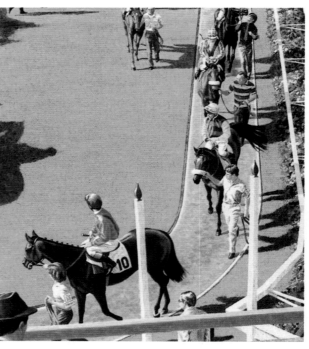

Artist: **Elizabeth Kitson BEFORE THE START** _Courtesy of:_ **The Artist**

Travelling the Turf
in
Ireland

National Hunt

Sunday 21st January	AIG Europe Champion Hurdle - Leopardstown
Thursday 25th January	Thyestes Chase - Gowran Park
Sunday 4th February	Hennessy Cognac Gold Cup Chase - Leopardstown
Monday 16th April	Powers Gold Label Irish Grand National - Fairyhouse
Tuesday 17th April	Powers Gold Cup Novice Chase - Fairyhouse
Tuesday 24th April	BMW Chase - Punchestown
Tuesday 24th April	Evening Herald Champion Novice Hurdle - Punchestown
Wednesday 25th April	Heineken Gold Cup - Punchestown
Wednesday 25th April	Stanley Cooker Champion Novice Hurdle - Punchestown
Thursday 26th April	IAWS Champion 4-year old Hurdle - Punchestown
Thursday 26th April	Ballymore Properties Champion Stayers Hurdle - Punchestown
Thursday 26th April	Swordlestown Cup Novice Chase - Punchestown
Friday 27th April	Shell Champion Hurdle - Punchestown
Friday 27th April	David Austin Memorial Chase - Punchestown
Wednesday 1st August	Compaq Galway Plate Handicap Chase - Galway
Thursday 2nd August	Guinness Galway Handicap Hurdle - Galway
Wednesday 26th September	Guinness Kerry National Handicap Chase - Listowel
Sunday 2nd December	Hatton's Grace Hurdle - Fairyhouse
Sunday 2nd December	Drinmore Novice Chase - Fairyhouse
Sunday 2nd December	Royal Bond Novice Chase - Fairyhouse
Sunday 9th December	John Durkan Memorial Chase - Punchestown
Wednesday 26th December	Denny Gold Medal Chase - Leopardstown
Thursday 27th December	Paddy Power Handicap Chase - Leopardstown
Friday 28th December	Ericsson Chase - Leopardstown

Flat

Saturday 26th May	Entenmann's 2000 Guineas - Curragh
Sunday 27th May	Entenmann's 1000 Guineas - Curragh
Sunday 1st July	Budweiser Irish Derby - Curragh
Sunday 15th July	Kildangan Stud Irish Oaks - Curragh
Sunday 12th August	Independent Heinz 57 Phoenix Stakes - Leopardstown
Sunday 2nd September	Moyglare Stud Stakes - Curragh
Saturday 8th September	Esat Digifone Irish Champion Stakes/part of the Emirates World Racing Championship Series - Leopardstown
Saturday 15th September	Jefferson Smurfit Memorial Irish St. Leger - Curragh
Sunday 16th September	Aga Khan Studs National Stakes - Curragh

Introduction
by J A McGrath

Some of my very favourite racing experiences have taken place on Irish racecourses. The first time I went racing in Ireland was in 1974, when I was sent by my then employers, the China Mail, an evening newspaper in Hong Kong, to report on the Irish Derby. I arrived in Dublin with no prior knowledge of the people, place or customs. But it did not take long to learn. I took a bus to the Curragh from my hotel on the quays – there was a train strike at the time – and shared a taxi back to O'Connell Street with a few racing folk I met over my first pint of Guinness in a Newbridge pub. It was a never-to-be-forgotten experience, and one that I would not expect to be repeated anywhere else.

Ireland and its racing people are unique. It always seems to me that those connected with the turf are actively involved in celebrating their good fortune, usually on a daily basis. It is impossible not to get caught up in a discussion on racing, especially if you carry the essential 'clues,' the Racing Post or a copy of the Irish Independent open at the racing page, into any hotel lobby or bar. Everybody, it seems, has not just an interest, but a friend or relation with a leg in a horse, bred or trained by somebody of note.

Grottos have been erected to Irish racing, and its great heroes and heroines, not dominating to the extent of statues some saints of the Catholic Church have in their memory – but only a couple of lengths behind them. Arkle, for example, is revered in a variety of different drinking establishments. I love the old black and white pictures of 'Himself,' with Pat Taaffe in the saddle, and also some of the correspondence the horse received through the post. One memorable post card to the great horse was addressed simply: 'Arkle, Ireland.' It arrived at the stables of Tom Dreaper, probably quicker than the trainer's monthly gas bill.

Although more than three decades ago, this era marks a special period in Irish racing, a time when the greatest steeplechaser the game has ever seen was followed quickly on centre stage by Flat champions, Sir Ivor and Nijinsky, both trained at Cashel, Tipperary, by the soft-spoken genius, Vincent O'Brien. Ballydoyle, the famous training establshment Vincent built with the proceeeds of several major gambles in the late-1940s and early-1950s, is still thriving today under the management of Aidan O'Brien, no blood relation but a trainer who displays the same brand of painstaking dedication to his job.

More recently, the horse who has done most to advertise the professionalism and quality of Ireland and its great racing industry is Dr Michael Smurfit's Vintage Crop. It is now acclaimed in the history of international racing how Dermot Weld ignored the critical jibes of fellow trainers in Australia and took Vintage Crop from a win in the 1993 Jefferson Smurfit Irish St Leger at the Curragh in September to victory in the Foster's Melbourne Cup at Flemington, Australia, in November that year. The locals said Weld was mad to even consider running a horse in 'the Cup' on his first outing for seven weeks. The Irishman knew his horse better than the locals, who were made to revise their thoughts on how horses should be trained for their big race.

There are times I wish I could take a month's leave of absence to go on an extended racing tour of Ireland. But planning such a tour, looking to guarantee all the highlights of the calendar year, would be near-impossible. For there is a racing highlight of some description in Ireland every month.

While I thoroughly enjoy watching the Classics at the Curragh, which provide such a quality test of a thoroughbred on a very fair

course, the Festivals are what really captures the imagination, and most interest, as a racegoer.

Galway is a fabulous racing Festival, which extends a unique Western brand of hospitality and warmth. You may have to battle to get a drink in some of the packed bars, but there will be no shortage of 'craic' along the way. And the horses? Why you might even see the winner of the following year's Whitbread at Sandown.

Tralee is fun and very enjoyable, while Killarney, with its beautiful scenery and lively night life, has a lot to offer. Punchestown, in late April, often spilling over into May, has steadily grown into the third 'un-missable' jumping Festival, being outranked only by Cheltenham and Aintree. But as Punchestown does not seek to compete directly with those, choosing to provide an extra dimension of enjoyment more than anything else, it has been an overwhelming success.

Travelling the Turf in Ireland is fun. It is also thoroughly enjoyable, distinctly memorable, and, sometimes, profitable. I hope that those who read this book will agree that to go racing in Ireland is to gain an insight into a unique country and its people.

*Artist: **Jay Kirkman JOCKEY***
*Courtesy of: **Park Walk Gallery***

Travelling the Turf in Ireland
*Artist: **Peter Smith STRETCHING FOR HOME***
*Courtesy of: **Frost & Reed***

For many years now the best Irish thoroughbred National Hunt horse is eagerly sought overseas, but to nowhere is it as consistently and regularly exported than to Great Britain. This trend, which has proved most profitable and beneficial to buyer and seller over the years, shows no signs of tapering off and indeed if one looks at the facts and figures, it seems to be very much on the increase. Whilst the Irish-bred has long been exported to England to the point-to-point fraternity, it is in the area of Park racing where the most growth has occurred in the past 10-12 years. Whilst the older type of animal has long graced the English point-to-point field, it is the success of the better Irish animal, particularly the one from the point-to-point academy, which has hit the headlines in recent years.

Recent Gold Cup winners including **Mr Mulligan and Cool Dawn** - were ex point-to-point performers, while this years Aintree Grand National has been captured by the Tommy Carberry trained **Bobbyjo**. Other top recruits to the ranks in the past five years include this year's Whitbread Gold Cup victor **Call It a Day**, Welsh National winner **Belmont King**, Grand National runner up **Suny Bay**, in addition to such top class winners as **Ask Tom, Island Chief, Gales Cavalier, Unguided Missile, General Crack, Wandering Light** and **Yes Man** to name but a few.

It would be difficult to find better value at any sporting fixture than that which is found at the some 80 plus point-to-point meetings which take place throughout Ireland from the first day of January up to the last weekend in May. On the Northern Ireland scene, a day's racing will cost the racing enthusiast about a tenner, which covers admission to the course and a racecard with detailed and ample information - ample enough to ensure that the punter's ongoing battle with the 'Auld Enemy' is more than an exercise in 'hit and miss'. In the South, admission is either £3 per head or £5 a Car, whilst a comprehensive racecard only costs a pound. Most meets in the South are usually run on a Sunday, with a few on Saturdays and similarly a couple in mid-week, although competition from Park Sunday racing appears to be about to hit an all time high. The traditional day for competing in the North of Ireland is Saturday with a few mid-week dates. At present the number of horses competing in the point-to-point field continues to rise steadily and the 1998 season saw a record number of some 2,480 hopefuls coming before the starter. As with most sports events run during the winter months, one is inclined to be somewhat at the mercy of the elements, but the point-to-point brigade are invariably a hardy bunch. There are some seventy five courses sprinkled throughout the country with about five or six utilising the inside of courses in Park venues such as Dundalk and Listowel. In addition there are four venues which stage more than one point-to-point fixture during the season. Also there are 2 two day Festivals held here with the East Antrims running a two-day fixture in Loughanmore and the season usually winds up with the South Unions availing of the last weekend in May staging another popular Saturday/Sunday double header. Indeed the latter has tried with some success to make this an annual International fixture with a few races open to U.K. runners, making this a pleasant and somewhat laid back gathering - with the emphasis on fun and craic!

However, if one expects this apparent low-key attitude to permeate through the rest of the season, then one is in for a big surprise, as nothing could be further from the truth.

Though the sport basically purports to be amateur, very little from the organisation, the running and the competitive attitude leads one to believe that it is anything other than professional in the main.

The standard of rider, and in particular the leading ones, is of a particularly high standard and one only has to mention the names of Adrian Maguire, Norman Williamson and Timmy Murphy who have joined the professional ranks subsequently, to highlight the standard which the sport has achieved in regards to jockeyship.

For overseas National Hunt and point-to-point enthusiasts, visitors could easily ensure that they take in either a Saturday or Sunday point-to-point, in addition to a weekend Park fixture (there are many excellent National Hunt meets at this time of year) and in the process sample both sides of the racing spectrum. One thing is for sure however, whether it is wearing the wet gear at an inclement point-to-point in the Pigeons or at the more comfortable surroundings of Leopardstown, you are sure to enjoy the atmosphere and racing that is unique to an Irish National Hunt meeting.

Artist: **David Dent** *ISTABRAQ Courtesy of:* **The Artist**

JANUARY

Mon	1	Fairyhouse
Mon	1	Tramore
Thu	4	Thurles
Sat	6	Cork
Sun	7	Naas
Wed	10	Punchestown
Sat	13	Navan
Sun	14	Leopardstown
Wed	17	Down Royal
Thu	18	Tramore
Sat	20	Punchestown
Sun	21	Leopardstown
Thu	25	Gowran Park
Sat	27	Naas
Sun	28	Fairyhouse

FEBRUARY

Thu	1	Clonmel
Sat	3	Naas
Sun	4	Leopardstown
Thu	8	Thurles
Sat	10	Punchestown
Sun	11	Punchestown
Thu	15	Clonmel
Sat	17	Gowran Park
Sun	18	Navan
Thu	22	Thurles
Sat	24	Fairyhouse
Sun	25	Naas
Wed	28	Limerick

MARCH

Sat	3	Tramore
Sun	4	Leopardstown
Wed	7	Downpatrick
Sat	10	Navan
Sun	11	Naas
Sat	17	Down Royal
Sat	17	Limerick
Sun	18	Fairyhouse
Sun	18	Limerick
Mon	19	Limerick
Mon	19	Wexford
Thu	22	Clonmel
Sat	24	Navan
Sun	25	Curragh
Wed	28	Downpatrick
Sat	31	Down Royal
Sat	31	Gowran Park

APRIL

Sun	1	Limerick
Wed	4	Tipperary
Sun	8	Curragh
Wed	11	Clonmel
Sat	14	Leopardstown
Sat	14	Cork
Sun	15	Cork
Sun	15	Fairyhouse
Mon	16	Fairyhouse
Mon	16	Cork
Tue	17	Fairyhouse
Wed	18	Fairyhouse
Thu	19	Ballinrobe
Sat	21	Listowel
Sun	22	Listowel
Sun	22	Navan
Tue	24	Punchestown
Wed	25	Punchestown
Thu	26	Punchestown
Fri	27	Punchestown
Sun	29	Cork
Mon	30	Sligo (e)

MAY

Wed	2	Tipperary (e)
Fri	4	Dundalk (e)
Sat	5	Limerick
Sun	6	Navan
Sun	6	Gowran Park
Mon	7	Curragh
Mon	7	Down Royal
Mon	7	Limerick
Fri	11	Cork (e)
Sat	12	Fairyhouse
Sun	13	Leopardstown
Sun	13	Killarney
Mon	14	Killarney (e)
Tue	15	Killarney
Wed	16	Gowran Park (e)
Fri	18	Cork (e)
Fri	18	Downpatrick (e)
Sat	19	Downpatrick
Sun	20	Navan
Sun	20	Clonmel
Mon	21	Roscommon (e)
Wed	23	Leopardstown (e)
Thu	24	Tipperary (e)
Fri	25	Dundalk (e)
Sat	26	Curragh
Sun	27	Curragh
Mon	28	Kilbeggan (e)
Wed	30	Fairyhouse (e)
Thu	31	Clonmel (e)

JUNE

Fri	1	Wexford (e)
Sat	2	Cork
Sun	3	Cork
Sun	3	Sligo
Mon	4	Naas
Mon	4	Tralee
Wed	6	Leopardstown (e)
Thu	7	Gowran Park (e)
Fri	8	Kilbeggan (e)
Sat	9	Limerick
Sun	10	Limerick
Sun	10	Navan
Mon	11	Ballinrobe (e)
Tue	12	Ballinrobe (e)
Wed	13	Leopardstown (e)
Thu	14	Tipperary (e)
Fri	15	Wexford (e)
Sat	16	Navan
Sun	17	Roscommon
Mon	18	Roscommon (e)
Tue	19	Laytown (e)
Wed	20	Clonmel (e)
Thu	21	Naas (e)
Fri	22	Down Royal (e)
Sat	23	Down Royal
Sun	24	Gowran Park
Mon	25	Kilbeggan (e)
Tue	26	Tramore (e)
Wed	27	Leopardstown (e)
Fri	29	Curragh (e)
Sat	30	Curragh

JULY

Sun	1	Curragh
Mon	2	Sligo (e)
Tue	3	Cork (e)
Wed	4	Bellewstown (e)
Thu	5	Bellewstown (e)
Fri	6	Bellewstown (e)
Fri	6	Limerick (e)
Sat	7	Leopardstown
Mon	9	Roscommon (e)
Wed	11	Naas (e)
Thu	12	Dundalk

Fri	13	Dundalk (e)
Fri	13	Wexford (e)
Sat	14	Curragh
Sat	14	Wexford
Sun	15	Curragh
Mon	16	Killarney (e)
Tue	17	Killarney
Wed	18	Killarney (e)
Wed	18	Leopardstown (e)
Thu	19	Killarney
Fri	20	Kilbeggan (e)
Sat	21	Leopardstown
Sun	22	Dundalk
Sun	22	Tipperary
Mon	23	Ballinrobe (e)
Tue	24	Ballinrobe (e)
Wed	25	Naas (e)
Fri	27	Tipperary (e)
Sat	28	Curragh
Mon	30	Galway (e)
Tue	31	Galway (e)

AUGUST

Wed	1	Galway
Thu	2	Galway
Fri	3	Galway (e)
Sat	4	Galway
Sun	5	Galway
Mon	6	Cork
Mon	6	Naas
Tue	7	Roscommon (e)
Wed	8	Fairyhouse (e)
Wed	8	Sligo (e)
Thu	9	Sligo
Fri	10	Kilbeggan (e)
Sat	11	Wexford
Sun	12	Leopardstown
Sun	12	Tramore
Mon	13	Tramore (e)
Tue	14	Tramore (e)
Wed	15	Tramore
Wed	15	Dundalk
Fri	17	Cork (e)
Sat	18	Tipperary
Sun	19	Curragh
Mon	20	Roscommon
Wed	22	Sligo
Thu	23	Gowran Park
Fri	24	Kilbeggan
Sat	25	Curragh
Sun	26	Ballinrobe
Mon	27	Downpatrick
Tue	28	Tralee
Wed	29	Tralee
Thu	30	Tralee
Fri	31	Tralee (e)

SEPTEMBER

Sat	1	Tralee
Sun	2	Tralee
Sun	2	Curragh
Mon	3	Roscommon
Thu	6	Clonmel
Sat	8	Leopardstown
Mon	10	Galway
Tue	11	Galway
Wed	12	Galway
Fri	14	Downpatrick
Sat	15	Curragh
Sun	16	Curragh
Wed	19	Fairyhouse
Thu	20	Gowran Park
Fri	21	Down Royal
Sat	22	Cork
Sat	22	Down Royal
Mon	24	Listowel
Tue	25	Listowel

Wed	26	Listowel
Thu	27	Listowel
Fri	28	Listowel
Sat	29	Listowel
Sun	30	Punchestown

OCTOBER

Thu	4	Thurles
Fri	5	Fairyhouse
Sat	6	Curragh
Sun	7	Tipperary
Mon	8	Roscommon
Wed	10	Downpatrick
Thu	11	Gowran Park
Fri	12	Gowran Park
Sat	13	Gowran Park
Sun	14	Curragh
Sun	14	Limerick
Wed	17	Navan
Thu	18	Punchestown
Sat	20	Tipperary
Sun	21	Naas
Wed	24	Fairyhouse
Thu	25	Thurles
Sat	27	Leopardstown
Sun	28	Galway
Sun	28	Wexford
Mon	29	Leopardstown
Mon	29	Galway
Wed	31	Tipperary

NOVEMBER

Thu	1	Clonmel
Sat	3	Navan
Sun	4	Punchestown
Mon	5	Limerick
Thu	8	Thurles
Fri	9	Down Royal
Sat	10	Down Royal
Sat	10	Naas
Sun	11	Leopardstown
Sun	11	Cork
Thu	15	Clonmel
Sat	17	Punchestown
Sun	18	Navan
Wed	21	Downpatrick
Thu	22	Cork
Sat	24	Naas
Sun	25	Clonmel
Thu	29	Thurles

DECEMBER

Sat	1	Fairyhouse
Sun	2	Fairyhouse
Sat	8	Clonmel
Sun	9	Punchestown
Wed	12	Fairyhouse
Sat	15	Navan
Sun	16	Cork
Sat	22	Navan
Sun	23	Thurles
Wed	26	Leopardstown
Wed	26	Limerick
Wed	26	Down Royal
Thu	27	Leopardstown
Thu	27	Limerick
Fri	28	Leopardstown
Fri	28	Limerick
Sat	29	Leopardstown
Sun	30	Punchestown

(e) Denotes Evening Fixture
Dates of fixtures may be subject to alteration.

Sligo

Down Royal

Downpatrick

Dundalk

Ballinrobe

Roscommon

Navan

Laytown

Bellewstown

Galway

Kilbeggan

Fairyhouse

Curragh

Leopardstown

Naas

Punchestown

Limerick

Thurles

Listowel

Tipperary

Gowran Park

Tralee

Clonmel

Killarney

Tramore

Wexford

Cork

© *MAPS IN MINUTES*™(*2000*)

Ballinrobe

Contact: **Mr John Flannelly, Manager, Ballinrobe Race Committee, Ballinrobe, Co Mayo Tel: 00 353 92 41811, 00 353 87 289 5974. Secretary, N. Molloy, Convent Road, Ballinrobe, Co. Mayo Tel: 00 353 92-41219 Clerk of course: P.R. McGouran, 39 Barton Road, Rathfarnam, Dublin 14 Tel: 00 353 1 4931548 Racedays: Tel: 00 353 92 41052, Fax: 00 353 92 41406**

Ballinrobe has a very old tradition of racing in various forms with meetings recorded in 1774 and steeplechases included in the 1834 meeting. The present course was purchased in 1921.

Possessing a slightly elevated track, Ballinrobe boasts an exceptional view of the whole course. General facilities updated in 1998.

Location
One mile from Ballinrobe Town N84.

Refreshment Facilities
Bars and restaurants

Local Hotels
Ashford Castle, Tel: 00 353 92 46003, internationally renowned 5 star Hotel; Ryans Hotel Tel: 00 353 92 46243.

Local Restaurants
Flannerys, Ballinrobe, in top 100 pubs; Red Door, Ballinrobe; Echoes, Cong, among the 100 best restaurants in Ireland.

Places of Interest/Activities
Angling in 60,000 acres of brown trout fishing, golf - 18 hole championship course. Also a major area for items of historical and archeological interest.

Bellewstown

Contact: **Mr Kevin Coleman the Secretary/Manager, 9 Palace Street, Drogheda, Co Louth, Tel: 00 353 41 9842111, Fax: 00 353 41 9837566. Racecourse address Bellewstown Racecourse, Bellewstown, Co Meath, Tel: (Racedays only) 00 353 41 9823301 Fax: 00 353 41 9823644.**

Bellewstown racecourse, on the Hill of Crockafotha in Co Meath, is beautifully situated in a rural setting with magnificent views of the Mountains of Mourne to the north and the Irish sea to the east.

Bellewstown is an annual three day meeting which takes place in the first week of July. The races have always been associated with the smell of freshly mown hay and the taste of strawberries and cream. We do not know exactly when racing started in Bellewstown, but the first record of races appears in the August edition of the Dublin Gazette and the Weekly Courier in 1726.

George Tandy, a former Mayor of Drogheda and brother of the famous Napper Tandy, persuaded King George III to sponsor a race at Bellewstown in 1780. The race was called His Majesty's Plate and was valued at £100.

All the English monarchs continued to sponsor a race at Bellewstown until 1980, when Queen Elizabeth II decided to discontinue the race. However, the Queen continues to sponsor a race at the Curragh called the Royal Whip.

Location
The racecourse is 23 miles north of Dublin, off the main Dublin/Belfast road and seven miles south of Drogheda.

Public Transport
There is a special bus service from Dublin (Busarus) Tel: Bus Eireann 00 353 1 836 6111 for departure time. Buses also run from Drogheda.

Other Facilities
There is a free area beside the track which includes a carnival for children.

Local Hotels
Neptune Beach Hotel Tel: 00 353 41 982 7107, Bettystown; Old Mill Hotel and Glen Side Hotel, Julianstown; Rosnaree Park Hotel, Westcourt Hotel Tel: 00 353 41 983 0965 and Boyne Valley Hotel Tel: 00 353 41 9837737, Drogheda; Conyngham Arms Hotel Tel: 00 353 41 24155, Slane; Ashbourne House Hotel, Ashbourne. Contact the Irish Tourist Board Tel: 0171 493 3201 for an accommodation list.

Local Restaurants
Bacchus at the Coast Guard, Bettystown; Black Bull Inn, Buttergate and Monasterboice Inn (all Drogheda); Forge, Collon, Co Meath.

Places of Interest/Activities
The racecourse is close to the historic sites of Tara, Slane, Newgrange, Dowth and Knowth and the beautiful Boyne Valley. There are several 18 hole golf courses nearby.

Artist: **Roy Miller** SNOW TUNNEL Courtesy of: **The Artist**

Bettystown in Co. Meath is attracting much interest these days with the development of the new deluxe Neptune Beach Hotel and Leisure Club. The hotel has the most spectacular setting on the beautiful sandy beach at Bettystown.

All 38 spacious and luxurious en-suite bedrooms, most of which will command breathtaking views of the sea, are complete with trouser press, ironing facilities, hair dryer, satellite television and direct dial telephone.

The large comfortable foyer, with its glowing log fire and relaxing leather furniture, provides a warm and welcoming atmosphere for all guests. Morning and afternoon tea is served in the foyer and a relaxing drink can be enjoyed in the Victorian style Neptune Bar.

The elegant restaurant 'Le Pressage', is the ideal setting for a business luncheon or an intimate dinner. The cuisine is always of the highest standard with fine food and superb wines to suit all tastes. After dinner guests can also enjoy a cocktail in the stylish Seaview Lounge.

The Neptune Beach is the perfect venue for conferences and banquets of any size from small business meetings to exhibitions or seminars for up to 200 people. The main conference/banqueting room boasts spectacular sea views and is equipped with the most up to date audiovisual equipment.

The leisure club provides the very best in health and fitness equipment, with a spectacular 20 metre swimming pool, jacuzzi, steam room and a hi-tech fitness suite.

The Hotel is ideally located just 30 minutes north of Dublin Airport and 5 miles from Drogheda. The Neptune Beach is a golfer's delight with three championship courses in the surrounding area, while the racing fraternity will be perfectly placed for the courses at Fairyhouse, Bellewstown, Dundalk, Laytown and Navan.

Neptune Beach Hotel & Leisure Club
Bettystown
Co. Meath
Tel: 00 353 41 982 7107
Fax: 00 353 41 982 7412
e mail: info@neptunebeach.ie
web site: www.neptunebeach.ie

Clonmel

Contact: **Mr J L Desmond, Manager, Clonmel Racecourse, Davis Road, Clonmel, Co Tipperary, Tel: 00 353 52 22611/22032 Fax: 00 353 52 26446 Racedays: 00 353 52 25719 Fax: 00 353 52 25719.**

Clonmel, an historic town, lies at the foot of the Comeragh Mountains and is situated in the valley of the beautiful River Suir. To the north east lies Slievenamon.

Clonmel racecourse (Powerstown Park) is located in a picturesque setting north of the town. Racing, which had been open and free to spectators for over a hundred years at Clonmel, was enclosed in 1913 by Villiers Morton Jackson and became the commercially run Powerstown Park racecourse.

Morton Jackson also roped in the bookies to a distinct area of the course, banned gaming sideshows, brought in detectives and police to deter pickpockets and provided entry to a roofless grandstand accommodating 1500 at a charge of two shillings a head!

Since then Clonmel has grown and developed and today it is not uncommon to have in excess of 120 horses running at any one meeting. Extensive refurbishment has been carried out at Clonmel Racecourse during 1998. A new grandstand including a Bar and catering complex has been constructed. Along with a new computerised turnstile entrance, the weighroom/jockeys room has also been extensively upgraded and refurbished.

Location
Clonmel racecourse (Powerstown Park) is situated within two miles of the town centre, off the Waterford-Clonmel road. It is 100 miles from Dublin, 30 miles from Waterford, 24 miles from Tipperary and 12 miles from Cahir.

Refreshment Facilities
Self service restaurant, snack bars and bars

Local Hotels
Hotel Minella Tel: 00 353 52 22388, Clonmel Arms Hotel Tel: 00 353 52 21233 and Hearns Hotel Tel: 00 353 52 21611

Local Restaurants
Include La Scala, Emerald Garden (Chinese), Jasmine Court (Chinese), Mulcahys and Sean Tierney's Bar & Restaurant.

Places of Interest/Activities
Cahir Castle, Rock of Cashel, Kilkenny Castle and Mitchelstown's Caves, together with scenic drives also golf and pony trekking.

Cork

Contact: **Mr Michael Lane Executive Director/ Secretary, at Cork Racecourse (Mallow) Limited Killarney Road, Mallow, Co Cork Tel: 00 353 22 50207 Fax: 00 353 22 50213.**

There is a long tradition of horse racing in the region. The first ever steeplechase took place in 1752 between the church steeples of Buttervant and Donerail, just a few miles from Mallow. In 1777, six consecutive days of racing were on offer in the Mallow area, "all to be run according to the King's Plate articles".

With the demise of Cork Park in 1917, the need for a new racecourse in Ireland's largest county was apparent. Mallow, formed at the instigation of and under the control of Lieutenant Colonel F F MacCabe, commenced racing in 1924.

The racecourse re-opened at Easter 1997, following a £7 million refurbishment backed by the Irish Horseracing Authority, the Irish Government and local private and industry sponsorship.

Location
The racecourse is situated one mile from Mallow town on the Mallow-Killarney road (N72). Racegoers travelling from Cork and Limerick (N20) should go under the railway bridge at the roundabout. Patrons coming from Dublin and Waterford (N73 and N72) should take the town park bypass to reach the roundabout.

Public Transport
Mallow is well served by bus and rail. Most trains from Dublin (Heuston Station) to Cork stop at Mallow. Tel: Irish Rail (Iarnrod Eireann) 00 353 1 836 6222 for train timetable. Taxi service from Mallow Station to the racecourse.

Refreshment Facilities
Corporate restaurant (pre booked) , self service restaurant, snack bar

Local Hotels
Hiberian Hotel Tel: 00 353 22 21588, Mallow Park Hotel Tel: 00 353 22 21527, Longueville House Tel: 00 353 22 47156 and Springfort Hall Tel: 00 353 22 21278, Mallow; Assolas House Tel: 00 353 29 50015 in Kanturk

Local Restaurants
The Roundabout Inn & Restaurant, The Black Lamb and Kepplers in Mallow

Places of Interest/Activities
Mallow Castle and herd of white deer in Mallow; Doneraile Park in Doneraile; Blarney Castle in Blarney; also fishing, golf and pony trekking.

*Artist: **Jonathan Trowell** THE FAVOURITE*
*Courtesy of: **Osborne Studio Gallery***

Hotel Minella

A beautiful former Quaker Mansion, Hotel Minella is an impressive stately home presiding over a stretch of the rippling River Suir. Tasteful modernisation blends into the background of the original 1863 building which commands nine acres of lovingly maintained land. All in all, a rare example of a hotel able to combine the comforts of the 20th Century with the dignity and elegance of a bygone age which time, and three major wars, have tossed aside. Opened in 1962 by Mr and Mrs Nallen the Minella is now run by the second generation of Nallens - John and Elizabeth.

Clonmel itself - Cluain Meala - the Meadow of Honey, has aptly been described as the "sportsman's paradise". Long associated with many great names it is a renowned horse and greyhound breeding area. Few countries offer as much for a serious golfer with courses ranging from parkland pleasure of Thurles to the justly famous and demanding hills of Clonmel - a mere two miles from the hotel. Both of these are 18 hole, par 71 courses. The hotel is happy to arrange an all inclusive mini-holiday to ensure a more relaxed day.

For the racing enthusiast, this premier country is ideal. The Clonmel racecourse is just two miles from the Minella and less than an hour's drive away are the courses of Gowran, Tipperary, Wexford, Tramore and Cork. For a diversion from these temptations why not try your hand at swimming, boating and canoeing on the Suir, mountain climbing in the Comeragh Mountains and the beautiful Knockmealdown range. Club Minella, an exclusive 5 star Health & Leisure Complex, opened in 1999. Awaiting you is a 20 metre pool, outdoor Canadian hot tub, aerobics room, sauna, gymnasium, outdoor tennis court and a putting green as well as cruising on our pleasure boats on the Suir.

With a wealth of beautiful countryside in the area, you could take a walk, or step up the pace a little, by going pony trekking in the Nire Valley.

The Minella offers a warm and friendly welcome at the end of a whirling day. Enjoy a quiet drink in the cocktail bar, overlooking the lawns and the banks of the Suir, and then move to the oak panelled dining room to sample some of the Minella dishes. Enjoy traditional Irish cuisine at its best: prime roast beef, grilled steaks and fresh fish, all complemented by a fine selection of wines.

The 70 bedrooms offer the perfect end to the perfect day. All have an en-suite bathroom, colour televisions, direct dial telephone, hair dryer and alarm clock radio. Eight executive suites have a private jacuzzi or private steam room and all offer a stunning morning view over the river or Comeragh Mountains.

The Minella Stables are just 5 miles from the hotel and Mr Nallen Senior will be delighted to offer guided tours of the stables and the famous "Minella" horses at any time.

A home away from home ...the Nallen Family awaits your visit.

Hotel Minella
Clonmel
Co Tipperary Ireland
Tel: 00 353 52 22388/24381 Fax: 00 353 52 24381
e mail: hotelminella@tinet.ie
web site: www.tipp.ie/hotel-minella.htm

The Stand House Hotel is the ideal location whether you are taking a trip to the races, having a relaxing break or an active holiday.

The hotel, which is only 30 minutes from Dublin in the heart of the Curragh, offers excellent accommodation, entertainment and leisure facilities.

With 63 luxurious en-suite bedrooms, complete with direct dial telephone, trouser press, hair dryer and satellite television, and an acclaimed restaurant featuring top-class international cuisine, there is no doubt that a stay at the Stand House Hotel will be a luxurious one.

Should you wish to mix business with pleasure you will be attracted to the corporate racing deals. We can tailor packages to meet the needs and budget of the specific client, ensuring that you get exactly what you're looking for.

With a total of eight conference rooms catering for any number from 3 to 800, the Stand House Hotel is the perfect venue for weddings, banquets or for any special occasions. All the rooms reflect the elegance and atmosphere of the original 18th century building.

The Stand House Hotel is surrounded by a number of great attractions. As well as the following racecourses: The Curragh, Naas, Leopardstown, Punchestown, there are the golf courses: Cill Dara, The Curragh, Naas, K Club, Castle Warden, and Kilkea. There is car racing at Mondello Park, while the National Stud and the scene of the hit movie Braveheart are also located nearby.

For the last word in comfort all guests have use of the luxurious leisure centre with its 20 metre deck level swimming pool, sauna, steam room, Jacuzzi and fully equipped gymnasium. Guests may also relax in the Beauty Salon and L'Oreal Hair Salon (extra charge).

The Stand House Hotel
Leisure and Conference Centre
The Curragh
County Kildare
Tel: 00 353 45 436177
Fax: 00 353 45 436180
e mail: standhse@indigo.ie

Curragh

Contact: **Mr Jason Mottis, Manager** at **Curragh Racecourse, The Curragh, Co Kildare Tel: 00 353 45 441205 Fax: 00 353 45 441442**

E mail: info@curragh.ie
Web site: www.curragh.ie

In a country where breeding classic racehorses is almost as widespread as the green grass on which they thrive, the Home of the Classics is the Curragh racecourse. The ancient Gaelic name Curragh actually means racecourse and in the very earliest Irish manuscripts, the Curragh figured as a place of sport for Celtic Kings and their people.

The 17th century saw the Curragh become a sporting resort of the chief governors and administrators of Ireland. Every summer Dublin Castle was almost deserted as the lord lieutenant and his entourage came to Kildare to watch or compete in the racing at the Curragh. The number of King's Plates varied over the two centuries from 1700, but the vast majority of them were contested on the Curragh. Not surprisingly therefore the Curragh became the social centre and administrative headquarters of racing in Ireland over that time.

At the end of the 18th century, the Curragh had become permanently fringed by the lodges and stables of the most prominent owners, breeders and trainers in the country. These lodges and stables in name and even in fabric have survived in the hands of an equally illustrious racing community today. The first Irish Derby took place at the Curragh in 1866—this famous Classic has a legendary reputation for bringing out the best in horses and riders. It also ranks as Ireland's premier sporting and social event.

Today, as the headquarters of thoroughbred racing in Ireland, the Curragh caters for all five classic races in the country, as well as fourteen other prestigious meetings during the Irish racing calendar.

Location

The Curragh racecourse is situated 29 miles south west of Dublin on the main Dublin-Cork-Limerick road. It is nine miles from Naas and two miles from Newbridge.

Public Transport

By rail you can buy a combined admission and return ticket at Dublin (Heuston Station) for £14, for all Saturday and Sunday meetings. To check train schedules contact Iarnrod Eireann on 00 353 1 836 6222. A special bus leaves Busaras, Store Street, Dublin 1, for the Curragh on racedays and departs the racecourse after the last race. For further information on departure times contact Bus Eireann 00 353 1 836 6111. Special coaches can be hired for group outings, for further details contact 00 353 45 879007.

Admission Rates

For regular meetings in 2000 prices were as follows: Saturdays £8, Sundays £10, Classic and Group One meetings £12. Prices for 2000 Irish Derby Festival Weekend are as follows Friday meeting £10, Saturday £12 and Sunday in the West End Enclosure £15, Reserved Enclosure £35. Senior citizens and students have a 50% concession except for Irish Derby Day. Children under 14 who must be accompanied by an adult are admitted free to all meetings except again for Irish Derby Day when the charge is £5 Grandstand and £10 reserved enclosure. For seating and balcony access reservations call the racecourse.

Annual badge prices which admit to all meetings are adults £115, senior citizens £60 and under 25's £60. A portion of the main stand is reserved for annual badge holders. Badge holders also have access to the Members Bar and free parking in car park 'B'.

Corporate Hospitality

Private suites and hospitality rooms are available to cater for 10-160 people. All-in hospitality packages include: top level badge, racecard, reserved seat, pre-lunch reception, four course lunch with wine, complimentary bar, afternoon tea. Contact the Marketing Manager at the racecourse on 00 353 45 441205. Suites can be viewed on line at www.curragh.ie.

Artist: **Peter Curling FROSTY MORNING** *Courtesy of:* **Rosenstiel's**

Refreshment Facilities

The Horseshoe Restaurant at the Curragh is open from noon on racedays. To reserve tables for lunch and afternoon tea call 00 353 1 626 1466. Within the Tote Hall there is a self service area with hot meals and snacks served from noon onwards. There are five bars. The Curragh View Bar and Horseshoe Bar on the first floor have clear views of the course and the finishing post. The Curragh View Bar also serves hot and cold food from a deli and baguette bar. The Vintage Crop Bar is located under the West Stand next to the bookmakers ring, The Railway Bar is in the Tote Hall and the Paddock Bar is on the reserved upper balcony.

Other Facilities

A PA system relays full race commentary to all areas of the course. There is a closed circuit TV in all public areas and results of UK races are displayed beside the weigh room.

For children a crèche and outdoor playground are provided at the west end of the stand. In both these areas children are supervised by qualified nursing and child care staff. On Irish Derby Day both the crèche and playground are closed.

Local Hotels

Keadeen Hotel Tel: 00 353 45 431666 in Newbridge; Stand House Hotel Tel: 00 353 45 436177, Curragh Lodge Hotel Tel: 00 353 45 522144, Kildare; Kilkea Castle Tel: 00 353 45 503 45156, Castledermot; Ardenode Hotel Tel: 00 353 45 864198, Ballymore Eustace; Tulfarris House Tel: 00 353 45 867555, Blessington; Barberstown Castle Tel: 00 353 1 628 8157, Kildare Hotel and Country Club Tel: 00 353 1 601 7200, Straffan; Red Cow Morans Hotel Tel: 00 353 1 45 93650, Dublin.

Local Restaurants

Lumville House, Red House Inn and Togher's Roadhouse, all in Newbridge; Silken Thomas in Kildare; The Hideout, Berney's, McTernan's, Kilcullen and Poulaphouca House, all in Ballymore Eustace. Contact the Irish Tourist Board Tel: 0171 493 3201 for a full accommodation list.

Places of Interest/Activities

Irish National Stud; Japanese Gardens in Kildare; Castletown House in Celbridge; Lakeside Leisure Centre in Blessington; also golf, fishing, hunting, horse riding.

Artist: **Hubert De Watrigant** **ATTITUDES** *Courtesy of:* **Osborne Studio Gallery**

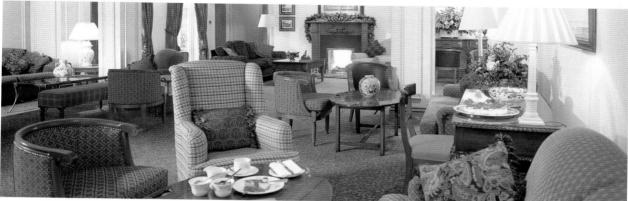

Tucked away amid the lush green countryside of County Kildare–Ireland's 'home of the horse'–Keadeen Hotel is located in Newbridge town just two kilometres from the internationally acclaimed Curragh racecourse. This family run hotel, established over 26 years ago is well known to all racegoers, both nationally and internationally, and is certainly no stranger to the hunting season. Racecourses at Naas and Punchestown are also close by.

Beautifully appointed and completely refurhished in 1996, Keadeen is situated in eight magnificent award-winning Kildare gardens. Adjacent to the primary Dublin-Cork-Limerick road, 40 kilometres west of Dublin city, Keadeen hotel enjoys an ideal location and is easily accessible off the main M7 motorway which links up with the newly built motorway to Dublin airport.

An enclave of tranquillity, Hotel Keadeen invites guests to savour a relaxing and comfortable stay in the first class family run hotel. Similarly the spectacular award-winning design of the Keadeen Club health and fitness centre, newly opened in September 1996 is a temptation that beckons to all. Each of the luxurious en suite bedrooms and the ten newly built executive rooms is designed with the comfort of guests in mind and is equipped to the highest of international standards.

The newly renovated foyer, drawing room and cocktail bars are the perfect venue for a relaxing evening while the renowned restaurant serves an excellent range of international cuisine, prepared from the finest of fresh Irish ingredients.

Hotel Keadeen's gateway location offers the tourist unrivalled access to the beauty spots of Kildare and Wicklow as well as a convenient stopover to or from Dublin airport.

Some of the many and varied activities on offer by arrangement through the hotel include: hunting - from a choice of six well established packs, golfing - choose from Kildare's very plentiful list of first class championship courses, walking the famous canal 'towpath trails' of the Grand and Royal Canal, flying - at Captain Darby Kennedy's Weston Aerodrome founded in the 1930s, cycling, fishing parachuting, clay pigeon shooting, archery, windsurfing, water skiing, motor racing-at Mondellos-or visit the magnificent Japanese Gardens or the National Stud . . . to name but a few of the many attractions on offer in this picturesque location.

Whatever the reason for visiting this enchanting part of the world, you are always assured of the warmest of welcomes at this delightful hotel.

The Keadeen Hotel
Newbridge
Co Kildare Ireland
Tel: 00 353 45 431666
Fax: 00 353 45 434402
e mail: keadeen@iol.ie
web site: keadeenhotel.kildare.ie

Down Royal

Contact: **Mr Michael Todd,** at **Down Royal Racecourse, Maze, Lisburn, Co Down BT27 5BW Tel: 02892 621256 Fax: 02892 621433**

The history of Down Royal goes back over 300 years to the reign of James II. Created by Royal Charter in 1685, The Down Royal Corporation of Horse Breeders was tasked with "Encouraging the Breed in the County of Down". Undoubtedly the most famous horse to race at Down Royal was the "Byerly Turk" one of the three foundation stallions of the Stud Book.

Down Royal Racecourse is the home of the Northern Ireland Festival of Racing.

Location
Down Royal Racecourse is situated 2 ¹/₂ miles from Lisburn and 10 miles south of Belfast. It is adjacent to the A1 which is the main Belfast/Dublin route. The Racecourse is twenty minutes from Belfast International Airport and thirty minutes from Belfast City Airport.

Corporate Hospitality
Corporate hospitality packages are available for all race meetings.

Refreshment Facilities
The Racecourse has a modern Grandstand with a capacity for 2500 people and incorporates the following public amenities: Large Island Bar, Fast Food Counters, Carvery Counter, Tote Hall, Seating and Tables, Toilets, Close Circuit T.V., Viewing Windows overlooking Parade Ring

Local Hotels
Beechlawn Hotel Tel: (02890) 612974, Dunmurry; White Gables Hotel, Hillsborough; Ballymac Hotel Tel: (02892) 684313, Stoneyford, Lisburn

Local Restaurants
The Racecourse Inn, Maze, Lisburn; The Hillside Restaurant, Hillsborough (Egon Ronay Recommended); The Plough, Hillsborough (Egon Ronay Recommended); The Tidi Doffer, Ravernet, Lisburn (Winner of the British Airways Award for best hostelry).

Places of Interest/Activities
Irish Linen Centre/Lisburn Museum, Lisburn (Award winning attraction). Tourist Information available - (02892) 660038. Hillsborough - a beautiful Georgian village with many speciality shops, pubs and restaurants.

Downpatrick

Contact: **Mr Iain Duff, Doonhamer, 71 Lismore Road, Downpatrick, Co Down Tel: 01396 841125 Fax: 01396 842227.** c/o **Ballydugan Road, Downpatrick, Co Down,** Racedays: **01396 612054 Fax: 01396 615923**.

The first race meeting to be held at Downpatrick was over 300 years ago - 1685. Racing has continued to take place with few breaks since, and on the present course for the last 200 years which is situated one mile away from the centre of this historic town.

A tight, undulating track of 1 ¹/₄ miles; many top National Hunt horses have started their careers at Downpatrick including the dual National winner Rhyme n' Reason, Cheltenham winners Rathgorman, Tourist Attraction and Sparky Gayle.

Downpatrick is possibly the friendliest course in Ireland with a strong local following. It has a supporters club which was formed in the early '70s and has raised substantial sums since its inception. Notably, Downpatrick is one of the four racecourses where all races are sponsored.

Artist: **Heather St Clair Davis** **DOWN AT THE START** *Courtesy of:* **Frost & Reed**

Artist: **Malcolm Coward COMING IN** Courtesy of: **Sally Mitchell Fine Arts**

Local Hotels
Burrendale Hotel and Country Club, Newcastle Tel: (01396) 722599

Dundalk

Contact: **Mr Norman Colfer, Manager, at Paddock Lodge, Ratoath, Co Meath, Tel: 00 353 1 825 6618.** The racecourse address is **Dundalk Racecourse, Dowdallshill, Dundalk, Co Louth, Tel/Fax: (Racedays only) 00 353 42 9334800**

Dundalk is derived originally from the Great Fortress, now called the Moat of Castletown, which was the residence of Cuchullin, the legendary hero and chief of the Red Branch Knights in the first century. This 'Dun-deal-gan' was the fortress of Delga, a Firbolg chief who had originally built it. The racecourse, founded in the early part of this century, is in a lovely setting at the foot of the Cooley mountains and beside Carlingford Lough.

Location
Dundalk is located 52 miles North of Dublin. The racecourse is situated one and a half miles from the town centre, off the Newry Road.

Corporate Hospitality
Hospitality room available to cater for 40-120 people. There is a wide variety of structured sponsorship packages to cater for all budgets.

Refreshment Facilities
Self service restaurant, snack bars and bars.

Local Hotels
Derryhale Hotel Tel: 00 353 42 9335471, Imperial Hotel Tel: 00 353 42 9332241 and Fairways Hotel Tel: 00 353 42 9321500 in Dundalk, Ballymascanlon Hotel Tel: 00 353 42 9371124 in Ballymascanlon; Carrickdale Hotel Tel: 00 353 42 9371397 in Ravensdale.

Fairyhouse

Contact: **Dick Sheil, Chief Executive** at **Fairyhouse Racecourse, Ratoath, Co. Meath, Tel: 00 353 1 8256167 Fax: 00 353 1 8256051**. e mail: info@fairyhouse-club.com

Fairyhouse is the home of Ireland's premier National Hunt race, the Powers Gold Label Irish Grand National, which is run every year on Easter Monday. In 2001 it will be on the second day of our popular Easter festival which will run from April 15th to 17th.

The first meeting held in Fairyhouse was in 1848 when the Ward Union Hunt held their point-to-point at this venue. From these small beginnings Fairyhouse quickly established itself as one of Ireland's premier racecourses. In 1870 the Irish Grand National was run and the winner was 'Sir Robert Peel'. The Grand National quickly became Ireland's most valuable and prestigious steeplechase and each success has its own rich tale, none more amazing that the win in 1929 of a six year old mare 'Alike', owned and ridden by 5'4" Frank Wise who was missing three fingers and who rode with a wooden leg.

Fairyhouse has always been one of the finest and fairest racecourses and continues to attract the leading horses both on the flat and over jumps. Arkle, Desert Orchid, Flying Bolt, Captain Christy, Prince Regent, Persian War, L'Escargot, and more recently Istabraq, See More Business and Bobbyjo are just some of the legendary greats that have graced the almost 2 mile circuit.

The racecourse is located 12 miles north west of Dublin, just off the N2 or the N3. The racecourse is within half an hour's drive from Dublin Airport and City Centre, and is easily accessible via the Westlink motorway and Blanchardstown bypass. Bus Eireann provides a special bus service from Busaras for racemeetings. Tel: 00 353 1 8366111.

In 2001 Fairyhouse will host 18 days racing with the feature being our four day Easter Festival featuring the Irish Grand National, the Powers Handicap Hurdle and the Powers Gold Cup. The pre-Christmas festival (Dec 1st - 2nd), features three Grade 1 races and is now firmly established as Ireland's first major National Hunt fixture of each new season. Fairyhouse also races on New Year's Day (Jan 1st).

Fairyhouse has an exclusive membership package which includes admission to all race meetings, private member's room looking onto the racetrack with an exclusive members' area in the stand, and members' car park. Fairyhouse is linked with two English racecourses, namely Uttoxeter and Newcastle. This enables members from each of the aforementioned courses complimentary admission to all meetings throughout the year.

Fairyhouse has a fully supervised and equipped crèche for children aged up to 9 years of age, with both indoor and outdoor play areas.

The racecourse opened its superb new grandstand and the refurbished Jameson Stand in November 1999. These new facilities will offer increased comfort to the racegoer. The new development includes new grandstand, weighroom building, Tote hall, betting shop, bars, restaurants, private suites and corporate hospitality rooms.

Throughout the year these Corporate facilities are available for numbers from 10 to 1,000. All suites and function rooms will have Tote, CCTV and either silver service or buffet style dining.

Local Hotels
The Newgrange Hotel Tel: 00 353 46 74100, Navan, The Great Southern Hotel Tel: 00 353 1 844 6000 and the Red Cow Morans Tel: 00 353 1 45 93650 are just some of the many hotels within a short distance from the racecourse. Contact the Irish Tourist Board Tel: 0171 493 3201 for a full accommodation list.

Refreshment Facilities
The Powers Gold Label Stand silver service restaurant, self service restaurants, seafood bar, fast food outlets and a choice of six bars.

Local Restaurants
Ryan's Steak House and Chez Francis Restaurant in Ratoath; Mill House in Clonee; The County Club in Dunshaughlin

Places of Interest/Activities
The racecourse is close to the historic sites of Tara, Slane and Newgrange as well as the beautiful Boyne Valley. Fishing and golf are available nearby.

Artist: **Peter Smith HURDLERS BEFORE THE OFF** *Courtesy of:* **Frost & Reed**

Four star Red Cow Moran Hotel combines classic elegance with modern design. A magnificent staircase sweeping from the marble lobby welcomes guests to this hotel of character and distinction. All the hotel's 123 executive bedrooms are fully air conditioned with teletext TV, voicemail phones, trouser press and tea/coffee making facilities. Eight luxuriously appointed suites ensure that Red Cow Moran Hotel can cater for the most prestigious and discerning guests.

Strategically located only 15 minutes from the airport and ten minutes from Dublin city centre, Red Cow Moran Hotel is ideal for those going racing. The Curragh, Punchestown, Naas, Leopardstown and Fairyhouse courses are all within convenient driving distance of this deluxe hotel. The hotel offers extensive free parking for guests.

The Winter Garden Restaurant, with warm wood, airy conservatory and modern lighting, offers imaginative Irish cuisine with an array of international dishes and an extensive wine list. Guests may also choose to sample the traditional ambience of the renowned Red Cow Inn, a 200 year old pub situated within the hotel's grounds which has a choice of two restaurants, the Carvery and the Carriage.

After a thrilling day at the races what better way to unwind than with a drink in one of the four bars within the complex including the spacious and tranquil surroundings of the hotel's resident's bar. For those who want to continue on into the night the Red Cow Inn also offers Club Diva, one of Dublin's premier nightspots within the hotel's grounds.

For corporate entertainment the hotel has extensive banqueting and conference facilities for up to 700 delegates as well as private syndicate and boardrooms for smaller parties.

Red Cow Moran Hotel
Naas Road
Dublin 22
Ireland
Tel: 00 353 1 45 93650
Fax: 00 353 1 45 91588
e mail: sales@morangroup.ie
web site: www.redcowhotel.com

Ardilaun House Hotel
Conference Centre & Leisure Club

Ardilaun House or Glenarde House as it was originally known was built around 1840 as a Town House for the Pearse Family who were Distillers and had large estates in South Galway.

Many of the Pearse family hold a place in local history. Augusta became Lady Gregory and was co-founder of the Abbey Theatre. Burton was founder of the Galway Blazers and a well-known racehorse trainer whose best horse was probably The Tetrach. Henry S. Pearse, who also resided at what is now Ardilaun House Hotel, was one of the stewards of the first Galway race meeting in Ballybrit in August 1869, and his horse won the first race on that day.

In 1922 the distillery closed and soon afterwards the Glenarde House and Estate was sold to Mr. Patrick Boland of the Biscuit Family. In 1961, the property, with 5 acres, was acquired by Mr. & Mrs. Patrick D. Ryan (Former Chairman of the Galway Race Committee) and its conversion into an hotel commenced - the hotel opened on St. Patrick's Day 1962.

1999 saw major investment and upgrading of the hotel and its facilities. A state of the art leisure centre was created, complete with a deck level swimming pool, jacuzzi, sauna, steam room, gym, aerobics room and a health and therapy suite and billiard room.

Golf, tennis, pitch & putt, the beach and the city centre are all within five minute's drive of the hotel.

Renovations also took place in the public areas and conference centre, with the addition of a designated board-room. The hotel relaunched itself as the Ardilaun House Hotel, Conference Centre & Leisure Club.

The Ardilaun is now a 90 bedroom, 4 star hotel, with five acres of grounds and gardens, offering superb facilities and comforts for the racegoer.

Special rates are available to readers of "Travelling the Turf in Ireland" for the September and October Meetings.

Brochures on request.

Ardilaun House Hotel
Taylors Hill
Galway
Co. Galway
Tel: 00 353 91 521433
Fax: 00 353 91 521546
e mail: ardilaun@iol.ie
web site: www.ardilaunhousehotel.ie

Galway

Contact: **Mr John Moloney, Manager** at **Galway Racecourse, Ballybrit, Co Galway** Tel: 00 353 91 753 870 Fax: 00 353 91 752 592, Web site: http:// www.iol.ie/galway-races, E-mail: galway @iol.ie

Records of organised race meetings in Co Galway go back to the middle of the 18th century and, according to local tradition, steeplechase races were run annually at Kiltulla, east of Ballybrit, for many years prior to 1868. In 1868, due to flooding of the course, they were transferred to Bushfield, beyond Oranmore. These, we are told, were the forerunners of the Galway races.

Sources record that there was an attendance of around 40,000 on the opening day at Ballybrit on Tuesday, 17th August 1869, and that 35,000 people turned up on the second day of the meeting. It is reported that the park in Eyre Square was used as a camping site to accommodate the huge crowds that arrived for the occasion. The first meeting was an overwhelming success and the Galway Races have gone from strength to strength ever since. The Galway Plate is one of the most important steeplechases in Ireland. The new Millennium Stand with its viewing terrace for 8,000 people and a second floor seating balcony for 2,000 people also features a wide range of amenities. The 1999 summer festival meeting became the first festival in Ireland to run for a full week - where new records for both attendances and betting were set.

Location
Galway is 136 miles from Dublin. The racecourse is situated four miles outside the city centre off the Galway-Tuam road. Directions to the course from the city are clearly marked with AA signs.

Public Transport
Regular train service to Galway from Dublin (Heuston Station). Tel: Irish Rail (Iarnrod Eireann) 00 353 1 836 6222 for train timetables. Special continuous bus service from Galway city centre during racing.

Admission Rates
Admission for the festival in July will be £10 and £12. September, October festival admission £8. For further information contact Galway Racecourse Tel: 00 353 91 753870.

Corporate Hospitality
Throughout the festival week the programme of National Hunt and flat racing including the famous Galway Hurdle and Galway Plate guarantees exciting racing for seven days. The Galway races 'Hospitality Village' offers a choice of packages in the Blazers Pavilion (ideal for groups of 6 or more) or Blazers Private Suite (for groups of 40 or more). Marquees are erected for the Summer/Autumn Festival, providing hospitality suites for all entertaining guests. There is also a new panoramic restaurant on the top level of the new Millennium Stand which caters for 200 people.

Refreshment Facilities
Self service carvery restaurant, seafood wine bar, snack bars and bars within the Millennium Stand.

Other Facilities
Children's crèche

Local Hotels
Ardilaun House Hotel Tel: 00 353 91 521433, Corrib Great Southern Hotel Tel: 00 353 91 755281; Galway Ryan Hotel Tel: 00 353 91 753181, Oranmore Lodge Tel: 00 353 91 794400; Victoria Hotel Tel: 00 353 91 564924; Great Southern Hotel Tel: 00 353 91 564041; Park House Hotel Tel: 00 353 91 564924; Quality Inn Tel: 00 353 91 792244; Oyster Manor Hotel Tel: 00 353 91 796777; Renvyle House Hotel Tel: 00 353 95 43511 and Connemara Coast Hotel Tel: 00 353 91 592108, Galway; and Ashford Castle Tel: 00 353 92 46003, Cong.

Local Restaurants
Park House and Eyre House in Galway; Twelve Pins, Donnelly's and Ty ar Mor in Barna; Drimcong House in Moycullen

Places of Interest/Activities
Walking tours of Galway, Connemara, Burren, Co Clare, Coole Park, Gort and the Aran Islands; also golf, fishing and pony trekking

Gowran Park

Contact: **Mr Tom Carroll, Manager** at **Gowran Park Race Company Limited Gowran, Co. Kilkenny** Tel: 00 353 56 26225 Fax: 00 353 56 26173.

Since the first race meeting was held in June 1914, the course has become recognised as one of the best trial courses for both steeplechasing and flat racing in the islands. Levmoss, who pulled off the unique double of the Ascot Gold Cup and the Prix de L'Arc de Triomphe, first won on the flat at Gowran. Arkle, Nicholas Silver and Foinavon all ran at Gowran before going on to greater success overseas. Recently, Danoli and Doran's Pride have raced against each other at the brand new October Kilkenny Racing Festival.

The Thyestes Chase (January) is the big event of the calendar, the first major steeplechase in the year. The Red Mills trial Hurdle (February) has become one of the classic Cheltenham Trials, and if Cheltenham week has not satisfied your taste for racing, the Tetratema Cup, which has been run since 1918, takes place on the Saturday after the big English meeting. In May the flat racing kicks off with The Glanbia Classic trial over the bank holiday weekend, and in June the Victor McCalmont Memorial Stakes and the McEnery Cup are run. The ever popular mid-June Jack Duggan Handicap Hurdle keeps the national hunt fans happy. Mid-October is the Kilkenny Racing Festival, a 3-day event which draws big crowds, featuring the Denny Cordell Lavarack Memorial Race, The Powers Gold Label Handicap Hurdle and the National Lottery Agents Champion Stakes.

Location
The racecourse is approximately 1/4 of a mile outside Gowran village on the Dublin-Waterford road. Gowran is 8 miles from Kilkenny, 80 miles from Dublin, 15 miles from Carlow and 5 miles from Thomastown.

Public Transport
Bus Eireann provides a special bus service from Dublin (Busaras) for most race meetings. Tel: 00 353 1 836 6111 to check times of departure. Also Rapid Express Tel. 00 353 51 872 149 and Tom Duffy (special raceday coaches from Dublin) Tel. 00 353 1 832 8169

Corporate Hospitality
The Helen Sheane suite caters for 30 - 100 people; the cocktail bar caters for 20 - 40 people; hard standing 'pads' are also available for siting of marquees.

Refreshment Facilities
Self service restaurant, snack bar and bars

Local Hotels
Club House Hotel Tel: 00 353 56 21994 and Hotel Kilkenny Tel: 00 353 56 62000, Kilkenny; Mount Juliet Hotel Tel: 00 353 56 73000, Kilkenny River Court Hotel, Thomastown; Kilkea Castle Tel: 00 353 503 45156, Castledermot, Dinn Ri in Carlow.

Local Restaurants
Laugton House and Kyteler's Inn in Kilkenny; Lord Bagenal in Leighlinbridge; The Long Man of Kilfane in Kilfane

Places of Interest/Activities
Kilkenny Castle, St Canice's Cathedral, Rothe House, Castle Yard, all in Kilkenny; also fishing, horse riding and golf, shopping and plenty of festivals.

Kilbeggan

Contact: **Mr Patrick J Dunican, Manager** at **Kilbeggan Racecourse, Kilbeggan, Co Westmeath Tel: 00 353 506 32176 Fax: 00 353 506 32125**

Kilbeggan Races is a truly Irish occasion. The quiet midlands town is transformed on race evenings into a festival of social and sporting pleasure, drawing admirers from every corner of Ireland. You can meet friends, circulate freely; you can eat drink or cheer without restriction, you can bring the family or whoever; where for your few pounds the odds are much better than a lottery ticket, and where you can boast afterwards it was sheer skill that made you pick the winner.

If you are bright, witty and rich you will enjoy Kilbeggan Races and if you are not, you will enjoy them just the same.

Westmeath C.C. sponsor a feature hurdle race in May. The Lean Midlands National is a July highlight and Bank of Ireland sponsor a major hurdle race during the season, also Max Premium Dog Food sponsor a Handicap Steeplechase in September, attracting hundreds to the racing the Irish love best, National Hunt. The only racecourse in Ireland where all races are over jumps under National Hunt Rules.

The friendship and atmosphere gives Kilbeggan the edge over other events. The neighbourly attitude makes it even easier for visitors to join in and savour the excitement of real racing enjoyment.

In the heart of Ireland a unique course with a natural setting, both easy on the eye and ideal for viewing.

The development of Kilbeggan Racecourse is a great credit to the local community which is reflected in the increasing numbers of visitors who attend - it really is worth a visit.

Location
Kilbeggan is situated on the cross roads of Ireland and the racecourse is 1 mile from the town centre. It is 13 miles from Mullingar, 20 miles from Athlone, 8 miles from Tullamore, 56 miles from Dublin, 131 miles from Cork and 198 miles from Belfast.

Public Transport
Bus service from Dublin (Busaras) Tel 00 353 1 8366111 for time of departure. Taxis from town centre to racecourse.

Corporate Hospitality
Superb tented village area on the hill overlooking the entire racetrack and also adjacent to the parade ring and main tote and which has facilities to cater for groups from 100 people to 2,000 people. The Balcony Suite, in the new pavilion and hospitality room is also able to cater for 30-250 people.

Refreshment Facilities
Self service restaurant, snack bars and bar.

Local Hotels/Restaurants
Bridge House Hotel Tel: 00 353 506 22000, Tullamore. Bloomfield House Hotel Tel: 00 353 44 40894, and the Greville Arms Hotel Tel: 00 353 44 48563, Mullingar.

Places of Interest/Activities
Locke's Distillery, Museum, Belvedere House and Gardens, Mullingar (Genesis) Tullynolly Castle, Birr Castle and gardens, also numerous golf courses and lakes for both coarse and fly fishing.

Killarney

Contact: **Mr Michael Doyle, Manager** at **Killarney Race Co Ltd, Racecourse, Killarney, Co Kerry Tel: 00 353 64 31125 Fax: 00 353 64 31860**

Renowned in verse, song, literature and paintings, the lakes of Killarney together with the background mountains give the racecourse one of the most natural settings in Ireland.

Race meetings were held frequently in Killarney on two different racecourses between the years 1827 and 1901. In 1936, after a lapse of 35 years, racing was resumed at the present racecourse. Killarney's celebrated four day Summer Festival commenced in 1947. The races are run along the bank of the River Flesk on ground where the Fianna (Celtic Warriors) roamed over 2000 years ago.

Throughout the years a host of famous people and international celebrities have enjoyed their visit to Killarney races, particularly the Summer Festival meeting.

Location
Killarney racecourse is half a mile from Killarney town centre, off the Kenmare road. Cork Airport, 50 miles; Farranfore Airport, nine miles.

Public Transport
Regular train service from Dublin (Heuston Station). Tel: Irish Rail (Iarnrod Eireann) 00 353 1 836 6222 for train timetables. Regular bus service from Dublin (Busaras). Tel Bus Eireann 00 353 1 836 6111 for times of departures.

Corporate Hospitality
Hospitality rooms available to cater for 20-100 people

Refreshment Facilities
Self service, restaurant, bars and snacks

Local Hotels/Restaurants
There are numerous hotels, guesthouses, B&Bs and self-catering units in Southern Kerry. There are also over 100 restaurants, many of which are to be found in the Good Food Guides. Contact the Irish Tourist Board Tel: 0171 493 3201 for a full accommodation list.

Places of Interest/Activities
Muckross House and Abbey, Killarney National Park, Ross Castle, Gap of Dunloe and Torc Waterfall. There is a 9 hole golf course within the racecourse. Also golf (eight major courses in South Kerry), pitch & putt, pony trekking, swimming, fishing, boating, mountaineering and magnificent beaches within 20 miles

*Artist: **Harry Matthews** ALL GOING WELL Courtesy of: **The Artist***

Laytown

Contact: **Mr Kevin Coleman**, the **Secretary/Manager**, at **9 Palace Street, Drogheda, Co Louth, Tel: 00 353 41 9842111, Fax: 00 353 41 987566.**

Local folklore has it that it was the parish priest who, in 1876, organised the first race meeting on Laytown's three miles of golden strand. Held intermittently since then, it was not until 1901 that local landowner, Paddy Delaney, established the meeting as we know it today. Nothing, not even two World Wars, has stopped it taking place since then.

Laytown races have not changed very much through the years, but they are unique because they are the only grandstand races held in Europe which have the approval of the governing bodies. The enclosure consists of a three acre field, elevated above the beach. Steps which have been built up into the face of the sand dunes and these form the Grandstand. Marquees are erected on the day before the races and these are used to provide a weigh room, bars and snack bars.

On Race Day, the strand is closed from early morning and work on the course then commences. By the time the first race is ready to start the tide has gone out, and racing can begin.

Location

Laytown is a small seaside resort on the east coast of Ireland, 29 miles north of Dublin. To reach the course, turn off the N1 Dublin-Belfast road at Julianstown.

Public Transport

Regular train services from Drogheda and Dublin (Connolly Station). Special bus service from Drogheda. Tel: 00 353 1 836 6111 Irish Rail (Iarnrod Eireann) for train timetable.

Refreshment Facilities

Snack bars and bars provided in the marquees

Local Hotels

Neptune Beach Hotel Tel: 00 353 41 9827107, Bettystown; Old Mill Hotel, Julianstown; Rosnaree Park Hotel, West Court Hotel Tel: 00 353 41 983 0965 and Boyne Valley Hotel Tel: 00 353 41 9837737, Drogheda; Conyngham Arms Hotel Tel: 00 353 41 9884444, Slane; Ashbourne House Hotel, Ashbourne

Local Restaurants

Bacchus at the Coast Guard, Bettystown; Monasterboice Inn, Drogheda; Forge-Collon Anchor, Mornington

Artist: **Peter Smith** **RUNNING THE SANDBAR** *Courtesy of:* **Frost & Reed**

Contact: **Racing Manager, Tom Burke** for specific information on racing fixtures or updates on the state of the "going" at; **Leopardstown Racecourse, Foxrock, Dublin 18, Tel: 00 353 1 2893607, Mobile: 0862347183, Fax: 00 353 1 2892634, E-mail: info@leopardstown.com, Website: www.leopardstown.com Aertel page 277.** Office hours are 9.30am - 5.30pm Monday to Friday and from 8am on each race day.

Leopardstown Racecourse is the only remaining racecourse in the greater Dublin area. It is set in superb surroundings, nestled in the foothills of the Dublin mountains, overlooking Dublin bay, six miles due south of the Dublin city centre. Access to the racecourse is via the M50 - coming from the north, west and south-west of the city, the N11 southbound from the city centre and the N11 northbound from Co. Wicklow. The racecourse's website gives updated directions to the track, including an interactive map.. We advise those planning to visit the racecourse to leave ample time for the journey as traffic can be congested approaching the track. There are free parking facilities at the racecourse for approximately 6000 cars and a designated area for coach parking.

The racecourse operates throughout the year with a total of 23 meetings culminating with the hugely successful post Christmas 4-day National Hunt Festival.

The racing calendar in Leopardstown can, broadly speaking, be broken down into 9 National Hunt meetings and 14 Flat meetings. The National Hunt Season opens with the 4 day Christmas festival, 26-29 December and closes with our post Cheltenham meeting in March. The flat season runs from April to November with the key meetings in this period including the Independent Heinz 57 Phoenix Stakes and the Esat Digifone Irish Champion Stakes, a race which is now part of the Emirates World Series Racing Championship.

Racing at Leopardstown has become a popular and effective vehicle for corporate sponsors. All of the major national hunt and flat meetings have sponsors, many long-standing and others recently becoming involved in race sponsorship. The Hennessy Gold Cup, The AIG Europe Champion Hurdle, The Ladbroke Hurdle, The Derrinstown Stud Derby Trial, The Independent Heinz 57 Phoenix Stakes, The Golden Pages Handicap and The Esat Digifone Irish Champion Stakes, are some of Leopardstown's most prestigious races. In December The Ericsson Chase, The Paddy Power Handicap Chase and The Denny Gold Medal Novice Chase are all integral parts of the four day post Christmas Festival. Ladies' Day is held in May, a meeting sponsored annually by The Jurys Doyle Hotel Group, long time supporters of Leopardstown.

Leopardstown Racecourse on its 171 acre site has, in recent years, been the focus of a major upgrade and renovation programme. Many of the facilities have been completely upgraded and this upgrading is continuing in other areas. The "Members Bar" which overlooks both the parade ring and the racetrack has become an integral part of the course and caters for the 1000+ Annual Members. The Box Holders' Bar with its minimalistic interior and prime viewing of the parade ring continues to serve the needs of the 300+ boxholders. In the Grandstand, Madigans Bar with its stripped pine floors and high tables now buzzes on race days with the younger patrons. Jodami's is always a firm favourite with racegoers, while Fillies Cafe Bar, with its "delicious dishes and liquid delights" is open all day Monday to Sunday, on racedays and non-racedays.

Leopardstown has 27 private suites many of which are rented out on

Artist: **Heather St Clair Davis** *SCHOOLING CHASERS* *Courtesy of:* **Frost & Reed**

an annual basis. A number are retained for daily bookings and they can accommodate up to 24 people. Catering at Leopardstown is provided by Fitzers Catering under the name of "Leopardstown Hospitality". A wide-ranging choice of menus is available from finger buffets to full à la carte. Each suite is equipped with a private bar and Tote facilities are within close proximity.

The Silken Glider Restaurant on the first floor is always busy on race days where patrons can enjoy a silver service meal. The restaurant accommodates approximately 300 people and advanced booking is always advisable. Bookings can be made with Fitzers at Leopardstown on Tel: 00 353 1 2893691 Fax: 00 353 1 2893659 E-mail: leopardstown@fitzers.ie Monday - Friday 9.30am - 5.30pm. The Paddock Food Hall, serving up hot snacks and quick meals throughout the day is located in the Tote Hall area on the ground floor and the traditional "steak sandwiches" are available throughout the building in various locations.

A number of corporate rooms are available for hire including the Centenary and Levmoss Rooms, together accommodating approximately 250 people. The Leopardstown Pavilion, one of the three elements which incorporate the Baileys Centre, overlooks the final fence with a stunning vista of the entire racetrack. This new facility shows off Leopardstown to its full potential and has proved hugely popular with corporate groups since its opening in April 1999. This glass fronted Pavilion boasts an entirely flexible space on 2 floors accommodating groups from 50 up to 1000 on the two floors in an open plan scenario.

The Baileys Centre is a £15 million development incorporating three seperate areas - the Leopardstown Pavilion, the Kilkenny Shop and ICON - a unique food and drink experience created by Baileys.

Close neighbour, Westwood - Dublin's most popular health and fitness centre - plays host to a state of the art creche and children's play area. Sitting in the middle of the racecourse is Leopardstown's 18 hole Golf Course which also incorporates a 48 bay floodlit driving range

Leopardstown Racecourse, Foxrock, Dublin 18-23 days racing per year, state of the art pavilion, corporate facilities, Dublin's best health and

fitness centre-Fitzone, child's play area, an 18 hole golfcourse, 9 bars and a night club.

Public transport

Raceday buses leave the city centre, Busarus, every one and a half hours and one hour before the first race. For further information contact 00 353 1 703 4400. On the return to the city, buses leave the racecourse 15 minutes after the last race. Additional buses 46, 46a, 63, 84 and 86 from town. The Icon bus runs daily between the city centre and Leopardstown racecourse. This stops at various locations en route to the track. The bus leaves O'Connell Street (opposite Dublin Bus) on the hour from 10am until 9pm. Return trip hourly from 11am to 10pm. Telephone 00 353 1 289 1000 for further information.

Local Hotels

Stillorgan Park Hotel Tel: 00 353 1 288 1621, Stillorgan; Fitzpatrick Castle Hotel Tel: 00 353 1 284 0700, Killiney; The Jurys Doyle Group has a chain of eleven hotels in Dublin, many of which are in easy reach of the racecourse. Central reservations: 00 353 1 607000, Davenport Hotel Tel: 00 353 1 607 3500, Mont Clare Hotel Tel: 00 353 1 607 3800 and Red Cow Moran Hotel Tel: 00 353 145 93650

Local Restaurants

Leopardstown Inn in Leopardstown; Lavins Thatched Restaurant and Beaufield Mews in Stillorgan; The Goat Grill in Goatstown; Lamb Doyle's in Sandyford; Palmers Golden Ball, in Kilternan.

Places of Interest

Leopardstown racecourse is only 15 minutes from Dublin which provides a myriad of attractions for visitors - galleries, museums, theatres, cinemas, churches, cathedrals and shops, as well as Dublin Zoo in Phoenix Park, the largest enclosed public park in Europe. The course itself offers a wide range of activities on non-racedays. These include an 18 hole golf course, driving range, squash and indoor tennis. Tel: 00 353 1 289 5341 for information on golf and 00 353 1 289 5665 in relation to squash and tennis.

We can with certainty say that Leopardstown has something for everyone!

Artist: **David Trundley** ***CHRISTMAS LEOPARDSTOWN*** *Courtesy of:* **The Artist**

Limerick

Contact: **Mr Angus Houston, Manager** at **Limerick Racecourse, Greenmount, Patrickswell, Limerick Tel: 00 353 61 355055 Fax: 00 353 61 355766. Website: www.limerick-racecourse.com.**

The new Limerick racecourse is situated at Greenmonnunt, Patrickswell, off the recently constructed Limerick City Bypass, a mere 5 miles from the city. The Grade 1 track will cater for both NH and Flat enthusiasts and after a recent visit by trainers, jockeys and the press, it received very favourable comments. Champion jockey Charlie Swan said "It looks tight and when you walk it you get a completely different picture. I like it a lot and think it will be a great test for horse and rider. I could not believe the difference when I walked it and would even go so far as to describe it as a galloping track."

The magnificent new stand, on four levels includes excellent Tote facilities and an S.P. Shop on the ground floor and a state of the art panoramic restaurant with a capacity for 500 guests located on the third floor. There are also 3 bars, fast-food outlets and self service restaurants within the complex. These will be available for hosting Corporate Functions, Exhibitions, Conferences, Banquets, and Product Launches. On the fourth floor there are thirteen boxes which may be rented on an annual or daily basis and accommodate up to 30 in each.

The view of the racetrack and the man-made lake in the inner area is spectacular and greatly enhances the vista.

The track itself is 70 metres wide and fields of 30 runners can be accommodated. The Fixture List for 2001 is for 15 days racing the highlight of which will be the annual 3 day Christmas Festival, the three day St. Patricks weekend and the Munster National meeting in October.

The Limerick Race Company is very proud of the new course, stand and ancillary buildings and looks forward to providing the mid west region with the very best in horse racing and general entertainment

Local Hotels
Limerick Inn Tel: 00 353 61 326666 and Castletroy Park Hotel Tel: 00 353 61 335566 in Limerick; Clare Inn, and Dromoland Castle Tel: 00 353 61 368144 in Newmarket-on-Fergus; Adare Manor Tel: 00 353 61 396566, and Dunraven Arms Tel: 00 353 61 396633 in Adare; Fitzpatrick's Bunratty Hotel Tel: 00 353 61 361177 in Bunratty; the Great Southern Hotel Tel: 00 353 61 471122 in Shannon. Contact the Irish Tourist Board Tel: 0171 493 3201 for a full accommodation list.

Local Restaurants
Matt The Thresher, Little Italy and Punch's Pub & Restaurant, Limerick; Durty Nelly's, Bunratty; The Gooser, Killaloe

Places of Interest/Activities
King John's Castle in Limerick; Bunratty Castle & Folk Park in Bunratty; the Burren and Cliffs of Moher in Co Clare; also golf, fishing, hunting and shooting.

Listowel

Contact: **Mr Brendan Daly** is the **Secretary, c/o William Street, Listowel, Co Kerry, Tel/Fax: 00 353 68 21144**

Racing commenced at Listowel in 1858. The races were held previously at Ballyeagh, near Ballybunion, but due to faction fighting they had to be moved and Listowel was chosen as the new venue. Due to the popularity of races, known originally as the North Kerry Hunt Steeplechase, the meeting was extended from the original one day event until it became a six day fixture in 1992.

Listowel Races is one of Ireland's oldest and most successful racing festivals and is held in the last week of September. In addition there is a 3 day weekend race meeting in April.

Location
Listowel is 16 miles from Tralee and 50 miles from Limerick. The course is situated five minutes from the town centre.

Public Transport
Regular train services from Dublin (Heuston Station) to Tralee and Limerick. Tel: 00 353 1 836 6222 Irish Rail (Iarnrod Eireann) for train timetables. Special bus services are provided daily from Tralee and Limerick railway stations to Listowel during the festival meeting.

Corporate Hospitality Rooms
Hospitality room available to cater for 40-100 people. In April of this year the new grandstand complex officially opened offering great facilities for all racegoers.

Refreshment Facilities
Dining room, self-service restaurant, snack bars, fast food outlets and bars.

Local Hotels
Listowel Arms Hotel Tel: 00 353 68 21500, Listowel; Cliff House Hotel Tel: 00 353 68 27777, Golf Hotel and The Marine Links Hotel Tel: 00 353 68 27139, Ballybunion. Contact the Irish Tourist Board Tel: 0171 493 3201 for a full accommodation list.

Local Restaurants
Three Mermaids, Horseshoe Bar, Elite Grill Room, Quirkes and Mamma Mia - all in Listowel.

Places of Interest/Activities
Town Park and Listowel Castle in Listowel, a local festival is held to coincide with the races providing nightly entertainment in the town; also golf and fishing.

Naas

Contact: **Mrs Margaret McGuinness, Manager** at **Naas Race Company Plc, Tipper Road, Naas, Co Kildare, Tel: 00 353 45 897391 Fax: 00 353 45 879486**

Naas racecourse is located on the main dual carriageway on route N7 southbound. Dublin is just 20 miles away. It is just 35 minutes, drive from the Airport and an hour's drive from the Ferryports.

Naas is a Grade 1 National Hunt Track and a Grade 11 Flat track, the stiff uphill finish making a true test for Cheltenham bound contenders.

The new £2 million stand complex includes restaurants, bars, corporate suites, indoor tote betting, and an S.P. shop. Patrons will be able to book tables for lunch in the new restaurant which is overlooking the racecourse and with tote betting at this level you need never leave your table. The betting ring has been improved and lowered to facilitate viewing from the stands and a new surface put in. Patrons wishing to have a bet with the bookmakers have easy access from the restaurant to the ring. Phase two will include upgrading of the stable yard and all other buildings.

Admission rates are adults £8/£10, students and senior citizens £4/£5. Free car and bus park.

Special Bus Eireann Service for race meetings from Dublin (Busaras) Tel: 00 353 1 8366 111 for time of departure. Arrow trains (Irish Rail 00 353 1 836 6222) run from Monday to Saturday from Heuston station to Sallins. From there a feeder bus will take you to Naas.

Local Hotels
The Ambassador Hotel Tel: 00 353 45 877064, Kill. Lawlors Hotel, Naas. Court Hotel, Naas. Town House Hotel, Naas. Harbour View Hotel, Naas. Hotel Keadeen Tel: 00 353 45 431666, Newbridge. Kildare Hotel and Country Club Tel: 00 353 1 601 7200, Straffan and Setanta House Hotel, Celbridge.

Local Restaurants
Manor Inn, Butt Mullins, Johnstown Inn, and Joe Olives

Places of Interest
Irish National Stud. Japanese Gardens in Kildare. Fishing, golf, hunting and pony trekking.

The 15th of July 1991 saw the official opening of the Kildare Hotel and Country Club, widely acclaimed as Ireland's premier resort development and a five-star complex to rival the very best that Europe can offer.

The Kildare Hotel and Country Club has been developed at a cost of £27.5 million by Jefferson Smurfit Group plc. Ireland's world class hotel and sporting facility encompasses an 18 hole golf course designed by the legendary Arnold Palmer, salmon and trout fishing, indoor and outdoor tennis, exercise, swimming and croquet.

The entire project was created in less than three years and involved the complete renovation of the existing Straffan House. A new wing was added in the style of the existing house, establishing in the process a 45 bedroom hotel, with a further 33 bedrooms scheduled for opening in April 2001, whose exacting standards have few equals.

The bedrooms and suites are complemented by exquisitely appointed self-contained apartments and a magnificent three bedroom lodge in the grounds. Meetings and private dining take place in the Tower and River rooms, where work can happily be combined with play by taking advantage of the wide range of leisure and recreational activities. The Kildare Country Club, simply known as The K Club, is a multi-facility sporting paradise. Members, hotel guests and visitors alike can enjoy the championship golf course, river and lake fishing, indoor and outdoor tennis, squash, gym, swimming pool, beauty treatment rooms, sauna and solarium.

The Arnold Palmer designed golf course has received many accolades and is home to the Smurfit European Open - one of the richest tournaments on the European Tour. In January 1999 it was announced that The K Club would be the host for the Ryder Cup 2005, its first visit to Ireland. The course covers some 177 acres of former stud farm land and has a total length of 7,227 yards, par 72.

Among eighteen exquisitely and imaginatively sculpted holes, particularly outstanding memories could stem from the huge par five 7th, the water-clad 8th or the spectacular par three 17th. Every hole, however, has its own individual challenge and beauty.

In the words of Arnold Palmer himself, reflecting proudly on his creation whilst standing on the terrace of the elevated clubhouse sited behind the eighteenth green; "We could draw for 100 years and not come up with as good a vision as we have here."

The K Club
Straffan
Co Kildare Ireland
Tel: (00 353 1) 601 7200 (Hotel) 601 7300 (Clubhouse)
Fax: (00 353 1) 601 7299 (Hotel) 601 7399 (Clubhouse)
e mail: golf@kclub.ie or hotel@kclub.ie
web site: www.kclub.ie

Navan

Contact: **Richard Lyttle Racing Manager c/o, Navan Racecourse, Proudstown, Navan, Co. Meath. Tel: 00 353 46 21350, Fax: 00 353 46 27964. E mail: info@navangolfandracecourse.com**

1999 was an exciting year for Navan Racecourse when it completed the first phase of its development and investment plan. The Proudstown Racecourse situated 2 miles from Navan town, 30 miles due north of Dublin City on the N3, had an extremely successful year with attendances and sponsorship all on the increase. Also in 1999, Navan was twinned with Newbury Racecourse.

The Racecourse will play host to 14 meetings in 2001 between October and June. Its main meeting is the Pierce Group Troytown Chase in November, named after the famous Aintree Grand National winner who was bred close by. The track is well respected by owners and trainers who often prep their horses here prior to the Cheltenham Festival. Often the horses who win at Navan, go on to perform well in major races in the UK.

Navan's recent £2 million development has provided new bars, a large self-service restaurant and new corporate facilities overlooking the racetrack. These new facilities which opened at the end of 1998 have been welcomed by Navan's loyal patrons who come again and again to this friendly welcoming track. Admission to the racecourse varies between £8 to £10. Day membership is also available. There is on course catering ranging from snack bars to full dining facilities. Corporate tables and private function rooms can be booked by arrangement. Restaurant and bar facilities are open seven days a week.

In addition to its racecourse, Navan has a fantastic 18 hole Golf Course with 9 holes lying alongside the track and the newer 9 being within the track itself. The thriving Golf Course brings new people to the racetrack throughout the year and membership is currently available - please contact the Administration Office at 00 353 46 72888 for more details. A Golf Driving Range is also in operation.

Public Transport

Buses from Dublin depart from Busaras from 7.30am (9.00am on Sundays) and leave at approximately 1 hour intervals, arriving at the Mercy Convent in Navan approximately 1.5 miles from the racecourse. Full details from Bus Eireann at 00 353 1 8366111 Web site - www.buseireann.ie

Local Hotels

Navan now has a number of excellent hotels, namely the Newgrange Hotel Tel: 00 353 46 23119, and the Ardboyne Hotel Tel: 00 353 46 73732 within the town offering excellent accommodation opportunities. Navan Tourist Information Office is located in the town centre Freephone 1850300789, or by e mail at info@meathtourism.ie, they will be very happy to provide advice on accomodation, bookings and attractions in the Meath district.

Local Restaurants

Being located close to Dublin, Navan has benefited from some exciting developments in the town. There are many excellent pubs and restaurants. The popular restaurants include Hudson's Bistro Tel: 00 353 46 29231, the Loft Tel: 00 353 46 71755; China Garden Tel: 00 353 46 23938 and Southbank Bistro Tel: 00 353 46 72406 .

Places of Interest

Other local attractions include the Passage Tomb of Newgrange (only 10 miles from the racecourse). Older than the Pyramids of Egypt, the tomb is over 5,000 years old and is one of the most famous megalithic monuments in Western Europe. Visit the recently renovated Trim Castle, parts which have been restored to its origional state, and also the Kells Heritage Centre which will host the famous 'Book of Kells' at certain times of the year. Nestled in the Meath Valley is of course the River Boyne, which lends itself to many scenic walks and fishing opportunities. The famous Battle of the Boyne took place in 1690, and its site is now a popular tourist attraction.

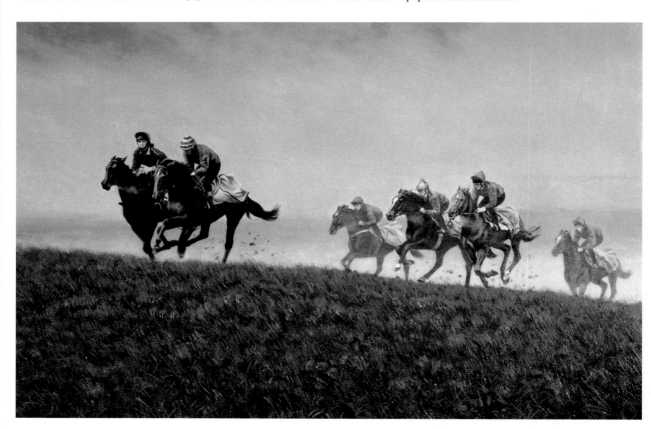

Artist: **Roy Miller** *OUT OF THE GLOOM* *Courtesy of:* **Private Collection USA**

Artist: **Heather St Clair Davis** RACING *Courtesy of:* **Frost & Reed**

The management at **Punchestown** is headed by **Chief Executive Charles Murless** who together with his capable team is contactable at the racecourse office. **Tel: 00 353 45 897704 Fax: 00 353 45 897319.** The address is **Punchestown Racecourse, Naas, Co Kildare. e mail: racing@punchestown.com web site www.punchestown.com**

As everyone already knows, Ireland is renowned for its unique and friendly atmosphere. No place is this seen to better effect than at Punchestown where even banks and schools are closed without question or complaint to enable everyone to participate in the festivities that take place each year! Peerless Punchestown, as it is often referred to, conjures up something special in the minds of all who have been fortunate enough to attend and sample the unique atmosphere that has made it famous. It has been a huge success story with growth beyond the stone walls and big banks which were used at the first meeting held in 1854 over two days, to what is today one of the premier National Hunt venues in the British Isles. Fences and hurdles were first introduced in the early 1860s but nearly 150 years on, Punchestown still maintains its famous bank course which is seen at its best in late April when it is raced over twice in three days for the Ernst & Young

Certified Hunters Steeplechase for the Ladies Perpetual Cup and the Quinns of Baltinglass Steeplechase for the La Touche Cup. These races are truly unique to Punchestown and provide a great challenge for horse and rider as well as a wonderful spectacle for all National Hunt enthusiasts.

The racecourse has recently undergone a £20m re-development, which has seen it transformed into a state of the art complex, capable of catering for the huge crowds which are now attracted each year. It boasts top class restaurant facilities in the panoramic, glass-fronted restaurant overlooking the racecourse, the de Robeck restaurant together with a self-service restaurant, seafood bar, and champagne bar as well as numerous snack food outlets throughout the grandstand. These are supported by the various hospitality marquees which are always packed to capacity and have a special atmosphere all of their own.

Punchestown has become a major attraction for overseas visitors, especially from the UK, who come in their thousands to sample the unique Irish atmosphere and 'craic' during the National Hunt Festival

Artist: **Heather St Clair Davis** THE STEEPLECHASE *Courtesy of:* **Frost & Reed**

which takes place in late April or early May each year. This is one of the principal National Hunt events of the season including the BMW Steeplechase, The Heineken Gold Cup, the LAWS Champion Four Year Old Hurdle and the Shell Champion Hurdle. Together with a top class supporting card, this meeting attracts a plethora of the very best equine talent from all corners of the British Isles.

The racecourse is easily accessible and is only 30 minutes from Dublin City centre travelling via the N7 to Naas which is only 3 miles from Punchestown. During the four day National Hunt Festival a special bus service is available from the Central Bus Station (Busarus), Store Street, Dublin 1 Tel: 000 353 1-836 6111. Punchestown is well signposted with well laid-out car parking facilities to ensure the ever increasing attendances are continually satisfied and sufficiently well catered for. The racecourse has a landing facility suitable for helicopters, however the office must be notified prior to your intended arrival.

Racegoers will be able to enjoy 15 racedays in 2001, including the four-day National Hunt Festival (24th - 27th April). Rates of admission vary throughout the year starting from £7 to £16 for entry to the Grandstand Enclosure and £24 for access to the Reserved Enclosure. Prices are naturally at the higher end of the scale for the National Hunt Festival but discounts are available for advance and group bookings by contacting the ticket office at the racecourse. Senior citizens and children are also allowed entry at reduced admission rates on the day. Car parking is free, however to avoid any possible delays it is advised to arrive early. Annual membership is £120 which provides access to the members car park and Reserved Enclosure for all racedays, representing great value for the regular racegoer. Disabled racegoers are well catered for with a reserved car park close to the entrance. The racecourse is completely wheelchair friendly with reserved areas overlooking the parade ring and racecourse, and lifts provide access to all levels of the grandstand.

Location
Punchestown racecourse is approximately three miles from Naas on the Naas-Ballymore Eustace Road. It is just 45 minutes (23 miles) from Dublin (Route N7), just over an hour's drive from Dublin Airport and Dun Laoghaire, and two hours from Rosslare.

Corporate Hospitality
Corporate hospitality packages are available in the tented village at the Spring National Hunt Festival. For further information contact Elaine Nolan at Punchestown Racecourse 00 353 45 897704.

Refreshment Facilities
Panoramic restaurant dining room/self service restaurant, snack bars, bars, and a reserved dining room facility available at the Spring Festival.

Local Hotels
Hotel Keadeen Tel: 00 353 45 431666, Newbridge; Moyglare Manor in Maynooth; Rathsallagh House Tel: 00 353 45 403112, Dunlavin; Ambassador Hotel Tel: 00 353 45 877064, Kill; Naas Court Hotel, Harbour View Hotel and Gregory Hotel, all in Naas; Kildare Hotel and Country Club Tel: 00 353 1 601 7200 in Straffan; Curryhills House and Country Club in Prosperous. Contact the Irish Tourist Board Tel: 0171 493 3201 for a full accommodation list.

Local Restaurants
Lawlors and Butt Mullins, Naas; Silken Thomas, Kildare; Johnstown Inn, Johnstown; Ballymore Inn, Ballymore Eustace, The Thatch, Ballymore Eustace.

Places of Interest/Activities
Irish National Stud; Japanese Gardens in Kildare; Castletown House in Celbridge; Russborough House, Lakeside Leisure Centre in Blessington; also fishing, pony trekking and golf.

Artist: **David Dent** **THE STONE WALL AT PUNCHESTOWN** *Courtesy of:* **The Artist**

Roscommon

Contact: **Mr Michael Finneran, Manager** at **Roscommon Racecourse, Racecourse Road, Roscommon Tel: 00 353 903 63494 Fax: 00 353 903 63608 Racedays Tel: 00 353 903 26231 Fax: 00 353 903 26231.**

Roscommon racecourse is steeped in National Hunt tradition. The first ever recorded race meeting took place in 1837 and was organised by the British military which then had a base in the town. Racing proper began in 1885 and has continued ever since, with the exception of a 12 year period from 1936 to 1948.

Location
The racecourse is situated one mile from Roscommon on the Castlebar Road. Roscommon is 90 miles from Dublin, 47 miles from Galway, 20 miles from Athlone and 50 miles from Sligo.

Public Transport
Regular train services from Dublin (Heuston Station) to Roscommon. Tel: Irish Rail (Iarnrod Eireann) 00 353 1 836 6222 for train timetable. Taxi service from Roscommon Station to the racecourse.

Corporate Hospitality
Hospitality rooms available to cater for 20-100 people.

Refreshment Facilities
Dining room, self service restaurant, snack bar, tea room, bars.

Local Hotels
Abbey Hotel Tel: 00 353 903 26240 and Royal Hotel Tel: 00 353 79 62016 in Roscommon.

Local Restaurants
Gleeson's and Westdeli in Roscommon.

Places of Interest/Activities
Lough Key Forest Park in Lough Key; County Heritage and Genealogical Centre in Strokestown; burial place of the kings of Ireland and Connacht in Rathcroghan; Arigna scenic drive; also boating, fishing, wind-surfing in Hudson Bay; Munsboro Equestrian Centre; River Shannon Cruises.

Sligo

Contact: **Mr Brian Kennedy, Manager** at **Ballymote, Co Sligo, Tel: 00 353 71 83342 Fax: 00 353 71 83342 Racedays Tel: 00 353 71 62484.**

Sligo town, in the heart of Yeats country, boasts one of the most scenic racecourses in the country. William Butler Yeats regarded Sligo as the Land of Heart's Desire. On either side of Sligo town stand the giant sentinels—Benbulben and Knocknarea. Round about are all the other places immortalised in Yeats' poetry—Hazelwood, Inisfree, Lisadell, Slish Wood, Dooney, Drumcliffe, etc.

Racing at Sligo has been taking place for over 180 years, being founded at the time when racing enjoyed great prosperity in the country. Indeed so great was the proliferation of race meetings over the period 1805 to 1815 that the organising committee of the Sligo Races decided that its 1814 meeting "will commence in August so as to give the racehorses time to travel to Bellewstown, Maze, Derry and Monaghan, and to come to Sligo".

The programme at all meetings is comprised of National Hunt and flat races.

Corporate Hospitality
The Cleveragh Room available to cater for 60 to 100 people.

Location
The racecourse is situated at Cleveragh, half a mile from the town centre, just off the Dublin-Sligo Road. Strandhill Airport is six miles away and Knock Airport is 35 miles.

Public Transport
Regular train service to Sligo from Dublin (Connolly Station). Tel: Irish Rail (Iarnrod Eireann) 00 353 1 836 6222 for train timetable. Taxi service from train station to the racecourse. Also served by Bus Eireann from Dublin (Busaras) Tel: 00 353 1 836 6111 for departure times.

Refreshment Facilities
Bar, restaurant, snack bar.

Local Hotels
Sligo Park Hotel Tel: 00 353 71 60291, Silver Swan Hotel and Southern Hotel Tel: 00 353 71 62101 in Sligo; Ballincar House Hotel Tel: 00 353 71 45361 and Yeats Country Hotel Tel: 00 353 71 77211 in Rosses Point

Places of Interest/Activities
Within a five mile radius of Sligo town are the contrasting beaches of Rosses Point and Strandhill; also golf at Strandhill, Tubbercurry and Ballymote Golf Clubs, surfing, angling and horse riding also at Strandhill

Thurles

Contact: **Mr Pierce Molony** at the **Racecourse, Thurles, Co Tipperary Tel: 00 353 504 22253 Fax: 00 353 504 24565 Racedays Tel: 00 353 504 23272 Fax: 00 353 504 23245. E mail: thurles@iol.ie**

Thurles, situated in the sporting county of Tipperary, is celebrated as the centre of the Gaelic Athletic Association. It is also the heart of the famous Scarteen hunting county.

Earliest records show a three day meeting in June 1732. In October 1760, there was a six day meeting .

The February meeting is renowned as a major trial for the forthcoming National Hunt Festival meetings at Cheltenham, Fairyhouse and Punchestown.

Location
The racecourse is situated one mile west of Thurles town, five miles west of the main Cork-Dublin Road. Thurles is 10 miles north of Cashel, 30 miles west of Kilkenny, 40 miles east of Limerick, 60 miles north of Cork and 60 miles south of Athlone.

Public Transport
Regular train service from Dublin (Heuston Station) and Cork. Tel: Irish Rail (Iarnrod Eireann) 00 353 1 836 6222 for train timetables. Free minibus service to racecourse.

Corporate Hospitality
Hospitality room available to cater for 50-100 people

Refreshment Facilities
Self service restaurant, bars, tea room

Local Hotels
Hayes Hotel Tel: 00 353 504 22122 and Anner Hotel Tel: 00 353 504 21799, Thurles; Cashel Palace Hotel Tel: 00 353 62 62707, Cashel; Dundrum House Hotel Tel: 00 353 62 71116, Dundrum; Horse & Jockey Inn

Local Restaurants
Park Avenue House and Inch House both in Thurles; Chez Hans and Legends in Cashel

Places of Interest/Activities
Rock of Cashel; Holycross Abbey; Devil's Bit Mountain; also hunting, local equestrian centres and an excellent 18-hole golf course in Thurles

Tipperary

Contact: **Peter Roe** at **Tipperary Racecourse Limerick Junction, Co Tipperary, Tel: 00 353 62 51357 Fax: 00 353 62 51303**

The first recorded meeting of Tipperary Races at Barronstown Course was Monday, 27 March 1848. In 1871/72, the races were abandoned due to smallpox, but were revived in 1881. In the early days of Barronstown (the predecessor to Limerick Junction racecourse) there was only one bookmaker, who also had a roulette table.

The first races at Limerick Junction took place in September 1916 promoted by Mr T Gardiner Wallis, the celebrated racing personality, and his trainer Senator J J Parkinson and colleagues Stephen Grehan and Charles Moore.

A major incentive to the commencement of Limerick Junction was the promise of a special railway siding from the Great Southern and Western Railway Company.

The name was changed from Limerick Junction to Tipperary Racecourse for a meeting on 8 May 1986. In December 1999 Tipperary Supporter's Club in conjunction with local businessmen took a three-year lease on the racecourse from the Irish Horseracing Authority. The aim of the newly formed company is to re-establish Tipperary as a leading provincial racecourse. The facilities underwent a major refurbishment in the spring of 2000.

Tipperary stages the only Group Race, the Gr.3 Coolmore Concorde Stakes, outside the metropolitan area. It also stages the John James McManus Hurdle in October, which has been won for the last 2 years by Champion Hurdle winner Istabraq.

Location
Situated off the main Tipperary-Limerick road, the racecourse is two miles from Tipperary, 24 miles from Limerick, 40 miles from Shannon Airport, 64 miles from Cork and 112 miles from Dublin.

Public Transport
Regular train services from Dublin (Heuston Station) and Cork to Limerick Junction Station, which is within easy walking distance of the track. Tel: Irish Rail (Iarnrod Eireann) 00 353 1 836 6222 for train timetables. Mini Bus service on certain racedays from Tipperary Town to the racecourse, phone racecourse for details.

Corporate Hospitality
Corporate hospitality is available for groups from 10-150. The newly refurbished hospitality area has Tote facilities, CCTV and either silver service or buffet style dining. The room overlooks the parade ring and racetrack.

Refreshment Facilities
The Winning Post Bar has full drink selections while the Istabraq Bar and Members Bar have full snack facilities as well as usual drinks. There is also a self service restaurant.

Local Hotels
The Ballykisteen Golf and Country Club opposite the racecourse has restaurant and bar facilities. There's also the Royal Hotel Tel: 00 353 62 33244, Tipperary; Aherlow House Hotel Tel: 00 353 52 56153, Glen of Aherlow; Dundrum House Hotel, Dundrum; Cashel Palace Hotel Tel: 00 353 62 62707, Cashel

Local Restaurants
Tipperary Town has a diversity of restaurants ranging from traditional to Chinese. Donovans (O'Brien Street) is excellent for lunch and hosts Irish music. Others include the Brown Trout (Bridge Street), Chaser O' Brien (Pallas Green) and Chez Hans (Cashel)

Places of Interest/Activities
Rock of Cashel; Cahir Castle; Mitchelstown Caves; scenic Glen of Aherlow; also golf, fishing, hunting and shooting

Tralee

Contact: **Patrick Crean, Secretary** at **Tralee Racecourse, Ballybeggan Park, c/o The Spa, Tralee, Co Kerry , Tel: 00 353 66 7136148 Fax: 00 353 66 7128007 Tel: (Racedays only) 00 353 66 7126188 Fax: 00 353 66 7126090.**

Racing is recorded in Tralee as far back as 1767, when a week-long meeting was held, the results of which are recorded in the Turf Club.

Great pride was taken in these meetings as is indicated by the organisers of the August 1805 meeting when they observed "The thanks of the meeting was unanimously given to the Steward for his uniform politeness and attention and his daily punctuality in paying the plates." Various venues in the locality were used until the present site, in Ballybeggan Park, was first opened to racing in 1889.

The park was formerly a deer park, and the stone for the surrounding limestone wall was quarried out of the land in the infield area of the course. The estate was formerly the property of Daniel O'Connell, The Liberator, in whose honour the Liberator Handicap is run annually.

The Tralee August meeting is the centrepiece of the International Rose of Tralee Festival. The festival sparkle spreads to the course for six days of great racing—this is a unique experience and is not to be missed. The two day June bank holiday meeting is an ideal way to get into the summer with traditional Kerry hospitality and scenery.

Location
Tralee racecourse is one and a half miles from the town centre, off the Tralee-Killarney road.

Public Transport
Regular train service from Dublin (Heuston Station). Tel Irish Rail (Iarnrod Eireann) 00 353 1 836 6222 for train timetable. Tralee railway station is approximately 1 mile from the racecourse. A special bus service from the railway station to the racecourse is provided on racedays.

Corporate Hospitality
Hospitality suite available to cater for 60-120 people

Refreshment Facilities
Dining room, snack bars and a new fast food outlet

Local Hotels
Abbey Gate Hotel Tel: 00 353 66 7129888, Brandon Hotel, Tel: 00 353 66 7123333 the Earl of Desmond, the Grand Hotel Tel: 00 353 66 7121499, Imperial Hotel, Ballygarry House Hotel, Meadowlands Hotel, and Quality Benners Hotel Tel: 00 353 66 7121877—all in Tralee. Contact the Irish Tourist Board Tel: 0171 493 3201 for a full accommodation list.

Local Restaurants
Aisling Geal, Numero Uno and the Oyster Tavern in Tralee; The Tankard in Fenit; Nick's in Killorglin

Places of Interest/Activities
A nine hole golf course at the racecourse opened in June 1997. The town also boasts the highly acclaimed high-tech county museum, a refurbished working windmill, an aquadome, the Geraldine Experience, Tralee Steam Railway, Siamsa Tire, and the National Folk Theatre

Tralee is the gateway to the Dingle Peninsula and the starting point for the Ring of Kerry. There are also magnificent beaches nearby at Banna and Inch; an 18 hole golf course designed by Arnold Palmer at Barrow; and sea angling at Fenit.

Tramore

Contact: **Sue Phelan Waterford & Tramore Racecourse, Tramore, Co Waterford, Tel: 00 353 51 381425 Fax: 00 353 51 390928. e mail: racing@tramore website: www.tramore-racecourse.com**

From 1806, racing was taking place at Tramore in what was known as 'the Black Strand'. It was right beside the sea and, before the First World War, had succumbed to the waves.

In 1914, Martin Murphy commenced racing again on his own property where all meetings still take place today. Those race meetings, held under the aegis of the Red Cross, were continued by Mr Murphy until his death in 1920.

In that year a new company made up of the renowned Senator J J Parkinson, Francis Murphy and Thomas Fleming took over control.

For many years the Fleming family were synonymous with Tramore Racecourse. In 1997 a new race company was formed, headed by Peter Queally. The improvements which have been carried out on the track have received very favourable comments from both trainers and jockeys. The facilities for the racegoers have also been upgraded. Tramore Festival in August ranks among one of the most popular meetings of the summer.

Location
The racecourse is situated eight miles from Waterford city on the main Tramore road and one mile inland from Tramore town centre. Waterford Airport is nine miles from Tramore.

Public Transport
Regular train service from Dublin (Heuston Station) to Waterford. Tel: Irish Rail (Iranrod Eireann) 00 353 1 836 6222 for train timetables. Local bus service to the track.

Corporate Hospitality
Hospitality room available to cater for 20-100 people

Refreshment Facilities
Self service restaurant and bars.

Local Hotels
Jurys Hotel, Tower Hotel and Granville Hotel in Waterford; Majestic Hotel and Grand Hotel in Tramore; Waterford Castle in Ballinakill. Contact the Irish Tourist Board Tel: 0171 493 3201 Fax: 0171 493 9065 for a full accommodation list.

Local Restaurants
The Esquire in Tramore; The Ship in Dunmore East

Places of Interest/Activities
Funfair and Amusements in Tramore; Waterford crystal factory in Waterford; also golf and fishing.

Wexford

Contact: **Michael Murphy, Roseville, New Ross, Co. Wexford, Tel: 00 353 51 421681 Fax: 00 353 51 421830 Racedays Tel: 00 353 53 42307 Fax: 00 353 53 43702.**

Steeped in tradition and deriving its name from its Viking heritage, Wexford has always been foremost in the breeding of horses in Ireland. Jumping is particularly associated with Wexford and many of Wexford's native sons as well as her horses have achieved outstanding National Hunt success.

The earliest records of racing here took place on reclaimed boglands in the 1870s. By 1902, however, this had ceased and racing commenced again on the present course in 1951.
The course is only 15 miles from the major sea port of Rosslare.

Location
Wexford racecourse is situated just outside the town off the Dublin-Rosslare bypass, 15 miles from Rosslare ferry port.

Public Transport
Regular Dublin-Rosslare train service. Tel Irish Rail (Iarnrod Eireann) 00 353 1 836 6222 for train timetables. Good taxi service from Wexford train station to the racecourse.

Corporate Hospitality
Hospitality rooms available to cater for 15-100 people

Refreshment Facilities
Self service restaurant, snack bar and bars

Local Hotels
Talbot Hotel, Wexford Lodge Hotel, Whites Hotel and Whitford House Hotel in Wexford; Tuski House Hotel and Hotel Rosslare in Rosslare; Ferrycarrig Hotel in Ferrycarrig

Local Restaurants
The Granary, Lobster Pot, Oyster Restaurant and Tim's Tavern—all in Wexford

Places of Interest/Activities
Wexford Wildlife Reserve in Wexford; Irish National Heritage Park in Ferrycarrig; Johnstown Castle Park in Johnstown; John F Kennedy Arboretum in New Ross; also golf and fishing.

For further information contact:
Irish Horseracing Authority,
Marketing & Promotions Department,
Leopardstown Racecourse,
Foxrock,
Dublin 18,
Ireland

Betty O'Connell
(Promotions/Tourism Manager)
Tel: 00 353 1 8351965
Fax: 00 353 1 8351964

Shirley Finnegan
(Administrator)
Tel: 00 353 1 2892888
Fax: 00 353 1 2898412
E mail: Info@irishracing.iba.ie
Web page: www.iba.ie/ibarace

For a full list of accommodation contact the
Irish Tourist Board,
150 New Bond Street,
London,
W1Y OAQ
Tel: 0207-493-3201
Fax: 0207-493-9065

Point to Point Racing in Ireland

For many years now the best Irish thoroughbred National Hunt horse is eagerly sought overseas, but to nowhere is it as consistently and regularly exported than to Great Britain. This trend, which has proved most profitable and beneficial to buyer and seller over the years, shows no signs of tapering off and indeed if one looks at the facts and figures, it seems to be very much on the increase. Whilst the Irish-bred has long been exported to England to the point-to-point fraternity, it is in the area of Park racing where the most growth has occurred in the past 10-12 years. Whilst the older type of animal has long graced the English point-to-point field, it is the success of the better Irish animal, particularly the one from the point-to-point academy, which has hit the headlines in recent years.

This season just past has been an exceptionally good year with respect to the success of former Irish point-to-point horses. Three of the most prestigious races in the English National Hunt calendar, namely the Tote Cheltenham Gold Cup, The Royal and Sun Alliance Novice Chase and the Whitbread Gold Cup were all captured by former, once-raced point-to-pointers, who incidentally failed to score between the flags on the point-to-point field. Looks like Trouble, Lord Noelie and Beau were the respective horses in question.

Other successful graduates from the point-to-point field were some of the better English novice hurdlers in Celtic Native, Bindaree and Best Mate. No Language Please, a former confined point-to-point winner, scored for the first time on record in a flat race. New Kid on the Block and Kings Castle further enhanced the point-to-pointers' reputation by both going on to win bumpers, with the former scoring three wins in total, including a Hurdle.

It would be difficult to find better value at any sporting fixture than that which is found at some of the 80 plus point-to-point meetings throughout Ireland from the first day of January up to the last weekend in May. On the Northern Ireland scene, a day's racing will cost the racing enthusiast about a tenner, which covers admission to the course and a racecard with detailed and ample information - ample enough to ensure that the punter's ongoing battle with the "Auld Enemy" is more than an exercise in "hit and miss". In the South, admission is either £5 per head or £10 per car, whilst a comprehensive racecard costs only a pound. Most meets in the South are usually run on a Sunday, with a few on Saturdays and similarly a couple in mid-week, although competition from Park Sunday racing appears to be about to hit an all time high. The traditional day for competing in the North of Ireland is Saturday with a few mid-week dates. At present the number of horses competing in the point-to-point field continues to rise steadily and the 2000 season saw some 2,314 hopefuls coming before the starter. As with most sports events run during the winter months, one is inclined to be somewhat at the mercy of the elements, but the point-to-point brigade are, invariably, a hardy bunch. There are about seventy-five courses sprinkled throughout the country with about five or six utilising the inside of courses in Park venues such as Punchestown, Naas, Fairyhouse, Dundalk and Listowel. In addition there are about four venues which stage more than one point-to-point fixture during the season.

Also there are 2 two-day Festivals held here, with the East Antrims running a two-day fixture in Loughanmore and the season usually winding up with the South Unions availing of the last weekend in May to stage another popular Saturday/Sunday double header. Indeed the latter has tried with some success to make this an annual International fixture with a few races open to U.K. runners, making this a pleasant and somewhat laid back gathering – with the emphasis on fun and Craic!

However, if one expects this apparent low-key attitude to permeate through the rest of the season, then one is in for a big surprise, as nothing could be further from the truth. Though the sport is basically purported to be amateur, very little from the organisation, the running and the competitive attitude leads one to believe that it is in essence professional in the main.

The standard of rider, and in particular the leading ones, is of particularly high level and one only has to mention the names of Adrian Maguire, Norman Williamson and Timmy Murphy who have joined the professional ranks subsequently, to highlight the standard which the sport has achieved in regard to jockeyship.

For overseas National Hunt and point-to-point enthusiasts, visitors could easily ensure that they take in either a Saturday or Sunday point-to-point, in addition to a weekend Park fixture (there are many excellent National Hunt meets at this time of year) and in the process sample both sides of the racing spectrum. One thing is for sure, however, whether it is wearing the wet gear at an inclement Point to Point in the Pigeons or at the more comfortable surrounds of Leopardstown, you are sure to enjoy the atmosphere and racing that is unique to an Irish National Hunt meeting.

*Artist: **Heather St Clair Davis** EASY WINNER Courtesy of: **Frost & Reed***

On the road southwest from Limerick, you come across what is probably the prettiest village in Ireland. This is Adare - straddling the River Maigue, picturesque with sturdy cottages, deep-set windows and mellow thatch. Here too is the Dunraven Arms Hotel, one of Ireland's premier hotels, carefully restored and renovated in keeping with the old-style village, which is something of a visitor attraction itself. The Dunraven Arms welcomes you to not only spacious and tastefully refurbished bedrooms (with TV and direct dial telephone) but to the highly-rated award-winning Maigue Restaurant which offers exceptional cuisine and a very good cellar. The newly opened leisure centre comprises a 17m swimming pool, therapy clinic, steam room, and Computerised Gym Studio. The river itself affords good salmon and trout fishing, and for equestrian enthusiasts, the Dunraven Arms caters famously for riding and fox hunting. For golfer's, there's the beautiful 18 hole Adare Golf Course (designed by Robert Jones) and Adare Manor Golf Club.

Lahinch and Ballybunion Championship Golf Courses are within driving distance. Shannon Airport is just a short 25 minute drive away. Our highly professional staff guarantee to make your stay a memorable one!

For racing enthusiasts, Limerick, Mallow, Listowel, Tralee and Killarney are all within half an hour to 45 minutes of the hotel. Hunting holidays are a speciality, with the County Limerick Foxhounds, Limerick Harriers, Scarteen-Black & Tans, Tipperary Foxhounds and Galway Blazers on the doorstep.

AA Three Rosettes, Gilbey's Gold Medal Award, Egon Ronay, RAC Hospitality, Service & Comfort Award, Mouton Cadet Award, Bord Failte Awards of Excellence.

"Dunraven Arms, the best hotel in Ireland" David Nicholson, Racing Post '98.

Dunraven Arms Hotel
Adare
Co. Limerick
Tel: 00 353 61 396633
Fax: 00 353 61 396541
E-mail: dunraven@iol.ie

Your horse is in the lead, racing with your colours, under a name you chose.

And all for less than £20 per week.*

When you share the cost of keeping a horse in training as a member of a syndicate, you can get closer to the action than ever before. In a syndicate of twelve members, each member can expect to spend less than £20 per week for the year.

Providing information on syndicate membership is just one of the services we offer at Irish Thoroughbred Marketing.

We are an industry/government-funded organisation and can provide impartial advice on everything from choosing a horse to engaging an agent or trainer.

So go on. Get a piece of the action.

For more information, call us on +353-1-2897302.

*Price does not include initial purchase of horse.

IRISH THOROUGHBRED MARKETING
Leopardstown Racecourse, Foxrock, Dublin 18, Ireland.
Tel: + 353 1 289 7302, Fax: +353 1 289 7297, Email: info@itm.ie www.itm.ie

Please send me information on racehorse ownership in Ireland.

Name:_____

Address:_____

_____

_____

Telephone: _____ TTT

Travelling the Turf
Around the World

*N*ever before has it been easier to hop on a jet and experience the thrills and colour of racing in another country. The babble of the crowd and the punting currency may seem foreign at first, but once your horse comes down the stretch to win in a photo finish, you will feel just as much at home at Sha Tin as Sandown.

Naturally there is a huge amount of smaller racecourses around the world that we have not been able to cover as yet but if you know of any gems that we should include please let us know. Similarly the odd restaurant or hotel discovery would be of great interest to us. Indeed we are hoping to add to this section of the book in our website: www.racecourseguide.com and in future editions of Travelling the Turf, so any assistance would be appreciated.

Since the launch of the Emirates World Series, top horses, jockeys, trainers and owners are taking to the skies in search of one of the turf's new holy grails. A new, hopefully true, world champion horse will be crowned after a series of races as diverse as the Dubai World Cup, the King George and Queen Elizabeth Diamond Stakes, the Breeders' Cup and the Japan Cup, and several more in between.

Travelling the Turf has always encouraged racegoers to go in search of green pastures beyond their own horizon and find a comfortable bed for the night after sampling some of the best of local fare. Now you can do it on the other side of the world! Wherever you might go, we hope our guide to world racing gives you the winning edge.

Artist: **Hubert De Watrigant** **THE SPIRIT OF RACING** *Courtesy of:* **Osborne Studio Gallery**

Wellington Cup	January	**Trentham, New Zealand**
Barbados Gold Cup	March	**Garrison Savannah, Barbados**
Dubai World Cup	March	**Nad Al Sheba, Dubai**
Australian Derby	April	**Randwick, Australia**
Derby Italiano	May	**Rome, Italy**
Poule D'Essai des Poulains	May	**Longchamp, France**
Poule D'Essai des Pouliches	May	**Longchamp, France**
Kentucky Derby	May	**Churchill Downs, USA**
Preakness Stakes	May	**Pimlico, USA**
Belmont Stakes	June	**Belmont Park, USA**
Prix du Jockey Club	June	**Chantilly, France**
Prix de Diane	June	**Chantilly, France**
Japanese Derby	June	**Tokyo, Japan**
Deutsches Derby	July	**Hamburg, Germany**
Prix du Jacques Le Marois	August	**Deauville, France**
Prix Morny	August	**Deauville, France**
Travers Stakes	August	**Deauville, France**
Prix du Moulin	September	**Longchamp, Paris**
Prix de La Salamandre	September	**Longchamp, Paris**
Prix Vermaille	September	**Longchamp, Paris**
Grosser Preis Von Baden	September	**Baden Baden, Germany**
Prix du Cadran	October	**Longchamp, Paris**
Prix de L'Arc de Triomphe	October	**Longchamp, Paris**
Velka Pardubicka	October	**Pardubice, Czech Republic**
Canadian International	October	**Woodbine, Toronto**
Cox Plate	October	**Flemington, Melbourne**
Melbourne Cup	November	**Flemington, Melbourne**
Japan Cup	November	**Tokyo Racecourse**
Breeders' Cup	November	**Gulfstream Park, Florida, USA**
Hong Kong International Races	December	**Sha Tin, Hong Kong**
New Zealand Derby	December	**Ellerslie, New Zealand**

Artist: **Paul Hart DANCING BRAVE** *Courtesy of:* **The Artist**

While most of our Racing Around the World concerns seeing the great events in the international racing calendar, there are other times and places during the year when you might want to get away for a quick sporting fix in a somewhat unusual locale. No one would pretend that places such as Barbados, the Czech Republic or Switzerland are worth visiting solely for the quality of horses, jockeys or trainers, but as racing occasions they are all first class places to visit at the right time of the year. True racing people have taken them to their heart and celebrate them in style.

BARBADOS GOLD CUP

While steeplechase fans will be in their element come January, many of the flat world's leading owners and trainers look to sunnier climes for a bit of rest and relaxation. Nowhere has been more popular with the sun worshippers than Barbados in recent years because that warm Barbadian welcome mixed with a few rum punches is the perfect antidote to the winter blues. The sun, sea and sand might be perfect, but the icing on this cake comes with a bit of racing thrown in as well. Given that the timing is right, you might even be able to take in a cricket Test match.

Barbados is the place where Sir Michael Stoute got his start in the training business and the local racetrack also has a familiar ring about it too - Garrison Savannah - the same name of the horse that won the Cheltenham Gold Cup for Jenny Pitman in 1991! You'll find the course just a couple of miles outside the capital of Bridgetown and it has been the home of horse racing here since 1845 when British officers raced their horses on what was then the parade ground. Things are a bit more organised now with three racing seasons a year, from January to March, May to August, and October to December, organised by the Barbados Turf Club, St Michael, Barbados, West Indies. Tel: (246) 426 3980, Fax: (246) 429 3591, e mail: barturf@sunbeach.net web site: barbadosturfclub.com.

The track is a six furlong oval grass strip, with races from five to 11 furlongs. The most important races in the calendar are the '5000' run in February, the Sandy Lane Gold Cup and the Banks Guineas in March, the United Barbados Derby in August and the Heineken Stakes on Boxing Day. Although this is the serious information for the dedicated fan, the emphasis at all meetings is on family entertainment and you can enjoy a picnic under the shade of the tall trees ringing the course and sample some Barbadian cuisine in the form of pudding and souse, rice and stew or fried fish and fish cakes. All of this can be washed down with a Planter's Punch, the main ingredient of which is the local rum.

The more serious punter can enjoy the view of racing from either the Grand Stand, Field Stand, Sir John Chandler Stand, or if you can wangle an invitation, one of the corporate boxes overlooking the paddock bend. Admission to the Grand Stand will set you back $10 BDS or about $5 US on normal race days, which rises to $20 BDS on Gold Cup day. The Club House charge is $25 BDS and $50 on Cup day.

Its economy depends more on importing tourists than

Artist: **Hubert De Watrigant ROUGE TOQUE BLANCHE** *Courtesy of:* **Osborne Studio Gallery**

exporting sugar and rum these days, so as you would imagine there is a wide range of places to hitch your hammock on this tropical isle. Many are on the south and west coast, the 'Caribbean' side of the island where the white sand gives way to calm blue waters. Here you will find the Almond Beach Club & Spa at Vauxhall, St James (246 432 7840), a low-key group of pastel buildings set amidst palms right on the beach. It has all the facilities and three pools, but families with children under 16 will have to look elsewhere. Any age, however, will be welcomed at its sister hotel the Almond Beach Village near Speightstown, St Peter (246 422 4900) which has equally fine accommodation. Club Rockley at Worthing (246 435 7880) is set in 70 acres of tropical gardens, has seven swimming pools and a nine hole golf course; a free shuttle bus will take you to the hotel's beach side bar and restaurant. If you don't mind a bit of self catering, you could try the Rainbow Reef at St Lawrence Gap (246 428 5110). Its apartments are right on the beach and there's also a pool and nine hole golf course. One of Barbados' landmark hotels is the famous Sam Lord's Castle (246 423 7350) at St Philip on the south-east coast which has a large complex of rooms, pools and tennis courts around the castle. A few other choices which are definitely in the luxury category, are that watering hole of the rich and famous, the Sandy Lane Hotel, as well as the Colony Club, Royal Pavilion and Treasure Beach, all of which are in St James on Barbados' 'platinum' east coast.

VELKA PARDUBICKA (Czech Republic)

It's known as the "European Grand National", and the sight of a large field of jumpers negotiating the 31 obstacles which include stone walls, banks, hedges and a monster known as the Taxis fence that are strung out along the twists and turns of this four and a quarter mile race is a truly thrilling experience. Thanks to international television coverage and the sporting participation of a regular flow of horses, trainers and jockeys from Britain, Ireland and France during the past few years, the event has grown in stature to a 'must do' for the ardent jump racing enthusiast.

You can swill as much of the local Pilsner brew as you wish in the pleasant confines of the quaint old town of Pardubice itself before taking in the Czech St Leger on the Saturday and if your stamina matches that of the horses, return the next day for the Velka Pardubicka itself. The best connections to get there are probably through the delightful city of Prague, just an hour to the west.

Held each October, 1999 marked the 125th running of the Velka Pardubicka and interestingly it was a British professional jockey, L Sayers who won the very first race in 1874 on Fantome. Another well-known rider in his day who rode in the Velka was Count Karel Kinsky; he is the only Czech to have also won the Grand National at Aintree in 1883. That should be good enough to win any pub quiz!

The course operates its own betting system, like the Tote in Britain or the Pari Mutuel in France or North America, here known as the SCARS Tip. Better do your homework before you go, because there are some pretty complicated each way bets on offer, as well as one where you can bet that the favourite will be beaten! The minimum stake is 50 crowns, or about £1, but the maximum pay out on any single bet is 10,000 crowns or £200, so don't dream in lottery figures about your winnings. Admission to the course ranges from £4 in one of the open air stands, to £60 in private boxes with catering. Racing here also

takes place in May, which features a British Day at the end of the month, June, August and September.

The capital of the Czech Republic, Prague, is a lively city to visit and one that has become extremely popular with visitors from the west since the Iron Curtain came crashing down a decade ago. Here you will find a wide range of hotels and restaurants from which to choose, as well as many pubs and bars where you can sample the famous Pils.

Closer to the racecourse itself, take a few hours and visit Pardubice Castle, a renaissance castle and Museum near the old Pernstyn square in the old part of Pardubice. Just a few miles outside the town is the Kuneticka Hora, a Gothic castle from the 15th century. A bit further away, about 12 miles west of Pardubice, real horse people will find Kladruby nad Labem - the original six hundred year old stables established in 1579 for breeding the famous Kladrubian white horses; another must see is Slatinany Castle with its Museum of the Horse. It's located in a large old park with walks through the forest about 10 miles south from Pardubice

Some of the hotels recommended by locals in Pardubice include: the 160 room Hotel Labe, which has its own large restaurant and casino; the smaller Clubhotel Harmony, Belehradska, 00420- 40- 6435020; the Hotel Zlata Tika on Trossova, 00420-40-6613478; the 17 room S.M.G. Sporthotel, Sukovo 00420-40-512082 which has a sauna and spa facilities; Hotel u Andela Zamecka 00420-40-514028; the 50 room Hotel Bohemia Masarykovo in Chrudim 00420-455- 620351; or the larger 200-room Hotel Cernigov Riegrovo, 00420-49-5814111, e-mail: cernigov@hk.anet.cz, http://www.cernigov.cz which has its own night club, restaurant and casino right on the premises. If you are getting a bit hungry after the races try U Nouzu, Hradite na Pmsku 22, restaurant, with its terrace and wine cellar, about 3 miles north of Pardubice towards Kuneticka Hora, 040 45005; or right in the old part of Pardubice near the castle on Zamecka 24 is Na Kovarne with its restaurant, pub and terrace, 040 514028.

ST MORITZ (Switzerland)

Swiss racing might sound like a contradiction in a land better known for skiing and fondue, but each year mother nature completely freezes over the lake at St Moritz and the good burghers of the town stage a racing spectacular on ice! The sight of horses and jockeys flying across the white packed snow against an Alpine backdrop is truly a unique experience, and the hospitality adds a new dimension to apres racing.

Of course you'll have to be here in January and February to take in the action and hope that a sudden thaw doesn't halt the proceedings! This is one of the few places in the world where you can go skiing in the morning and racing in the afternoon. Surprisingly, the quality of the racing is probably a far cry better than that on show at Lingfield at the same time of the year, and the horses adapt remarkably well to the conditions under foot. Several top jockeys from other countries are also usually on hand and the meetings have a winter carnival air about them. Some jump races over hurdles are also usually put on to keep fans of racing over the sticks happy.

The Swiss practically invented good hotel keeping so you won't be pressed to find some excellent accommodation. It's best to book early though, as St Moritz is a traditional watering hole for the rich and famous at this time of the year and of course skiing is the name of the true winter game. Although it's usually not cheap, and nothing is in Switzerland, there is a good choice of hotels, apartments and guest houses in St Moritz itself. Some favourites include: Badrutts Palace Hotel, a luxurious resort with old world hospitality overlooking the lake, (41 81837 1000); also overlooking the lake and mountains is the recently renovated Carlton Hotel (41 81832 1141); the excellent Kulm Hotel (41 81832 1151) on Via Veglia which has welcomed guests since 1856 and also has a fine view of the lake; or the elegant five star Park Hotels Waldhaus (41 81928 4848) which features art nouveau fireplaces and is set in its own 60 acre private park.

Artist: **David Dent** **REACH FOR GLORY** *Courtesy of:* **The Artist**

If accommodation is booked up here, you could also try another ski resort, Davos, which is not too far away, or the very toney Klosters. The nearest big city and major international airport is to be found in Zurich, which also offers a wide choice of accommodation and is quite interesting in its own right; here the family-run Baur au Lac Hotel (220 5020) on Talstrasse combines luxury with old-world elegance, while just outside the city the Dolder Grand Hotel (251 6321) on Kurhausstrasse is a fairy-tale castle set in the woods with pretty views over the Zurichsee. Right in the centre of the city you could also try the Savoy Baur En Ville (215 2525) on Am Paradeplatz, Zurich's oldest hotel, or the cosy elegance of the Widder (224 2526), a converted row of townhouses on Rennweg.

CAROLINA & COLONIAL CUP

(South Carolina)

When 50,000 jump racing fans assemble each spring at Springdale Race Course near Camden, South Carolina for the Carolina Cup, it's probably the world's biggest point to point. Timber fences, some five feet high, are the name of the game and it has become such an event that people come from hundreds, if not thousands, of miles to enjoy a massive tail-gate party while they witness the thrills and spills of some of the best steeplechasers in North America. Grab your picnic hamper, pack the beer in ice and you can be a good ol' boy or girl for the day.

You'll probably fly in to the South Carolina state capital of Columbia, which is just a half hour's drive from Camden on Interstate Highway 20, or you could take the more leisurely and historic US Route 1.

Springdale Race Course is part of a 600-acre training facility that was given by Marion duPont Scott to the State of South Carolina. The Carolina Cup is part of a six-race card and dates back to 1930; the formula of steeplechasing over a long galloping

course with stiff timber fences has been brought to Britain in the last few years in the form of the Marlborough Cup, which, like its American counterpart, is beginning to attract huge crowds.

The Carolina Cup is held at the end of March, while in the autumn at the end of November, the Colonial Cup is also held on the same course. A $100,000 steeplechase, it has produced some good winners such as Lonesome Glory who went on to win at Cheltenham, and usually attracts some good horses from the UK. The whole day has a fairground atmosphere with terrier trials, a market, classic cars, rides and special exhibitions. To find out more, contact their web site at www.carolina-cup.org. General admission for the Colonial Cup is $10-15, with general parking at $5 or $50 for preferred parking which includes two tickets. Reserved parking in the infield is $75, which also includes two tickets, or $125 for Front Row Paddock Side. $300 will get you a six-seater box in the Grandstand and covers all admission and parking, while $400 will get you the same deal with lunch included. While you're in the area you should also pay a visit to the Carolina Cup Racing Museum, which has interactive exhibits and memorabilia relating to the history of steeplechasing in North America.

Part of the Confederate old south, South Carolina has a lot going for it to entertain and amuse the visitor. If you want more information on where to see or what to do from your armchair, just log into the excellent web site at www.travelsc.com. Camden itself is in the state's 'Olde English District', which perhaps not surprisingly has counties such as Lancaster and York! Here you can find a room for the night at the Colony Inn on US 1 (803 432 5508), the Knights Inn on DeKalb St and US 1 (803 432 2453) or the Plantation Motel on Jefferson Davis Highway (803 432 2300). There are lots of other smaller guesthouses and b & bs to choose from. Columbia is the nearest main city and also has lots of hotels and restaurants. South Carolina's coast is not to be missed and we strongly suggest a visit to historic Charleston which dates back to 1670 and has lots of Civil War connections, as well as Georgetown, and the seaside beach resorts of Myrtle Beach and Hilton Head Island.

Artist: **Hubert de Watrigant** *LE ROND DE PRESENTATION* *Courtesy of:* **Osborne Studio Gallery**

Racing in France

Long before Le Chunnel was completed, making it easier than ever to hop across the channel for a day or weekend at the races in France, thousands of British racing fans have swarmed to Paris' Longchamp for the Arc weekend in early October, or drifted lazily to Deauville in the summer for some sea air with their sport.

Now the traffic travels in both directions, and on any given Saturday in the UK you will be able to see top French jockeys such as the bubbly Olivier Peslier compete head to head with his Italian/English counterpart Frankie Dettori. On Sunday in France, the location might have changed but the action often repeats itself, adding a fascinating elan to the racing action. The entente cordiale stretches to several of each country's top trainers and there are few Group races run in France without a representative from the top English yards, or alternatively, with horses sent from France to try and take the top prizes in British flat racing. And it continues year-round through the winter in the National Hunt game, with Martin Pipe taking his cheque book to pick up a top class hurdler at Auteuil or Francois Doumen bringing top French steeplechasers to English shores to try and win yet another top prize.

The common denominator in all this cross channel activity is often the owners who have significant strings of horses with trainers in both countries. The Aga Khan, Sheikh Mohammed, Sheikh Hamdan and the Maktoum family have long led the way, not to mention Khalid Abdullah, and others such as Daniel Wildenstein, the Niarchos family of France and Britain's Robert Sangster who have also encouraged the two-way traffic by

taking a sporting chance with their top steeds.

Despite some problems in recent years which saw the closure of one course at Evry, French racing has taken some positive steps in the last few years to improve the viability of the sport, and has never been keener to welcome the visiting racegoer from abroad. Taking into account the very high class racing on offer and the first class facilities for the visitor, racing in France is good value. What's more you can load up your car with some first class Bordeaux and Brie for the trip home. What are you waiting for?

The organising body for much of thoroughbred racing is France-Galop and they can provide details on the courses and fixtures. Drop them a line at France-Galop, 46 place Abel Gance, 92655 Boulogne, France. Tel: 1 49 10 2030. Fax: 1 47 61 9332. If you are into the Internet, they also have a web site at WWW. paristurf. tm. fr.

There are a number of British companies which run regular trips to French racecourses such as Longchamp, Chantilly and Deauville. They enjoy the benefit of being able to block book whole sections of the course for their clients to enjoy private facilities at big events such as the Arc weekend. In October literally thousands take up the offer and the British presence can often dominate proceedings at Longchamp. If you wish to let someone else make all the arrangements you could contact Horse Racing Abroad, 24 Sussex Road, Haywards Heath, West Sussex RH16 4EA. Tel: (01444) 441661. Fax: (01444) 416 169. A typical two-day Arc weekend by either Eurostar train or air, with a hotel room, course admission transfers and some extras, runs to about £220. The company are experts in arranging racing trips around the globe and Paris is their most popular venue.

LONGCHAMP

The surrounding Bois de Boulogne gives Longchamp a country feel and it is sometimes hard to remember that you are close to the centre of Paris. Reflecting its pre-eminence as the course of France's capital city, Longchamp is the course for many of the most important races in the country's racing calendar. From the French Guineas for colts and fillies in the spring, to the end of season European championship that is the Prix de L'Arc de Triomphe, Longchamp is the home of French racing at its best.

The Clerk of the Course at Longchamp can be contacted at Hippodrome de Longchamp, Route des Tribunes, Bois de Boulogne, 75016 Paris. Tel: 1 44 30 7500. Fax: 1 44 30 7599.

To get to the course, you can either take the number 244N Bus (Pte Maillot) or hop on the free shuttle bus provided by the racecourse from the Porte d'Auteuil. If the Metro is your choice, take the direction Porte d'Auteuil-Longchamp. Once you have reached the racecourse, compared with most major British courses it is relatively inexpensive to get in. There is one large public enclosure which covers the entire course and it costs FF 25 (about £2.50) to attend for a mid-week meeting and FF 40 (£4) for weekend fixtures or bank holidays. About FF 50 is asked for some of the biggest fixtures of the year such as the Arc de Triomphe. Even better still, those 18 years old or younger get in for nothing, while if you are 18-25 years old or over 60 years young, the price of admission is reduced by half. There is also a large public enclosure in the centre of the course, which is free to everyone!

There will be additional costs if you wish to reserve a seat in one of the restaurants, which you can do by telephoning ahead on 1 42 88 9138 or 1 44 30 7590. For those who enjoy the luxury of a private box, you can arrange one by contacting 1 49 10 2287.

Each year Longchamp hosts over 30 racing fixtures. Prime amongst these will be Arc day itself on the first Sunday in October, with a fine supporting card that also includes the Abbaye sprint over five furlongs, a race that often goes to an English invader. Get there a day earlier and you can watch one of the best stayers' races of the year, the Prix du Cadran which has attracted some of Britain's best long distance specialists. Leading up to the Arc, in early September is a number of Arc trials that try to establish some form for the big race itself. They are fascinating contests in themselves and well worth going to see live. If you do go on the first Sunday in September, you will be able to watch the Prix du Moulin de Longchamp, the race named after the windmill that provides a unique land mark at the far bend. Come to Longchamp in the spring and you will be able to take in the first of the French classics for colts in the form of the Dubai Poules d'Essai des Poulains and its counterpart for fillies, the Essai des Pouliches. A couple of weeks earlier, and one of the first Group races in the calendar awaits you in the form of the Prix Ganay.

Longchamp is a right handed track of 2,400 metres (about a mile and a half) whose principal characteristic is the sweeping bend before the finishing straight. So there is in effect, a turn for home into a 'false straight', and then another turn for home in the run to the finish line itself. Just to add some interest there are actually two finishing lines, so don't tear up your ticket on the tierce until the race is well and truly over! The outside course is bisected by a straight course upon which the famous Prix de l'Abbaye sprint is held over five furlongs.

Paris Local Favourites

What can be said of Paris that has not already been said? No doubt if you are a racing fan, you will be coming either in the Spring or the Autumn when the major races at Longchamp take place, and it is also a time when this vibrant city is at its finest. The Arc de Triomphe, Champs Elysees and Eiffel Tower are Paris' most famous landmarks but the way to really feel Paris is to walk amongst some of the smaller streets in either Montmartre, Le Marais or the Quartier Latin, the famous left bank on the other side of the Isle de Notre Dame. For anyone surfacing from the Metro for a very first view of Paris, it should be taken at night from the Trocadero overlooking the Seine and the Tour Eiffel. Hopefully the fountains will be playing under coloured floodlights to ensure a magic moment any visitor to this city of lovers will never forget.

There is an incredible number of excellent restaurants in Paris, and hotels by the bucketfull, so recommending just a few is tricky. Naturally, a lot depends on your budget. If time is tight and money no object then try The Crillon (1 44 711500), The Bristol (1 53 43 4300) or the Hotel Vernet (1 44 31 9800), all outstanding hotels with restaurants of superb quality. The Parc (1 44 05 6666) is also excellent and conveniently situated, as is the St-James Paris (1 44 05 8181). Finally, if you are into art nouveau try Alain Ducasse (1 47 27 1227) - a real jewel!

CHANTILLY

With its connections to French royalty going back centuries, Chantilly is perhaps the most elegant of French racecourses and home to some of the country's, and Europe's, leading Group races for three-year-olds such as the United Arab Emirates Prix du Jockey Club (French Derby) for colts, and the Prix de Diane Hermes (French Oaks) for fillies. A dramatic backdrop is provided by the magnificent 18th century chateau and the Grandes Ecuries, the stables which housed the steeds of nobility in days gone by.

Chantilly also has added interest as the locale is one of the top training centres in France, and home to the operations of such notables as Andre Fabre, Criquette Head or the English transplant John Hammond - the French Newmarket, one could say, but vive la difference!

If you wish to get in touch with the course write to Hippodrome des Princes de Conde, Route du Pesage, 60500 Chantilly. Tel: 3 44 62 4100. Fax: 3 44 57 3489.

Chantilly is situated about 30 miles north of Paris and is easily accessible from the capital. It also handy for Charles de Gaulle airport if you are flying in directly. If you are driving from the direction of Paris, take the A1 autoroute and exit at Survilliers. Alternatively, you could take the trains which run directly to Chantilly from Paris' Gare du Nord station. There are also trains which make other stops along the way and it might be best to check before you set off with the SNCF, Tel: 3 42 80 0303.

Despite the architectural opulence of the surroundings at Chantilly, like most French racecourses, it is quite cheap to get in. The public enclosure in the centre of the course is absolutely free, while general admission to the remainder of the course and grandstand area costs a mere FF 25 (about £2.50) during the week, or FF 40 (£4) on Sundays and bank holidays. Children and teenagers under 18 are free and those 18-25 years old and over 60s enjoy a fifty per cent reduction on the normal price. If you wish to book a seat or table in the restaurant, call ahead on Tel. 3 44 58 9001.

Chantilly holds 20 days of racing spread from the end of April until the third week of September. This is quite a comeback, as it was just a few years ago that this wonderful venue was cut back to only six days racing because of financial constraints - such was the sad state of French racing then. Thankfully now its all systems go and you could get off to an early start with a visit on a Sunday in May to see the running of the Prix Hocquart. The main action of the year of course takes place in June with the running of the French Derby and Oaks on consecutive Sundays. Other fixtures are scattered throughout May, June, July and September, but most often on weekdays.

Chantilly is a sweeping, right handed course of 2,000 metres (about a mile and a quarter) and provides a true test of ability.

Chantilly Local Favourites

As an overall place to pay a visit in the area just outside Paris, Chantilly ranks right up at the top along with such other marvellous venues as Fontainbleau or Versailles. It is connections with the horse though, that make it a must for those with an interest in racing and you should really make a point

Artist: **Jonathan Trowell** *CHANTILLY*
Courtesy of: **Osborne Studio Gallery**

of visiting the highly-regarded Musee Vivant du Cheval (the Museum of the Living Horse). Other notable places to visit nearby include the Abbaye de Chaalis at Hermenonville, the town of Senlis, and of course the Musee Condee and the park and Chateau de Chantille itself.

If you wish to find a bed for the night in a place that maintains the aristocratic theme of Chantilly, try the Chateau Mont Royal (Tel: 3 44 54 5050) a charming chateau hotel that was built at the turn of the century as a hunting lodge and sits in its own forest about six miles outside Chantilly. It has an excellent restaurant and the hotel will very kindly arrange golf, riding or fishing for you nearby. Another highly rated hostelry is the Golf Hotel Blue Green de Chantilly (3 44 58 4777) a good place for an extended stay if you like to try a round on the fairways. Although perhaps not quite as luxurious as these choices, either of the Hotel du Parc (3 44 58 2000), close to the centre of the town, or the baronial Chateau de Montvillargenne Hotel situated in the midst of a pretty forest, will not see you stuck for a bed for a night. For fine dining, one restaurant to put into the notebook is the Chateau de la Tour (3 44 62 3838). Other first class restaurants include the Tour d'Apremont (3 44 25 6111) and Verbois (3 44 24 0622) on the route de Creil.

If you wish to get more information on what to do while you are in the Chantilly area, contact the local tourist office on, Tel: 3 44 57 08 58.

DEAUVILLE

Everyone loves to go to the seaside for the summer, and with Deauville you can paddle your feet in the sea in the morning, gorge yourself on fine cuisine and wines at lunch, play the ponies in the afternoon and then try to double your winnings at the casino all night. Though not as ancient as say Chantilly, Deauville is not without its connections to royalty as racing here was first started here in 1864 by the Duc de Morny, the Emperor's younger brother and after whom one of the major races of the year, the Prix Morny is named.

The Clerk of the Course at Deauville may be contacted at Hippodrome de Deauville-La Touques, 45 avenue Hocquart de Turtot, 14800 Deauville, France. Tel: 2 31 14 2000. Fax: 2 31 14 2007.

To get to Deauville from Paris where you might begin your journey when in France, you could drive there taking the A 13 Autoroute that goes from Paris to Caen. By train, you would start your journey at the Gare St Lazare, getting off at Deauville Station. Of course you could also fly there directly if you had your own plane and then you would head for the airport at St Gatien. For landing information, Tel: 2 31 65 1717. Alternatively, mariners may enjoy a trip on the ferry which docks at Le Havre, fairly close to your destination.

The surroundings and hotels in Deauville might be on the luxurious side, but like most French courses, it won't cost you very much to get into the course. FF 25 (£2.50) is the price of general admission during the week and it goes up to FF 35 (£3.50) on Sundays and bank holidays. Those under 18 and over 60 are free, while the 18-25 year-olds get in for half price. Of course a private box would be more and if you would like to arrange one, call ahead on Tel: 1 49 10 2287. Deauville has three fine restaurants, La Toque, Les Jardins du Paddock and Les Haras, and if you would like to book a table call Tel: 2 31 14 3114

Racing at Deauville takes place from the middle of July to the end of August, and again for an all too brief couple of days in October. The main action takes place though in August when all of Paris has deserted its streets to find a place for the annual vacation. Racing is put on just about every Saturday and Sunday during the month and the big day is the Sunday when the Group 1 Prix Morny is staged, one of the top races for two year olds in France. In the past this race has been won by such stars as Machiavellian, Arazi and Hector Protector and almost always throws down vital clues to the future classics.

Another top class race is the Prix Jacques le Marois for older horses. Perhaps you too could find a future star here if you go to the Agence Francaise Yearling Sales which are held each August in Deauville. If all this doesn't satisfy your appetite for looking at horses, you could always take in a polo match!

In 2000, this right-handed course of about 2,000 metres (a mile and a quarter) will host 19 fixtures, the bulk of which are in August, the month when many take place on both Saturday or Sundays of 'le weekend'.

Deauville Local Favourites

Being an elegant seaside resort that has always attracted the well-heeled Parisian, it is not surprising that Deauville boasts a good complement of excellent hotels. After you've spent some time on the beach, perhaps bought a yacht at the sales, done some shopping at designer boutiques and gambled the day and night away at the course and casino, you might consider bedding down at any one of the following recommended hostelries: the Hotel du Golf (Tel: 2 31 14 2400) is a rambling Tudor chateau that has been recently renovated and enjoys splendid views of the River Seine as it meets the sea. True to its name, you can also get in a round of golf on the hotel's own course; the Golf's sister hotel, the Royal (2 31 98 66 22) is also run by the Lucien Barriere group, enjoys sea views and is handy

for the centre of town and the Casino; others you could try are the Mercure (2 31 98 6633), the L'Amiraute (2 31 88 6262) and the Hotel Yacht Club (2 31 87 3000) overlooking the quay side near the town centre, or L'Augeval (2 31 81 1318). You don't have to be Greek to stay at the Helios Hotel (2 31 14 4646), but you might take home your winnings to the Hotel Le Trophee (2 31 88 4586). Deauville accommodation tends to get fully booked up when the racing is on during the summer, so it's best to reserve ahead if you can.

There is a delightful atmosphere in Deauville and there are numerous restaurants - many are very relaxed and dinner just seems to go on and on. Try Ciro's (2 31 14 3131) or the appropriately named Yearling (2 31 88 3337) which is well regarded. At nearby Touques the Village (2 31 88 0177) is good, as is Aux Landiers (2 31 88 0039) - a real gem in which to plan your winning bets in real peace.

If the pace is a bit hectic in Deauville, you might take a break and do a bit of a tour to nearby Trouville, the delightful Honfleur, with yet even more outstanding restaurants, or Caen both of which offer some interesting sight-seeing and some museums worth a visit. If your horse has won or money is no object come what may, try the Ferme St-Simeon (2 31 89 2361), a spectacular restaurant. If you can't get enough of the equine action in Deauville, you might pay a visit to the nearby course at Clairefontaine which usually offers a mixed card of both flat and jump racing.

If you need any advice on some of the many attractions that Deauville has to offer, contact the Office du Tourisme on Tel: 2 31 14 4000.

Racing in Germany

After some years in the doldrums, racing in Germany has made a real come-from-behind finish in the nineties and now is

*Artist: **Klaus Philipp** **BADEN BADEN** Courtesy of: **The Artist***

one of the top places in Europe to go for some quality racing. Since unification a few years ago, Berlin's historic Hoppegarten has been brought back into the illustrious fold of German racecourses, a list which also includes Hamburg, the home of the German Derby held each year on the first Sunday of July; Cologne, where the German 2,000 Guineas is staged and one of the country's leading training centres; as well as other major tracks at Munich, Hanover, Bremen, Dortmund, Dusseldorf and Frankfurt which provide a variety of top notch flat and jump racing.

With their high prize money, German Pattern races have become major targets for top European owners and trainers since they were opened up to foreign competition in recent years and there are few Group races which will not see a runner from the John Dunlop or Clive Brittain stables, and probably ridden by a Dettori or Fallon if they take place on a Sunday! The Maktoum family of Dubai set up a training operation there in the 1990s and although relatively modest compared with their operations in France and England, this also adds to the international flavour and the class of racing. Germany has long had some top trainers of its own and with the right breeding stock they are now going overseas to take on the world at meetings such as the Breeders Cup - and with the success many British trainers would envy. German bloodstock continues to improve and it will be interesting to see what will be achieved in the coming years.

By most yardsticks, top amongst German racecourses for racing, hospitality, scenery and a generally great time comes Baden Baden, a real gem of a place on the edge of the Black Forest.

BADEN BADEN

Baden Baden is one of Germany's most popular and prettiest of courses, with a long history of racing going back to 1858. Back in Victorian times it was visited by those who came originally to take the waters at the town's spa, but is now really a year-round resort. Nestled between the Black Forest and the Rhine, it's a delightful place to escape to no matter what the time of year, but for the racing fan, it is the spring and late summer/autumn when Baden Baden's two main racing festivals take place that make a visit to the town particularly appealing. The racecourse is considered by many to be the country's number one course: Germany's answer to Ascot in a beautiful parkland setting.

The course is run by the private Internationaler Club, which has about 130 members, and can be contacted at Internationaler Club e.V., Lichtentaler Allee 8, 76530 Baden Baden, Germany. Tel: 07221 21120. Fax: 07221 211222. On racedays you can reach the course on Tel: 07221 211216.

If you are driving there the quickest way is to take the A5 Autobahn which links Basel in Switzerland with Karlsruhe and take the exit signed Baden Baden-Iffezheim and you will find the course about 8 miles north west of the town, next to the village of Iffezheim. If you are travelling by train, head for the Baden Baden-Oos station and board the special buses laid on for racedays which will take you the last five miles to the course. Otherwise, a taxi will cost you only about DM 20 (£7). If you are lucky enough to come by private aeroplane, you should land at the new airport at Solingen which is only about 20 minutes away. For those taking commercial flights, Strasbourg is the nearest airport with regularly scheduled

flights and it is about a half hour's drive away. Foreign owners and trainers are treated particularly well here and if you let the officials know in advance, they'll line you up with a badge and even make arrangements to collect you from the airport or railway station.

Less elevated visitors though won't find the tariff too high to spend a day at the races, with general admission only DM 10 (about £3). If you want a reserved seat it will cost you a bit more, with prices ranging up to DM 70 (£23), depending upon where you sit. There are six days of racing during each of the two annual meetings and you can buy badges which cover the entire meeting: for example, a six-day badge for the Schwarzwald Terrace restaurant, with its fine views of the course from the top level of the stands, would set you back about DM 230 (£75) or DM 180 (£60) for the Wein Terrace restaurant just below it. Box seats come in at about the DM 200 (£70) level for all six days, or about DM 50 (£17) on a daily basis. Children are allowed into the course for a modest DM 4 (a little over £1) and they will find various things to entertain them during their visit, including a children's playground. There is also a baby care room which is free.

Although the whole course and setting really is first class, Baden Baden lets you enjoy your racing any way you like it, from the casual pleasure of a beer and bratwurst on a park bench next to the track, to a fine meal in the more formal surroundings of a private box. You could start the day with an early morning breakfast on the Clubhouse Terrace and watch the horses work out on the course and come back later for a big lunch in the Black Forest Terrace with a view of the real racing action in the afternoon.

Although Baden Baden is probably best known for its flat racing, the course also holds jump racing over hurdles and fences. In fact, there are no fewer than five different courses here, including the Old Course, New Course and Straight Course, which have a total of two miles of excellent turf racecourse between them, with a two furlong final straight. The Steeplechase Course is two miles and three furlongs around, with sixteen fences with a short, steep hill known as the Kapellenberg, while the Hurdles Course is a tighter one with a quarter mile circumference and completely flat.

There are usually nine races a day on each of the twelve days of racing held at Baden Baden of different classes and distances. Included in these are no fewer than ten European pattern Group races, so the standard of racing is really quite high. Highlight of the spring meeting is the Group 2 Baden Airpark-Grosser Preis der Wirtschaft. In late summer and early Autumn, the Mercedes-Benz Grosser Preis von Baden is a Group 1 contest that has been won by some outstanding horses.

Putting a bet on your selection on the Tote here will be familiar to most punters, with win, place, Forecast and Tricast wagering from a minimum stake of DM 2.50 (just under a pound). If your German is good enough, the racing paper "Sport-Welt" will help you with your selection. For those used to racing in Britain, Ireland or Australia, there are also on-course bookmakers who will take your bet. If you aren't in the stands when the stalls fly open, there are over 100 TV monitors to help you follow the race. Don't worry if you get to the course without having changed your pounds or francs into local currency as there is a foreign exchange and cheque cashing service at the on-course Deutsche Bank branch.

With some of the finest racing in Europe at the highest level, a visit to Baden Baden is a must for every racing enthusiast. Like the spa town, the racecourse prides itself on looking after its guests!

Baden Baden Local Favourites

If you are visiting Baden Baden for the races, you will be fortunate to be staying in a place that has some of the finest hotels and service in the world, with over a century of catering for just about anyone's personal whim. Spa towns tend to pamper their guests and this is one of the ultimate places to be pampered. You could take the waters before or after racing, play a round of golf at one of the resort's many courses or if you are on a roll with a few winners, try your luck at the world famous casino in the Kurhaus.

The Caracalla-Therme and the Friedrichsbad are the two best known bathing spots where a garden of earthly delights awaits those wishing to take the cure before taking in a more cultural experience at the theatre or concert hall. Right in Baden Baden, the Lichtentaler Allee and historic old town is filled with elegant boutiques and shops just waiting to relieve you of your winnings from the course or casino.

Baden Baden is right on the doorstep of the region's wine growing district, the Rebland, which has some of the finest wines in Germany as well as some extremely good eating places in addition to some glorious scenery. A day touring around here, or a short hop over the Rhine to neighbouring Alsace would be sure to prompt a trip to the gym when you return home.

In the very top rank of hotels here, there is the famous Brenner's Park Hotel (07221 9000) which is firmly in the luxury category and is an excellent nearby hotel on the outskirts of Baden Baden. Also top class is Monch's Posthotel (07083 7440) in nearby Bad Herrenalb. First-class accommodation can be found in either the Europaischer Hof Hotel (07221 23561) or the Badischer Hof hotels, both run by the quality Steigenberger hotel chain which also provides on-course catering services at Baden Baden.

If you fancy a stay in the heart of the Black Forest, try the Hotel Bareiss (07442 470) near Baiersbronn-Mitteltal - it's a complete resort with all kinds of sports facilities. Here you won't be too far away from the fabulous Restaurant Schwarzwaldstube (07442 4920) with its classic fine French cuisine.

One thing you should really do before leaving home though is to book ahead, as racing at Baden Baden has had a resurgence in popularity in recent years and you might be disappointed if you don't have a reservation at the hotel of your choice. Despite the architectural opulence of the surroundings at Chantilly, like most French racecourses it is quite cheap to get in. The public enclosure in the centre of the course is absolutely free, while general admission to the remainder of the course and grandstand area costs a mere FF 25 (about £2.50) during the week, or FF 40 (£4) on Sundays and bank holidays. Children and teenagers under 18 are free and those 18-25 years old and over 60s enjoy a fifty per cent reduction on the normal price. If you wish to book a seat or table in the restaurant, call ahead on Tel. 3 44 58 9001.

Artist: **Roy Miller LONGCHAMP** *Courtesy of:* **The Artist**

Racing in Canada

WOODBINE

When it was built in the 1950s, the sprawling complex that is Woodbine Racetrack lay in peaceful countryside amid farms to the north west of the city of Toronto. Now this booming city of almost three million people has all but swallowed it up and as you sit in the grandstand the roar of jet engines overhead signals the approach to the busy international airport close by, bringing visitors from around the world.

Woodbine is a first-rate, modern complex that, while filled with punters only a few times a year for major races such as the Queen's Plate in late June and the Canadian International in October, offers an excellent day at the races at a very reasonable cost - in fact admission to the course itself is free!

Run by the Ontario Jockey Club, Woodbine can be contacted at Woodbine Racetrack, PO Box 156, Rexdale, Ontario, Canada, M9W 5L2. Tel: (416) 675 6110. Fax: (416) 213 2126. Web site: ojc.com/attrack/woodbine.html. The web site is an excellent way to visit Woodbine, if you can't get there in person.

The course is very easy to drive to by car. Just a few minutes from Toronto International Airport, take Bellfield Road to Carlingview Drive if you wish to avoid the traffic and enter via the backstretch or follow Highway 409 to Highway 27 and the main entrance. Allow about a half hour or more to cover the 15 miles from downtown Toronto, taking the Queen Elizabeth Way west to Highway 427 right to the track. Valet parking is also available at a small charge at the Clubhouse entrance. Alternatively you could take Toronto's efficient subway system and hop in a taxi or connect with the free Racetrack buses which leave from Kipling Station just under an hour before the first race to the main entrance and returning after the last race. Seating is on a first-come, first served basis. If you need any assistance with directions, give the course a ring on (416) 675-RACE.

Thoroughbred racing takes place at Woodbine from the end of March through to the first week in December, although there is Harness Racing here seven months of the year. There are usually ten races a day of varying calibre and distances, mostly on the dirt track but some held on the turf course. There are big stakes races held on Saturdays, Sundays and holidays throughout the year, with the Queen's Plate for Canadian bred three year olds, the first leg of the Canadian Triple Crown in late June providing the highlight of the summer season and the EP Taylor Stakes and Canadian International with a guaranteed purse of Can$1.5 million attracting some of the best turf horses from around the world in mid October. In 1996 Woodbine played host to the Breeders' Cup and trainers and jockeys all seemed to agree that the track's new mile and a half turf course provided one of the fairest tests to equine ability in North America. Woodbine also operates a simulcasting system with other racetracks in North America beaming in live racing on TV from other courses, complete with pari-mutuel betting.

Admission to the large Grandstand and course itself is free, but there are admission charges to access various bars, restaurants and other facilities. There are also thousands of free seats in the Grandstand on several levels offering excellent views of all parts of the track. Some sections have reserved seating at a small charge on big race days. A race programme costs $2.50 and contains past performances plus a brief form guide; for the purist handicapper, a copy of the Daily Racing Form is also a must. The minimum bet on the pari-mutuel is $2 Canadian (about $1.50 US), so you don't have to bring loads of cash to enjoy yourself.

At the top end of the scale is the Woodbine Club, an exclusive member-only private club whose panelled lounges and bars offer luxurious accommodation. If you are just visiting Toronto for a few days it might be worth your while to find a member who can take you as a guest. If you get lucky and cash in a big daily double, you might want to stump up the $1,000 for your own membership!

Woodbine has a number of restaurants and bars to choose from but reservations are advised for busy weekends and holiday meetings, Tel 888-675 7223. Favourite on the second floor is a new dining room with panoramic views which overlooks the finish line. Each table has its own TV monitor showing track odds and racing. On the third floor Clubhouse level is Champions, a bar and delicatessen counter serving soup and sandwiches, which has an outdoor patio and casual dining. No reservations required here but there is a $5 admission surcharge. On the first floor, the Finish Line bar also offers light snacks; the Oaks Lounge on the second level and the Walking Ring patio on the first floor offer serious liquid refreshment possibilities and a view of the saddling paddock. At the east end of the grandstand are three other bars, Willows, Silks Lounge and the Winners Circle, which will also whet your whistle, but have no views of the track. The grandstand complex also contains a food court with a wide choice of snack and fast food outlets, the hot roast beef sandwiches at the carvery are a safe bet.

Having fully satisfied your appetite, why not spend a while visiting the Canadian Horse Racing Hall of Fame on the ground floor of the grandstand. In addition to celebrating such equine heroes as Northern Dancer and the great 'Big Red' Secretariat, who had his last race at Woodbine, winning as he pleased by more than 6 lengths, you can explore the rich history of the turf in Canada.

Toronto Local Favourites

Toronto is well worth a visit in itself, with a multitude of first class hotels and a fabulous range of restaurants that reflect the city's multi-ethnic population. In fact, there are more restaurants per capita in Toronto than any other city in the world! You might never leave the airport strip of hotels and eateries, but you would be missing much if you did not try and stay downtown. It's a clean, safe walking city with lots of shopping, sites and nightlife, so why not enjoy it to the maximum? The Yorkville area in mid-town Toronto is an excellent bet with hotels such as the classic Park Plaza (416 924 5471) on Avenue Road with its fifties roof garden bar. The Four Seasons Hotel (416 964 0411) opposite offers all the luxury that chain usually provides. For a fun night out and a lot of local colour try the Brunswick Tavern on Bloor Street West, a favourite watering hole. Dip south on Spadina Avenue and you are in Chinatown. The Pink Pearl on Dundas Street is only one of many excellent restaurants here, or for a bit of jazz and some delicatessen delights drop into Grossman's Tavern on Spadina. A fun place to dine and a local landmark is Ed's Warehouse, handy for taking in a musical at the Royal Alex Theatre next door.

There are many hotels right downtown and a safe bet is the Royal York Hotel (416 368 2511) opposite Union Station or for a bit of turn-of-the-century elegance try the King Edward Hotel (416 863 3131) on King Street, handy for shopping in the vast Eaton Centre or exploring the nightlife. Toronto is right on Lake Ontario and the Harbourfront area hops night and day. Stay at the Radisson Hotel (416 203 3333) right on the water and take a ferry to the Toronto Islands for a bit of green quiet and the best view of the city skyline. See the sites from the top of the CN Tower or take in a baseball game in the covered Sky Dome at its foot. Toronto and Woodbine are a winning daily double.

Racing in New York

The three principle thoroughbred racetracks of Belmont and Aqueduct near New York City and Saratoga in upstate New York are run by the New York Racing Association Inc., PO Box 90, Jamaica, New York, 11417. Tel: (718) 641 4700. E Mail: nyra@nyra.com. They also have an excellent web site giving details of all three tracks, updates on big race entries and general news; well worth a visit at nyracing.com/contact.html.

BELMONT PARK

Any way you look at it, Belmont, like New York City itself, is a big place. The main grandstand which was built as part of a major refit in the late 1960s is awesomely large and stretches most of the finishing straight. On big race days such as the Belmont Stakes they can fit in upwards of 90,000 people and at least 33,000 of those will not have any trouble getting a seat. By North American standards the course itself is also pretty impressive with a mile and a half dirt track, while the Widener turf course is just over a mile and a quarter. Of all racetracks in America Belmont is probably the one best suited to the running style of British and European horses, so visitors from across the Atlantic might have an even chance of making a few bob if they spot any imported runners here.

Belmont is on Long Island and to get there from Manhattan take the Queens Midtown Tunnel to the Long Island Expressway, east to Cross Island Parkway and south to Exit 26-D. From Connecticut take any route to the Throgs Neck Bridge to the Cross Island Parkway, or from New Jersey you can use the George Washington Bridge from the north or from the south the Interstate bridge to the Staten Island Expressway and the Verazzano Bridge. From Manhattan you could also take the 8th Avenue subway to connecting buses at 169th or 179th streets,

or by rail via the Long Island Railroad from Penn Station to make connections at Jamaica.

Once you've reached the track it will cost a mere $2 to park the car, or an additional $2 for preferred parking closer to the entrance. A courtesy shuttle bus will take you to the admission entrance. If you're feeling really quite lazy it's worth paying an extra $4 for valet parking. There is special parking available for both the grandstand and clubhouse. Admission to the Grandstand is only $2, but it's probably worth spending another $2 to get into the Clubhouse, then you can go anywhere you like. Children under 12 are free.

Racing is held at Belmont over long stretches in the spring and summer and again in the autumn and, apart from the month of August when everyone moves to Saratoga, alternates with Aqueduct. So if you're visiting New York City at any time other than August, you can get some local action. No racing is usually held on Mondays (except bank holidays) and Tuesdays, as well as the occasional Wednesday on a bank holiday week. Watch out for Palm Sunday and Easter Sunday though, as they are both 'dark', as is Yom Kippur.

There are big races just about every weekend, but one to catch in April would be the Wood Memorial, a Kentucky Derby trial for three year-olds, followed by the highlight of the season, the Belmont Stakes in June, which forms the third leg of the American triple crown. It's by far the biggest day of the year with a supporting card of excellent Group 1, 2 and 3 races. The crowds pack in and the course looks at its glorious best. Of course Belmont has held the Breeders' Cup and will very probably do so again sometime soon: however, the regular autumn programme has its own rewards with the Man O'War and the Woodward weight-for-age stakes providing excellent quality racing in September followed by the Jockey Club Gold Cup in October and its fine supporting card of Group races.

Belmont is big, but even on the biggest races days there seem to be acres of space in the cavernous Grandstand and getting something to eat or drink is little problem. The Clubhouse has several restaurants including the glass-enclosed Garden Terrace Dining Room on the fourth floor with its great view of the track. There is a $2 seating charge, a $10 minimum order and you are required to wear a sports jacket or suit. The Paddock Dining Room on the second floor overlooks the

Artist: **Katie O'Sullivan** *FINAL ADJUSTMENTS* *Courtesy of:* **Osborne Studio Gallery**

paddock (naturally!), while the Belmont Cafe on the first floor offers lighter fare and also breakfast for those who like to get up early and watch the horses go through their morning paces. On weekends its best to reserve, so call ahead on (516) 488 1740. There's also a food court with a choice of fast food snacks and the backyard picnic area for you to bring your own picnic. There are bars throughout the complex on all levels, some as long as your mother- in- law's last visit!

If you happen to be in New York City during the winter, from December to early March, and are desperate for some action, you could spend an afternoon at Aqueduct. which is not that far from Manhattan in Jamaica (Long Island that is!). It's probably easiest to go by subway - take the 'A' train to the Old Aqueduct station and pick up a free bus to the track. The big "A" will always be a favourite with some Noo Yawkers, but it's really a bit like the all-weather at Lingfield on a cold, wet January day. Come to think of it, you should be where anyone else with a bit sense in the Big Apple has already gone - to Florida!

New York City Local Favourites

For New York City, you've really got to be in the heart of the action, and that means mid-town Manhattan. Shopping at Saks, Bergdorff-Goodman or Brooks Brothers on Fifth Avenue, taking in a concert at Carnegie Hall or seeing a show at Radio City Music Hall, it's all right here. Put a bit of breathing space between you and the skyscrapers by taking a stroll through Central Park (by day, please!) and drop down to Greenwich Village or SoHo at night for some great dining, drinking and music. The flagship of Manhattan hotels is of course the Plaza Hotel (212 546 5493) at Central Park South and Fifth Avenue, made famous by scores of movies - remember Lisa Minelli and Dudley Moore in "Arthur"? If you find the tariff for the night a bit steep, try lunch in the Palm Court instead or sample a few oysters Rockefeller in the Oyster Bar downstairs.

Sunday lunch could take you to the Tavern on the Green in Central Park; it's a rambling, way-over-the-top sort of place but

lots of fun. A visit to Rockefeller Plaza is a must and the cafe overlooking the skating rink in the late autumn and winter is a great place to people watch over lunch. In the evening dine and dance in art deco style in the magnificent Rainbow Room - a great way to blow your winnings. Late night hunger pangs can be satisfied at one of the many delis around town; try Wolfs Famous Delicatessen on Sixth Avenue where the wafer thin roast beef is piled high on rye. Wherever you stay in New York, go out in the morning to one of the many local diners for breakfast where a couple of dollars will get you eggs sunny side up or easy over with your bottomless cup of coffee. New York offers an incredible choice when it comes to hotels of every size and description. Wouldn't it be better to stay in a place that offers some character with a convenient location? For some Edwardian elegance and connections to the New York literati try the Algonquin (212 840 6800) on West 44th street. The Carlisle (212 744 1600) on Madison Avenue is a real gem and only one block from Central Park. Although it has a mere 60 rooms The Lowell (212 838 1400) on East 63rd Street has working fireplaces to enjoy in its bedrooms and art deco elegance. For a great afternoon tea and fine views over Central Park go to The Pierre (212 838 8000) on famous Fifth Avenue.

SARATOGA

The song might say "I like New York in June", but you will love Saratoga in August. That's the month that this sleepy Victorian spa town in upstate New York is transformed into the racing centre of North America. Virtually the whole of the Big Apple is transported three hundred miles north to escape the swelter of the city in summer, joined by many racing professionals and enthusiasts from around the world attracted by the quality of racing, sporting art exhibitions and summer yearling sales. There has been racing at Saratoga since 1863 and the racetrack just like the town itself oozes Victorian charm.

Saratoga is just under an hour's drive north of Albany in upper New York state and is easily reached from New York City or western New York using the New York Thruway to Exit 24 at Albany, then the Northway (87) to Exit 14 and Route 9P to just

Artist: **Gill Parker** **CAPTAIN LEO & LUCKS LADY DIANE** *Courtesy of:* **Lord & Lady Baden Powell**

outside the track entrance. From Vermont or New Hampshire take Route 40 to Schuyerville and Route 29 to Saratoga. When you arrive, $5 will get you trackside parking but it's only $2 in the main parking areas where many pack a picnic and barbecue and have a tailgate party.

A great way to start the day is to have breakfast on the Clubhouse porch and watch the early morning workouts. Admission is free and breakfast is served between 7:00 and 9:30 am every racing day. Expert commentators describe the training sessions; afterwards you can hop on a tram for a free tour of the barn area or catch the Paddock show and starting gate demonstration.

A holiday atmosphere pervades Saratoga, with lots of people bringing their fold-up chairs and coolers into the track to sit among the tall pine trees, listening to the strains of a Dixieland band while watching the betting shows and races on TV monitors slung from the trees. It costs only $2 to get into the track, or $4 for the Clubhouse with children under 12 admitted free. To be sure of a seat overlooking the course it's best to reserve one in advance - $6 in the Clubhouse and $4 for the Grandstand. Write before July 1st to Saratoga Reserved Seats, PO Box 030257, Elmont, NY USA 11003 Tel: (718) 641 4700. A few Grandstand seats do go on sale each morning at the track entrance from 8:00 am, or you can buy them the night before at the Holiday Inn in the centre of Saratoga.

Any day at Saratoga is a great day, even though it's just as hard as any other place to pick a winner. Racing starts at the end of July and runs through to the Labour Day bank holiday which is the first Monday in September - six days a week (Tuesday's are 'dark' days). The quality of the racing is excellent with a top handicap or group race almost every day. Highlights of the meeting include the Group 1 Whitney Handicap and Sword Dancer Invitation Handicap and the Travers Stakes for three year olds over a mile and a quarter run towards the end of August. Thrown in here and there are also some steeplechases, just to make things even more interesting if you're a jumping fan at heart! If you have an hour or so to spare before racing, a visit to the racing museum

near the main entrance is also a good bet.

Saratoga offers a wide choice of fast food outlets and you can get just about anything you want from steaks to grits and ice cream. There are also several restaurants and bars from which to choose including the Turf Terrace, Club Terrace, Carousel Restaurant and Lounge, Paddock Tent and At The Rail Pavilion most of which should be reserved in advance and carry seating charges. Call Service America (718) 529 8700 before July 20 or (518) 587 5070 during the race meeting.

Saratoga may be very laid back, but America does insist on a little formality with its racing and Gentlemen are expected to wear suits or sports jackets in certain areas such as Box Seats, the Turf Terrace and the At The Rail Pavilion. Show up here in shorts or jeans (even designer labels) and you will be turned away! The rest of the course is a lot more relaxed, but you're supposed to keep on your shoes and shirts at all times - that goes for the ladies too!

Saratoga Local Favourites

Saratoga Springs is extremely busy during the entire month of August when the racing community descends en masse, many people staying in the same place every year. If you want to stay right in town then it is advisable to book as early as possible - up to a year before you visit! One top-notch hostelry right in Saratoga is the Ramada Renaissance (518 584 4000). With demand so high for accommodation, it's not surprising that the prices are also high compared with other places not that far away. After taking in a day's racing you could do a neat escape for the night to the cool mountains in neighbouring Vermont. There are lots of great inns here, especially around Woodstock, but the Rutland Inn is a real gem in the sleepy town of the same name and it's just under an hour away. There are also many hotels in New York's state capital of Albany, just a half hour south, as well as small towns such as Ithica, the home of Cornell University, in the Finger Lakes region. A visit here could also include a trip to a winery to sample some of the local tipple - some of it surprisingly good.

Artist: **Heather St Clair Davis FINAL BEND, SARATOGA** *Courtesy of:* **Frost & Reed**

Racing in Florida

When the temperature dips on the late Autumn, sensible North American racing folk pack their binoculars and forward their Daily Racing Form to the sunny climes of the sunshine state of Florida. Decades before Godolphin decided to experiment by wintering their horses in the Arabian Gulf, American trainers and owners moved their horses here and raced them under the waving palms. Racing in Florida is centred around the Miami area and the two tracks which host the main winter season are Hialeah and Gulfstream Park. If you do end up near Miami at other times of the year, you could also catch some thoroughbred action at Calder, just south west of the city, where racing is held from the end of May.

HIALEAH PARK

Built in the 1920s when Miami first took off as a winter tourist destination with Northerners wishing to escape the snow and winter, Hialeah has bags of atmosphere. The complex of buildings was built in mock 16th-century French Mediterranean style, with lots of arches and red tiled roofs. They are surrounded by lush tropical gardens and, fringed by palm trees, the course itself contains a lake with a resident flock of flamingos which usually explodes into flight when the starting gates burst open, signalling the start of a race. Hialeah in the 1950s saw such greats as Eddie Arcaro riding Nashua and Bold Ruler to victory, followed by one Willie Shoemaker on board Northern Dancer and Buckpasser a few years later - the very stuff of legend.

The course is located at 2200 East 4th Avenue, Hialeah, Florida, USA 33011. Tel: (305) 885 8000. Michael Mackey is General Manager, while Stephen Brunetti is Director of Racing. There is lots of regularly updated information on Hialeah's web site: www.hialeahpark .com.

Hialeah is only 5 minutes north of Miami International Airport and is easily reached via highway I-95 by car. On weekends you can take a bus from Miami Beach, or any day from Broward or Palm Beach use Metro Rail right to the door, which also gives you free admission and a free ride home! Parking costs from $1 in the general grandstand to $4 for valet parking at the Clubhouse.

Admission is only $2 to the Grandstand, $4 to the Clubhouse. If you go during the week, it's half price and on opening and closing day, it's free! At other times, save those tickets to Panther, Marlin and Heat games as well as many movie ticket stubs as they also give you free admission. Programmes are only $1, or $2 if you want the full simulcast card to bet on televised races from other tracks, including the Dubai World Cup and the Kentucky Derby.

Racing is held at Hialeah almost every day over a two month period from the middle of March to the third week in May with a nine race card during the week, ten races on weekends and eleven on big stakes days. Thursdays after the first week in April are usually 'dark'. Highlights of the meeting are the Widener Handicap at the end of March, the Kentucky Derby trial Flamingo Stakes for three-year olds in early April, won by such racing greats as Chief's Crown and Seattle Slew, and the Turf Cup a few weeks later. There's a special breakfast at Hialeah on Flamingo day which is the biggest day of the year.

If you're wondering who those people are in the private boxes, well they've rented them for the whole season, paying anywhere from $200 to $600 to entertain their friends and guests. If you strike it lucky on the Superfecta, why not splash out and join the Turf Club at $350 single or $600 double and enjoy your cocktails in the stylish surroundings of its private bar and restaurant. Otherwise there are lots of bars, cafes, restaurants and fast food outlets to satisfy your thirst or appetite throughout the Grandstand or Clubhouse. If you need any information on how to place your bet, a taxi or hotel, or directions, check with any of the Customer Service Centres. The course also provides a variety of children's entertainment as well, including a video game room, carousel and bouncy castle as well as puppet shows

Artist: **D M Dent** COLOURS _Courtesy of:_ **The Artist**

and pony rides on certain days.

With the Florida sun blazing down and just a gentle breeze to keep the palms in motion, there's no doubt that racing at Hialeah is excellent value for money.

GULFSTREAM PARK

While it may not have the charm or character of Hialeah, there is some seriously good racing at Gulfstream and it holds the prime time of Florida racing when the weather is at its worst in the rest of North America. Its lush, tropical setting also makes Gulfstream one of the world's most beautiful courses and it offers a variety of entertainments and a great day out in the sunshine for the serious or casual racegoer.

Gulfstream is located in Hallandale, between Fort Lauderdale and Miami and it's very handy for both places using the I-95, US 1 and Hallandale Beach Boulevard. You could use either Miami International or Ft Lauderdale/Hollywood International airports to reach your destination.

For information write to Gulfstream Park, 901 South Federal Highway, Hallandale, Florida, USA 33009. Tel: (954) 454 7000. Fax: (954) 454 7827. E mail: marketing@gulfstreampark.com.

Gulfstream holds its major meeting of the year from early January to the middle of March. There is racing every day except Tuesdays and post time is 1:00 p.m. Admission to the Grandstand is $3 or $5 for the Clubhouse. Both include a free programme and parking. As many trainers use the Florida racing season as a prep for the US Triple Crown for three year olds, the highlight of season at Gulfstream is the Grade 1 Florida Derby held in the middle of March. It carries a purse in excess of $750,000 and usually attracts some top members of the classic generation.

Artist: **Harry Matthews ONE MILE ROUND** *Courtesy of:* **The Artist**

Artist: **Harry Matthews SECRETARIAT** *Courtesy of:* **The Artist**

There are three gourmet dining rooms to satisfy your hunger, two in the Clubhouse and one in the Turf Club, all with terraced seating for a view of the track. There is also a large, air-conditioned (of course!) cafeteria in the Grandstand as well as no fewer than 21 other restaurants and snack bars here and 14 bars.

Florida Favourites

There's no shortage of places to stay, eat or drink in South Florida, after all it has been the favourite sun destination for North Americans for almost a century now. First time visitors might be surprised at the amount of Spanish that is spoken everywhere, but it gives Miami its unique flavour as the major gateway to Central and South America and provides the Latino punch in the pina colada. Two great centres of interest are the Art Deco revival area of Miami Beach and the laid-back delights of Key West, a hundred and odd miles to the south. Both are sure bets for accommodation, food, drink and fun people-watching.

Handy for either Hialeah or Gulfstream are several top notch hostelries including the Turnberry Isle Resort (305) 932 6200 on West Country Club Drive and just 10 minutes from the track, the Sheraton Bal Harbour (305) 865 7511 on Collins Avenue about 20 minutes away in Bal Harbor, and the Marriott Harbor Beach (954) 525 4000 and Pier 66 Hyatt Regency (954) 525 6666 both in Fort Lauderdale, a half hour away. Closer to the track, in fact only five minutes away and a bit less expensive, is the Hollywood Beach Clarion Hotel (954) 459 1900 on South Ocean Drive. The nice people there also give discounts to people connected with racing. There are many top notch restaurants in the Miami area and just a few that come highly recommended are: Manero's on East Hallandale Beach Boulevard (954) 456 1000; Chef Allen's (305) 935 2900 on NE 29th Avenue in North Miami Beach, Las Brisas (954) 923 1500 on Surf Road in Hollywood or Joe's Stone Crabs (305) 673 0365 on Buskin Set in Miami Beach. If you need any advice on where to stay or what to do close to the racing action you could contact either the Greater Miami Convention & Visitors Bureau Tel: (305) 539 3000 or that of Fort Lauderdale (954) 765 4466.

Florida really does have everything for the visitor - sun, sand and lots to see. If you have time to spare, take the Tagmeme Trail through the Everglades to the west coast and collect some sea shells on Signable Island. Of course if the kids are along on the trip you won't be able to leave the sunshine state without a stop off at Disney World in Orlando. Actually, big kids seem to like it too!

Racing in Kentucky

Kentucky is the spiritual home of racing in America. This is Bluegrass Country and perhaps the most important breeding place for top notch thoroughbreds on the continent. The annual Keeneland Sales attract horse people with fat wallets from all over the world and yearlings sold here go on to fame and glory in most parts of the globe. Of course the racing is top notch here, but just to tour around the countryside following mile after mile of white fencing around the stud farms is the experience of a lifetime for those who love horses and racing, a feeling similar to that found around Newmarket or in much of Ireland.

CHURCHILL DOWNS

There are five racetracks in Kentucky but the daddy of them all is Churchill Downs, home of the Kentucky Derby, held on the first Saturday in May and the first leg of the US triple crown for three year-olds. Around one hundred and forty thousand people pack the Downs on Derby Day and as the first strains of My Old Kentucky Home waft over the crowd as the horses come out to parade for the big race, spirits and emotions run high. This is mint julep time, when everyone can be a Kentucky Colonel for the day. Louisville lies on the banks of the Ohio River and is about an hour's flying time from Chicago, just under two hours from New York and about four from Los Angeles and is served by many different airlines so there isn't much problem getting there.

The world famous twin spires of Churchill Downs can be found at 700 Central Avenue, Louisville, Kentucky, USA 40208. Tel: (502) 636 4400. Fax: (502) 636 4430. Web site: kentuckyderby.com. The track first opened in 1875 and has one of the longest and most illustrious histories in the annals of the American turf and the Derby has been held here every year since.

The Kentucky Derby is actually a week long affair, with many other activities going on. For early risers there's 'Dawn at the Downs' where you can breakfast track-side each day and watch the contenders and other horses go through their morning workouts. There are special jockeys autograph sessions, the 'Festival in the Field' concerts with rock bands, handicapping contests and seminars and backstretch tours, just to mention a few. Away from the track, all of Louisville gets into the swing with hot air balloon races, one of the largest firework displays on the continent and a steamboat race down the Ohio River - all part of the Kentucky Derby Festival.

Like most tracks in North America, admission to Churchill Downs on racing days won't break the bank, but on Derby and Oaks days general admission rises to $30 and $15 respectively. If you wish to sit down anywhere it's best to reserve a seat ahead of time - contact the course for details; prices range from $42 for a seat in the First Floor Grandstand Bleachers on Derby Day to $4,400 for an eight seater box in the Clubhouse. On Oaks day there are 12,000 bleacher seats available free in the infield on a first-come, first-served basis. A great tradition of the Oaks and Derby days is the tailgate party which sees 80,000 people enjoying their barbecues and beer in the forty acres of the infield. The main grandstand area has many bars and restaurants for those non-tailgaters and a mint julep on Derby day will cost you about $5, but that's not bad because you get

Artist: **Jonathan Trowell** **BUSINESS AS USUAL** *Courtesy of:* **Osborne Studio Gallery**

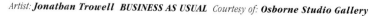

to keep the souvenir glass!

Of course the Kentucky Derby week is the highlight of the year at Churchill Downs, but the track stages many more days racing in both the Spring and the Autumn. The Spring meeting covers abut 48 days racing, from the end of April until the end of June. Race days are normally Wednesday through Sunday, all week during Derby Week, and with a few Mondays and Tuesdays thrown in. The Autumn meeting has 24 days racing held daily except Mondays and runs for the month of November. Post time is normally 3:00 pm on weekdays in the Spring and 1:00 on weekends and holidays but on Kentucky Derby and Oaks days the first race is moved up to 11:30 am. The Autumn meeting has a daily 1:00 pm start, except on Thanksgiving (the third Thursday in November) and closing weekend when it is brought forward to 11:30 am. No excuses now to miss the daily double!

In the Spring, the annual 'Run for the Roses' is just the icing on the cake of a whole week of great racing here which kicks off the Saturday of the week before with the Derby Trial stakes, the last prep race for the big event itself and runs through the Kentucky Oaks for three year old fillies on Derby eve Friday. Each of these and other graded races are championships in their own right. If all of this flat racing is a bit much for those who prefer the jumps, take heart and stick around for Churchill Downs annual Steeplechase Racing day on Sunday at the end of June. Three jump races are part of a ten race card including the $100,000 Grade 1 Hard Scuffle Steeplechase.

Kentucky has several other racetracks which host racing at other times of the year. Keeneland at Lexington of course also holds the annual summer yearling sales in July and is the centre for breeding; you could spend days or weeks visiting famous stud farms such as Gainesway, Shadwell Stud, Darby Dan Farm, Calumet Farm, the Kentucky Horse Center or Spendthrift Farm. Tours can often be arranged if you enquire ahead of time.

Kentucky Local Favourites

Getting around Louisville can be an experience in itself. For something different, why not hop on a horse drawn carriage for a tour by Kentucky Carriage (802) 944 6065 or by horse drawn trams by Louisville Horse Trams (502) 581 0100. There are lots of choices of places to stay in Louisville. The Aleksander House B&B on First Street (502) 637 4985 might be the cosy spot for the November racing at Churchill Downs as it features open fireplaces, gourmet breakfasts and four-poster beds in an old Victorian house. The Camberley Brown Hotel on West Broadway (502) 583 1234 is much larger with 300 four-star rooms. Another Victorian house hotel is the Columbine Inn (502) 635 5000 on South Third Street, where you can sit on the porch overlooking the gardens. The Inn at The Park on South Fourth Street (502) 637 6930 also offers Victorian elegance with your B&B.

Within walking distance right downtown are a host of eateries. You could go for a pizza and beer with some live entertainment at Bearno's by the Bridge on West Main Street (502) 584 7437 or if seafood is your choice try Joe's Crab Shack on River Road (502) 568 1171 which is loud, lively and a lot of fun. A bit more up-market is the Bristol Bar & Grille at Riverfront Plaza (502) 562 0158 serving American and international cuisine; slightly more relaxed and reasonable is Deke's Marketplace Grill on West Market Street (502) 584 8337. Right on the river you can dine aboard the Star of Louisville at West River Road (502)

581 7827 or on the decks of Towboat Annies River Cafe (502) 589 2010 with its great view of the Ohio River.

If you'd like to take home a souvenir of your visit to Kentucky, why not stop off at The Festival Gallery on Fourth Avenue in Louisville (502) 581 1986 which stocks a wide range of racing art on the Derby and its heroes. Another place to relive some memories and pick up some memorabilia is the Kentucky Derby Museum (502) 637 1111 which has three floors of exhibits on thoroughbred racing and the Derby itself, as well as a gift shop.

If you need any information on where to stay or what to do, contact the Louisville Convention & Visitors Bureau, 400 South First Street, Louisville, Kentucky, USA 40202. Tel:(502) 584 2121 or visit their web site at www.louisville-visitors.com.

Racing in California

Southern California's normally benign climate makes racing a year round pleasure. Don't worry about earthquakes or the El Nino effect, here in lotus land some of North America's top trainers such as D Wayne Lukas ply their trade, sometimes venturing farther afield to pluck top prize money. Actually it's surprising that they actually leave at all given the level of racing right at home. This is a spot to go racing under the palms in first class comfort before you head off to Malibu for some surfing, tour the big movie company's lots, see the original Disneyworld, shop on Rodeo Drive or cruise down Sunset Strip. California's got it all, and more! This State actually has nine racecourses and if you were visiting San Francisco for example it would be a shame not to not to put on a few exactors at Golden Gate Fields, or do the daily double at Del Mar in San Diego. The two top bets though are Hollywood Park and Santa Anita in the Los Angeles area.

SANTA ANITA

Racing at Santa Anita goes back to 1907 but it was in 1933 that the present course was built and, while many changes have been made over the years, it still maintains its classic Art Deco design and park-like setting.

Santa Anita Park covers 320 acres and is situated in the suburb of Arcadia, about 14 miles north east of downtown Los Angeles and 30 miles from LA International Airport. Any one of a number of freeways will connect to the Interstate 210 Freeway to take you there by car; exit at Baldwin and turn right. When you arrive there is a choice of three parking areas: General Parking is $3, Preferred (a bit closer to the track) is $5, or you can have someone else park your car for $8 for Valet Parking.

You can contact the track at Los Angeles Turf Club, PO Box 808, Arcadia, California, USA 91066-0808. Tel: (626) 7223. Fax: (626) 574 9860. E mail: sainfo@santaanita.com. Web site: santaanita.com.

Two race meetings are held here each year. The Oak Tree meeting runs for six to seven weeks in October and November, with about 32 days of racing. The longer winter/spring meeting traditionally opens just after Christmas and runs through mid-April. The Grade 1 Santa Anita Derby is California's 'Spring Classic' for three year-olds and is a major stepping stone to the Kentucky Derby. It is held on the first Saturday in April, exactly a month before the Derby, and many winners such as

Triple Crown hero Affirmed have gone on to win the Run for the Roses after success in California. Other top races are the Santa Monica Handicap for older fillies and mares, also a Grade 1 race run at the end of January, the half million dollar Strub Stakes in early February, the San Luis Obispo Handicap over a mile and a half on the turf for four year olds and up in mid February and the $1 million Santa Anita Handicap over a mile and a quarter in early March. Santa Anita hosted the Breeders' Cup in 1984 and 1993 and will probably do so again, a testimonial to this excellent venue.

There are three levels, and prices, of admission to Santa Anita. A $5 General Admission allows you to wander around the Grandstand with its excellent views of the track and finishing line, the Infield, with its picnic grounds and playground for the kids, the Paddock Room which is the ground floor of the grandstand with lots of betting, food and beverage facilities as well as the Paddock Gardens around the parade ring. The Club House will set you back $8.50 and also has excellent facilities including dining tables overlooking the first turn on the track after the finish line. At the upper end of the scale at $10 on weekdays and $15 on weekends and holidays, the Turf Club is quite luxurious if a bit more formal, with reserved seats at the finish line and fine dining while you put on your bets. Reserved Club House and Grandstand seats are available only at busy weekends and holidays. If you go into the Grandstand and wish to upgrade to other areas you can do so by going to the Reserved Ticket Booth and Terrace Gate for the Club House or the Turf Club. Children under 17 are allowed in free if accompanied by an adult, as are those over 65 on certain special days. Box seats holding four to six people are also available for hire and most include a private television set. If you would like to reserve one, call (626) 574 6400.

There is a number of dining rooms and terraces, snack stands and bars located throughout the park. Dining facilities with full-service menus are located in the Club House and Turf Club. The Terrace Food Court, near the main grandstand entrance, feature a variety of self-service food. In the infield at the centre of the track, the Wine Shed offers deli-style food, beer and wines.

Santa Anita runs a number of programmes for people who like racing, including a 'Clocker's Corner' where you can watch the early morning workouts and have a bit of breakfast as well as handicapping classes with experts who will share their wisdom in picking winners. They are all free of charge. In fact if you need any information about anything at the track, check with the Patron Service Desks that are located throughout the grandstand.

HOLLYWOOD PARK

You certainly don't have to be a movie star to visit Hollywood Park, but you might just bump into a few while you are there. The course has been nicknamed "The track of Lakes and Flowers" and you will see why when you step inside. It has a beautifully picturesque setting and a spectacular view of the hills surrounding Hollywood. The movie star connection is in fact a very real one as the Hollywood Turf Club was founded by Jack L Warner of Warner Brothers films in 1938 and its original shareholders included Walt Disney, Bing Crosby and Sam Goldwyn. Always one step ahead of the pack, Hollywood boasts a number of 'firsts' including the introduction of the film patrol camera for use by the stewards in 1941, the first Sunday racing in 1973 and now the first racetrack to have its own casino.

Hollywood Park is to be found just three miles east of Los Angeles International Airport at the intersection of Century Boulevard and Prairie Avenue. Take the 105 or 405 Freeways to get there. If you need to contact the course, write to PO Box 369, Inglewood, California, USA 90306-0369, otherwise the street address is 1050 South Prairie Avenue, Inglewood, California USA 90301-4197. Tel: (310) 419 1500. Fax: (310) 419 8022. A virtual visit to their Web site can be arranged at www.hollywoodpark.com.

Hollywood gives you a choice of three different places to watch the racing, dine or have a drink. General admission to the Grandstand and parade ring is only $6, while you could pay $9.50 to step up into the Clubhouse. For those wishing a little bit more luxury, try the Turf Club which carries a $25 admission charge. Parking is all free no matter where you go and you get a free programme on entry. If you arrive by foot or bus, they knock $1.50 off these prices. Anyone under 30 years old gets in on Friday nights for only $1 and if you're over 62 you can attend on Wednesdays and Thursdays for a $3 discount. If you bring the kids, they are free of charge under 17 years and there is lots to keep them occupied with a playground and carousel at the North Park. Once you're inside, Hollywood offers a choice of over 30,000 seats in the grandstand and clubhouse, with another 3,000 in the Turf Club. There is also a wide variety of places to eat and drink, from a hot dog and beer to a four course meal in the Winners Circle dining room in the Clubhouse.

Hollywood has seen some notable stars of the equine variety over the years including the great Citation, the perennially tough John Henry and champion Affirmed who became racing's first $2 million winner in 1979 with a victory in the Hollywood Gold Cup. This was also the course that hosted the very first Breeders' Cup meeting in 1984, the first of three held here, when 65,000 people jammed the place and bet almost $12 million! Hollywood completed a $100 million expansion in 1994 which included a golf and sports centre and the Hollywood Casino where you can play poker, blackjack or bingo as well as bet on the simulcast races from as far away as Hong Kong - 24 hours a day of gambling pleasure.

There are two seasons of racing at Hollywood Park, from the end of April to July and November through December. Daily post times are 1:00 pm except Friday when racing moves to the evening with the first race at 7:00 pm. The big race of the spring and summer meeting is the $1 million Hollywood Gold Cup staged at the end of June with a fine supporting card. Some legendary horses have won the Gold Cup over the years, including the great Cigar, Round Table, Swaps, Citation and Sea Biscuit. In the Autumn there is a three day Turf Festival held over the Thanksgiving Weekend that features six group races on the grass and attracts turf stars from across North America and Europe - a sure winner. There are lots of stars in Hollywood, but Hollywood Park has to be one of the biggest and brightest!

Southern California Local Favourites

There are so many things to see and do in southern California, you could spend a lifetime here - small wonder so many people move here for the good life. Hollywood Park is only ten minutes from the beach and 20 minutes from Beverly Hills and there are thousands of hotel rooms close at hand.

Despite the traffic jams on the freeways, you really do need a car here to get around. Handy for either racetrack, the Beverly Wilshire Hotel (310) 275 5200 on Wilshire Boulevard in Beverly Hills offers the ultimate in luxury and star spotting possibilities. Also firmly in the top bracket are the Beverly Hills Hotel (310) 276 2251 also on Wilshire and the Radisson Plaza (310) 546 7511 in Manhattan Beach. A bit further away from Los Angeles, you could try the Ritz-Carlton (310) 823 1700 on Admiralty Way in Marina Del Ray. If you wanted to save a bit of money to play the ponies, try the budget priced Embassy Suites Hotel (310) 215 1000 on Airport Boulevard in LA or Motel 6 (310) 419 1234 on West Century. If you need any assistance with local information or hotels, there is a tourist information bureau in Los Angeles Airport

There is a wide choice of hotels that are all handy for a trip to Santa Anita, including the Doubletree Hotel (626) 792 2727, Ritz-Carlton Huntingdon Hotel(626) 568 3900 or Hilton Hotel (626) 577 1000, which are all in Pasadena. In Arcadia where the track is located you could stay at the Embassy Suites (626) 445 8525, the Hampton Inn (626) 574 5600 or the Santa Anita Inn (626) 446 5211. Arcadia also has a good choice of restaurants. You could try Anthony's for Italian food (626) 446 3171, go to Peppers (626) 446 5529 or the Arroyo

(626) 821 2021 for Mexican specialties. If you like steak and seafood (known here as 'Surf and Turf') drop in to The Derby (626) 447 2430. A taste of the orient can be found at Tokyo Wako for Japanese (626) 351 8963 or the Panda Inn for Chinese in Pasadena (626) 793 7300. For more information about the Santa Anita area, call the Pasadena Convention and Visitors Bureau on (626) 795 9311.

If shopping is your game, you can do it 'til you drop and rub shoulders with the movie stars on Rodeo Drive in Beverly Hills. The Farmer's Market on West 3rd Street in Hollywood is also lots of fun and probably a lot less expensive, as is the Olivera Street area downtown with its Mexican-style marketplace with lots of shops, artisans and restaurants. Little Tokyo, the largest Japanese area in the USA is not far away, on First and San Pedro Streets, as is Chinatown, north of Sunset Boulevard between Almeda and Hill streets. While you're here you should make a pilgrimage and wish upon a star at Disneyland (714) 999 4565, stroll along the Hollywood Walk of Fame on Hollywood Boulevard and Vine Streets or take the tour at Universal Studios (818) 622 3801. If you've got time, hop on down to San Diego and play a few horses at Del Mar or cross the desert to Las Vegas for unlimited action, day and night.

Artist: **_David Trundley_ TROTTERS** _Courtesy of:_ **_The Artist_**

Racing in Australia

The Australian horse race that everyone in the world seems knows best is the Melbourne Cup. Held at the beginning of November at Flemington Racecourse in the city that gives its name to the prize, the Cup is the event that caps a month long series of races and brings the entire country to a halt for the day. In antipodean terms it's Royal Ascot, The Derby and Kentucky's Run for the Roses all rolled into one big blast of fun.

From an international perspective, it is also a race that more and more trainers and horses are taking a tilt at from far afield. At face value, the conditions for foreign contenders are horrendous - a long and tiring trip probably half way around the world to a different hemisphere, and then you face a two mile handicap probably carrying near top weight against a field of twenty or so top locals who have been primed to their best condition for weeks. But an Irish horse lifted the prize a few years ago and the names of Vintage Crop and Dermot Weld will forever be etched in Australian racing history.

For the foreign visitor the equine action leading to the Cup begins a month earlier at Caulfield with the 1,000 Guineas and Caulfield Cup, moves to Moonee Valley for the WS Cox Plate and continues at Flemington for the Victoria Derby. All of these races are major local events that bring out the Aussie punters in droves and provide a holiday atmosphere to some pretty top-notch racing action.

There are about twenty major racecourses in this sports loving nation and they are spread from Tasmania to the Northern Territory and across to Western Australia. The foreign punter though, can find many a day's pleasure in those located in and around Sydney and in Melbourne, which has four courses including Flemington, Caulfield, Sandown and Moonee Valley, where they hold night racing under the lights.

The thoroughbred racing season stretches year round in Australia, with action both over the sticks and on the flat. The major flat races that will catch the visitor's eye, though, take place between the middle of August and the end of May, which is summer 'Down Under'. As the breeding season flip-flops with the Northern Hemisphere there is also a growing business in shipping stallions from Europe and North America to the land of Oz to do double hemisphere duty. There are many stud farms around the major Australian racing and training centres and they are well worth a day out in themselves. If you want more information on the breeding side or stud farms, contact Thoroughbred Breeders Australia, 571 Queensberry Street, North Melbourne, 3051, Victoria Tel (+613) 9326 3966 Fax (+613) 9326 3866

To get into the mood before you go racing in Australia, try to dig out the video of the film that was made about the Aussie wonder horse, Phar Lap. He won just about everything worth winning in Australia, including the Melbourne Cup in 1930 under record top weight, before being shipped to the USA where his career ended somewhat tragically.

FLEMINGTON RACECOURSE

Flemington is situated about four miles west of the state of Victoria's capital city, Melbourne, next to the Maribyrnong River. It is easily accessible from the city by car or tram and on race days by special trains or by boat along the river. The train arrives upsides the back of the main stands; if you're driving use Entrance A on the opposite side at the junction of the Smithfield and Ballarat roads to enter the large free parking area in the centre of the course; trainers and their horseboxes, and the disabled can use Entrance B, which takes them right next to the stand to the "Birdcage". This is the stabling area where horses are installed before racing and it got its name because it's here that Gentlemen racegoers used to show off their 'birds' or lady friends. You don't have to take your bird these days and it is open to the public.

The track is run by the Victoria Racing Club and can be reached at 400 Epsom Road, Flemington, Australia, 3031. Tel: (03) 9258 4666. Fax: (03) 9258 4605. If you need to get in touch with the track itself call (03) 9371 7171. They also have a helpful website at www.vrc.net. au

Flemington has been the home of the Melbourne Cup since it was first run in 1861 and the race has been run each year here since on the first Tuesday in November. The main course itself is a wide, sweeping ellipse of about a mile and a half in circumference and is used for both flat and hurdle races. There is also a steeplechase course, with all brush fences, used for jump racing. Although it can hold up to 100,000 people (and does on Cup day!) it's a pretty course with a country feel to it. The best viewing of the course is from the Hill Stand opposite the winning post, which has four levels and has full facilities for betting both with the bookmakers the Tote, as well as restaurants, bars and snack bars. The newer Prince of Wales Stand next to it was opened by Prince Charles in 1985. There are also on-course shops selling souvenirs, clothes, books and videos, so you have no excuses not to bring something back for a friend.

Australia is one of the few places in the world outside Britain and Ireland that has private bookmakers on course and you can either bet with them or the Tote. The bookies here have already entered the computer age though, using electronic boards to record the bets. They also take bets by phone from off-course punters.

Although getting into the course on regular race days only costs a few dollars, understandably admission prices do go up a bit when it comes to the big days of racing at Flemington for the four day Melbourne Cup Carnival which features the Cup itself, the Derby and the Oaks. Admission on Cup day with a reserved seat in the Lawn Stand will set you back A$82 (about £34), while admission alone is about A$25 (£10.50). The course offers various package deals which include reserved seats on each of the big race days and a four day package of admission and a reserved seat in the covered Hill Stand will cost you A$197 (£82) for example. The Hill Stand also has two top notch restaurants, The Panorama and The Skyline, but you will have to fork out about A$925 (£385) for a Panorama/Skyline 4-day package (Single days N/A).

Melbourne Cup day brings out all kinds of people to the racetrack and offers lots of fun and entertainment, a lot like Australia and its people themselves. It's both the formal recognition of a champion in the making and a great excuse to squeeze a few tinnies, put a shrimp on the barby and let your hair down, so no matter how conservatively or crazily you dress to go there, you will be sure to have a good time. Just be sure to say G'day to your neighbour!

Melbourne Favourites

Despite the high rise buildings which first catch the eye, Melbourne still retains much of its Victorian architecture and this gives the city a pleasant, old fashioned feel at street level. You can 'go walkabout' here as there are lots of pedestrian malls with interesting shopping and a wide variety of restaurants and bars. The Sovereign Hill area of the city is a place where you can go to relive the city's gold rush days. If you are a real sports fan, be sure to visit the Melbourne Cricket Ground, which is Australia's biggest sports stadium and can hold 100,000 spectators. It was built for the 1956 Olympics which were held here and also contains a fascinating Cricket Museum. Not far away from Melbourne is the Yarra Valley which is famous the world over for its vineyards and wineries, some of which you can visit to sample the tipple before its exported. For those who'd like to see the local wildlife a bit closer, take a trip to Philip Island where you can cuddle a Koala, try to catch a Kangaroo or just watch the seals or penguins at play.

To find a bed for the night in Melbourne, you could try either the Grand Southern Cross Hotel (03 9653 0221) or The Sofitel Melbourne (03 9653 0000). Accommodation is also available at the popular Crown Towers Hotel (+613) 9292 8888 which is part of the Casino. Other possibilities are The Windsor (03 9653 0653) or the Hotel Como (03 9824 0400) in South Yarra. If you want to step out of an evening and sample some local brew, try the Victoria Hotel in Albert Park, the Palace Hotel, a favourite local hang-out, or the Fawkner Club which has an open-air courtyard. Restaurants abound in this city, with a wide choice of different types of cuisine. The Melbourne Oyster Bar

(03 6702745) on King Street will do for seafood lovers, or they could try The Last Aussie Fishcaf (03 6991942) on Park Street in South Melbourne. For a taste of the orient try the Bamboo House (03 6621565) or the Flower Drum (03 66325313) which are both on Little Bourke Street.

Racing in Japan

If racing in Hong Kong seems all about large amounts of money changing hands, in Japan its more yen than most people can count. Huge crowds generate equally huge betting turnover and that in turn makes for exceptional prize money. The average prize money on offer for each race at top courses like Tokyo rings up well in excess of £100,000. If you were a foreign owner this might seem like the veritable pot of gold, but racing in Japan has long been closed to foreign horses except for a few Group races such as the Japan Cup. There are moves afoot however to open up racing to horses from other countries and this should add some interest for the visiting punter in the future. Japanese breeders have spent the rich pickings at the courses buying some expensive horse flesh for many years and you can go and visit studs such as Shadai Farm.

Japan has ten racecourses run by the Japan Racing Association spread around the country, including two, Tokyo Racecourse and Nakayama, which are near the capital. Racing takes place largely around the weekends from mid-March to mid-June and again from October to the end of the year when the international flavour is added in the form of the Japan Cup. There are also another thirty or so racecourses that are run by local authorities which offer various levels of thoroughbred

Artist: **Susan Crawford PILSUDSKI** *Courtesy of:* **Rosenstiel's**

racing in settings that range from large urban centres to small country courses.

TOKYO RACECOURSE

Tokyo Racecourse, or Fuchu as it's known to local punters, is the Newmarket of Japanese racing. Originally built in 1933, it has been updated and expanded ever since, most recently in 1993, to a commodious complex that attracts equally huge crowds of people when racing is held on Saturdays and Sundays during the season. The course actually lies in the Forest of Fuchu from which it derives its local name and from the stands you get a superb view of the famous Mount Fuji and you will be able to enjoy the racing in complete comfort either live or captured on huge television screens around the park. It's here that they hold the Japanese Derby for local three year-olds in the spring and cap it all off in the autumn with the International Japan Cup which sees horses from all over the world going for glory under their equally famous jockeys.

The General Manager of Tokyo Racecourse can be contacted on. Tel: 423 63 3141. Fax: 423 40 7070. You can visit the Japan Racing Association website, which has information on all the courses they run on www.jait.jrao.ne.jp which will give you the English language version.

To get to the racecourse it's probably best to take the metro underground train. Fuchu-keibaseimonmae Station on the Keio Line which departs from Shinjuku Station has a concourse that directly connects with the racecourse. It takes about thirty minutes to get there from Shinjuku. Alternatively, Fuchi-Honmachi Station also has a direct overhead passageway leading into the track's West Gate.

Basic admission to the course is only Y200 (about £1) which gives you access to all areas of the course except the reserved enclosure. Y500 (£2.50) gives you a reserved seat in the E area, while prices from Y1,500 (£7.50) (C area) to Y3,500 (£17) (S area) will provide you with admission and a reserved seat in various areas of the reserved enclosure. Some of the S reserved seats on the fifth and six floors are in pairs for couples (sounds cosy) and have a built-in TV monitor. The Grandstand can hold a staggering 200,000 people, just to put some scale on things and what's really amazing is that they actually have room to move around, see the horses and place their bets. It's called Memorial 60 as it was completed to commemorate the 60th anniversary of Tokyo Racecourse in 1993 and extended to stretch 460 metres or almost three furlongs - practically the entire length of the home stretch. Small wonder that this is the largest grandstand in the world! The course itself has four tracks. The turf track is the biggest at about a mile and a half around and inside are a dirt track, a steeplechase course (jump fans take note) and a training track. State-of-the-art might be an over-used expression these days but the facilities for fans here really qualify. Two giant Turf Vision screens give you an excellent view of the action down the backstretch and the run to the finish line from any part of the grandstand. There is a large amphitheatre around the paddock so you can check on the condition of the horses before the race. Some of them wear some pretty strange looking headgear, but don't be put off! The winner's circle is a large area directly in front of the grandstand.

There are no fewer than 1,100 closed circuit TV monitors scattered throughout the racecourse and these provide information on the horse's weight (not a bad idea), pari-mutuel odds and dividends, as well as paddock views of the horses and the

racing itself. In the first floor of the basement is a Video Hall with a giant screen. The course has its own video and book store called the PR Corner as well as an FM radio station just for racegoers on track. Try a bit of sushi in the Fast Food Plaza downstairs in the basement or for something a bit more formal there is the Restaurant New Tokyo on the third floor or the Restaurant Hotel Okura on the sixth floor.

No doubt you might come to Fuchu for the Japan Cup in November as it usually attracts a top-notch field of international stars with their owners, trainers and jockeys. Under the guidance of Sir Michael Stoute in 1997 Pilsudski capped an incredible season by doing the Breeders' Cup - Japan Cup double, a truly remarkable achievement for a British horse. The top races of the spring season are the Yushun Himba (Japanese Oaks) for home bred three year old fillies, the Tokyo Yushun (Japanese Derby) for local colts and the NHK Mile Cup which is also open to foreign bred horses. Other Grade 1 races which also attract invited international horses are the Yasuda Kinen over a mile for older horses and the Emperor's Cup for three year olds and up. For National Hunt fans, there is at least one jump race included in the programmes for both spring and autumn, but you'd have to go to Nakayama to see the Japanese version of the Grand National!

While you're here be sure to visit the JRA Racing Museum at the racecourse. It has some incredible hands-on displays where you can experience what it's like to be a jockey riding in a race and shows depicting the world's great races. Go into the Epsom Promenade where they have a 1/50 scale walk-through of Epsom Racecourse, Tokyo's sister course, where British punters can check out a bit of old Blighty. There's lots of things for children of all ages to do here as well, with pony and carriage rides in the infield as well as a miniature railway to take you around. If all this becomes a bit much and you need a bit of peace and quiet to study the form or contemplate zen and the art of motorcycle maintenance, sneak away to the Japanese Garden in the woods behind the paddock.

Tokyo Favourites

There's no shortage of things to see and do in sprawling Tokyo. The Ginza is this city's famous shopping area and most famous landmark for visitors and it's busy both day and night. You might want to leave your cheque book or credit card at home though as many of the imported goods are more expensive here than at home. No wonder Japanese tourists do some hard shopping when they are out of the country on holiday. Still you could just go into some of the big Japanese department stores and enjoy being greeted by the staff with a bow when you enter or take the elevator - that doesn't happen in too many places anywhere else, but it certainly does in Japan! No trip to Japan would be complete without sampling some of the local fare and there are sushi bars dotted around everywhere. If you are daring try a bit of the Fugu. It's a puffer fish and if the chef has left in just a bit of the liver, you won't see the next sunrise! Perhaps a safer bet and often more palatable to western tastes is tepanyaki cooking where your party sits around a horse-shoe table sipping sake while the chef grills prawns or Kobe beef in front of you. Too much sake and the karaoke will no doubt beckon!

Not too far away from the racecourse, there is a number of superior hotels in Shinjuku, all catering to western tastes, including the Hotel Century Hyatt Tokyo (3 3349 0111), the Hotel Park Hyatt Tokyo (3 5322 1234), the Tokyo Hilton (3

3344 5111) and the Keio Plaza InterContinental Tokyo (3 3344 0111). Of course these are just a few of the many possible places to stay and if you wanted something a little bit closer to the Tea House of the August Moon, take a trip outside Tokyo to the countryside and you will have little problem finding a place to leave your shoes at the door. While eminently worthwhile, visiting Japan is certainly not cheap and let's hope you have a few winners at the races to help replenish your wallet!

Racing in Hong Kong

Perhaps it is the counterfoil to their otherwise industrious and conservative natures, but the people of Hong Kong love a punt on the horses and this makes racing, and betting, a big business in this former British colony. Of course it was the Brits who exported their rules and regulations for the Sport of Kings back in the early nineteenth century and thoroughbred racing is organised here by the Hong Kong Jockey Club. You can contact them at 1 Sports Road, Happy Valley, Hong Kong. Tel: (852) 2966 8111. Fax: (852) 2577 9036. E mail: jcinfo@hkjc.org.hk. web site: www.hongkongjockeyclub.com

Some might say sadly not 'Royal' any more, but even though the Union Flag was lowered a few years ago, it's business as usual under the new regime and it will probably see thoroughbred racing spread rapidly throughout China during the coming years. Racing means money, money, money and here the profits from racing not only generate a thriving sport, but are used to support social services and run good causes which directly benefit the local population, including hospitals, clinics, schools, parks and swimming pools. The Jockey Club operates the Tote as well as the local lottery and generates a surplus after taxation of about HK$2 billion per season. Racing here, though, is also a lot of fun and the quality of racing is excellent, with many trainers, horses and jockeys coming from around the world to capture some big prize money.

Hong Kong has two racecourses in Sha Tin and Happy Valley and between them 78 race meetings will be held between early September and late June. Meetings are held most Saturdays and Wednesdays and some Sundays, each attracting an average crowd of 38,500 racegoers on-course who stake several million betting tickets a race meeting. Betting turnover here is the highest in the world per person and added up to a massive HK$81 billion last season. The highlights of the year and probably of most interest to visitors are the Hong Kong International Races which attract leading horses, trainers and jockeys from all over the world.

SHA TIN RACECOURSE

Sha Tin is the modern showpiece of Hong Kong racing, having been built on reclaimed land and opened in 1978. It's here during the first half of December that the big races are held around the course's large sweeping oval. The big date of the year here is the Hong Kong International Races which include the Hong Kong Cup (G1), Hong Kong Mile (G2), Hong Kong Vase (G2) and Hong Kong Sprint (L). Horses competing in these races come from Australia, Europe, New Zealand, Malaysia & Singapore as well as North America, Japan and the United Arab Emirates, so you might be excused if you don't get the form right at first try. Accompanying the race meeting is also a top international sale of thoroughbreds which attracts buyers from almost as far afield. Other highlights of the year include the Hong Kong Derby run in March, the Hong Kong Gold Cup in March and the Queen Elizabeth II Cup held in the middle of May.

Hong Kong prize money is well endowed by the high tote turnover and some of the world's top jockeys are invited to come here to compete for a season or two on a regular basis, while others fly in for the big races.

Located in Hong Kong's New Territories, you can get to Sha Tin from the centre of town very easily by bus, train or taxi. Once there it will cost you HK$10 (about £1 or US$1.60) to get into the course or HK$50 (£5) to get into the Members' Enclosure. If you are a visitor to Hong Kong, take your passport with you if you wish to buy admission to the Members' at the main gate.

Sha Tin hosts a total of about 45 race meetings throughout the season, split between day and night racing. Most are run over the main turf course, but others take place on the all-weather track and a few are mixed all-weather and turf. A nine-race card in the afternoon starts at 1:30 pm, while for a ten-race fixture the first race is moved back to 1:00 pm. Night meetings begin at 6:30 pm and take place on Saturday or Sunday.

Inside the course, which can hold up to 85,000 people, there are lots of restaurants and fast-food stalls to choose from. There are two huge grandstands where you won't have any problem finding a seat, as well as the Club Building overlooking the winning line with a view straight down the finishing straight. A huge colour TV screen also helps the view from ground level. Grandstand 2 connects directly with the railway station, while Grandstand 1 has the parade ring to its rear. There is also a special visitors box for tourists to use, as well as a number of private boxes.

HAPPY VALLEY

Despite its verdant, almost pastoral, name, Happy Valley's situation makes Longchamp or Belmont Park seem way out in the middle of the country. The course is right in the centre of the city, surrounded by tall buildings and making it an absolutely unique urban amphitheatre of equine action. Some have claimed the land on which Happy Valley is situated is the world's most expensive piece of real estate and it would be hard to disagree, judging by the buildings which frame it.

Happy Valley is so close to the centre of Hong Kong that you could just as easily walk there as take a bus, subway train or taxi. Admission follows the same pattern here as Sha Tin at HK$10 (about £1 or US$1.60) to get into the course or HK$50 to get into the Members' Enclosure. Don't forget to take your passport with you to buy admission to the Members' at the main gate. The course also has the usual array of wining and dining possibilities in restaurants and fast food stalls, as well as a visitors' box for tourists. There is a high-rise complex of stands overlooking the straight and the finish line and with a large colour TV screen in the middle of the infield, you won't miss a thing at this relatively tight track. Make sure you back a jockey who knows his way around!

Happy Valley holds about 30 meetings a year, also split between day and night racing and all on the turf. A nine-race card in the afternoon commences at 1:30 pm, while for a ten-race fixture the first race is moved back to 1:00 pm. Night meetings begin at 6:30 pm on Wednesdays and sometimes the odd Tuesday, and an hour later if held on a Saturday.

The course also contains the fascinating Hong Kong Racing Museum situated next to the Happy Valley stand which is well worth a visit if you can spare the time. For those more interested in flexing their credit cards than racing, the Causeway Bay shopping and entertainment complex is just a five minute walk from the course.

Hong Kong Favourites

There is so much choice in Hong Kong, you could easily spend weeks here and still not find your shopping list exhausted. Anything made to measure, from shirts to suits, are an absolute bargain compared with prices anywhere else and once they've got your measurements you can re-order from anywhere in the world (provided your shape stays the same!). If you want a suit try William Cheng (2739 7888) - outstanding value and they can make them in three days! There are hundreds of restaurants to choose from and a lot of the better ones are housed in the plethora of first class hotels that can be found in Hong Kong.

The Excelsior (2837 6840) situated in the harbour front in Causeway Bay is an excellent choice with numerous restaurants. Have a drink in Tutts on the 34th floor for a view that will take your breath away. Another choice is the Mandarin Oriental (2522 0111) for more fine dining, breathtaking views and true elegance. You could also try the Hong Kong Renaissance (2375 1133) or the Hotel Nikko (2739 1111). Closer to Sha Tin, the Regal Riverside Hotel and the Royal Park Hotel also come highly recommended. There is also a large shopping mall in Sha Tin, about a five minute ride from the racecourse.

The pace of Hong Kong is extremely frenetic. Visit the Banking Centre and if you can, go up the Peak in a tram - there's a fantastic harbour-view and find the little bar and restaurant which nestles here - it's an absolute beauty. When arranging a visit to Hong Kong , talk to the major airlines - they offer some tremendous fly and stay deals at some really first class hotels. The flag may have changed in Hong Kong but so much still remains the same - it is a city that is thoroughly recommended.

Racing in Singapore

Racing has been taking place in Singapore since the very first meeting contested a prize of $150 in 1842. The purse was a King's ransom in those days, and little has changed in what is today one of the most modern centres of commerce in the Far East. Prize money is still high in Singapore, a fact which has helped racing attract some of the best flat horses in this part of the world as well as a few globe-trotting European and American thoroughbreds for the year's big races. Racing is organised by the Singapore Turf Club and its an interesting testimonial to the colonial past that members of the public were only allowed to attend their meetings in 1960. Before then the only people allowed in were members and owners. We can only presume that jockeys and trainers were also in attendance!

Things have come along way since then in Singapore and female jockeys were given their licenses in 1981, the same year a new grandstand was built to provide facilities for up to 50,000 people at the Bukit Timah racecourse. The first million dollar (that's Australian dollars) race was held in 1993 and an entirely new $40 million racecourse and training complex was planned, built and opened in 1999 at Kranji, Tel: (65) 879 1000 Fax: (65) 879 1010, in the northern part of Singapore. State of the art technology enables the Singapore punter to get his bet on in what must be one of the most up to date horse racing

emporia in the world. Visit the Singapore Turf Club website at www.turfclub.com.sg if you'd like a tour.

KRANJI RACECOURSE

Kranji Racecourse is a massive new complex about a dozen or so miles from the centre of the city. Those who planned it borrowed the best features from the leading racecourses around the world. The four storey grandstand can hold 30,000 racegoers in comfort, with a fine view of the mile and a quarter, left-handed oval track. The slight incline to the finish line produces some exciting racing. Kranji also has three training tracks providing both turf and fibresand surfaces, as well as modern stables for 1,000 horses. Visiting trainers should take note that their horses are treated like kings here, with their own air-conditioned facilities and stabling that is guarded twenty four hours a day!

Kranji's about 30 minutes from the centre of Singapore and getting there is no problem. The easiest way is probably to take the MRT, the rapid transit system that takes you right to the course and provides links the rest of Singapore. Taxis, a private coach service and public buses also go to the track on race days. If you have a car, there's a multi-storey car park that will take over 2,000 cars and costs S$5.

Racing at Kranji is held at night under the floodlights when it's a bit cooler for punters and horses alike with meetings held on Wednesdays, Saturdays and the occasional Sunday throughout the year. Post time is 7:00 pm for the first race, except on Sundays when it's moved up to 5:30 pm. About 25,000 usually show up to take in the local action as well as live telecasts of racing from across the straights in Malaysia and Perth in Australia. Racing from other venues starts a bit earlier in the afternoon and it's best to check the local papers for exact times. There's a giant outdoor video screen, as well as monitors dotted throughout the grandstand. Admission to the lower grandstand will set you back a mere five Singapore dollars, while ten will buy you air-conditioned comfort upstairs. If you are just visiting Singapore, you can buy admission to the exclusive Hibiscus Room on the third level for 20 Singapore dollars, but you'll need your passport handy when buying the ticket. You won't have any problem getting a bet on the tote as there are over 400 windows, as well as electronic ACCESS terminal points. Electronic dividend boards constantly update the latest odds. Four food courts are located in the grandstand for snacks and drinks and if you want to dine a bit more elegantly try the restaurants in the Club level.

As you will find out, Singapore has a bit of an authoritarian streak in its culture. It wasn't that long ago that the government banned chewing gum and going racing is no exception. At Kranji there are dress codes that should be followed: no shorts, singlets (funny Australian sleeveless shirts) or slippers in the lower and upper grandstands; those attending in the Gold Card members, Hibiscus Room and Owners are not allowed to wear shorts, collarless t-shirts, slippers (best left with the dog at home anyway) sandals or jeans. Don't plan on bringing the kids either as you have to be 18 years old to get in to attend racing in Singapore.

Despite a bit of Ascot-like fussiness about dress, it's well worth leaving your slippers at home to go racing. The standard of horses competing here is getting better all the time and one local jockey, Saimee, has become a local superstar. He won the inaugural running of the S$3 million Singapore Airlines

International Cup held in March on the locally trained Ouzo, just beating Francois Doumen's Jim and Tonic. Other highlights of the racing calendar include the Queen Elizabeth II Cup which is held on the annual Ladies Day in August. The very first running was won by Lester Piggott on Jumbo Jet back in 1972. The Singapore Derby in May is open to international entries as are the Singapore Cup in September, Raffles Cup in October and the Singapore Gold Cup held later that month and worth over S$1 million.

Singapore Favourites

A visit to Singapore evokes the romance of its founder Raffles (337 1886), the intrepid British colonial officer who first developed this part of the Malay peninsula as a centre for trade. Raffles the man has been immortalised by the hotel of the same name, although today you may have to look a little harder to find that famous verandah on which to sip your pink gin as the property is now overshadowed by the looming skyscrapers that offer testimonial to Singapore's booming economy. Singapore is jammed with excellent restaurants, serving a unique blend of local and other oriental cuisine and its probably worth going there just to eat!

Of course, if you really want to step out in style and back in history, you can still stay at the Raffles Hotel and rub shoulders with the ghosts of Noel Coward, Joseph Conrad and the other illustrious guests of days gone by. You may need a few winners at Kranji to foot the bill though as room rates start at $650 and go up to S$850 per night. It's bang in the centre of the city and has been recently renovated to restore its former glory. Not too far away is the much more reasonable option in the Peninsular Excelsior Hotel (337 2200), and what it might lack in character is more than made up for by convenience and facilities. A bed for the night here is in the S$150 range. Also centrally located and of a superior quality is the The Mandarin Singapore (737 4411) on Orchard Road as well as the Four Seasons Singapore (734 1110) which is close to the main shopping area on Orchard Boulevard. A few more to consider are the 600 room Imperial Hotel which is perched on a hilltop surrounded by greenery and offers a panoramic view of Singapore; the Marina Mandarin (338 3388) on Raffles Boulevard which offers fine facilities or the Metropole Hotel (336 3611) on Seah Street—not far from the Raffles Hotel, but considerably less costly.

Artist: **Roy Miller** _ANOTHER DAY, ANOTHER DOLLAR_ _Courtesy of:_ **The Artist**

Imagine a green oasis in the middle of the desert; imagine also the finest selection of the world's thoroughbreds; imagine also a watering hole of genuine excellence - well this is racing in Dubai. The richest race in the world, the US $4 million Dubai World Cup, may attract your immediate attention, but in racing terms it is just a single barrel from the well in this land of oil, sheikhs and stallions. Although everything in Dubai might look shiny, new and modern on the surface, it really just masks the long history of racing in this part of the world. It is, after all, where the modern day thoroughbred originated and where the power behind one of the most successful thoroughbred operations in the world lies today in the form of the rulers of Dubai, the Maktoum family, led by its head Sheikh Mohammed.

It may be rather ironic that when British aristocracy went shopping for horses to be bred for racing in the eighteenth century they ended up in this part of the world and the sires they brought home formed the original stock from which all thoroughbreds racing today are descended. Now, fuelled by the wealth of black gold, Arab sheikhs and princes comb the world for the best horses money can buy and bring some of them home to breed and race.

During the past decade, Dubai has sprung up almost magically to be one of the top tourist destinations in the world, and now it's also a place where the visitor can enjoy some excellent racing during the winter months. The most important factors contributing to this have been the formation of the Godolphin Stable by Sheikh Mohammed which now sees some of the world's best horses returning here for a bit of rest and recreation each winter, the building of Nad al Sheba as the country's showpiece track, and the institution of the world's richest race, the US$4 million Dubai World Cup to tempt foreign owners and trainers to bring their champions here to win the big prize.

Racing in the United Arab Emirates is run by the Emirates Racing Association and you can contact them at Suite 203, City Tower 1, PO Box 1178, Dubai. Tel: (9714) 313311. Fax: (9714) 313322. Michael Osborne is the Chief Executive. Perhaps reflecting their keen interests in horses and racing the UAE actually has five racecourses, Nad al Sheba, Jebel Ali, Abu Dhabi, Sharjah, and the Ghantoot Racing and Polo Club and they all have fixtures on various days of the week during the winter season, run under the auspices of the Emirates Racing Association. If the action at these five doesn't quite satisfy your appetite, you could always take in a bit of camel racing which is held a stone's throw from Nad al Sheba at the Dubai Camel Racetrack - it's an amazing sport!

NAD AL SHEBA

A patch of scrubby desert on the edge of the town of Zabeel just a decade ago, Nad al Sheba now glistens in the sun as a green jewel for equestrian sport. Of course it has taken enormous amounts of money to build this fine complex, but it is now reaping dividends as a new centre of world class racing and, lured as ever by rich prize money, owners and trainers from around the world now bring their best stock to race each March, joined by some of the best international jockeys. Where the best go, the rest usually follow and Dubai is now firmly on the map as a place where the lover of horse racing is pencilling in his next trip.

Although he might be one of the richest men in the world,

Sheikh Mohammed is very much a hands-on horseman and he has applied the same approach to building and running Nad al Sheba. Since the first race was run here in 1992, there have been many improvements and additions that make the expression 'state of the art' an understatement.

Nad al Sheba is run by the Dubai Racing Club and you can contact them at Suite 203, City Tower 1, Sheikh Zayed Road, PO Box 1178, Dubai, United Arab Emirates. Tel: (9714) 329888. Fax: (9714) 329777.

You could probably spot this oasis from a satellite orbiting the earth, but to be a little more precise the racecourse is located about three miles south east of the city of Dubai and if you are driving there it is signposted on the Dubai to Abu Dhabi Road at the Metropolitan Hotel junction or from the roundabout close to the Dubai Polo Club and Country Club. When you get there you can park your car for nothing in the general area; if you already have a badge there is a special area reserved for you at the rear of the grandstand.

General admission to the course is free and this allows you to go just about anywhere. You also get a complimentary programme and form guide! However you will probably wish to go into the Club House area as well and you can buy a day badge for DHs 70 (about £12 or $19) at the entrance to it. Club House admission also gives you access to the Dubai Golf and Racing Clubs' members box on the second floor of the grandstand with its great view of the course. There is a total of 4,000 seats for spectators in the grandstand so you shouldn't have too much problem finding a seat. There is a wide variety of food and drinks in the Club House, as well as the Spike Bar and Links Steakhouse restaurant where you can dine surrounded by cowboy memorabilia. There are also some 14 private boxes for hire; the availability of these might be somewhat limited as they are sold primarily to the corporate market, but it might be worth enquiring with the course if you wish to entertain a group of people.

In the public enclosure you can dress casually, but those in the Club House or private boxes are encouraged to don 'smart casual' attire. Of course Dubai, being an Arab country, women are expected to dress 'modestly', which means the extremities should be appropriately covered. The course has a Ladies Day during the racing season and it's an event when the smartest clothing is pulled out of the wardrobe.

The high rolling punter will have a bit of difficulty getting a bet on here as gambling per se is not allowed under Islamic law. However, to give everyone a sporting chance at winning something, there is a free 'competition' to win big cash prizes. A Pick 6 (selected winners of all six races) competition is held every race meeting and carries a prize fund of DHs 40,000 (£7,000 or $11,000). There are also other prizes for picking the forecast in the Fifth race, as well as a Big 5 Jackpot where you have to name the first five horses home in correct finishing order. In the third and fourth races there is a Daily Double, although here you are invited to select the first three finishers in correct order to claim the loot. You may not be able to battle with the bookies or tap into the tote in Dubai, but you might just come away with some extra cash and one thing's for sure, as it's free to enter you won't lose your shirt!

There are usually six or seven races per fixture and as it would be unwise for man or beast to exert themselves in the heat of the desert sun, racing is held at night under the lights when things cool down a bit. Post time for the first race is at 7:00 pm, except during Ramadan in January when it moves to 9:00 pm. Four of Dubai's trainers use Nad al Sheba as their training base and they usually work out the horses between 6:00-9:00 am each morning. You can have breakfast at the track in the morning and watch them go through their paces.

Racing at Nad al Sheba is staged from the beginning of November until the third week in April on Sundays and Thursdays. The only exception to the usual fixture arrangements is the Dubai World Cup meeting itself which is held on a Saturday at the end of March. The World Cup has established itself as a major Group 1 fixture in the international racing calendar and, in addition to the 30,000 spectators on-course, it is beamed to millions around the world who watch eagerly on television. Tense anticipation and exciting finishes have been the order of the day so far. The first running of this mile and a quarter race on the sand saw the legendary Cigar extend a long winning streak and win narrowly under jockey Jerry Bailey. The second year saw the Sir Michael Stoute trained Singspiel stay on up the stretch to capture the prize for Sheikh Mohammed at his home track, while the third thrilling finish was provided by winner Silver Charm, who beat Swain by the width of a nostril.

The World Cup is supported on the same card by the mile and a quarter Dubai Duty Free, which, although it serves as a consolation race for horses not qualified for the World Cup itself, would be the feature race on any other card with US$ 500,000 in prize money to be won. Horses from Britain and Europe may always be at a bit of a disadvantage when running on dirt, but the way some of them have adapted gives hope for the future. If you want to see how the Sheikh Mohammed maroon and white silks or his Godolphin blue fare over the winter season this is the place to go. The added attraction of a host of world class jockeys in action is another great bonus.

For more information on the Dubai World Cup, write to Suite 213, City Tower 1, PO Box 1178, Dubai, United Arab Emirates. Tel: (9714) 322277. Fax: (9714) 322288. E mail: dubaiwcp@emirates.net.ae. Web site: www.dubai worldcup.com.

Dubai Favourites

Although the racing might be the sport that lures you to this part of the world, as many thousands of people have already found out it is now one of the top destinations in the world for an all round winter holiday with some almost-guaranteed great weather. The second running of the Dubai World Cup may have been a washout but it only serves to prove the general rule that in Dubai the sun always shines. This means that you can partake of any other sport at your leisure including sailing or windsurfing, golf on several different courses, polo, or treks into the desert on all-terrain vehicles or by camel! With many people coming here to work from all over the world, Dubai has quite a cosmopolitan flavour and the choice of restaurants, from Mexican

or Lebanese to Indian and Italian, as well as bars and nightlife is also pretty impressive.

If you have taken the children with you, or feel a bit young at heart yourself, you could visit the new Wonderland theme park on the edge of Dubai Creek. Not too far away, but worth a visit is Sharjah with its Arabic souk or marketplace where you can shop for antiques, jewellery or oriental rugs.

There should be little problem finding accommodation here as there is a wide range of choice and location, almost all of it to high international-class standards. Some to note in the luxury category would be the Hatta Fort Hotel ((085 23211), the Hilton Beach Club (9714 445333) or the Metropolitan Hotel (9714 440000) which is closest to the racecourse itself. The Jumeriah Beach (9714 480000) as its name suggests is close to the seaside. A little less luxurious perhaps and at a lower tariff, you could try the Imperial Suites Hotel (9714 515100), Astoria Hotel (9714 534300) or the Palm Beach Hotel (9714 525550). Anywhere you choose, you are likely to come to the conclusion that Dubai is a future winner for a holiday.

Artist: **Harry Matthews** **DETERMINATION** *Courtesy of:* **The Artist**

ROBERT AINSWORTH

Robert Ainsworth was interested in art and drawing from an early age, in fact he first exhibited his work at the age of 12.

He now concentrates his artistic skills on painting equestrian, sporting and wildlife scenes. He exhibits in London and at regional game fairs and shows, painting in watercolour, acrylic and pastels.

DOROTHY AIRTH

After growing up in the Vale of York where there were plenty of horses to study, Dorothy Airth studied at York Art School. By dint of covering the exam papers with drawings of horses Dorothy received her Illustration Diploma with notable marks and went on to spend a year at Newcastle under Roger de Grey.

After moving to Lancashire, Dorothy was able to keep horses for the first time and this, together with the fine skies and landscapes, encouraged her to try her hand at racing scenes as well as undertaking commissions for portraits of horses.

Dorothy also paints and exhibits small oil paintings and country scenes in pastels. In addition to horses she also paints portraits of dogs and other animals. Commission prices on application.

JOHN ATKINS

John Atkins is a painter and sculptor of animals and sporting subjects but specialises in horses and racing. His works in oils, water colour and acrylic are in many private collections in the United Kingdom and abroad.

He prefers to work direct from life as far as possible, painting and drawing at meetings, finding inspiration in the colour, movement and atmosphere of the racing scene. Commission prices on application.

MARGARET BARRETT

Born in a house overlooking the Derby course at Epsom, Margaret Barrett cannot remember a time when she did not draw and paint horses. She holds a degree in Fine Art and her paintings have since been exhibited in London, Tokyo and New York. She won the Society of Equestrian Artists prize for best Oil Painting in an exhibition held at Christies. Her work is published as limited edition prints and also appears as book illustrations.

Her work shows a lifetime's love of horses and the countryside, but her speciality is in racing scenes. She responds to the power and grace of these magnificent animals by capturing a sense of

movement that can almost be heard as well as seen!

Margaret accepts commissions for people, horses and racing scenes. Prices on application.

CLAIRE EVA BURTON

Claire Eva Burton has always been interested in horses and racing. She began by sketching horses at local point-to-points and this led to full-time study at Medway College of Art. On leaving college, Claire worked for trainers Mick Haines and Tommy Gosling at Epsom but after a nasty fall she decided to study horses from the ground. She attends many race meetings where she sketches scenes and later completes the paintings in her studio.

Claire has held many exhibitions in London and is kept busy with commissions, including one for 12 pictures to decorate the Queen Mother's Box at Cheltenham. Claire's work is extremely popular and many limited editions of her work have been published. Please see our print section for further details. Commission prices on application.

ROSEMARY COATES

Rosemary studied at the Ruskin School of Fine Art and Drawing in Oxford having been brought up in the heart of Berkshire where she spent her time with horses. Rosemary has worked on commissions for over ten years and specialises in equestrian field sports.

Her pictures sell in the USA and through sporting shops and the racecourses as well as through the National Horse Racing Museum in Newmarket. Commission prices on application.

PETER CURLING

Peter Curling was born in Waterford in Ireland in 1955; he was educated in England and Florence and now lives permanently in Ireland.

He has been fascinated by horses since his earliest childhood and began to sketch and paint at his local stables whilst he was still at school. He later lived for a time in Newmarket, riding out with the eminent trainer Michael Stoute. Peter Curling rode his own horse, Caddy, to Victory at Limerick Junction in 1985.

His originals are now exhibited all over the world.

TERENCE GILBERT

Born in London he began his artistic training at Camberwell Art School and afterwards used to frequent the National

Gallery (where his father worked) studying the techniques of the Old Masters. After a period working as a free-lance illustrator for film companies, advertising campaigns, leading publishers and magazines in Great Britain, Europe and America he decided after a successful exhibition in America in 1975 to paint fine art for galleries full time.

Among the more well-known commissions he has undertaken are a portrait of H M The Queen and President Reagan, Riding at Windsor, which was presented to the President in the White House and H M King Hussein of Jordan at Sandhurst, a gift on his birthday by Mrs Thatcher in 1985. Also equestrian portraits of Derby Winners, Nashwan and Generous.

He has a wide ranging interest in sport and painted many sporting heroes such as Damon Hill, John Daly, Stefan Edberg, Frankie Dettori and Sir Peter O'Sullevan. Other portrait subjects include Charlton Heston and Ronnie Scott.

Terence has exhibited widely including USA, Saudi Arabia, Oman, Royal Academy Touring Exhibition in Dubai, Royal College of Art, Society of Equestrian Artists, Mathaf Gallery, Osborne Studio Gallery and the Patterson Gallery.

Apart from racing prints, Terence has many other sporting prints which are available on application.

BRIAN HALTON

Brian Halton is a sporting artist who teaches painting and sculpture to A level students. His main interest lies in racing and he has been painting commissions for some twenty years.

Brian spends much of his time working on commissions of all sporting themes such as greyhound racing, tennis, golf, football, cricket and boxing as well as all aspects of racing. Commissions include Sir Stanley Matthews, Denis Law, George Best, Nigel Benn and Prince Naseem.

He and his wife run a small gallery that has a strong equestrian theme and includes work by other artists. Commission prices on application.

REFNA HAMEY

Refna is no stranger to horses. A keen observer of all equine sports and a natural draughtswoman, her paintings show innate composition skills, firmness of touch and vitality of colour.

She is immensely capable of showing the moods and movements of her subjects and they are depicted from a great variety of angles.

Refna studied at Cambridge and

Kingston Schools of Art. She trotted off to Newmarket regularly to paint from life. It was the painting of Mill Reef, which started the success story. This led to more commissions: Observe, Celtic Shot, Saxon Farm and Kibah Tictoc, to name a few.

Refna has had work accepted by the Royal Academy. Her most recent exhibition was at the Tryon and Swann Gallery.

PAUL HART

Paul Hart studied illustration at Medway College of Art and Design, learning mainly figure work in a variety of mediums. After leaving college I worked as a freelance illustrator carrying out commissions for companies such as IPC magazines, Longmans Educational Books and Readers Digest.

His first equestrian paintings were of shire horses at ploughing matches and he has had some of them reproduced as greeting cards by Medici and Gordon Fraser. Since then he has concentrated mainly on horse racing subjects, starting with a commission of Desert Orchid and more recently a commission for Sir Mark Prescott. Some examples of his work have been reproduced as limited edition prints.

MICHAEL HESLOP

Michael Heslop is one of the foremost sports artists in the world, having studied at Somerset College of Art and Design for four years, followed by a final year at Brighton College of Art and Design.

He has exhibited and won awards in England, America, Spain, Sweden, Switzerland and Australia, and is collected by many of the world's leading professional sportsmen and women. His career spans a period of some twenty-five years.

His commitment and intense love of the subject stems from his active participation in many sports, both as a competitor and a coach.

His work is meticulously researched and composed and is based on a sound technique and an interest in detail and atmosphere.

He now lives and works from Topsham, a picturesque village in Devon, having returned from a successful eighteen months as resident artist in Sweden. Michael now concentrates on sporting subject commissions and limited edition prints.

ELIZABETH HOWIE MCCRINDLE

Born in a country village in Ayrshire, Elizabeth has spent all her life painting and loving horses. After twenty-four years in the textile industry she now works as a full-time artist.

The bulk of her work consists of commissions but she has exhibited successfully in galleries throughout Scotland and south of the border.

Her paintings can be found in private collections throughout the UK, Northern Ireland, USA, Mexico, Canada, Germany, Zimbabwe and New Zealand. Prices start at £200 for a head study and £500 for a full study.

JACQUIE JONES

Jacquie Jones' responsive and enlightened style is a result of the incredible passion and confidence with which she paints, employing unnerving strokes of colour and joy in a variety of mediums. Her works range from the serene and tranquil, as seen in 'Salukis and Hawks', to the raw, energetic power of 'Racing Vigour'.

Jacquie's work is very much influenced by all cultures associated with the horse, especially that of the Arab world. The freedom that the horse enables man to enjoy is the primary focus of Jacquie's style and it is this freedom that she paints.

Alongside her special interest in racing and the racehorse, Jacquie portrays every aspect of the equine world, through equestrian sports into Arabian images, horse portraiture, hunting, eventing and dressage scenes. In addition Jacquie paints other countryside pursuits and is much influenced by her love of working dogs. This variety of subjects keeps her energy and artistic diversity at the highest possible level.

Jacquie is a Friend of the Equestrian Artists Society of England. She has illustrated three books, Racing Dreams, Ponies and Dreams and Badger Creek. Jacquie has previously exhibited in Newmarket and the United Arab Emirates. In 1997, Jacquie was appointed the first ever artist in residence to the National Horseracing Museum in Newmarket and had her first London solo exhibition in 1998 at The Park Gallery. Jacquie now has her own web site www.horseracingart.co.uk.

DENNIS KIRTLEY

Dennis Kirtley, born in Sunderland, is entirely self-taught. Throughout his life he has nursed a passion for horses, in particular the English thoroughbred, and his drawings and paintings of the noble animal are scattered worldwide. His patrons from the racing world are numerous and include the late Prince Aly Khan and the late Sir Victor Sassoon.

His subjects range from Derby winners Crepello and St Paddy in the fifties and sixties to champions Known Fact, Be my Guest and the brilliant Golden Fleece in more recent times. Dennis has exhibited at numerous galleries and in 1977 published a limited edition print entitled Lester showing the champion jockey surrounded by many of his greatest winners. Prices on application, web site: www.denniskirtley.co.uk

ELIZABETH KITSON

Elizabeth Kitson rode and taught riding from an early age, horses being a major part of her life. Later she started painting seriously, starting with military actions, then specialising in portraits of people and animals, particularly horses and dogs, in oils and pastels - always getting a good likeness - action, movement and light being her special interest. She works mainly for commission.

She has exhibited in London and the provinces. Commissions have included the 'Battle of Waterloo' which is now a limited edition print. Her pictures have sold in many different countries. She is a member of Society of Equestrian Artists and runs their Devon Art Workshop. She is also a member of the Society of the Armed Forces Art Society and the Army Art Society.

ASAD KURI MONTANA

Asad's interest in horses began at an early age when drawing cowboys and Indians. Since studying fine art in London, he has exhibited at the RHH summer exhibitions, and other galleries in Dubai and Canada, and he now teaches equestrian art in Salisbury.

His view is that painting horses is easy but capturing the movement and characteristics of each individual horse is the key point in equestrian art.

He attends some of the major horse shows and trials, but his main passion in life is British racing with all its beauty, colour, fullness and ups and downs.

Over the years he has painted for many breeders, owners and trainers in the UK, Dubai and Canada. Commission prices and other details are available on application.

JANE LAZENBY

Jane was born in Barnsley in 1969, and grew up horse mad, getting her first pony on her 13th birthday. She still competes in a variety of disciplines on her homebred mare.

She studied fine art at Newcastle, graduating in 1992, and was one of nine

UK finalists to have their work chosen for exhibition in New York.

Jane spends the majority of her time working on commissions, specialising in equestrian portraits and scenes. She has exhibited in London with the Society of Equestrian Artists, and throughout Yorkshire.

She has work in private collections in New Zealand, Australia, the USA and across the UK. Commission prices on application.

BARRIE LINKLATER

Barrie Linklater specialises in equine and human portrait work and a broad range of equestrian paintings, particularly racing scenes.

He has spent his entire working life with pencil and brush, first as an illustrator in England then four years in Australia, returning to London to build a reputation for portrait and equestrian painting in the classical style, with commissions for HRH The Duke of Edinburgh, Sheik Ahmed-al-Maktoum, Lady Beaverbrook, York Race Committee and others. Twelve of his paintings now hang in the Royal Collection, and others in the USA, Canada, Holland, the Far East, Dubai and Australia. He has exhibited widely and is a long standing member of the Society of Equestrian Artists

HARRY MATTHEWS

Harry Matthews was born on Merseyside, the son of a corner shop bookie and is consequently a racing fanatic. A self-taught portrait painter and professional illustrator, his many qualifications include a fine art honours degree in printmaking and colour theory.

A prize-winning artist he has exhibited at the Royal Academy, the Westminster Gallery and Mall Galleries, Goodwood House, Newmarket Racing Museum and many others worldwide. His work now hangs in the collections of royalty, well known international celebrities and, most notably, other artists.

Acclaimed for his exceptional figure work, Harry has no set style but being a natural gambler will always seek to experiment. Commission prices on application.

ROY MILLER

SEA, AAEA, one of the world's foremost equestrian artists, has won awards with the society of Equestrian Artists, and the American Academy of Equine Art, and is a full member of both organisations.

A native of Manchester, Roy Miller

began work as a commercial artist at the age of 14. In the evenings he studied at the Regional College of Art in Manchester. In 1959 he moved to London and worked as a freelance illustrator. Exhibited a racing picture in the Royal Academy summer exhibition 1961. Began specialising in equestrian painting about 1971, and has continued full time since 1974.

The Queen is among those who have a Miller in their private collection and he has painted for owners, trainers, jockeys and breeders worldwide. Was commissioned to paint the official pictures for the new racecourse at Sha Tin, Hong Kong and racehorses of year in Canada, Australia and Hong Kong. Has had one man exhibitions in USA, Canada, UK and Australia. He has also been commissioned to design and paint the originals for the Lester Piggott gates at Epsom racecourse. Roy Miller has also successfully published many limited edition prints. Please see our print section for further details. Commission prices on application.

KRISTINE NASON

Kristine Nason is an English artist whose talent has been passed down through generations of her family. Always entranced by the beauty of horses, she began accepting commissions for equestrian paintings by the age of fourteen.

In 1992, following a career in fine art publishing and design in which she forged a name for herself as an accomplished artist with work in collections all over the world, Kristine decided to concentrate once again on painting equestrian subjects.

She is rapidly building a reputation in this field for her sensitive interpretation of character, and skill in depicting the complicated anatomy of the horse. She also accepts commissions for portraits of people and dogs. Prices on application.

WILLIAM NEWTON

In 1987 following eight years as a professional National Hunt jockey, William Newton returned to his first passion of sculpture. Much of his work, and one of his greatest strengths, is in the portrait sculpture of animals, in particular horses.

Besides having taken part in numerous mixed exhibitions he has held two successful one man shows (1995 and 1997) both at Jonathan Cooper's Park Walk Gallery, London SW; the next being scheduled for June 2000.

He was responsible for sculpting the prestigious trophies for both the 1998 and 1999 Vodafone Derby and Oaks - Epsom Downs.

GILL PARKER

Gill cast her first bronze in 1983. An early association with the Sladmore Gallery led to her first one woman exhibition in November 1984. Successful exhibitions around Britain and the United States followed, as have two more solo shows with the Sladmore Gallery.

A member of the Society of Equestrian Artists, Gill won the President's Medal at their annual show in 1993. Entirely self-taught, she has kept horses for many years and has an appreciation and knowledge of all aspects of the equestrian world. Gill has completed commissions of some of the greatest horses in the racing and eventing world including Dancing Brave, Rainbow Quest and Mrs Moss. Limited edition bronzes are available, commission prices on application.

K G PARKER-BARRATT

This artist started drawing at a very early age. Fascinated by the movement of a horse, he always enjoyed drawing and painting horses. He had no formal art education and was completely self taught. In his teens he started to take an interest in the life and works of Sir Alfred Munnings and has done extensive studies on this artist. Most of his work is done in acrylic and oils.

Two years ago he moved to Penzance, Cornwall. In the short time he has lived there he has taken an interest in the local race meetings and he is now in the process of completing two paintings of St Buryan races and the Penzance Mounts Bay race meetings.

KLAUS PHILIPP

After the war, Klaus Philipp returned to the farm from which he had been evacuated and spent the majority of his time looking after the horses and competing in many competitions successfully. He used to sketch the horses on the farm and paint commissions for friends to supplement his earnings.

Klaus later joined the mounted police where he became Captain in charge of a troop of 30 horses. He continued to paint and found that his love and feel for the horse helped him to portray the animal naturally. He left the police force in 1980 and became a full-time artist. His work is highly regarded and is found in many private collections all over the world. Commission prices on application.

PHILIPPA PORLEY

Philippa started riding and competing

in the show ring from the age of two, thus beginning a lifelong interest in all equestrian disciplines. After gaining an honours degree in 1995, she decided to paint full time, with commissions now sold as far afield as Australia and America.

Philippa enjoys working with both pastels and oils and specialises in fine detail and true likenesses. The artist has painted British and Olympic team members in dressage, Showjumping and Eventing, Horse of the Year Show showing champions, and leading National Hunt horses Cool Dawn, French Holly and Addington Boy. Philippa loves the challenge of capturing each individual character. Commission prices on application.

MICHAEL ROBSON

Michael was born in Beverley in 1957, a stone's throw from the racecourse. He has been drawing and painting animals from an early age and has specialised in horses and racing scenes since turning professional in 1989. Michael spends a great deal of time working on commissions and will undertake any equestrian scene. Commission prices on application.

DIANE SARGEANT

Diane Sargeant's interest in horses began at an early age. A great love and respect of the horse was developed whilst working with them. She carried this passion with her and now, as an entirely self-taught artist, gains inspiration for her paintings by attending race meetings and point-to-points.

Diane enjoys working in a variety of media and, although her love for the horse provides the main impetus for her work, she also portrays many other subjects, including wildlife, for which she has won awards.

Her work is exhibited regularly in and around Leicestershire, and is held in high regard in private collections both abroad and in the UK. Commission prices on request.

PETER SMITH

Peter Smith was born in 1949 and has always been fascinated by horses. Having studied at the Carlisle and Glasgow Colleges of Art, he now lives near Ayr racecourse where he makes the preliminary sketches on which he bases his paintings. Originally influenced by Stubbs and Munnings, Peter's work now has a strength and directness that is completely his own. His mastery of colour and

his unique ability to capture on canvas the speed and movement of steeplechase racing is his hallmark.

Frost and Reed have exhibited Peter Smith's paintings for some years in the United States and, as a result, he has a large clientele there. Commission prices on application.

KATY SODEAU

Katy is a self-taught artist in her thirties. She originally trained and worked in architecture but became hooked on painting horses when she lived in Newmarket in the 1980s. Katy is still fascinated by the challenge of portraying the speed and excitement of horseracing in her painting.

Katy has now been working as a professional artist for five years. She has had successful solo shows in a variety of venues around East Anglia and has exhibited at the Society of Equestrian Artists.

Katy has her own web site at www.equinepainting.co.uk

BRIAN STANLEY

Brian Stanley is a self-taught artist specialising in painting horses. He has undertaken many commissions including the famous Lloyds black horse. He exhibits locally and also in London and the Cotswolds. His paintings have sold in North America and throughout Europe and the United Kingdom.

He has won two blue ribbon awards at the Three Spires Art Show in Truro and has exhibited at the Society of Equestrian Artists. Commissions undertaken.

HEATHER ST CLAIR DAVIS

It is our sad duty to report the death of Heather, last year. Born in the Cotswold Hills, Heather was brought up amid horses and art and, after graduating from Art College in Cheltenham, she moved to the United States, where she lived with her family on a farm in Vermont. Over the years she has established a distinguished reputation as a leading contemporary equine artist. Heather's outstanding ability as a painter of landscape and her professional knowledge of horses were fundamental to her success. She returned to England for her subjects: hunting scenes, racehorses exercising, the excitement of steeplechasing or flat racing, horses hacking home after a morning ride or quietly grazing in a sweeping Gloucestershire landscape. Her work is inspired, original and rewarding to own. Heather was a founder member of the American

Academy of Equine Artists. She will be greatly missed.

PHILIP TOON

An entirely self-taught artist who has been painting professionally for about seven years. His main interests lie with racehorses and racing scenes.

He has exhibited his work at Newbury and Warwick racecourses and many galleries up and down the country. Philip undertakes many private commissions: mainly equine, but he also covers many other subjects. Commissions are undertaken and prices are available on request.

JONATHAN TROWELL

Was born in Durham in 1938. He studied at the Sunderland College of Art and won a scholarship to the Royal Academy Schools. He received the Landseer Silver Medal for Painting, the Bronze Medal for drawing and the Sir James Knott Travelling Scholarship which enabled him to work in Spain and North Africa.

He has exhibited at the Royal Academy Summer Exhibition, the Royal Society of Portrait Painters, Young Contemporaries and the Fine Art Society. His work features in many private and public collections including those of HRH The Prince of Wales, Culham College, Oxford—Newnham College, Cambridge—The Royal College of Art, the Imperial College, The Bank of Japan, BP, de Beers and CIBA-Geigy.

DAVID TRUNDLEY

David Trundley, born in 1949, was bred in Cambridgeshire. He grew up a keen sportsman reaching county standard at football, cricket, squash and athletics. Later, he moved to Taunton from where he paints racehorses with a passion. Most of his spare time is spent at racecourses gathering material for his paintings and the result is a delightful enthusiasm shining through his charming pictures.

David paints mostly in acrylic and adopts a fresh, impressionistic approach to his work. He exhibits at the Tryon Gallery, London. Commission prices on application.

MARTIN WILLIAMS

After gaining a BA(Hons) degree in graphic design, Martin Williams worked in the creative departments of several major advertising agencies in London.

Since painting his first equestrian subject 'by pure chance' ten years ago, his fine art career has developed rapidly.

His work is now in the collections of many leading owners, trainers and jockeys around the world and he has been paid the ultimate compliment of having his work purchased by fellow artists and sculptors.

Martin's increasing reputation is based on an impressive use of colour and the ability to capture light, mood and atmosphere in a range of media. Although specialising in racing subjects, he is also an accomplished landscape and portrait painter.

Martin has recently exhibited in Tokyo but his work can be seen on a more regular basis at Equus in Newmarket and at the Osborne Studio Gallery in London. Commission prices on application.

ALISON RUTH WILSON

Alison studied Fine Art at the Slade School in London. She then spent several years working in London as a theatre Scenic Artist. She is committed to the survival of the practice of teaching formal Life Drawing to art students, and for some years she worked as a part-time specialist lecturer in the subject. Although she now paints full time, she still teaches the occasional life class.

Her work is predominantly in oils, but she also works in other media such as pencil, pastel, and silverpoint; a large proportion of her work involves horses. The precise structural drawing and exacting technical standards that characterise her work make her particularly in demand for portrait commissions.

SUE WINGATE

Sue Wingate studied at three art colleges over a seven year period which culminated in her becoming an M.A., RCA (Royal College of Art).

Initially concentrating on large landscapes, Sue widened her subject matter in 1980 to include animal studies of all kinds and especially subjects from the equine world. Over the years she has undertaken some prestigious commissions which have resulted in her painting some outstanding horses usch as Teenoso and Secreto (both Derby winners), Bosra Sham, Chief Singer, Dancing Brave, Desert Orchid, Direct Route, etc. In 1990 she had a large exhibition in the Museum and Art Gallery, Doncaster. The painting entitled 'The Spirit Of The St Leger' was specially commissioned as a centrepiece and now forms part of the museum's permanent collection. In 1999 she had another large exhibition at Palace House, Newmarket, where her paintings were hung in a suite of rooms formerly used by Charles II.

Sue is a director of her own business, Field Galleries which markets reproductions of her paintings on quality greetings cards and prints. Please see our print section for further details. Commissions accepted for conté drawings, pastels, watercolours and oils—prices on application..

Artist: **Malcolm Coward MUDLARKS** *Courtesy of:* **Sally Mitchell Fine Arts**

Please note the illustrations are for guidance only. The printing process may vary colours slightly. Sizes are not to a uniform scale throughout the list.

Sizes quoted are for paper size unless otherwise stated.

All prints are limited editions unless otherwise stated.

WE THREE KINGS
by Susan Crawford   14" x 25" or 7" x 12"

THE SNOW TUNNEL by Roy Miller   19" × 14"

SUDDEN BLIZZARD
by Roy Miller   12 ½" × 13"

DESERT ORCHID
by Claire Burton   17" × 15"

EVERGREEN CHAMPIONS
by Roy Miller   17 ½" × 22"

TURNING FOR HOME
by Stephen Smith   15" x 19½"

ALDANITI IN RETIREMENT
by Claire Eva Burton   19" x 22"

ALL OUT
by Constance Halford-Thompson   15" x 20"

LAMMTARRA/PENTIRE KING - KING GEORGE VI
& QUEEN ELIZABETH DIAMOND STAKES, ASCOT
by Mike Heslop   17¾" x 21¾"

OUT OF THE STALLS
by Constance Halford-
Thompson
12" x 16"

ON THE BEACH,
LAYTOWN
by Constance Halford-
Thompson
12" x 16"

DANCING BRAVE - PRIX DE L'ARC DE TRIOMPHE
by Mike Heslop   14" x 25" or 7" x 12"

GLORIOUS GOODWOOD
by Harry Matthews   16" x 22"

POST HASTE
by Johnny Jonas   16" x 22"

NO RECALL
by John King   12" x 15"

AFTER THE RACE THAT NEVER WAS
by John King   9" x 12"

GLORIOUS GOODWOOD
by Sue Wingate   19" x 14"

RARIN TO GO
by Sue Wingate   19" x 14"

HEAD ON
by Jonathan Trowell 17" x 21"

THE FINAL BEND
by Constance Halford-Thompson 15" x 20"

WARREN HILL 20" × 26"

THE DEVIL'S DYKE 20" × 26"

ALL TO PLAY FOR 18" x 13"

THE HIGH STREET 20" × 26"

THE JULY COURSE 20" × 26"

GLORIOUS GOODWOOD 1901
by Terence Gilbert 15¹/₂" x 23¹/₂"

SCENES OF NEWMARKET
by D. Trundley 24" × 30"

STUDIES OF CHELTENHAM
by D. Trundley 24" × 30"

GENEROUS
by Roy Miller   20" x 20"

ARKLE
by Roy Miller   15¼" x 17"

SHERGAR
by Roy Miller   12½" x 12½"

THE NATIONAL THAT NEVER WAS
by A J Dent   21" x 14"

STORMIN HOME
by A J Dent   21" x 14"

A CLASSIC FINISH (Silver
Patriarch and Benny the Dip)
by Sue Wingate   19" x 14"

VIKING FLAGSHIP
by Claire Eva Burton   18" x 25"

THE SPIRIT OF THE ST LEGER
by Sue Wingate   19" x 14"

THERE GOES YOUR SHIRT!
by Gilbert Holiday   11¼" x 19¼"

AT THE END OF THE RAINBOW
by Gilbert Holiday   12¼" x 19¼"

A POINT TO POINT
by Gilbert Holiday   14¾" x 17¾"

RETURNING TO PADDOCK
by Gilbert Holiday   12½" x 19¼"

WEATHERCOCK HOUSE
by Stephen Smith   21" x 15¾"

LAMMTARRA
by Roy Miller   17½" x 17"

INTO THE LEAD
by Margaret Barrett   12" x 10"

CHAMPIONS
by Roy Miller   15¼" x 18¼"

SHEER DELIGHT
by Margaret Barrett   9" x 12"

CHANTILLY
by Jonathan Trowell 20" x 16"

THE FINISH
by Mark Churms   12" x 8"

WEST TIP
by Mark Churms 8½" x 11½"

DAYLAMI
by Stephen Smith   21³/₈" x 15"

ONE MAN
by Stephen Smith   20" x 16"

MONTJEU
by Stephen Smith   21" x 15"

Print Order Form

Print	Artist	Size	Price incl.VAT	Edition Size	Qty.	Cost
Following prints are found on page 262						
We Three Kings	Susan Crawford	14" x 25"	£ 42.00	Open		
We Three Kings	Susan Crawford	7" x 12"	£ 17.00	Open		
The Snow Tunnel	Roy Miller	19" x 14"	£ 64.50	475		
Desert Orchid	Claire Burton	17" x 15"	£ 26.00	Open		
Sudden Blizzard	Roy Miller	12½" x 13"	£ 47.00	475		
Evergreen Champions	Roy Miller	17½" x 22"	£ 84.50	550		
Following prints are found on page 263						
Turning For Home	Stephen Smith	15" x 19½"	£ 53.00	500		
Aldaniti In Retirement	Claire Burton	19" x 22"	£ 66.00	600		
All Out	C. Halford-Thompson	15" x 20"	£ 76.00	500		
Lammtarra/Pentire King	Mike Heslop	17¾" x 21¾"	£ 88.00	500		
Out of the Stalls	C. Halford-Thompson	12" x 16"	£ 45.00	500		
On The Beach, Laytown	C. Halford-Thompson	12" x 16"	£ 45.00	500		
Dancing Brave	Mike Heslop	13" x 24½"	£ 99.00	500		
Following prints are found on page 264						
Glorious Goodwood	Harry Matthews	16" x 22"	£ 55.00	500		
Post Haste	Johnny Jonas	16" x 22"	£ 55.00	500		
No Recall	John King	12" x 15"	£ 47.50	850		
After The Race That Never Was	John King	9" x 12"	£ 47.50	850		
Glorious Goodwood	Sue Wingate	19" x 14"	£ 75.00	500		
Rarin' to Go	Sue Wingate	19" x 14"	£ 75.00	500		
Following prints are found on page 265						
Head On	Jonathan Trowell	17" x 21"	£ 65.00	325		
The Final Bend	C. Halford-Thompson	15' x 20"	£ 65.00	500		
Warren Hill	Neil Cawthorne	20" x 26"	£ 65.00	850		
The Devil's Dyke	Neil Cawthorne	20" x 26"	£ 65.00	850		
All to Play For	Margaret Barrett	18" x 13"	£ 45.00	250		
Glorious Goodwood 1901	Terence Gilbert	15½" x 23½"	£ 58.00	500		
The High Street	Neil Cawthorne	20" x 26"	£ 65.00	850		
The July Course	Neil Cawthorne	20" x 26"	£ 65.00	850		
Scenes of Newmarket	D. Trundley	24" x 30"	£ 61.00	500		
Studies of Cheltenham	D. Trundley	24" x 30"	£ 61.00	500		
Following prints are found on page 266						
Generous	Roy Miller	20" x 20"	£ 85.00	550		
Arkle	Roy Miller	15¼" x 17"	£ 78.00	850		
Shergar	Roy Miller	12½" x 12½"	£ 40.00	850		
The National That Never Was	A J Dent	21" x 14"	£ 65.00	480		
Stormin' Home	A J Dent	21" x 14"	£ 69.00	480		
A Classic Finish	Sue Wingate	19" x 14"	£ 80.00	500		
Viking Flagship	Claire Eva Burton	18" x 25"	£ 82.50	495		
Spirit of the St Leger	Sue Wingate	29" x 19½"	£ 75.00	575		
There Goes Your Shirt	Gilbert Holiday	11¼" x 19¼"	£ 65.00	500		
At the End of the Rainbow	Gilbert Holiday	12½" x 19¼"	£ 65.00	500		
					Sub-total	

Print Order Form cont'd

Print	Artist	Size	Price incl. VAT	Edition Size	Qty	Cost
A Point to Point	Gilbert Holiday	14³/₄" x 17³/₄"	£ 65.00	500		
Returning to Paddock	Gilbert Holiday	12¹/₂" x 19¹/₄"	£ 65.00	500		
Following prints are found on page 267						
Weathercock House	Stephen Smith	21" x 15³/₄"	£ 70.00	500		
Lammtarra	Roy Miller	17" x 17¹/₂"	£ 76.50	450		
Into the Lead	Margaret Barrett	12" x 10"	£ 41.50	850		
Champions	Roy Miller	15¹/₄" x 18¹/₄"	£ 68.50	500		
Sheer Delight	Margaret Barrett	9" x 12"	£ 35.50	850		
Chantilly	Jonathan Trowell	20" x 16"	£ 88.50	275		
The Finish	Mark Churms	12" x 8"	£ 25.00	1000		
West Tip	Mark Churms	8¹/₂" x 11¹/₂"	on application	1000		
Daylami	Stephen Smith	21³/₈" x 15"	£ 82.50	500		
One Man	Stephen Smith	20" x 16"	£ 58.00	500		
Montjeu	Stephen Smith	21" x 15"	£ 70.00	500		
The Racecourses of Britain	Rosemary Coates	16" x 20"	£ 25.00	Open		
Point-to-Pointing in Britain	Rosemary Coates	16" x 20"	£ 25.00	Open		
Postage & Packing						**£5.00**
					Total	

All prints are individually signed. limited edition unless otherwise stated.

I enclose a cheque for the sum of £_____ payable to Kensington West Productions Ltd.

Please debit my Access / Visa / Amex / Diners card by the sum of £_____

No. ☐☐☐☐☐☐☐☐☐☐☐☐☐☐☐☐

Name _____

Address _____

_____**Tel. No** _____

All orders should be sent to:
Kensington West Productions Ltd, 5 Cattle Market, Hexham, Northumberland, NE46 1NJ
Alternatively telephone your order on (01434) 609933

Book Order Form

Title	Hardback	Qty.	Softback	Qty.
The Spirit of Racing	£16.99			
The Tote Guide to Horse Racing	£ 6.99		£ 4.99	
Following the Fairways 13th edition	£18.99		£14.99	
Fishing Forays 4th edition	£17.99			
The Spirit of Football	£14.99			
Ports of Call	£18.99		£14.99	
The Spirit of Cricket	£16.99			
The Spirit of Rugby	£16.99			
Icons of Sport	£16.99			

Feature Directory

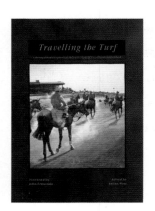

We have limited stocks available of
the previous editions of Travelling the
Turf. If you would like to purchase
any of the previous editions they are
available at
£10 per copy plus £3 P&P
(£5 P&P Eire).

To check availability or to place an
order please contact

Kensington West Productions Ltd
5 Cattle Market, Hexham,
Northumberland NE46 1NJ

Tel: (01434) 609933
Fax: (01434) 600066
E mail: kwp@kensingtonwest.co.uk

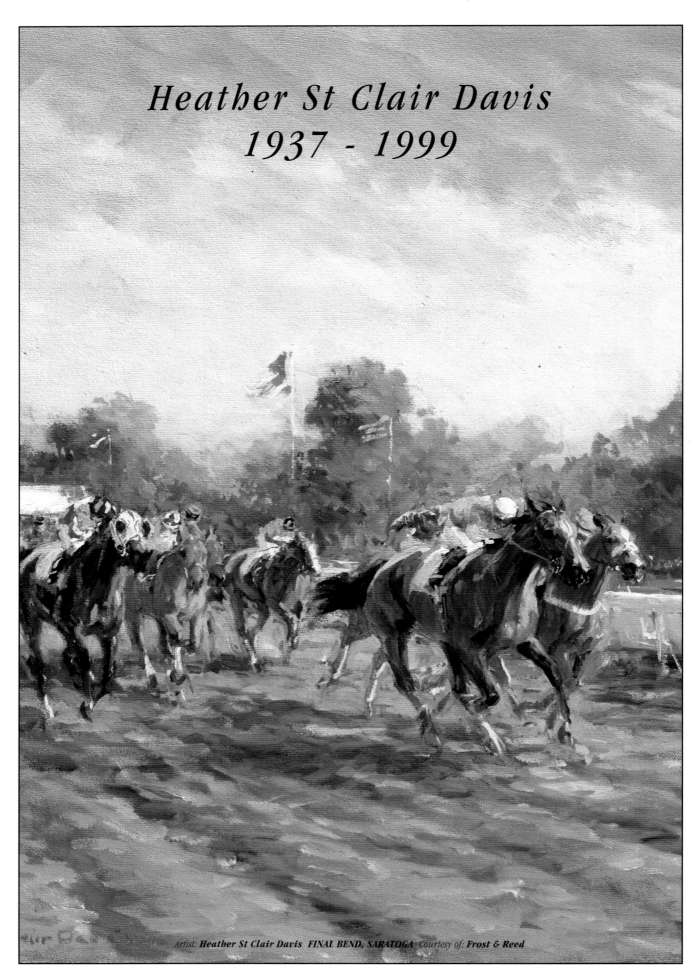

Heather St Clair Davis
1937 - 1999

Artist: **Heather St Clair Davis** **FINAL BEND, SARATOGA** Courtesy of: **Frost & Reed**